Beginning Drupal 7

TODD TOMLINSON

Apress®

Beginning Drupal 7

ISBN-13 (pbk): 978-1-4302-2859-2

ISBN-13 (electronic): 978-1-4302-2860-8

Printed and bound in the United States of America 9 8 7 6 5 4 3 2 1

President and Publisher: Paul Manning
Lead Editors: Michelle Lowman, Brian MacDonald
Technical Reviewers: Steve Edwards, Todd Kelsey
Editorial Board: Clay Andres, Steve Anglin, Mark Beckner, Ewan Buckingham, Gary Cornell, Jonathan Gennick, Jonathan Hassell, Michelle Lowman, Matthew Moodie, Duncan Parkes, Jeffrey Pepper, Frank Pohlmann, Douglas Pundick, Ben Renow-Clarke, Dominic Shakeshaft, Matt Wade, Tom Welsh
Coordinating Editor: Jim Markham
Copy Editor: Tracy Brown Collins
Compositor: Kimberly Burton
Indexer: BIM Indexing & Proofreading Services
Artist: April Milne
Cover Designer: Anna Ishchenko

Distributed to the book trade worldwide by Springer-Verlag New York, Inc., 233 Spring Street, 6th Floor, New York, NY 10013. Phone 1-800-SPRINGER, fax 201-348-4505, e-mail `orders-ny@springer-sbm.com`, or visit `www.springeronline.com`.

For information on translations, please e-mail `rights@apress.com`, or visit `www.apress.com`.

Apress and friends of ED books may be purchased in bulk for academic, corporate, or promotional use. eBook versions and licenses are also available for most titles. For more information, reference our Special Bulk Sales–eBook Licensing web page at `www.apress.com/info/bulksales`.

There are so many people to thank for making this book possible, including two very special people who had a huge influence on my life and my desire to write. This book is dedicated to them.

Grant Wiley (1925-1996), president of Sportland Distributing, gave me the opportunity to enter the world of information technology back in 1976. If it weren't for Grant's support and encouragement, I might be still slinging boxes in a warehouse somewhere. He took a chance by asking me to read through the IBM manuals so that I could take over the responsibility for the newly installed IBM System/32. Grant taught me everything about business that you don't learn in business school, concepts that I've carried with me and applied while consulting for dozens of the largest companies in the world.

I also want to thank my 98-year-old grandmother, Gladys Tomlinson, who at 96 published her first book. Thank you, Grandma, for all you've done for me over the years, and for the influence that you have had on my life.

Contents at a Glance

Contents

About the Author

Todd Tomlinson is the Vice President of eGovernment Solutions at ServerLogic Corporation in Portland Oregon. Todd's focus over the past 15 years has been on designing, developing, deploying, and supporting complex web solutions for public- and private-sector clients all around the world. He has been using Drupal as the primary platform for creating beautiful and feature-rich sites such as `http://arapahoelibraries.org/ald/`.

Prior to joining ServerLogic, Todd was the Senior Director of eBusiness Strategic Services for Oracle Corporation, where he helped Oracle's largest clients develop their strategic plans for leveraging the web as a core component of their business. He is also the former Vice President of Internet Solutions for Claremont Technology Group, Vice President and CTO of Emerald Solutions, Managing Director for CNF Ventures, and a Senior Manager with Andersen Consulting/Accenture.

Todd has a BS in Computer Science, an MBA, and is in the dissertation phase of his Ph.D.

Todd's passion for Drupal is evident in his obsession with evangelizing the platform and his enthusiasm when speaking with clients about the possibilities of what they can accomplish using Drupal. If you want to see someone literally "light up," stop him on the street and ask him, "What is Drupal, and what can it do for me?"

About the Technical Reviewer

A developer for Drupal Staffing and Consulting, **Steve Edwards** has been involved with the IT industry since 1995. He has held support, analyst, and project management roles serving industries that include banking software, trucking, and telecom. In 1998, Steve began developing websites, adding Drupal to his repertoire in 2006. Today, he is an active member of the Drupal community, contributing modules and core patches.

When not working on Drupal, Steve's time is spent with his family and church. He is active in sports, and he is a search and rescue volunteer.

Acknowledgments

I would like to thank the following people:

My parents for giving me the encouragement to explore new opportunities.

My sisters for putting up with a geeky brother, before geeky was cool.

My daughters for giving dad the time to write this book when they really would have rather gone to a movie or the park.

Todd K., Fran C., and Vicky S. for sharing their authoring experiences and expertise.

Steve for helping to convince me that Drupal is better than Joomla, and for tech editing the book.

Brian G. for stepping off the cliff with me to start a company focused exclusively on Drupal.

Paul H. for your development expertise and for showing me alternative ways of thinking about Drupal development.

Cynthia, John, Oli, Alyson, and the Arapahoe Libraries Team for thinking way outside of the box and picking Drupal for your new website's platform.

Carol and the entire team at the Bloomfield Township Public Library for having the vision and the passion to create something great on Drupal.

Bonnie and Peter for carrying the vision for a next generation platform for high school students and for believing that Drupal is the right platform.

Mike Mostafavi for sparking my passion to teach and giving me the opportunity to spend eight years teaching at the university.

Phil, Mike, Steve, and Terry for giving me the opportunity to build a consulting practice focused on Drupal.

Dries for having the vision and passion for creating Drupal.

The Drupal community for your dedication to making the platform the best CMS on the planet.

The Apress team for leading me through the jungle of authoring a book. Without your passion for publishing the best books on the planet, I wouldn't have had the opportunity to cross the "author a book" item off my bucket list.

Introduction

In its relatively short life, Drupal has had a tremendous impact on the landscape of the Internet. As a web content management system (CMS), Drupal has enabled the creation of feature- and content-rich websites for organizations large and small. As a web application framework, Drupal is changing the way that people think about web application development. When I experienced the power of the Drupal platform for the first time, I knew that it was something more than just another content management solution. When I saw how easily and quickly I could build feature-rich websites, I shifted gears and focused my entire career around Drupal. While working with clients, I was often asked, "Where can I go to find information for someone who is new to Drupal?" Unfortunately there wasn't a comprehensive resource that I could point them to, and thus began my journey of writing this book.

I'm also often asked, "What is Drupal?" The short answer is, "Drupal is an open source web content management system that allows you to quickly and easily create simple to complex sites that span everything from a simple blog, a corporate site, a social networking site, or virtually anything you can dream up." What you can build with Drupal is only limited by your imagination and the time you have to spend with the platform.

As an open source platform, Drupal's community is constantly improving the platform and extending the functionality of the core platform by creating new and exciting add-on modules. If there's a new concept created on the web, it's likely that there will be a new Drupal module that enables that concept in a matter of days. It's the community behind the platform that makes Drupal what it is today, and what it will become in the future. I'll show you how to leverage the features contributed by the community, making it easy for you to build incredible solutions with minimal effort.

The very act of picking up this book is the first step in your journey down the path of learning how to use Drupal. If you will walk with me through the entire book, you'll have the knowledge and experience to build complex and powerful Drupal based websites. You'll also have the foundation necessary to move beyond the basics, expanding on the concepts I cover in this book.

Learning Drupal is like learning any new technology. There will be bumps and hurdles that cause you to step back and scratch your head. I hope the book helps smooth the bumps and provides you with enough information to easily jump over those hurdles. I look forward to seeing your works on the web and hope to bump into you at an upcoming DrupalCon.

CHAPTER 1

■ ■ ■

Introduction to Drupal

This chapter provides a basic overview of what a content management system (CMS) is, how Drupal fills the role as a CMS, the major building blocks of Drupal, and how to create content on your new Drupal website.

Content Management Systems

In its simplest form, a CMS is a software package that provides tools for authoring, publishing, and managing content on a website. "Content" is anything from a news story, a blog post, a video, a photograph, a podcast, an article, or a description of a product that you are selling. In more general terms, content is any combination of text, graphics, photographs, audio, and video that represents something that visitors to your site will read, watch, and hear.

A CMS typically provides a number of features that simplify the process of building, deploying, and managing websites, including the following:

- an administrative interface
- a database repository for content
- a mechanism for associating information that is stored in the database with a physical page on the website
- a toolset for authoring, publishing, and managing content
- a component for creating and managing menus and navigational elements
- the tools required to define and apply themes
- user management
- a security framework
- Web 2.0 capabilities such as forums, blogs, wikis, polls, and surveys
- taxonomy and tagging
- online forms
- e-commerce capabilities

There are hundreds of CMSes available (check out `www.cmsmatrix.org`). They range from simple blogging-only platforms, such as WordPress, to complex enterprise class content management solutions, such as Drupal.

Drupal

Drupal is a free and open source CMS written in PHP and distributed under the GNU General Public License. Drupal stems from a project by a Dutch university student, Dries Buytaert. The goal of the project was to provide a mechanism for Buytaert and his friends to share news and events. Buytaert turned Drupal into an open source project in 2001, and the community readily embraced the concept and has expanded on its humble beginnings, creating what is now one of the most powerful and feature-rich CMS platforms on the web. Individuals, teams, and communities leverage Drupal's features to easily publish, manage, and organize content on a variety of websites, ranging from personal blogs to large corporate and government sites.

The standard release of Drupal, known as Drupal core, contains basic features that can be used to create a classic brochure website, a single- or multi-user blog, an Internet forum, or a community website with user-generated content. Features found in Drupal core include the ability to author and publish content; to create and manage users, menus, forums, and polls; and to manage your site through a web browser-based administrative interface.

Drupal was designed to be enhanced with new features and custom behavior by downloading and enabling add-on modules. There are thousands of additional modules (known as contributed or 'contrib' modules) that extend Drupal cores functionality, covering a broad spectrum of capabilities, including e-commerce, social networking, integration with third-party applications, and multimedia.

Drupal can run on any computing platform that supports both a web server capable of running PHP version 5.2+ (including Apache, IIS, Lighttpd, and nginx) and a database (such as MySQL, SQLite, or PostgreSQL) to store content and settings.

Drupal Core

When you download and install Drupal, you are installing what is commonly called as Drupal core. Core represents the "engine" that powers a Drupal-based website, along with a number of out-of-the-box features that enable the creation of a relatively full-featured website. The primary components of Drupal core include capabilities to create and manage

- content
- file uploads/downloads
- menus
- user accounts
- roles and permissions
- taxonomy
- blogs
- discussion forums
- online polls

Drupal core also includes a feature-rich search engine, multilingual capabilities, and logging and error reporting.

Contributed Modules

Although Drupal core can be used to build feature-rich websites, there are likely situations where core lacks the functionality needed to address specific requirements. In such cases, the first step is to search through the thousands of custom modules contributed by developers from all around the world to the Drupal project for a solution that meets your needs. It's very likely that someone else has had the same functional requirement and has developed a solution to extend Drupal core to provide the functionality that you need.

To find a contributed module, visit the Drupal.org website at `www.drupal.org/project/modules`. You will find a general list of categories and the current number of contributed modules contained within each. Here is a short sampling of the types of categories and the number of modules you can find in each:

- utility (926)
- content (900)
- content display (853)
- third-party integration (816)
- administration (557)
- Content Construction Kit (CCK) (420)
- developer (398)
- community (359)
- media (331)
- e-commerce (316)

A few of the most popular modules, and the ones that you will likely want to install, include:

- Ubercart: A full-featured web storefront module that provides all of the mechanisms required to sell products (physical as well as electronic downloads), collect credit card payments, and manage shipments. If you want to sell something on your website, this is the module you will want to use.
- Webform: A module that provides a simple to use mechanism for creating, publishing, and managing forms (such as for a volunteer application, or an "ask us" or request more information form). There's no programming involved in creating online forms; any user with a basic understanding of how to create content in Drupal can quickly master the creation of simple to complex forms.

- Views: This module provides a simple to use tool for extracting information from the Drupal database and displaying the results on your website. Views is extremely powerful and can be used for things like displaying events on a calendar, creating a photo gallery, creating a slideshow, creating a table that lists various attributes of content (such as the title, author, date published, taxonomy terms, the body of the article, and so on).

- Panels: This module provides the ability to create complex page layouts without having to create code. There are several predefined layouts (rows and columns), as well as flexible layout that allows you to define your own custom layout.

- Date and Calendar: These modules provide the ability to create and manipulate date fields, as well as rendering a list of events on a calendar.

- Content Construction Kit (CCK): CCK provides the ability to create custom content types in Drupal. In Chapter 2 I discuss the two basic content types that come with Drupal 7: the story and the page. There will likely be other types of content that you want to capture on your site: content that contains additional fields beyond just a title and the body of the article. An example of a custom content type might be an event, where an event has a title and description (body) plus fields for capturing the start date/time, end date/time, the location, the price, and a description of the method for acquiring a ticket. CCK provides the mechanisms you will need to create and manage custom content types on your website.

- Backup and Migrate: Handles scheduled backups of content in your Drupal database, with the ability to restore the database to a previous state based on one of the backup files created by this module. This is a must-have module for any production website.

- Google Analytics: Provides a simple to use form for setting up Google Analytics on your site. Google analytics is a free service that tracks the number of visitors to your website, where those visitors came from, what search terms they used to find your site, the pages they visited while on your site, how long they spent on your site, and many other useful metrics that will help you view and understand the usage of your website. For more information on Google Analytics, please visit `www.google.com/analytics`.

- ImageCache: A tool that automatically resizes, scales, and crops images on your website. A must have for any site that uses pictures that are uploaded by users. ImageCache will take, for example, a 4MB picture that was uploaded from a digital camera and automatically resize that picture to a predefined, web-friendly size, such as 200px by 200px, thereby reducing the overall file size significantly and speeding the page loading time.

- IMCE: A simple to use, web browser-based file manager that enables file uploads and downloads to and from your server.

- Pathauto: This module creates search engine-friendly URLs by automatically generating a "pretty" URL that is based on the page's title (such as `www.drupal7book.com/examples` instead of the default Drupal URL of `www.drupal7book.com?node=1234`).

- Scheduler: Provides the ability to specify the date that a node will become published on the site, and the date when a node will no longer be published. This allows a content author to create a node now and have it not appear on the site until some date in the future.
- WYSIWYG: Provides a simple to use feature for downloading, installing, and configuring "what-you-see-is-what-you-get" text editors.

Drupal Themes

A theme is the Drupal component that defines how the pages on your website are structured and the visual aspects of those pages. A Drupal theme defines attributes of your website such as:

- How many columns of information will be presented on a page (a 3-column layout with a left, center, and right column; a 2-column layout with a narrow left column and a wide right column for content; a 1-column layout, and the like).
- Whether a page has a banner at the top.
- Whether a page has a footer.
- Where navigational menus appear (at the top of the page, under the banner, in the right column, and so on).
- The colors used on the page.
- The font and font size used for various elements on a page (such as headings, titles, and body text).
- Graphical elements, such as logos.

Drupal core includes a number of off-the-shelf themes that you can use for your new website. You may also download one or more of the hundreds of free themes that are available at `www.drupal.org/project/themes`, or create your own theme by following the directions found at `www.drupal.org/theme-guide`.

Creating Content

A website without content would be like a book without words, a newspaper without news, and a magazine without articles: hardly worth the effort of looking at. Drupal makes it easy to create, publish, and manage content on your new website. Let's look at how simple it is by creating our first piece of content. If you haven't installed Drupal yet, please visit the Appendix and follow the step-by-step process for installing and configuring Drupal core.

There are multiple paths for getting to the content-authoring screens in Drupal. I'll focus on the simplest first, and then discuss other methods in Chapter 2.

On the front page of your new website, you will see an "Add new content" link in the Welcome article on your home page. In the left-hand column, you will also see an "Add new content" link in the Management menu (see Figure 1-1). Click either of the links: they both take you to the content editing form where you will create your first piece of content.

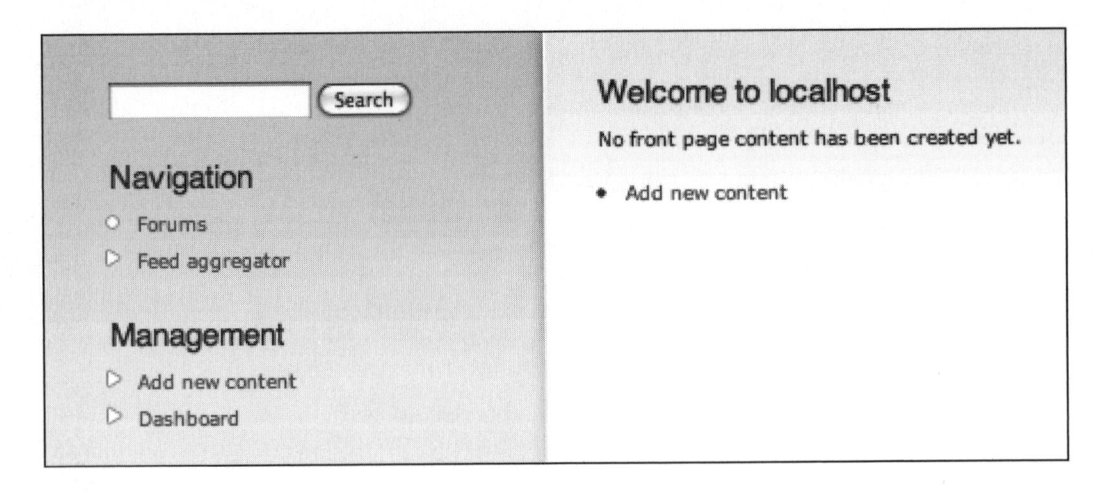

Figure 1-1. Click either "Add new content" link to get started

Next you'll see a listing of the content types that you can use (see Figure 1-2). Drupal 7 comes with two basic content types: an article and a basic page. Both content types provide you, the author, with a text field for entering the title of the content item, and a body text area where you can write. Different content types provide additional elements. In the case of an article, you have the ability to enter "tags" for categorizing your content. I will cover tagging and several other content types later in the book, as well as the capability for creating your own custom content types.

Article

Use *articles* for time-specific content like news, press releases or blog posts.

Basic page

Use *basic pages* for your static content, such as an 'About us' page.

Figure 1-2. Select your content type

Start with the simplest content type – a page – as the basis for your first content item on your new website. Click the "Basic page" link, which opens the content creation form for creating that content type (see Figure 1-3). On this form, enter the title of your first article and some text into the body area. After you have entered the title and body of your article, scroll down to the bottom of the page. On the left side of the screen you will see a vertical menu with several options. Click the "Publishing options" tab (I will cover the other options in Chapter 2), and check the Published and "Promoted to front-page" boxes. By checking the Published option, the article will be immediately displayed on your website the moment you click the Save button. Checking the "Promoted to front-page" box instructs Drupal to automatically display the article on the homepage of your new website.

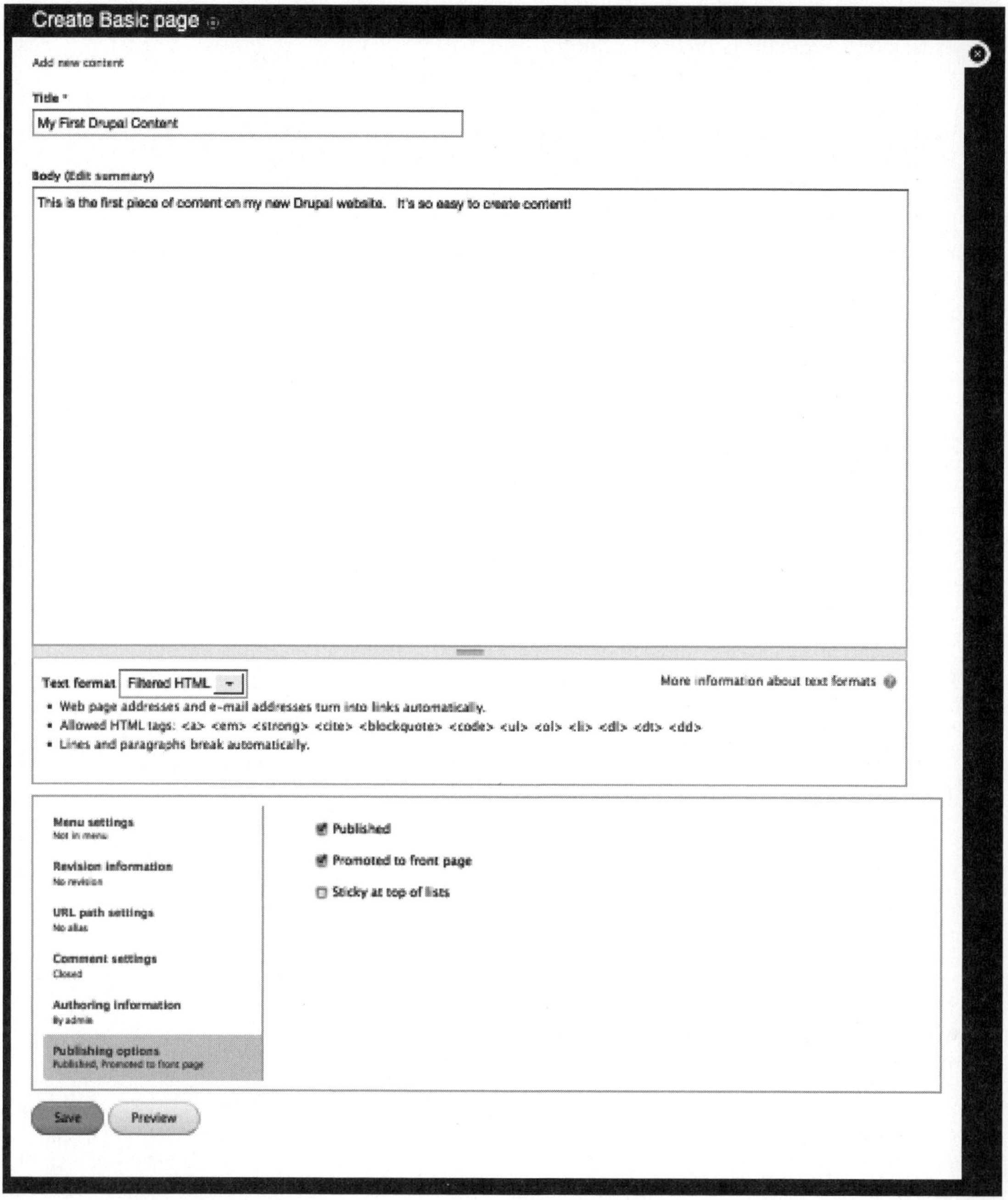

Create Basic page

Add new content

Title *

My First Drupal Content

Body (Edit summary)

This is the first piece of content on my new Drupal website. It's so easy to create content!

Text format Filtered HTML

More information about text formats

- Web page addresses and e-mail addresses turn into links automatically.
- Allowed HTML tags: <a> <em> <strong> <cite> <blockquote> <code> <ul> <ol> <li> <dl> <dt> <dd>
- Lines and paragraphs break automatically.

Menu settings
Not in menu

Revision information
No revision

URL path settings
No alias

Comment settings
Closed

Authoring information
By admin

Publishing options
Published, Promoted to front page

Published

Promoted to front page

Sticky at top of lists

Save Preview

Figure 1-3. Creating a basic page

Next click Save. Drupal will insert your new page into the database, and will then automatically redirect your browser to the homepage of your website, where you will see your new article (see Figure 1-4).

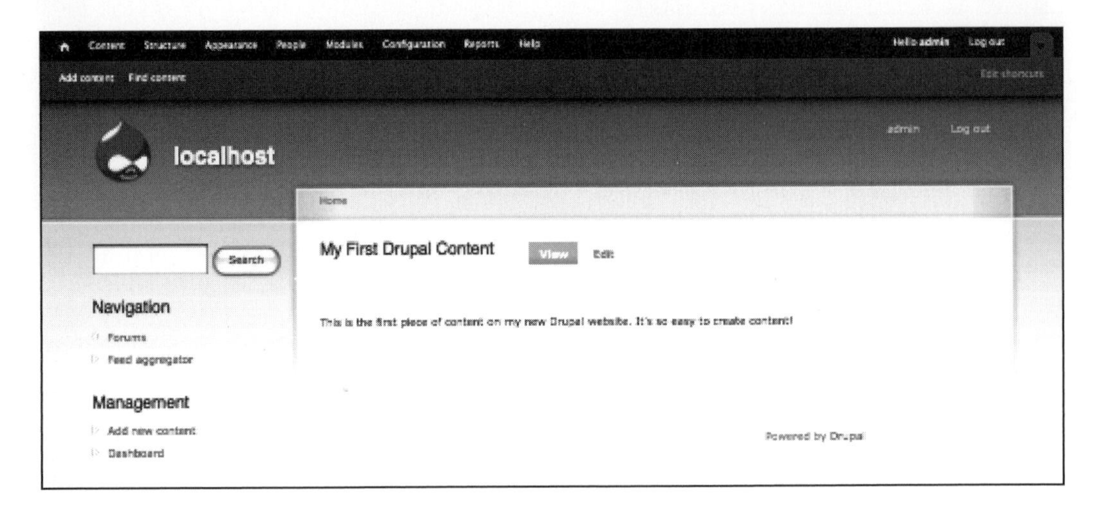

Figure 1-4. *Voila, you are published*

Congratulations! You've authored and published content on your new Drupal website. There are many other content authoring, publishing, and management features that I will cover throughout the remainder of this book. You are well on your way to building incredible websites on Drupal.

Summary

This chapter focused on the basics of what a CMS is, the base functionality available in Drupal core, how to extend the functional footprint of Drupal core by adding contributed modules, Drupal themes, and creating your first content item in Drupal. Chapter 2 will dive deeper into the content creation, publishing, and management capabilities of Drupal 7.

CHAPTER 2

■ ■ ■

Creating and Managing Content

Remember, a website without content is as interesting and informative as a book without words. In this chapter, I focus on Drupal's content creating, publishing, editing, and management features; providing you with the knowledge necessary to venture out and create, publish, and manage a wide variety of content on your new Drupal website. You started that process in the previous chapter; now let's see what you can add.

Understanding the Basics

Content is the primary building block of any website, whether it is constructed using Drupal or any other tool in the marketplace. Content is what visitors come to a website to find, and a lack of content is often the reason visitors fail to return to a website after the first time. In its most basic form, content is any combination of text, pictures, video, audio, and graphics. An individual piece of content may take a variety of different forms:

- news story
- blog post
- product description
- company overview
- forum post
- photograph
- wiki entry

Content on a Drupal-based website often starts with a title followed by body text. In Chapter 1, we created a basic page, which consisted of content with just a title and body. Drupal provides the ability to expand on this with a custom content type. A custom content type enables you to create additional fields that can be used to capture other relevant and related information. A common example is a calendar event. An event includes a title and body text (the description of the event), as well as other pertinent information, such as the date and time, the location, and possibly a map or photo. I'll cover creating custom content types in Chapter 10.

Creating Content in Drupal

In Chapter 1, I introduced Drupal's content creation capabilities by showing you how to create your first content item and publish it to your website. The content type that you used in Chapter 1 was the basic page. Drupal 7 includes a second content type – an article.

An article is identical to a basic page, with the single exception that an article has an image upload feature and an additional field where the author can enter what are called tags. Tags are simply words that help classify, organize, and search for related content on your site. They are a powerful Drupal feature that I will cover in detail in Chapter 4.

To create and publish your new article, click one of the "Add new content" links on your website and select Article from the list of content types. The form that is used to create an article looks identical to the form used to author a basic page, with the exception of the two additional fields. Proceed with the content creation process by entering a title. Next, upload a picture by clicking on the Browse button and finding a picture on your computer to upload and include in the article (see Figure 2-1).

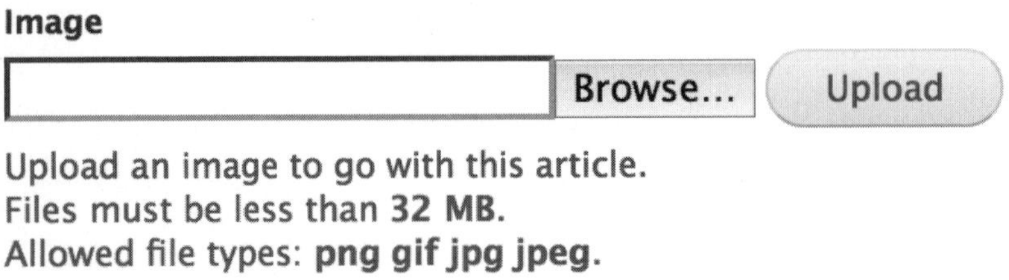

Image

Browse... Upload

Upload an image to go with this article.
Files must be less than **32 MB**.
Allowed file types: **png gif jpg jpeg**.

Figure 2-1. *Browse your computer for the image you wish to add to your article*

After you locate and upload an image, your article creation form should display a miniature version of the image on the form (see Figure 2-2), along with an alternate text field. It is a good idea to enter text into this field, especially if you expect to have visitors with visual disabilities.

Image

Apress

apress_logo.jpg (33.56 KB) Remove

Alternate text

The Apress Logo

This text will be used by screen readers, search engines, or when the image cannot be loaded.

Upload an image to go with this article.

Figure 2-2. *The image you wish to upload appears, and you are given the chance to add descriptive text*

The next step is to create the body text and the tags associated with your article (see Figure 2-3). Tags can be any list of words or phrases, separated by commas, that describe the general concepts covered in your article. I'll discuss these in more detail in Chapter 4.

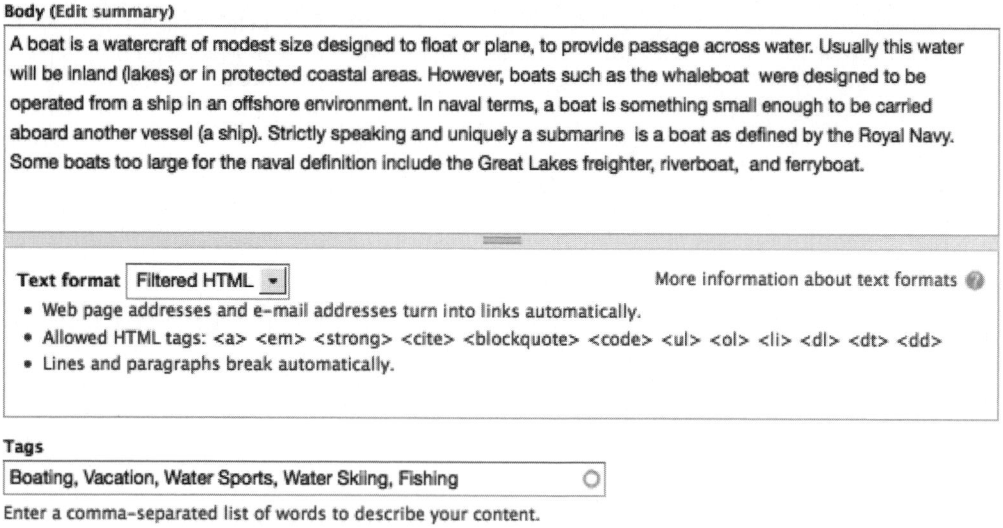

Body (Edit summary)

A boat is a watercraft of modest size designed to float or plane, to provide passage across water. Usually this water will be inland (lakes) or in protected coastal areas. However, boats such as the whaleboat were designed to be operated from a ship in an offshore environment. In naval terms, a boat is something small enough to be carried aboard another vessel (a ship). Strictly speaking and uniquely a submarine is a boat as defined by the Royal Navy. Some boats too large for the naval definition include the Great Lakes freighter, riverboat, and ferryboat.

Text format Filtered HTML   More information about text formats

- Web page addresses and e-mail addresses turn into links automatically.
- Allowed HTML tags: <a> <em> <strong> <cite> <blockquote> <code> <ul> <ol> <li> <dl> <dt> <dd>
- Lines and paragraphs break automatically.

Tags

Boating, Vacation, Water Sports, Water Skiing, Fishing

Enter a comma-separated list of words to describe your content.

Figure 2-3. *Creating article body text and adding tags*

From the vertical menu at the bottom of the page, select the Publishing Options, check the Published and "Promoted to the front-page" boxes, and click Save. The results of your actions should be an updated homepage that displays your new article (see Figure 2-4).

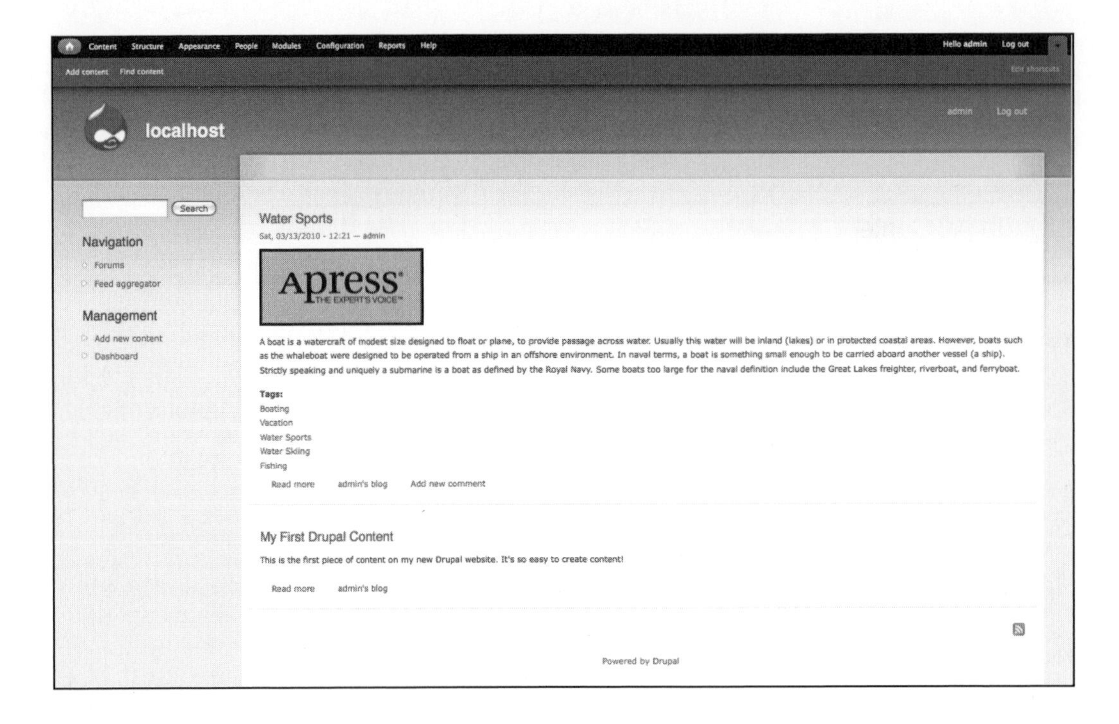

Figure 2-4. *You updated homepage appears*

As you can see in the figure, an article displays the image that was uploaded as well as the list of tags that were entered. I will cover tagging and taxonomy in detail in Chapter 4, but as a preview, clicking one of the tags automatically renders a list of all articles that were tagged with that same term.

Teasers and Full Nodes

One of Drupal's key content-related features is the ability to automatically display a content item in either "teaser" or "full-node" mode. A teaser is a shortened version of the article, typically the first 600 characters, whereas "full node" refers to the entire length of the content. In Figure 2-4, you'll notice a "Read more" link at the bottom of both articles. This tells you that Drupal is automatically rendering the content items in teaser mode. You can modify the length of teasers by setting the length by content type. I'll cover the details of how to set teaser length in Chapter 10.

Editing Content

The time will come where you need to change something about a piece of content that you've posted on your site. The process for editing content is nearly identical to the process for creating it, the only difference being the need to find the content that you want to change. If you are on the page where the content you need to change resides, and you are logged in as a user who has the correct permissions (see

Chapter 6), you will see an Edit and View link to the right-hand side of the content item's title (see Figure 2-5).

Figure 2-5. You can edit the content of your own site by clicking Edit

By default, Drupal allows the author of a content item to edit, update, and delete that item. Only site administrators or users with roles that permit them to edit, update, and delete other authors' content may make changes to your content. If you do not see Edit next to the title of a content item, then you are not logged into with an account with the proper permissions to make changes to that item.

To change a content item, click on the "Edit" link. Drupal will display that content item in edit mode where you can change or delete the item (see Figure 2-6).

Figure 2-6. Content is displayed in editing mode

Try updating the article you created in the previous step by navigating back to your homepage (simply revisit your site by returning to http://localhost or the URL of your hosted website) and clicking the Edit link next to the title of the content you created in the previous step. Change the title and/or the body and click the Save button at the bottom of that page (you may need to scroll down to see the Save button). The new version automatically appears on the homepage after you've saved it.

Other Content Options

At the bottom of the content editing form, we modified one of the vertical menu items – "Publishing options" – before we saved our new content item. Let's look at the other options associated with a content item before moving on to more advanced content topics.

Click the Edit link next to the title of the content item you just updated and scroll to the bottom of the screen. At the bottom you will see a vertical menu with the following options:

- Menu settings
- Revision information
- URL path settings
- Comment settings
- Authoring information
- Publishing options

Menu Settings

There may be instances when a content item is important enough to list on one of your site's navigational menus. By default Drupal creates a "Main menu" and "Secondary menu". The Main menu is typically displayed at the top of the page and the Secondary menu may appear in footer, left sidebar, or under the banner of your site – depending on the theme you selected. I'll cover menus in detail in Chapter 5, but for now I'll show you how to assign your test content item to the Main menu. While on the home page of your site click on the edit link associated with the sample content item you created in previous steps. Click the "lMenu settings" tab (see Figure 2-7). The "Menu setting" panel will appear. Check the "Provide a menu link" check box, and you will see three fields: "Menu link title," "Parent item," and "Weight." In the "Menu link title" field, enter a descriptive link title for your article (remember that this will appear in a menu, so use as few words as possible). From the "Parent item" drop-down, select "Main menu" (right now that is the only menu you have defined on your site). Leave the Weight field set to zero if you want your menu to sort alphabetically. You can override the alphabetical sort feature by selecting a weight from the list of values. The lower the number, the "lighter" the item will be on your menu. For horizontal menus, a lighter item appears to the left of a heavier item. For vertical menus, a lighter item appears above a heavier item. Setting the sort weight is useful in situations where you want, for example, the Home menu link to always appear as the first menu item. To force the Home link to the front of the list select the lowest number from the drop down list of values.

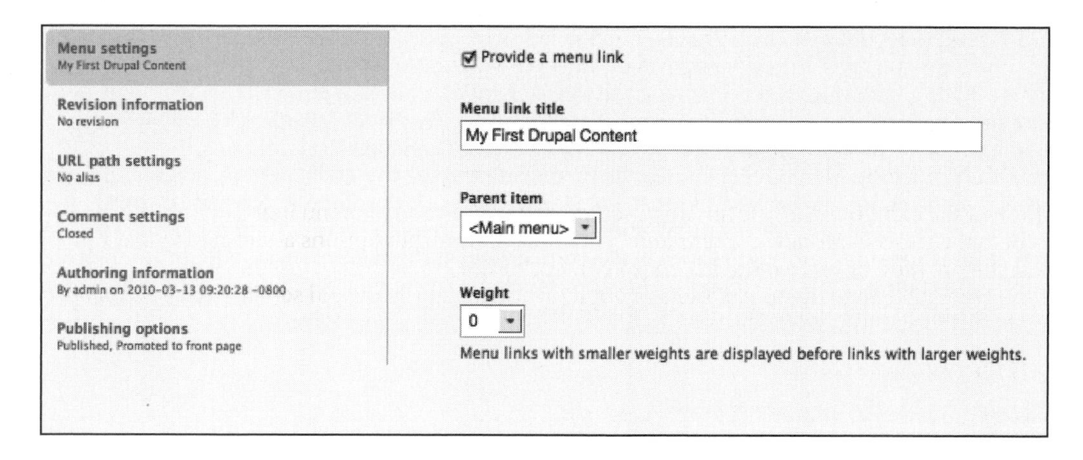

Figure 2-7. Click the "Menu settings" tab and select your preferences

Click the Save button. Drupal will save your content item, and the item will now appear on the main menu. Your menu item should appear at the top right-hand side of the heading (the blue area) on your website (see Figure 2-8).

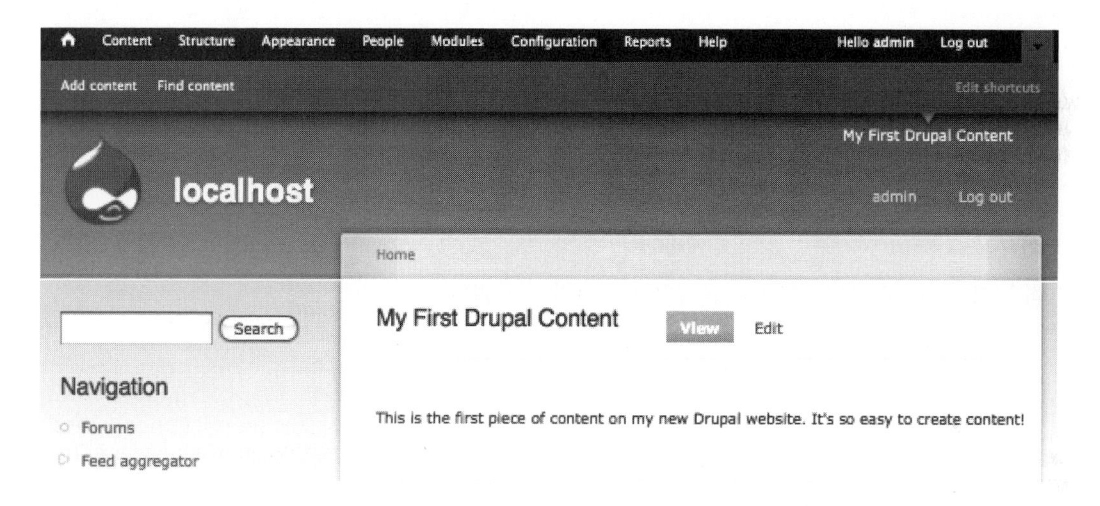

Figure 2-8. Your revised menu now contains your content item

Click the new menu item to be taken directly to that content item. If you delete the related content item, the menu item will automatically disappear.

Revision Information

Have you ever made a change to a document, saved those changes, and then realized that you made a mistake and need to "undo" the changes you made? Have you ever realized this *after* closing Microsoft Word, when it's too late to revert back to the document in its pre-changed state?

There will come a time when you or someone else makes changes to a content item, and you'll wish you had a copy of the content before it was changed. Drupal solves this problem by providing the ability to create a new version (copy) of your content when that content item is changed. Edit the sample article you created in previous steps and scroll down to the vertical tabs at the bottom of the edit form. Click on the "Revision information" tab, you will see a checkbox labeled "Create new revision." Check the box and enter a description of the changes that you made (see Figure 2-9).

***Figure 2-9.** Enter an explanation of the changes you made*

Once you have entered the description of what you changed, click the Save button. Drupal then displays your content item with a new Revisions link to the right of the title (see Figure 2-10).

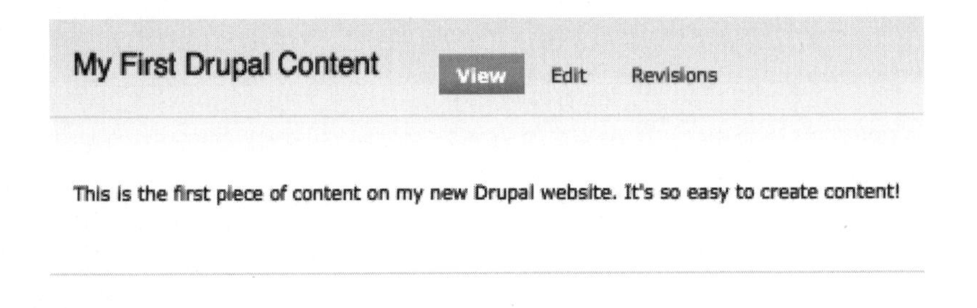
My First Drupal Content
View
Edit
Revisions
This is the first piece of content on my new Drupal website. It's so easy to create content!

***Figure 2-10.** Your item now includes a Revisions link*

Clicking the Revisions link takes you to a page that lists the current version and all previous versions of that content item (see Figure 2-11).

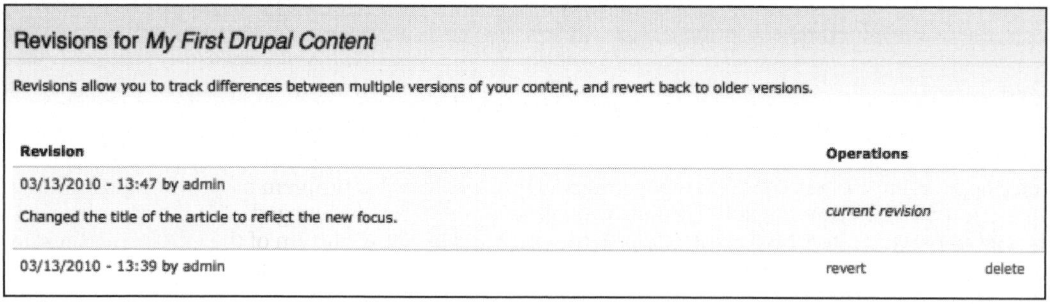

Revisions for *My First Drupal Content*

Revisions allow you to track differences between multiple versions of your content, and revert back to older versions.

Revision	Operations	
03/13/2010 - 13:47 by admin Changed the title of the article to reflect the new focus.	*current revision*	
03/13/2010 - 13:39 by admin	revert	delete

Figure 2-11. All the revisions to an item appear on this screen

You can view a previously published version of the article by clicking the date and time for a previous version.

Clicking the Back button in your browser returns you to the previous page where you can click the Revert link, changing the currently published version to a previously published version. Clicking Revert causes Drupal to display a page that asks you if you really want to revert back to a previously published version.

Clicking the Revert button results in Drupal unpublishing the current version and publishing the selected version.

In this process, you as the author had to request that a new version of the content item be created. You can also configure each content type so that it automatically creates a new version when updates are made to any piece of content that is authored using that content type. I'll discuss how to do that later in this chapter.

URL Path Settings

You may have noticed while working with the revisions feature that the URL that was shown in your browser's address bar looked something like http://localhost/node/1, where "node" in the URL tells us that Drupal is displaying a single piece of content (a node) and "1" represents the unique ID of the node that is being displayed. In this case, it's the first node that we created in the system, so the ID is 1. That number will increase by 1 for each node we add. Although http://localhost/node/1 gets us to the content that we wanted, the URL is not very people- or search-engine-friendly. Fortunately, Drupal lets us override the URL to something that is.

Click the Edit link next to the title of your content item and scroll to the bottom of the page. In the vertical menu, click "URL path settings." Drupal lets you create an alias, or an alternative URL, to the same content item as http://localhost/node/1. In the "URL alias" field, enter a more descriptive URL (see Figure 2-12).

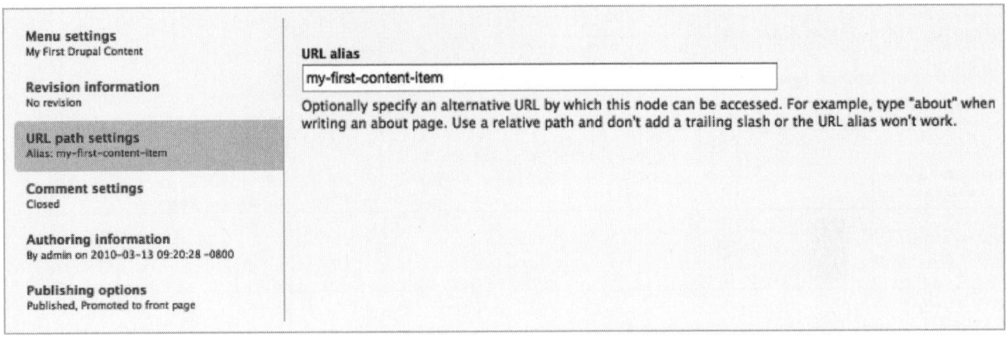

Figure 2-12. Changing your content's URL to a more descriptive one

---

■ **Caution** You must use hyphens to separate the words in your URL. Spaces between words will not work.

After entering the new URL alias, click the Save button at the bottom of the page. Drupal will redisplay the page using the new alias URL that you created on the previous page. In my example, the new URL is http://localhost/my-first-content-item. The new URL is easy for a human to understand and, more important, easy for a search engine to pick up: the URL better indicates the content that the page provides.

Creating alias URLs is an important aspect of creating content on your website. However, manually creating an alias for every content item is tedious. Fortunately, there is a Drupal module that automatically creates a URL alias for every content item saved on your site after the module is installed and enabled. That module is called "Pathauto." I'll cover the installation of modules like path auto in Chapter 8.

Comment Settings

Drupal provides the capability for visitors to your website to post comments on your site's content. To try it, click the Edit link next to the title of your content item and scroll to the bottom of the page. In the vertical menu on the left, click "Comment settings." Clicking the link reveals the screen shown in Figure 2-13.

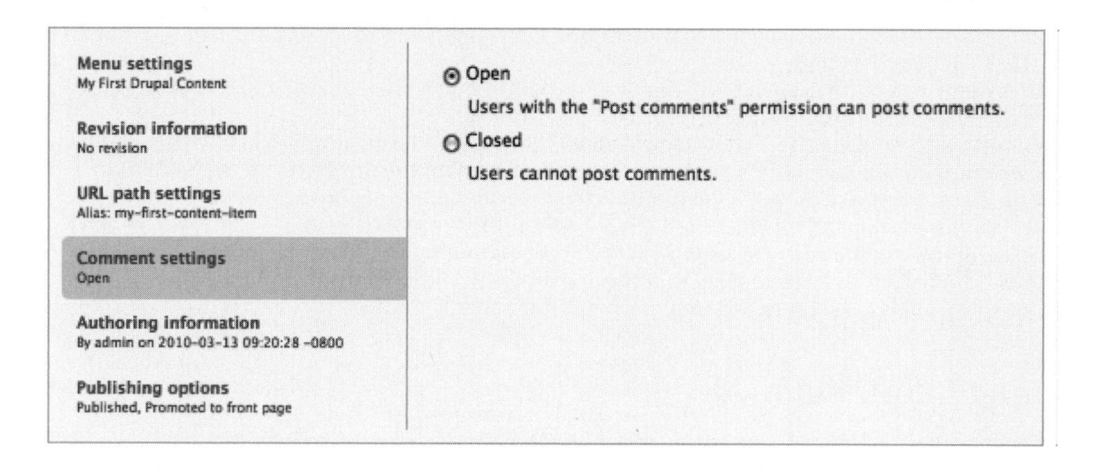

Figure 2-13. Setting your comments preferences

Select Open and click Save. You'll notice a significant change in how your content item is displayed. There is now a form at the bottom of the article where users can post comments (see Figure 2-14).

Add new comment

Your name

admin

Subject

Comment *

Figure 2-14. Users can now post comments on your site

Visitors to your site can now write and publish comments in response to your content item (assuming you have set the permissions to allow anonymous users to post comments, which I will cover in Chapter 6). Try entering a Subject and Comment and then click Save. Your comment should now appear in the Comments section.

As the content author (or as an administrator of the site), you can delete, edit, or reply to a comment by clicking the links under each comment.

Comments typically appear in chronological order. As the site administrator, you have the ability to specify how comments are displayed: either the newest comment at the top of the list or the first comment posted at the top of the list. I'll cover how to set the default order in Chapter 10.

Turning comments on and off at the individual content item provides absolute control over which items accept comments. You can also set whether to accept comments at the content type level, meaning every content item created using that content type will "inherit" that setting. I'll cover setting global parameters, such as accepting comments, in Chapter 10.

Authoring Information

Once again, click the Edit link next to the title of your content item and scroll to the bottom of the page. Click "Authoring information" in the vertical menu, and you'll see the screen shown in Figure 2-15.

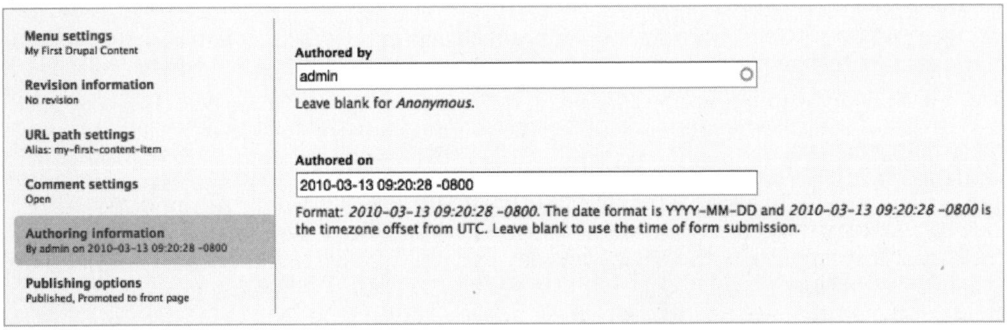

Figure 2-15. *Enter author information here*

This screen provides information about who created the content and the date that the content was authored. It's unlikely that you'll want to change this information, but you can if you need to.

Publishing Options

The final item on the vertical menu is "Publishing options." Click the Edit link next to the title of your content item and scroll to the bottom of the page. Click "Publishing options" to see the screen shown in Figure 2-16.

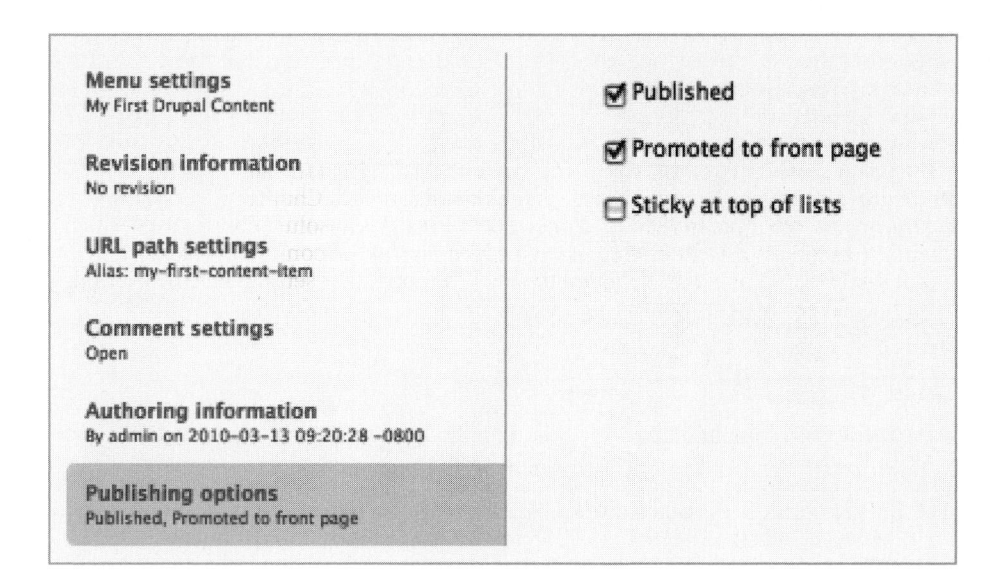

Figure 2-16. Checking out your publishing options

We used this screen when we created our page and selected to "Promote to front page." We can also use this form to "unpublish" a content item. Doing so makes that item "invisible" to visitors to your website, but visible to you, the author, and any other administrators on your website. This is an often overlooked feature that can help you as you build your website by allowing you to author content and see how that content will look on your site, without exposing the content to site visitors. It also allows you to author content in advance, before you actually want to "go live" with it.

We used the "Promote to front page" option to tell Drupal that we want this article to show up on the front page of our website. If you uncheck this box, your article will be removed from the front page, but will still be available through the URL that we set up in the previous steps, or directly through the http://localhost/node/X link, where X is the node ID of the content that we are seeking. I will cover alternative methods for having content show up on the front page in later chapters when I talk about advanced Drupal features.

The "Sticky at the top of list" option provides a mechanism for ensuring that this content item always appears at the top of lists. I will cover lists in detail in Chapter 10. This is a helpful feature when you have content that you want to highlight, such as an article on the rules for posting content on your site.

Deleting Content

I've covered how to create and edit content, but I haven't covered how to delete content. There may be cases where you have a piece of content that is no longer relevant to your site, and you want to delete it. The process for deleting a content item is fairly simple. First create a new article following the steps that we covered earlier in the chapter. The title and content isn't important as we're going to immediately delete the article after we've created it. In the publishing options make sure that you check both the published and promoted to front page check boxes as we want the article to appear on the homepage of our site. Once finished, click the Edit link to the right of the title of the content item that you created and scroll to the bottom of the page (see Figure 2-17).

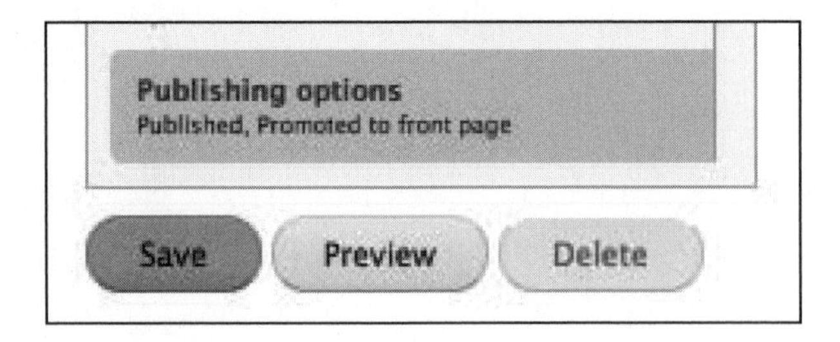

Figure 2-17. *Preparing to delete a content item*

At the bottom of the page you'll see a Delete button. Click it, and you'll be prompted with a "do you really want to delete it" screen. Click the Delete button, which will trigger Drupal to physically remove your content item from the Drupal database. Drupal will then take you back to the front page of your website, where you'll see that your content item no longer exists, and the menu item you created earlier in this chapter is also gone.

Finding Content

It is likely that your site will have dozens to hundreds of content items, and at some point you'll need the capability to look for an item that you want to view, change, or delete. To find that content item you could do any of the following:

- Navigate to the page where that item resides, and click the Edit button next to the title.
- Enter the URL for that item in the address bar of your web browser.
- Search for that item using your site's search feature.
- Use the content listing page.

Any of the methods would work, but one of the most common methods is to use the content listing page. To view this page, click the Content link in top black menu bar. You'll see the screen shown in Figure 2-18.

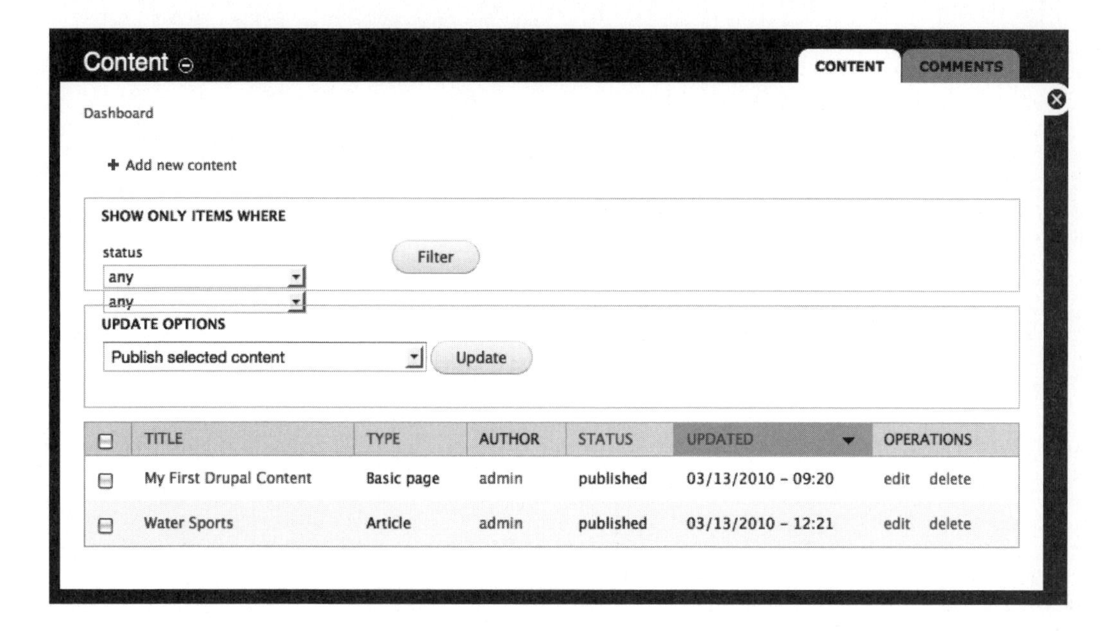

Figure 2-18. Viewing the Content screen

On this page you can sort the list by clicking on the title, type, author, status, or updated column headings. You can also filter the results (limit what is shown) by selecting the status from the top drop-down menu (for example, Published or Unpublished) and/or the content type drop-down menu (such as Article or Page). Clicking the Filter button will refresh the list to show only those items that meet the criteria you selected.

From any item in the list, you can click the title of the article to view that article, or you can click the Edit or Delete links to edit or delete that item. You may also publish, unpublish, delete, promote to the front page, unpromote to the front page, make sticky and remove stickiness on multiple content items at the same time. Just click the check box to the left of each content item and select the option to apply to all items you checked, then click Update.

Summary

This chapter focused on creating content, setting the various options that are available when creating a content item, updating and deleting content. You learned how to place a content item on a menu so users can easily find and view content, and how to create search-engine- and user-friendly URLs. At this point, you have the basic skills and understanding necessary to create a basic Drupal website, but stopping now means that you would miss out on all of the other rich and powerful features that Drupal has to offer. In the chapters that follow, I will describe the processes for creating complex page layouts, rendering lists of content, controlling who has access to various features and functions on your website, and share tips and tricks for managing your new site.

CHAPTER 3

■ ■ ■

Creating and Managing Users

Now that your site is up and running, you have a couple of decisions to make. First, will you have any administrators on the site other than yourself? Second, will your site be open to everyone, or will users need to log in to view content and other features? In this chapter, I cover the how Drupal treats visitors to your site, and how you as a site administrator can configure Drupal's user account features to restrict the capabilities of those who have user accounts on your system.

Users, Roles, and Permissions

Controlling who has the ability to do what on your website is performed through Drupal's security features. Drupal's security features provide the ability to define who has the ability to view, create, update, delete, and participate through a combination of individual user accounts, user roles, and permissions.

Users (or site visitors) in Drupal 7 are divided into two general categories: anonymous users and authenticated users. Anonymous users are individuals who visit your website and do not log in using a user ID and password. If you visit `www.cnn.com` and don't log in, you're classified as an anonymous user. With Drupal, you have the ability to support anonymous users, and you also have the ability to restrict what an anonymous user can do on your site. Authenticated users are visitors to your site who log in using a unique user ID and password. I'll cover how user IDs and passwords are created shortly, but understanding the difference between the two categories of users is important.

Roles are a Drupal mechanism that allows you, the site administrator, to define categories of authenticated users of your website. You may define roles on your website that are department specific (e.g., a role for human resources, purchasing, sales, marketing, and customer service), roles that are functionally oriented (e.g., content authors, content reviewers, content authors), roles that are associated with a specific section of your website (e.g., products, support, sales, homepage), or any other definition that you can dream up. Roles are simply a way of putting authenticated users into categories, where categories are associated with specific permissions. Any authenticated user of your website may be assigned to none, one, or more than one role (e.g., you may have a user who is assigned roles of sales department, content author, and products).

Permissions in Drupal are a mechanism for controlling what a user assigned to a specific role can do. There are dozens of permissions that you can enable or revoke for each user role you have defined. Examples of permissions that you might set for a specific role include: the ability to create a new page, the ability to create a new article, the ability to edit any article regardless of who authored it, the ability to search content on the website, and the ability to add a new user account. The combination of permissions that you set for each role define the capabilities that a user assigned to that role can do on your website.

When you combine user roles with permissions and individual user accounts, you end up with a highly configurable solution for securing access to key features and content on your website.

User Accounts

All Drupal websites have at least one user account: the system administrator. This account is created automatically during the installation process, and is the account that you will use to administer your site. For sites where the site owner is the only one who creates content and administers the site, having just the site administrators account is all that is required. If you anticipate having others who will administer or create content, then you'll need to decide which Drupal mechanism will be used to create user accounts. Drupal provides three alternatives for you to pick from:

- Users can create their own accounts without an administrator approving their account.
- Users can request a new account, but an administrator has to approve the account before it is activated.
- Only Administrators create user accounts.

The approach you take is dependent on how you anticipate visitors using your website. If your site is informational in nature and visitors don't need to log in to see content or participate in site features (e.g., posting comments), then option 3 is the best approach, as it doesn't confuse visitors to the site by making them think that you have to log in to your site to see content. If your site has content or features that are considered "not for public consumption" and require a user account, then you will want to pick an approach that works for you depending on whether you want users to be able to create their own accounts without verifying their credentials (option 1), or you want an administrator to perform some form of verification before the users account is activated (option 2).

Setting the approach that you wish to use is part of the process of setting up the various settings for user accounts on your system.

Configuring User Account Settings

Before creating your first user account, it is advisable that you visit the user account settings page and review or modify the general user account configuration settings. To access the settings page, click the Configuration link in the menu at the top of the page (assuming you are logged in as the administrator), and, on the Configuration page, scroll down until you see the section titled "People and Permissions." Click the Account Settings link, which will take you to the page that you will use to set various configuration options for user accounts.

The options that you can set on this page are:

- *What term you will use to identify anonymous users.* In most cases, leaving the default value is appropriate.

- *What role do you want to associate with administrator capabilities* (I will cover creating roles later in this chapter). The role selected will become the default role assigned as the administrator of new modules that you install on the system. Using the default value "administrator" is an appropriate action.

The next set of options, "Registration and Cancellation," define how user accounts are set up on your system. The first set of options define how new user accounts are handled.

- If only administrators can create accounts, select the first option "Administrators Only."
- If any visitor to your website can create their own account, select the "Visitors" option.
- If visitors can request an account but an administrator must approve that request before the account is active, then select the third option, "Visitors, but administrator approval is required."

For demonstration purposes I'll select the first option, so that only administrators may create user accounts.

The next option, "Require e-mail verification," is a good option to leave checked. This option requires that the user responds to a Drupal-generated e-mail that asks them to confirm their account. This helps to avoid "bot" created user accounts, as most bots do not have the intelligence or capabilities to respond to user account verification e-mails.

The next set of options allows you to define what happens to content on your site that was created by this user when you disable that person's account in the future. In most cases the default option, "Disable the account and keep all content," meets the needs of a majority of websites. You may, however, decide that one of the other options is more appropriate for your site.

The next set of options defines whether users can add pictures and signatures to their profiles. I will leave the default values for our test site; however, you may wish to enable or disable these options depending on whether you wish to provide those capabilities to users.

The remaining options at the bottom of the page define how e-mails generated by the system that inform users of their new account are formatted, and the content that is included in each of the emails that are generated by the system. You may modify the content of the e-mails to address your individual preferences. Simply click through each of the tabs in the vertical menu to view each of the e-mails that are generated by the system and sent to users.

You may also define what fields are included in a user's profile. You may wish to capture additional user details beyond Drupal's out-of-the-box profile (username and e-mail address) with details such as the user's address and phone number. Click on the Manage Fields tab at the top of the screen to see these fields.

You can add other fields to your user's profile by simply entering a new label for the field, defining an internal name for the field, and selecting the type of field you want to present to the user (such as a text box). In Figure 3-1, I've created a new field for capturing the "location" of the user. In this example, I used Location as the label, user_location as the field name, Text as the type of information to store, and "Text field" as the type of field to use to collect the location from the user.

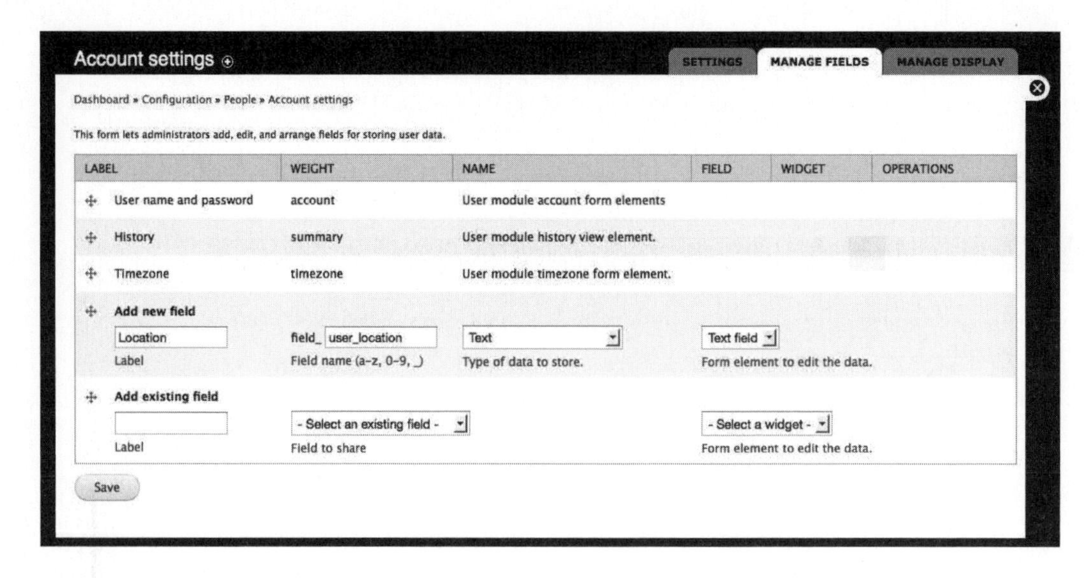

Figure 3-1. Updating user account settings

Clicking the Save button walks you through additional configuration screens where you can further refine the details of this field. For this demonstration, and for a typical field, selecting the defaults on these other screens is appropriate.

You now have the definition of user accounts completed and you are now ready to define roles and set permissions.

Creating Roles

User roles are a mechanism for categorizing groups of users with similar responsibilities and capabilities on your website. If your website is for an elementary school, you might have roles for teachers, students, and staff. If your website is a community website you might have roles for content authors, content reviewers, publishers, and forum administrators.

The hardest part about creating user roles is deciding what roles you'll need for your site. In general terms, it is easier to administer a site that has fewer roles than one that has lots of roles, as you must set the permissions for each individual role. However, fewer roles means less flexibility, so it is a balancing act, and often one that you have to adjust over time as you become more familiar with the types of users on your site. Unfortunately, there isn't a formula you can use to determine how many roles you'll need, but fortunately there isn't a right or wrong answer as to how many you will need. For our example, we'll create two general-purpose roles:

A role for users who are part of our organization and who will have responsibility for authoring, publishing, and managing content and menus on our site.

A role for site visitors who are provided access to "non-public" content that is intended only for authenticated users (visitors who have been assigned a user ID and password). These users can view content and add comments to content, but cannot author, edit, or delete content.

To create a new user role, assuming you are logged in with the administrator account, click the People link in menu at the top of the page. On the People page, click the Permissions tab. On the Permissions page, click the Roles link to navigate to the page where you view, create, edit, and delete roles. On this page there is a blank text box in the Name column, which is where you will enter the name of our new group. For demonstration purposes, enter "company user" as the name of the new role (see Figure 3-2).

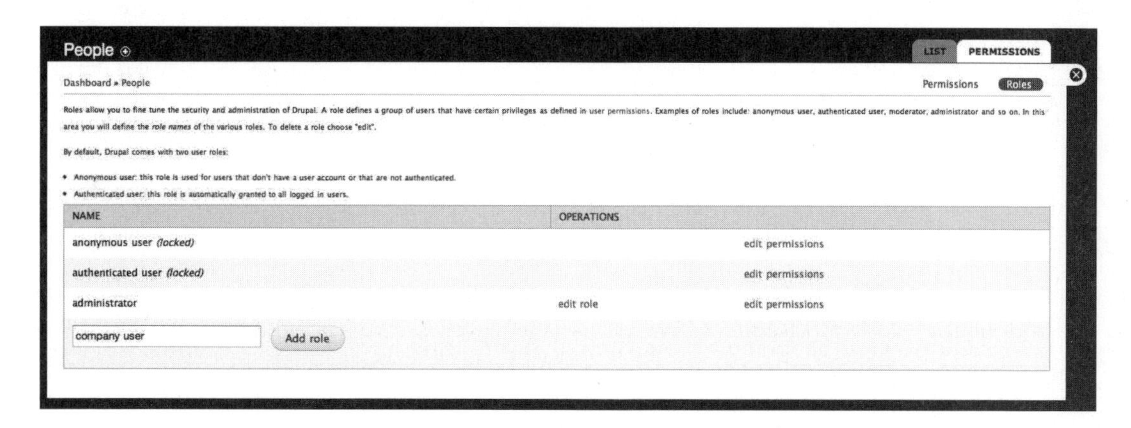

Figure 3-2. Working with roles in the People page

Click the "Add role" button. This results in the creation of the company user role and a new blank text box for creating another new role. For our second example user role, enter "restricted user." A restricted user is any user who has an account on the website and who can view restricted content and post comments to that content, but cannot create, edit, or delete content or perform any administration functions on our website. Once you've entered "restricted user" in the text box, click the "Add role" button to continue.

With both of your new roles defined, you're ready to assign permissions to the roles that you have created.

Assigning Permissions

Permissions provide a mechanism for controlling what users assigned to specific roles on the website can and cannot do. Drupal core and each contributed module provide a set of predefined permissions that you must either enable or disable on a role-by-role basis.

To assign permissions to a role, click the People link at the top of the page (assuming you are logged in as the site administrator). On the People page, click the Permission tab, which reveals the page that you will use to set permissions for each of the roles that you have defined (see Figure 3-3).

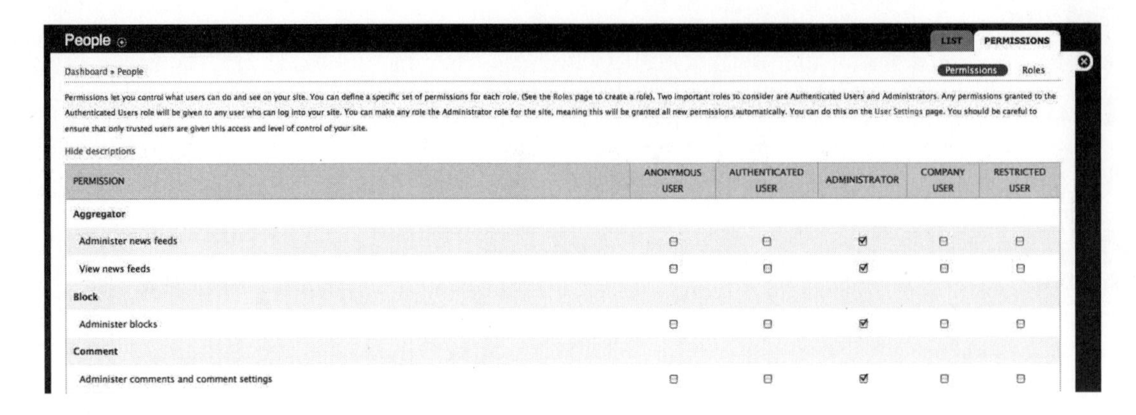

Figure 3-3. Setting permissions for each role

This page lists all of the permissions available for your site and the roles that you have defined. You can scroll down the page and check those permissions that you wish to enable for that role, and you can uncheck permissions that you would like to remove from this role.

For demonstration purposes, scroll down the page until you find a section titled Node, and in that section check the following boxes for the Company user role:

- Create new *Article* content
- Create new *Basic page* content
- Edit own *Article* content
- Edit own *Basic page* content
- Delete own *Article* content
- Delete own *Basic page* content

For the Restricted User role, scroll up to the Comments section and check the following permissions:

- View comments
- Post comments without approval
- Edit own comments

At this point, you have created roles and assigned permissions to those roles. You are now ready to create user accounts.

Creating User Accounts

You now have user roles defined, appropriate permissions set, and are ready to create user accounts. The process for creating a new user account is accomplished by first clicking the People link in the menu at the top of the page. Clicking this link reveals the page shown in Figure 3-4.

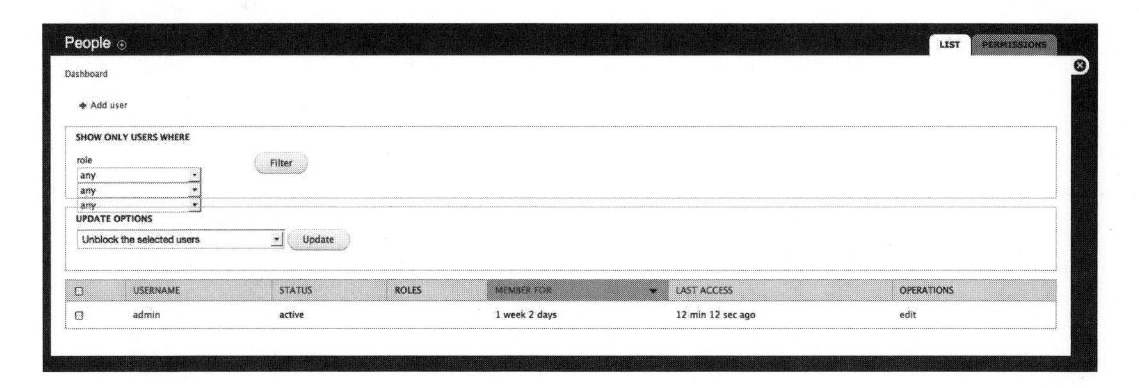

Figure 3-4. Creating user accounts

This screen lists all existing user accounts. At this point, the only account that is listed is the admin account, which was created when we performed the installation process. To add a new user, click the "Add user" link at the top left of this page. Clicking the link reveals the "Add user" form (see Figure 3-5).

People

LIST PERMISSIONS

Dashboard » People

This web page allows administrators to register new users. Users' e-mail addresses and usernames must be unique.

ACCOUNT INFORMATION

Username *

Spaces are allowed; punctuation is not allowed except for periods, hyphens, apostrophes, and underscores.

E-mail address *

A valid e-mail address. All e-mails from the system will be sent to this address. The e-mail address is not made public and will only be used if you wish to receive a new password or wish to receive certain news or notifications by e-mail.

Password *

Password strength:

Confirm password *

Provide a password for the new account in both fields.

Status

Blocked

Active

Roles

authenticated user

administrator

company user

restricted user

Notify user of new account

Create new account

Figure 3-5. *The "Add user" form*

For demonstration purposes, we will create a new user account by entering the following values:

- In the username field enter: johnsmith.
- In the password field enter: johnsmith@company.com.
- In the password field enter: 12johnsmith34.
- In the confirm password field enter: 12johnsmith34.
- For status make sure that active is selected.
- For roles check the company user box.
- Check the notify user of new account box (clicking this option causes Drupal to send an e-mail to the user notifying them of their new account).
- Click the Create New Account button to save the account.
- Click the List tab at the top of the screen to see the complete list of user accounts on your site (see Figure 3-6), including the account that you just created.

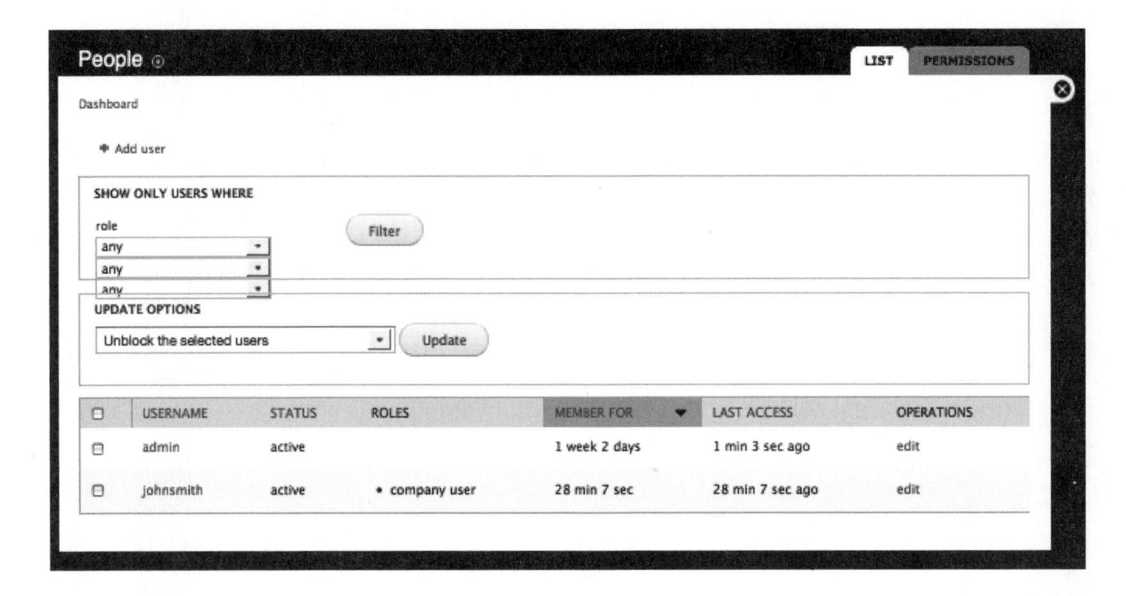

Figure 3-6. *All the user accounts of your site*

John Smith can now log onto your site and perform all the tasks associated with the company user role.

There may be instances where you need to update a user account. For example, resetting a user's password, changing his or her e-mail address, updating his or her assigned roles, or disabling the account. You can perform all of these actions by clicking the Edit link associated with the users account on the People page.

User Generated Accounts

If you configured your site so that users can create their own accounts, requiring that a site administrator review and approve their account, the process is slightly different than that of an administrator creating the users account. If you selected the user account option where a visitor can create their account but requires administrator approval, or the option where visitors can create their account without an administrator approving their account, the login form has an additional option under the Login button: "Create new account." See Figure 3-7.

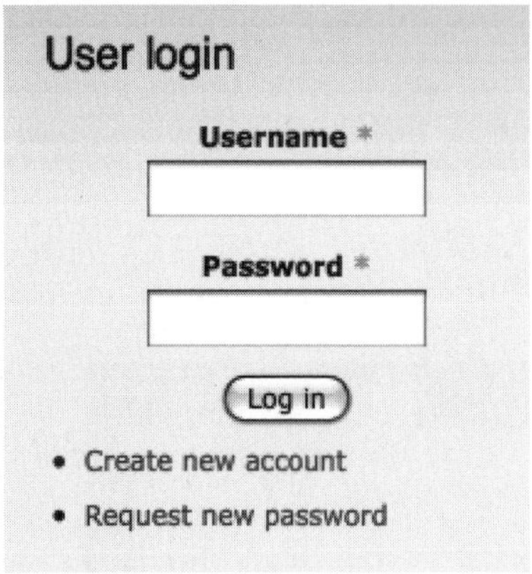

Figure 3-7. *The "Create new account" option*

Clicking this link (while not logged into the site) brings you to a screen where a visitor can enter their requested username and their e-mail address (see Figure 8). For this example, enter a username and an e-mail address for the new account and click "Create new account" (note: Drupal only allows you to use an e-mail address once across your entire site. Attempting to reuse an e-mail address that is already assigned to an account on your system will result in an error message).

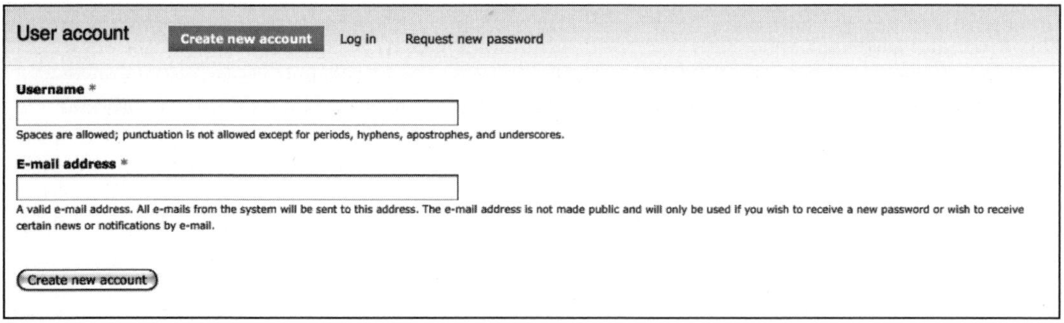

Figure 3-8. *Entering new account information*

As soon as the account is created Drupal sends an email to the e-mail address entered by the user and displays a success message displayed on the screen:

"Thank you for applying for an account. Your account is currently pending approval by the site administrator. In the meantime, a welcome message with further instructions has been sent to your e-mail address."

If you configured your system to allow users to create an account but an administrator must manually approve that account, you'll need to visit the People page and edit that users account, changing the users status from Blocked to Active. Until the user's status has been changed, they will be unable to log onto your site with their user ID and password. If you selected the option where users can create an account and the account does not require administrator approval, the user will be able to log onto your site immediately.

Resetting User's Passwords

One of Drupal's features that saves site administrators hours of work a year is the ability for users to reset their passwords without having to e-mail a site administrator asking someone to reset their password for them. If you log out of your site (clicking the logout link at the top right of the page), you'll note that in the right column, under the Login button, there is a link for requesting a new password (refer to Figure 3-7).

Clicking on this link reveals a page where the visitor can enter either their user ID or their email address.

Entering either a valid username or a valid e-mail address (where "valid" means that it exists as either a valid user ID on your site or a valid e-mail address associated with a user account on your site) results in Drupal generating an e-mail that is sent to the user with a "one-time login" link that allows them to reset their password.

Summary

In this chapter, I covered the process for configuring how Drupal handles user accounts and the approach for creating user roles and assigning permissions to those roles. I discussed the decisions that you as the site owner must make when setting up your site, including whether you will be the only person who has the ability to administer the site and create content, or whether you will have others who will be responsible for those areas.

If there will be others assigned to tasks of creating content or managing the site, then you'll want to configure the base settings for user accounts, create roles for those who will be performing activities on your site, and set the appropriate permissions. You'll also want to define whether users can create their own accounts without an administrator approving their accounts, or users can create an account but an administrator must approve it, or only administrators can create accounts. Once you've made those decisions and set the parameters discussed in this chapter you're ready to start adding users to your site. You can have all the users you can handle, but they probably won't stick around long if they can't find the content they're interested in on your site. That's where taxonomy comes in, which is what we'll talk about next.

CHAPTER 4

■ ■ ■

Taxonomy

One of the Drupal features new Drupal users under-use and misunderstand is Taxonomy. New Drupal users are overwhelmed with all of the other features and functions provided by the platform, and they bypass what may be one of the most powerful and useful features that Drupal has to offer. In this chapter you will create and use taxonomy terms to categorize content so that visitors can easily find information related to a specific topic.

Taxonomy Overview

At the simplest level, taxonomy provides a mechanism for categorizing content on your site. One of the benefits of a library is that the librarians have taken the time to examine every book, movie, periodical, and music item that they have on the shelves in their building. The librarians, or the publishers, have painstakingly thought about how to categorize each item so that it easy to locate. Not only is it easy to locate an item in the library, it is also easy to locate items that are similar to the item that you are interested in. For example, you could walk into a library and locate the section for all items related to web design. In that section, you could find books on topics ranging from using Photoshop to create graphics to programming in PHP, all thanks to the work of the librarians and the use of a system to categorize similar items.

Think of how painful it would be to walk into a library where everything is thrown on shelves without regards to subject, title, author, or category. Within a few minutes of searching haphazardly around the aisles for specific book, you would likely either leave out of sheer frustration or would ask a librarian, who would hopefully have some idea of where the book might be. Taxonomy is a lot like categorizing items that are in a library, but for the content that resides on your site. If you categorize the content, you make it easier for people to find what they're looking for, and you also make it easier for people to find things that are similar to an item that that they may be looking at.

In Drupal taxonomy is divided into two elements: a *vocabulary* and *term*. A vocabulary is simply a group of related terms, where a term is a word or phrase that describes a distinct aspect of a vocabulary. Another way to think of a vocabulary is as a category and a term as a "tag," which is a common tool used on blogs to categorize content. The benefits of Drupal's taxonomy over just tagging content is the ability to associate multiple terms (tags) as a single vocabulary, making it possible to display a list of all content for a vocabulary (multiple tags) instead of just a single tag.

Let's take a look at a real-world example. Let's say the site that we are creating is one that is focused on sports news. Our targeted audience is people who like to follow what is happening with their favorite teams. If we think about how people might want to search and navigate content on our site, we might think of organizing the content by the type of sport, for example:

- Football
- Baseball
- Basketball
- Hockey
- Soccer

People may also think about sports by team:

- Ravens
- Trailblazers
- Lakers
- Raiders
- Yankees

In this example, we would define a vocabulary for type of sport and assign terms to that vocabulary for each sport listed. We could also create another vocabulary for teams, and assign each of the teams listed to a term associated with that vocabulary. We could then use Drupal's taxonomy feature to associate each piece of content authored on the site with a sport (such as basketball) and a team (such as the Trailblazers). We could then use taxonomy's built-in features to list all content items that are associated with specific vocabulary on a page.

Creating Vocabularies

The first step in using taxonomy is to identify and create the vocabularies that you will use to categorize content on your website. Depending on the focus of your site and the breadth of subjects that you cover, you may only need a single vocabulary or you may need several vocabularies. There isn't a "correct" answer, nor is there a formula that you can use to determine how many vocabularies your site will need. The best approach is to think about the content that you will include and the subjects that the content will cover. If the subjects are all related (e.g., types of sports) then a single vocabulary is likely all that you will need. If the subjects are not related (e.g., a general news website with stories about various technologies, health care, jobs, and entertainment), then you may need several vocabularies, one per subject area.

Once you've identified at least one vocabulary, click on the Structure link in the admin menu at the top of any page on your site. You'll see a list of options that includes a link to Taxonomy. Click that to reveal a page that lists all of the vocabularies that have already been defined for your site. By default, Drupal creates a vocabulary called Tags as a default generic "container" for terms. See Figure 4-1.

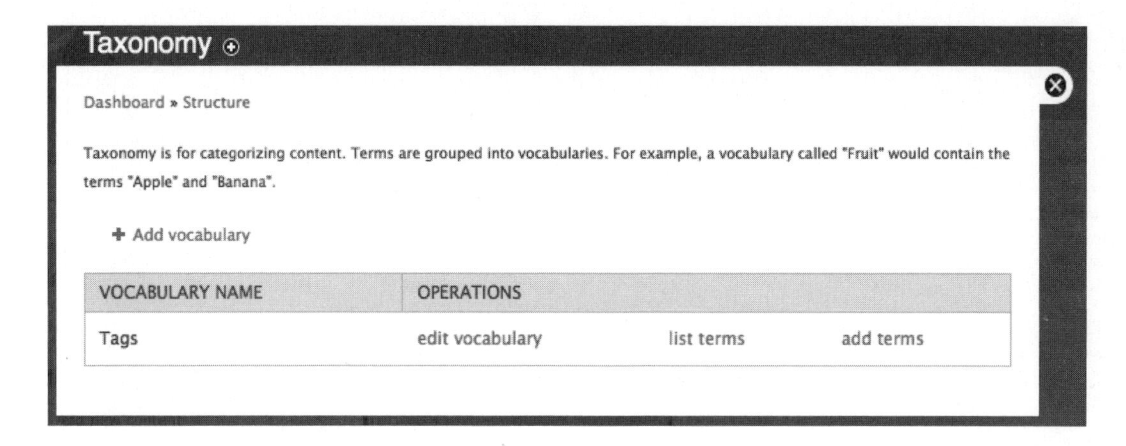

Figure 4-1. The Tags vocabulary

To add a new vocabulary, click on the "Add vocabulary" link at the top of the list, revealing the form shown in Figure 4-2. In the Name field, enter Type of Sport, and enter a brief description in the Decryption field.

Taxonomy
Dashboard » Structure » Taxonomy
Name *
Type of Sport
Machine name: type_of_sport [Edit]
Description
A vocabulary used to categorize sports
Save

Figure 4-2. Creating a new vocabulary

Once you've entered the values in both fields, click Save, which results in the list of vocabulary items to be displayed with your new vocabulary shown in the list. See Figure 4-3.

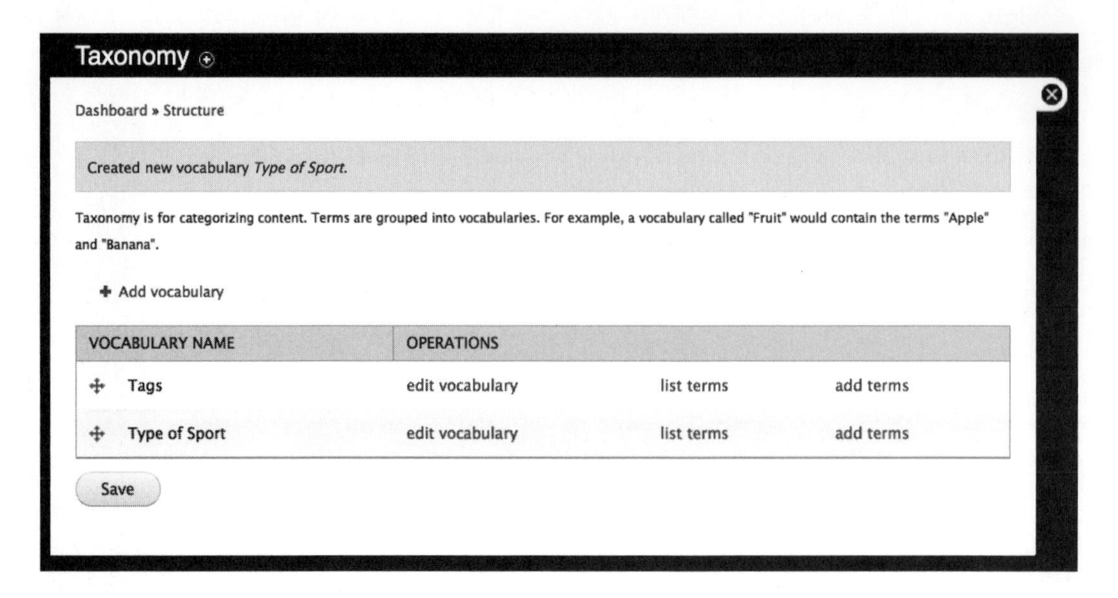

Figure 4-3. *Your newly created vocabulary*

The next step is to create a list of terms that are associated with the "Type of Sport" vocabulary. To create terms, click on the "Add terms" link for the vocabulary that you created. Clicking on that link reveals the form shown in Figure 4-4. Enter Basketball as the name of the term, and enter a brief description that expands on the meaning behind the term.

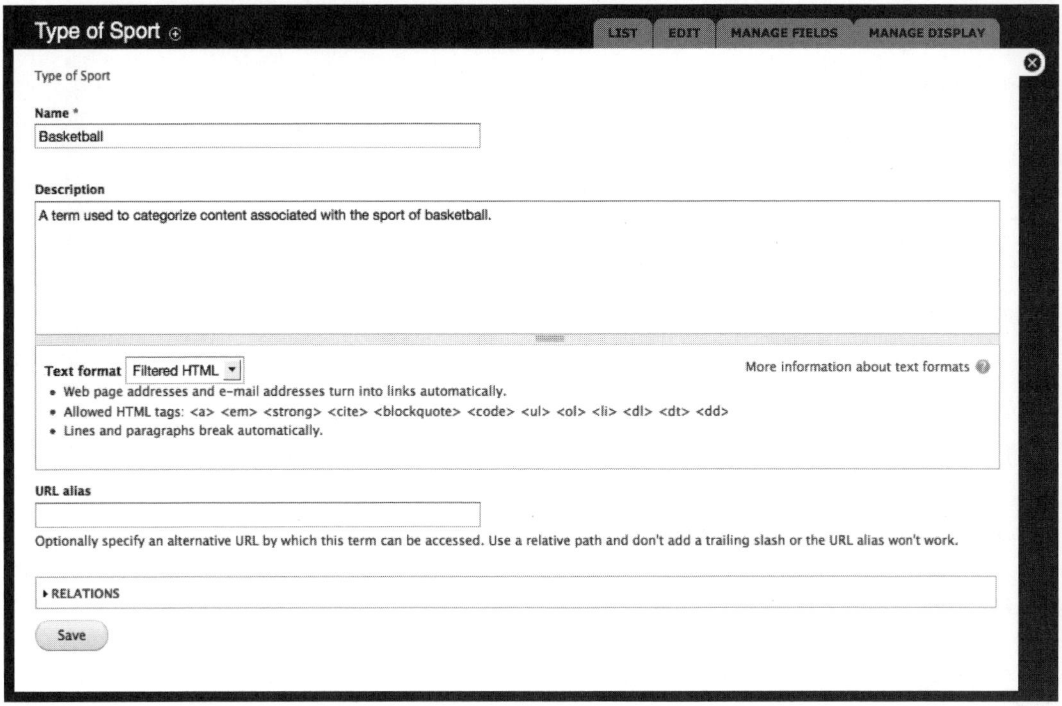

Figure 4-4. Adding terms

After entering the term and a description, click Save. Drupal then redisplays the form to enable you to enter another term. To practice, create terms for other sports, such as baseball, football, and soccer. Once you've completed the process of entering the terms associated with your vocabulary, click on the Link tab at the top of the page to see the complete list of terms for the vocabulary, shown in Figure 4-5.

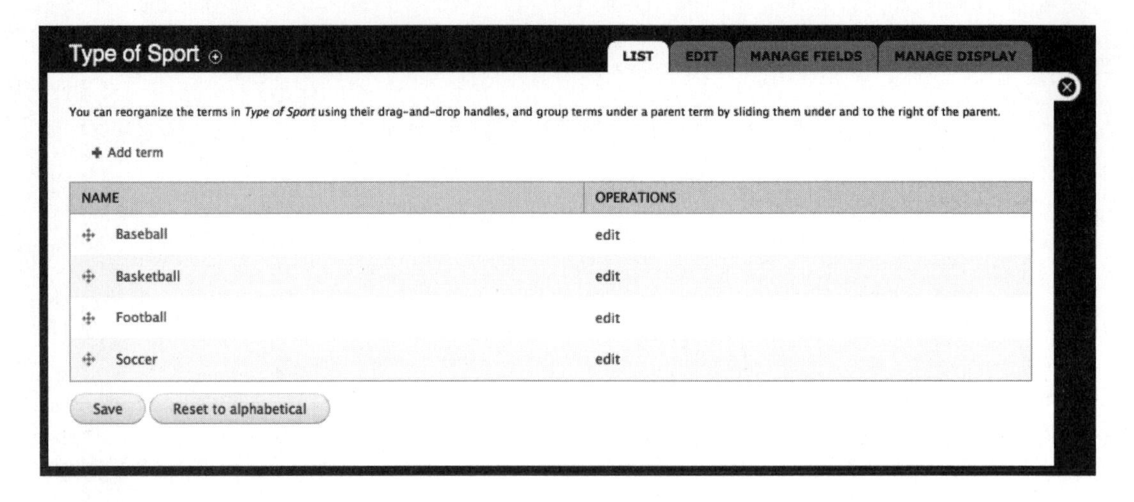

Figure 4-5. The complete list of terms

At this point we've created a vocabulary and the terms that we will use to categorize content. We now have to identify which content types will use this vocabulary as a method for categorizing content, and configure our vocabulary so that it will appear on the content creation screens for those content types.

Assigning a Taxonomy Vocabulary to a Content Type

Providing content authors with the ability to assign one of the terms to a new piece of content requires that a site administrator updates the all of the content types to include a reference to the vocabulary that we wish to link to content on our site.

The first step is to identify all the content types that you want to associate with the new vocabulary. You may decide that all content types will use the vocabulary to categories the content created on your site, or you may decide the vocabulary is only appropriate for one or a few content types. For example, you might want to restrict which content types would be used if you had a vocabulary that listed terms for event venues (e.g., cafeteria, gym, courtyard, soccer field, and so on). That vocabulary may only be appropriate for a calendar event content type and not your generic page content type.

As an example, let's update the "Generic page" content type on the test site to incorporate the ability to tag content with the type of sport vocabulary. The first step is to click on the Structure link in the admin menu at the top of each page of your site. Click on the "Content types" link to get to the page that lists the available content types (shown in Figure 4-6).

NAME	OPERATIONS			
Article (Machine name: article) Use *articles* for time-specific content like news, press releases or blog posts.	edit	manage fields	manage display	delete
Basic page (Machine name: page) Use *basic pages* for your static content, such as an 'About us' page.	edit	manage fields	manage display	delete

Figure 4-6. *Available content types*

On the list of content types, you'll see a link for managing the fields associated with this content type. We'll learn in Chapter 10 how to add several types of fields to our content type (e.g., you may wish to add a file upload, an additional text box to collect specific information, check boxes, radio buttons, or a select list to expand the content collected when someone uses that content type). For now we will concentrate on adding the taxonomy vocabulary to our content type so that an author can select one of the types of sports terms.

Click on the "Manage fields" link to expose the form used to add our vocabulary (see Figure 4-7). On this form, you will notice a section dedicated to adding a new field. Enter "Type of Sport" in the Label field, enter "type_of_sport" as the internal field name that Drupal will use to reference this field, and choose the field type that you wish to use to display the list of terms From the list of options choose "Select list" if you have a long list of terms in the vocabulary. If you have a short list of terms, "Check boxes/radio buttons" is a better option as Drupal displays all of the options on the screen rather than having to scroll through a very short select list. The last option is to render a text box where the author can enter the term. This option automatically begins to search the list of terms when the author enters the first character, and lists all terms that meet the characters that the author entered. If no term is found that matches the word entered by the author, a new taxonomy term is created. This option makes it easy to expand the list of terms by allowing authors to create a new term when the author creates a new article. If you have a tightly controlled list of terms and don't want authors to have the ability to expand upon the list (such as a list of job titles that are set by the HR department), you will not want to use this option. For our example, use the "Select list" option, as we don't want authors to have the ability to add new types of sports to our vocabulary.

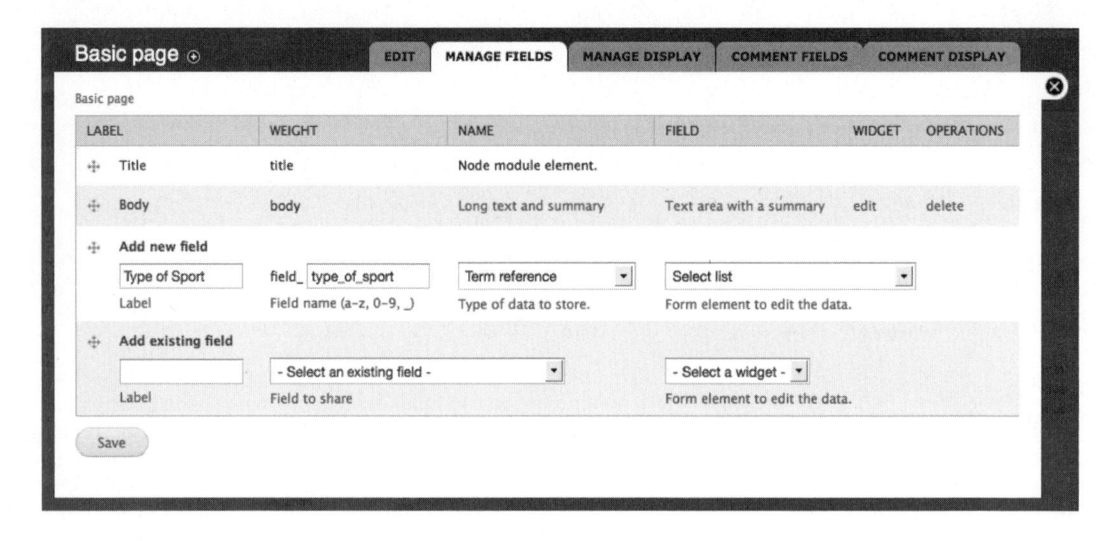

Figure 4-7. Managing fields

Click on the Save button. You'll next see a screen where you can specify the vocabulary that provides the source for the list of terms that will appear in the select list (see Figure 4-8). For this example, select "Type of Sport" and click on "Save field settings."

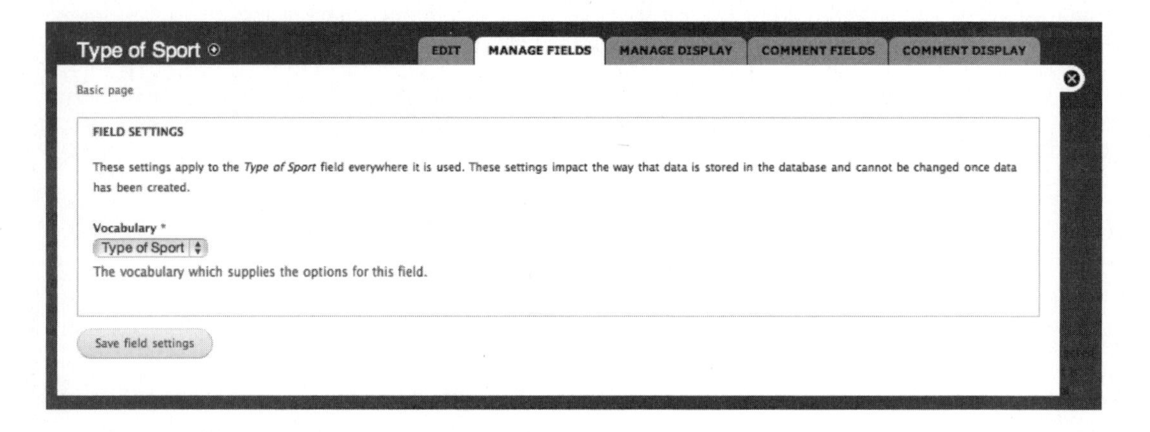

Figure 4-8. Determining field settings

The next screen you see after clicking save allows you to:

- Change the label that will be displayed next to this field.
- Specify whether the taxonomy term is a required field (whether the author must select from one of the items before saving the piece of content).

- Provide help text.
- Specify a default value that should be used in the case where the author does not select value.
- Specify how many values an author can select. If you used the radio buttons/checkbox widget type, selecting 1 will render the list as radio buttons. Selecting more than 1 will result in the list being rendered as checkboxes.
- You can change the vocabulary that will be used as the source of the list of values that will be displayed as options to the author.

After changing any of the values on this page, click Save.

Selecting a Taxonomy Term when Creating Content

Based on our actions in the previous step, creating a new content item using the Basic page content type will now present the author with a list of values that they can select from to categorize the content they are authoring. To test this feature, click on any of the "create content" links that we have described previously (such as the create content link in the gray bar near the top of the page). From the list of content types listed, click on the "Basic page" content type. When the Basic page creation page is displayed, notice that there is a new select list field where the author can select the type of sport to assign to this content item (see Figure 4-9).

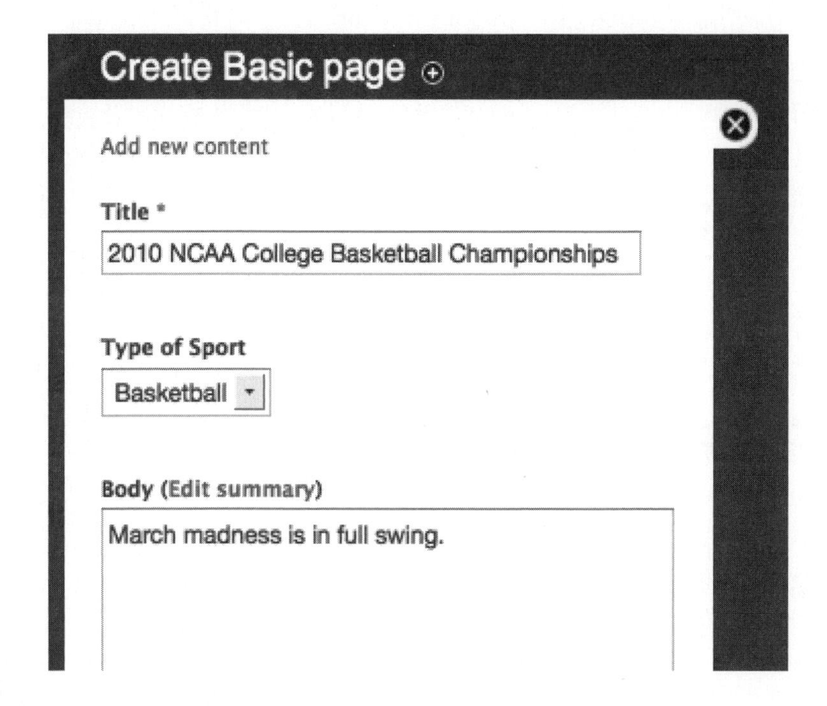

Figure 4-9. *Creating a basic page*

Clicking on Save results in Drupal displaying our new page with a new field, "Associated Sport," with Basketball listed as the option that was selected.

To demonstrate the power of taxonomy, create two additional pages using the same taxonomy term you selected in the first example. On the final content item that you created, once you have saved it, click on the term that you used. In Figure 4-10 you would click on Basketball.

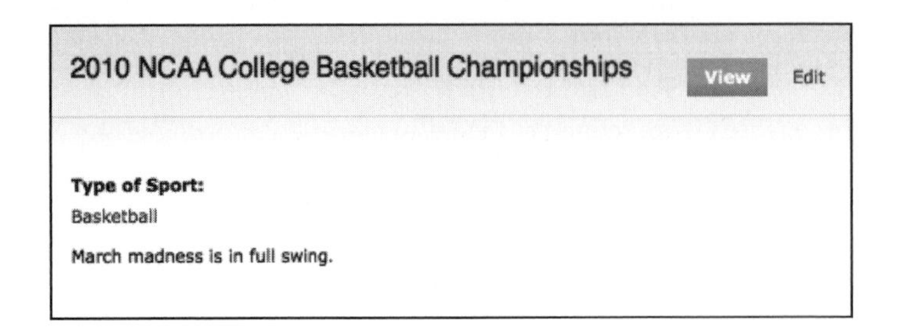

Figure 4-10. A new content item assigned to the Basketball taxonomy term

The result of clicking on the term is a page that lists all other pages that were created and assigned to the Basketball taxonomy term (see Figure 4-11).

Basketball View Edit

A term used to categorize content associated with the sport of basketball.

Collegate Woman's Teams to Compete for National Title

Type of Sport:
Basketball

Pellentesque congue, nisi sed iaculis pellentesque, neque eros molestie massa, a malesuada diam augue rhoncus felis! Morbi eu mollis arcu. Etiam nisl erat, tincidunt sit amet bibendum id, dapibus ac quam. Aliquam eget justo a metus viverra molestie. In auctor, diam vitae elementum interdum; diam nulla pellentesque eros, ut volutpat turpis lectus nec nibh. Suspendisse purus nisl, malesuada fermentum vulputate eget, tincidunt eu justo. Cras feugiat porta feugiat. Duis dictum, nulla et varius viverra, orci neque vulputate elit, nec varius ipsum libero at diam.

Read more

2012 Olympics to Exclude Basketball

Type of Sport:
Basketball

Pellentesque congue, nisi sed iaculis pellentesque, neque eros molestie massa, a malesuada diam augue rhoncus felis! Morbi eu mollis arcu. Etiam nisl erat, tincidunt sit amet bibendum id, dapibus ac quam. Aliquam eget justo a metus viverra molestie. In auctor, diam vitae elementum interdum; diam nulla pellentesque eros, ut volutpat turpis lectus nec nibh. Suspendisse purus nisl, malesuada fermentum vulputate eget, tincidunt eu justo. Cras feugiat porta feugiat. Duis dictum, nulla et varius viverra, orci neque vulputate elit, nec varius ipsum libero at diam.

Read more

Portland Trailblazers Extend Winning Streak

Type of Sport:
Basketball

Pellentesque congue, nisi sed iaculis pellentesque, neque eros molestie massa, a malesuada diam augue rhoncus felis! Morbi eu mollis arcu. Etiam nisl erat, tincidunt sit amet bibendum id,

Figure 4-11. All pages assigned to the term Basketball

Drupal automatically renders all of the articles that are associated with the selected term. The list is sorted in date/time order, with the most recently added basic page listed at the top of the list. You will also notice an RSS feed icon at the bottom of the page. Drupal also created an RSS feed for all the pages that are associated with this taxonomy term. Clicking on the RSS icon will render the list as a standard feed.

Creating Human- and Search-Engine-Friendly Lists

By default, Drupal creates URLs for lists of content that are related to taxonomy terms, as shown in Figure 4-12.

Figure 4-12. *Drupal-created URLs*

The structure of the URL is "taxonomy/term/X," where X is the "term ID" of the taxonomy term that you are referencing. While Drupal understands what this refers to, a human and, more important, a search engine wouldn't have a clue what this URL was related to other than looking at the title of the list and the content of the list. A simple remedy is to provide a URL alias. You can provide a URL alias by editing the taxonomy term and entering a value in the field that is shown on the form for adding a URL alias. To navigate back to your taxonomy term list, click on the Structure menu at the top of the page. On the Structure page, click on the Taxonomy link. On the Taxonomy page, click on the "List terms" link that is associated with the vocabulary where the term you wish to supply a URL alias resides. Locate the term you wish to update and click on the Edit tab. In the URL alias field (shown in Figure 4-13), enter a descriptive URL that is easily understood by humans and search engines. For consistency and simplicity, use all lowercase letters with hyphens between words. For our example, we're using a single word, "basketball." Click the Save button after entering your URL alias. In the address bar of your browser, enter the URL to your site followed by the URL alias that you just created for your taxonomy term. In the example above the URL would be http://localhost/basketball (see Figure 4-14).

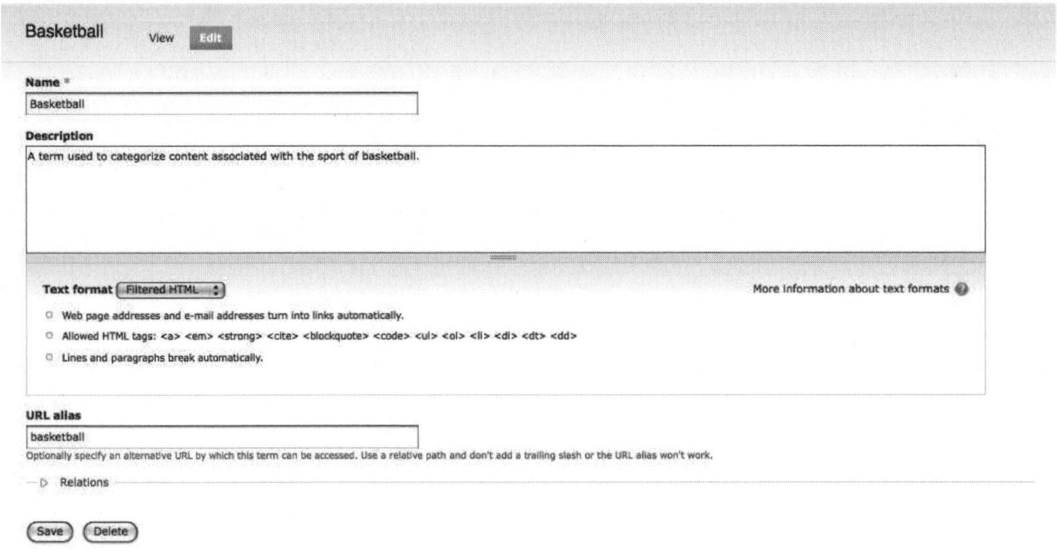

Figure 4-13. Setting the URL alias for a taxonomy term

Hierarchical Terms

What if you need to define a hierarchical structure of taxonomy terms, say, for example "basketball." You need the ability to further categorize basketball content by:

- Basketball
  - High School
  - College
    - Division 1
    - Division 2
    - Division 3
  - NBA
    - Eastern Conference
    - Central Conference
    - Western Conference

Fortunately, Drupal provides a simple mechanism for creating a hierarchical structure of taxonomy terms. To update our example, return to the "Add term" link next to the vocabulary for "Types of Sports."

Click on the Structure menu at the top of the page, and on the Structure page, click on the Taxonomy link. Click on the "Add term" link next to the vocabulary where you wish to add a new term, which reveals the term creation screen. Begin by adding the term for High School. Enter High School as the term name and then click on the Relationships link at the bottom of the form. In the list of terms, select Basketball as the parent term and then click Save. Continue the process by entering College and NBA, also selecting Basketball as the parent term. To create the third level of the hierarchy, enter Division 1 as the term name and, for the relationship selected, "College" as the parent. Continue the process until you've created all of the terms listed above. The resulting structure should look something like the list shown in Figure 4-14.

NAME	OPERATION
Baseball	edit
Basketball	edit
High School	edit
College	edit
Division 1	edit
Division 2	edit
Division 3	edit
NBA	edit
Central Conference	edit
Eastern Conference	edit
Western Conference	edit

Figure 4-14. *The resulting list*

We now have the ability to assign taxonomy terms to content items at the child level as well as at the parent level.

The resulting Page that is created using this method now shows the associated sport as "High School." Clicking on High School would render a list of all pages that are associated with the term "High School" under "Basketball."

This approach provides a finer level of granularity for categorizing content.

Assigning More Than One Vocabulary

There may come a time when categorizing content by a single vocabulary represents a constraint that you must overcome to address a complex requirement for content categorization. Fortunately Drupal does not constrain you on how many vocabularies you can assign to a content type. Simply follow the steps we performed earlier in this chapter to add a second field to the content type. Simply select a different vocabulary as the source for the values that you wish to present to the author.

Summary

Hopefully this chapter shed some light on the power and simplicity of taxonomy. I suggest that you start using taxonomy on your first site, because the more you use it the more comfortable you will be with its capabilities and the power that it brings to the content you deliver to your visitors. I will continue to leverage taxonomy throughout the rest of this book as I cover other advanced Drupal features.

CHAPTER 5

■ ■ ■

Creating Menus

Making it easy for visitors to find information on your website, and more important, making it easy for visitors to find the information that you want them to find, is a key factor in defining the success or failure of your new site. There are three basic mechanisms in Drupal to provide navigational capabilities to your site:

- Text links embedded in content that direct the user to a new page.
- Images and buttons that direct the user to a new page when clicked.
- Menus, which are horizontal or vertical lists of text or image links.

In this chapter, you will learn how to use Drupal's administrator's interface for creating and managing menus.

Ordering From the Menu

A menu, in its simplest form, is a horizontal or vertical list of links that direct a user to a new page. If you examine the home page of your new website, you'll see that there are at least six menus on that page alone. See Figure 5-1.

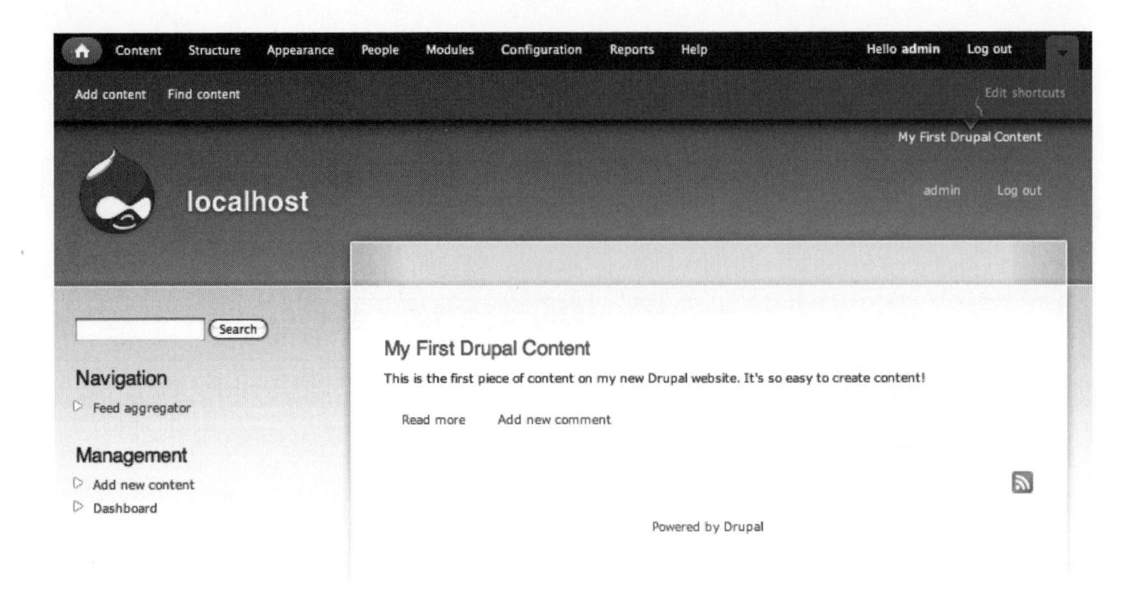

Figure 5-1. Menus on a site

From top to bottom, the menus are:

- the top black bar, starting with Content;
- the gray bar at the top of the page, starting with Add Content;
- the top site menu (top of the blue area), with Admin and Log out
- the secondary menu in the right column, starting with Home;
- the left hand column menu titled Management; and
- the menu that is embedded in the article on the page, starting with "Create content."

Menus help a visitor to a site understand (and access) the content, features, and functions that the site provides.

On our example site that we're creating in this book, the menus shown on the page are all text links. Drupal also provides mechanisms for creating menus that are button and/or image based. I created a dynamic image-based menu for the Bloomfield Township Public Library (`http://btpl.org`) that uses a combination of buttons and images (images appear above the menu item that is being highlighted; for example, the boy with the paint on his fingers in Figure 5-2 is the highlighted menu item).

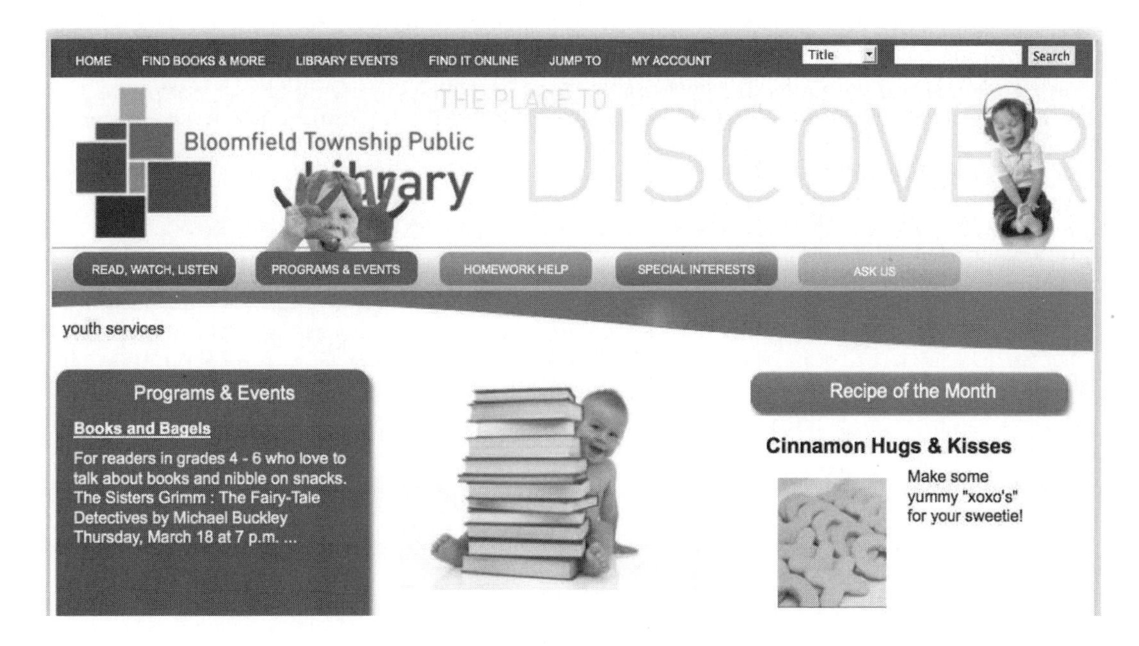

Figure 5-2. An example of an image-based menu

Creating menus is facilitated through a set of screens that are part of Drupal 7 core. There are three basic activities for creating items on menus

- Adding an item to an existing menu. Drupal 7 comes with several menus already created. All you need to do is to add items to those menus.
- Creating a new menu. If you need more than the two menus that come with Drupal 7, you can create a new menu.
- Assigning the menu to a region of on a page. If you created a new menu, you'll need to assign it to a region on the page.

Adding an Item to a Menu

There are two general items that we can add to our page as menu items: a link to an existing element on our site (a content item, a list of content associated with a taxonomy term, and so on), or a link to a page that is external to our site.

Adding a Content Item to a Menu

There are two approaches for adding items to menus: you can use the menu administration form (see figure 5-4) to create a new menu item, or you can create a menu link from the content item that you wish to reference from within the form used to create or edit that content item. The best practice is to use the content creation form (see figure 5-3) or, as we will see later in the book, other element creation forms such as a panel page or a view. The reason for using this approach is that when you delete that content item, Drupal automatically removes the item from the menu to which it was assigned. If you use the manual approach of creating a menu item using the menu administration form, you as the site owner must remember to remove that item manually from the menu.

To create a new content item, click on any of the Create Content links that are available on the home page of your website (assuming you are still logged in as the administrator), and select the "Basic page" content type. As an example, enter a title and body for the new content type and then click on the "Provide a menu" vertical tab at the bottom of the screen (see Figure 5-3). Check the "Provide a menu" box, which reveals the fields for defining your menu. Enter the title for the item as you wish it to appear on the menu, and select the main menu as the one where you want the item to appear. After entering the values for your menu item, click on the Save button at the bottom of the page. Drupal then displays the page that you just created, with the menu item associated with this page now appearing in the Main menu at the top right of the darker blue area of the page.

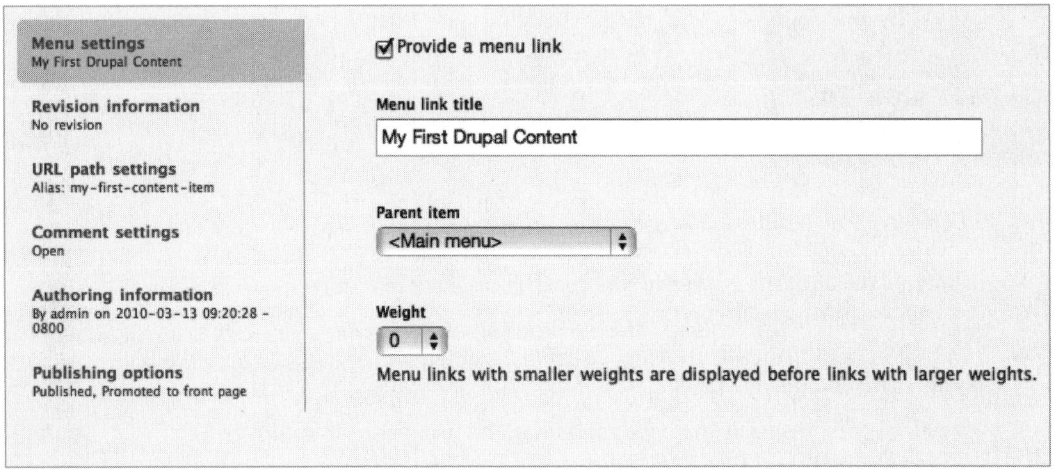

Figure 5-3. *Adding a content item to a menu*

Clicking on that link will take you directly to the page we just created, regardless of where you are on the website.

Adding a Menu Item for an External Page

You can add links to external sites by adding a menu item. To do so, click on the Structure menu item at the top of the page. On the Structure page, click on the Menu link. On the Menu page, click on the "Add item" link for the Main menu. You should now see the "Add menu item" form (see Figure 5-4). Enter a title (in this example, I used Apress as the menu title), the path, which is the full URL to the external page to which we want to link (in the example I used `www.apress.com`), ensure that the enabled check box is checked, and for demonstration purposes, select the Main menu from the parent item drop down list.

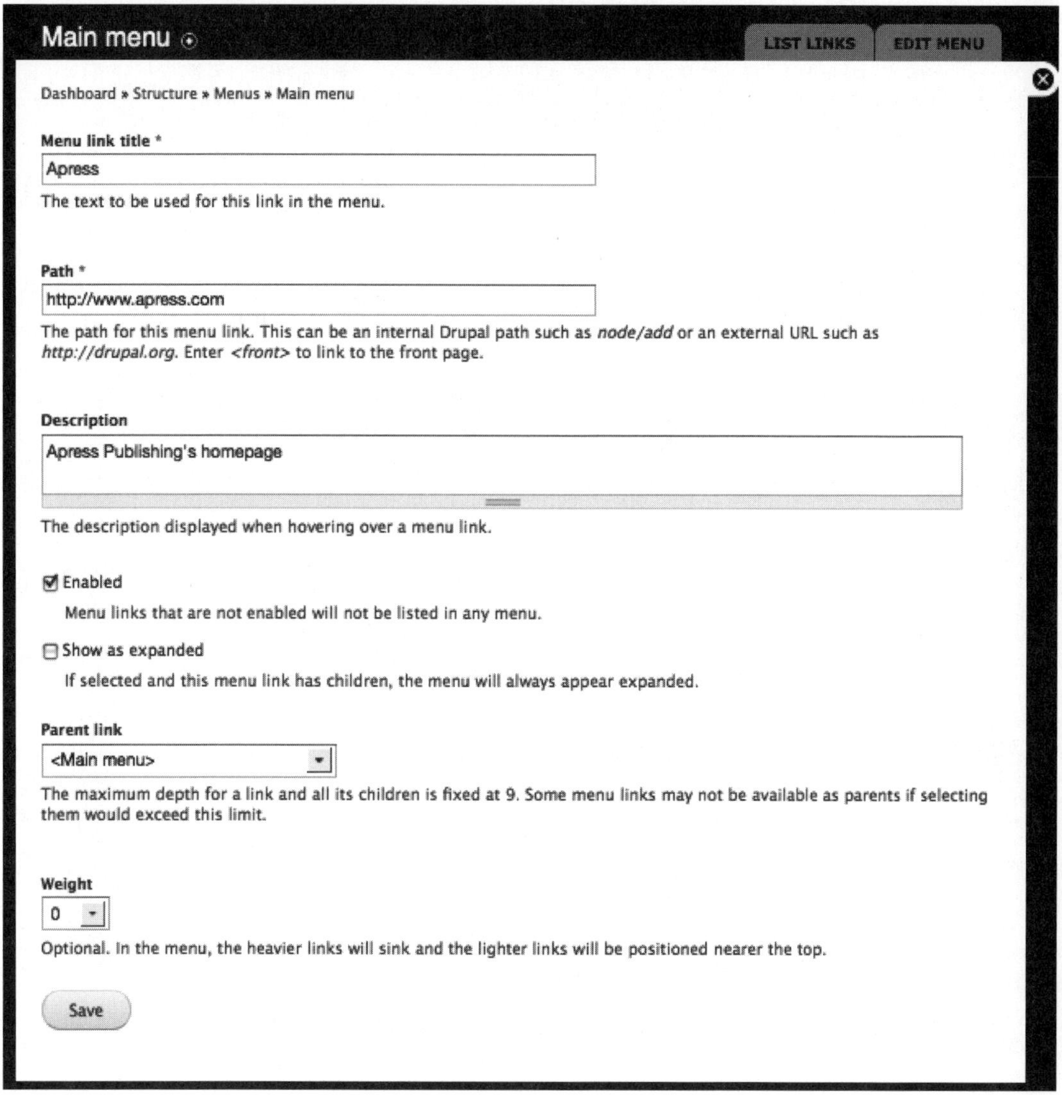

Main menu

LIST LINKS | EDIT MENU

Dashboard » Structure » Menus » Main menu

Menu link title *

Apress

The text to be used for this link in the menu.

Path *

http://www.apress.com

The path for this menu link. This can be an internal Drupal path such as *node/add* or an external URL such as *http://drupal.org*. Enter *<front>* to link to the front page.

Description

Apress Publishing's homepage

The description displayed when hovering over a menu link.

☑ Enabled

Menu links that are not enabled will not be listed in any menu.

☐ Show as expanded

If selected and this menu link has children, the menu will always appear expanded.

Parent link

<Main menu>

The maximum depth for a link and all its children is fixed at 9. Some menu links may not be available as parents if selecting them would exceed this limit.

Weight

0

Optional. In the menu, the heavier links will sink and the lighter links will be positioned nearer the top.

Save

Figure 5-4. *Adding a menu item for an external page*

Once you've entered all the values, click on the Save button at the bottom of the page (you may need to scroll down to see it). Drupal then displays the complete list of items that are assigned to the Main menu, including the new item that we just created.

You should now see the new menu item that you just added. Clicking on that menu item will take you to the external link that you entered when you created the menu item.

Creating a New Menu

There may be situations where you need to create additional menus beyond what ships with Drupal 7. As an example, when creating Drupal-based websites for public libraries, I am often asked to build unique menus for each department in the library (a menu for adult services, youth services, teen services, circulation, and so on). In such a case, the basic menus shipped with Drupal 7 are not enough to fulfill the library's requirements. To create a new menu, click on the Structure menu item at the top of any page on your site. On the Structure page, click on Menus, and on the Menus page click on the Add Menu link. The form for creating a new menu is displayed (see Figure 5-5). On the form for creating a new menu, enter the title of the menu and a description (which is optional). Click the Save button, and you now have a new menu ready to assign items to using the same methods as described earlier in this chapter.

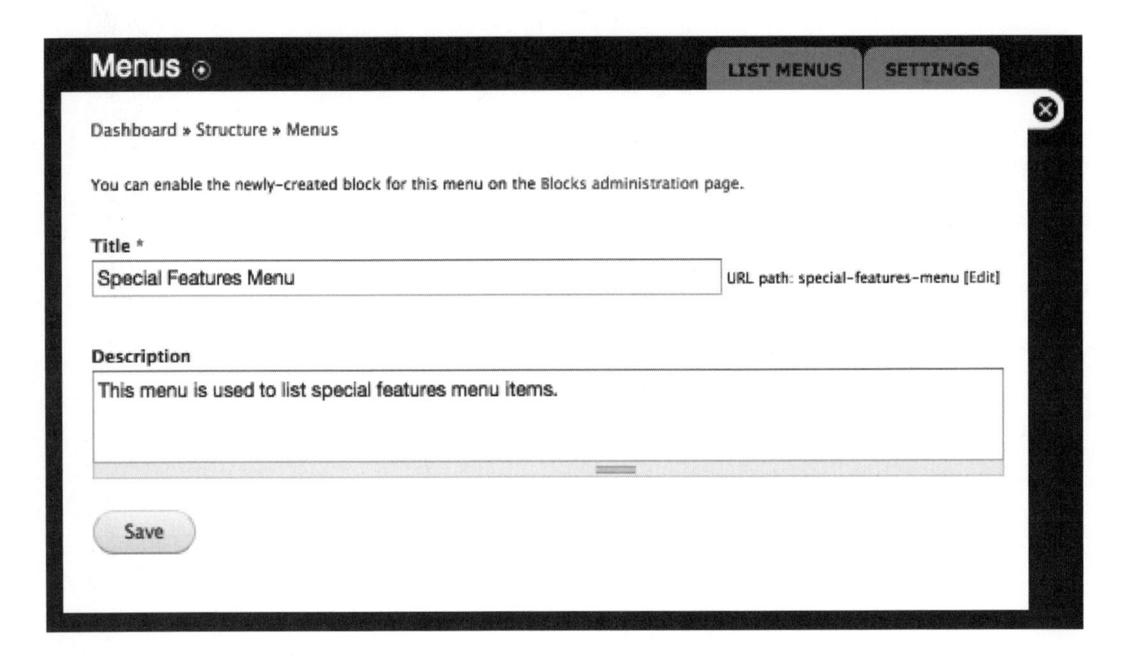

Figure 5-5. *Creating a new menu*

After saving the menu, you can now add items to it. As practice, create menu items for the following external links, using the process described in the section "Adding a Menu Item for an External Page": apress.com, yahoo.com, google.com, and bing.com. When completed, your menu should look something like that in Figure 5-6.

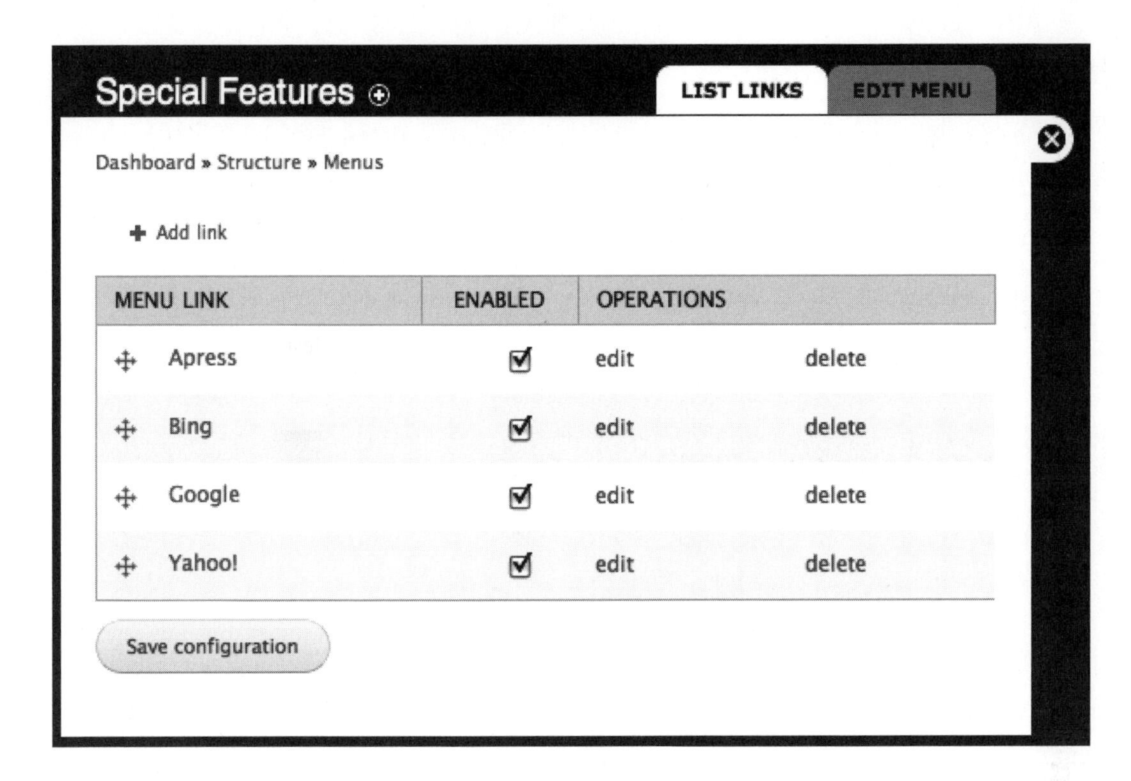

Figure 5-6. Your menu with items

At this point the menu exists in Drupal, but it isn't assigned to a region on a page and, therefore, isn't visible to site visitors. To make your new menu visible, click on the Structure link at the top of any page, and on the Structure page click on the Blocks link. On the Blocks page, scroll down until you find Special Features (see Figure 5-7). In the list to the right of Special Features, pick the left sidebar option and then click on the Save Blocks button at the bottom of the page.

Disabled

Author information	<none>	configure
Main menu	<none>	configure
Recent comments	<none>	configure
Recent content	<none>	configure
Secondary menu	<none>	configure
Shortcuts	<none>	configure
Special Features	<none>	configure

Figure 5-7. *Assigning menus to a block*

Click on the home icon at the top left of the screen to return to the home page and voila! There's your new menu. You may now place your order.

Summary

In this chapter I covered the basics of adding links to a menu and creating a new menu. I explained the process of adding content items to menus and adding links to external websites. I also covered how to enable a new menu so that it appears on your site.
In the next chapter I explain how to completely change the look of your website by installing and enabling a new theme. Be prepared to say "wow!"

CHAPTER 6

■ ■ ■

Installing Themes

In this chapter I will explain the process of changing the overall look and feel of your site by installing a new theme. I will walk you through the process of selecting, downloading, and enabling your selected theme. You've added some neat things to your site in previous chapters, and we've seen some exciting features of Drupal; but this chapter will have you going "wow!"

The visual layout and presentation of your new Drupal site is defined through a Drupal component called a theme. A theme defines:

- The colors used on the page.
- The fonts used for text, headings, links, and other elements.
- The placement of images and graphics that are present on every page of the site (images and graphics that are associated with the page itself rather than a content item).
- The layout of the page (such as a menu at the top, a banner area, a secondary menu below the banner, a column on the left, or a footer).

Drupal themes are designed and developed using HTML, cascading style sheets (CSS), and the PHP programming language. Themes can be as simple as a plain white canvas or as complex and visually energizing as your imagination can conjure up.

We have already worked with a Drupal theme; the basic Drupal 7 site that we installed as part of the earlier chapters in this book used the Garland theme. Garland is a predominantly "blue" theme (see Figure 6-1), with a relatively simple structure. There is a region (a rectangular area on the page where content, menus, widgets, and so on can be assigned) for a header, a left sidebar, a right sidebar, the general content area, and the footer.

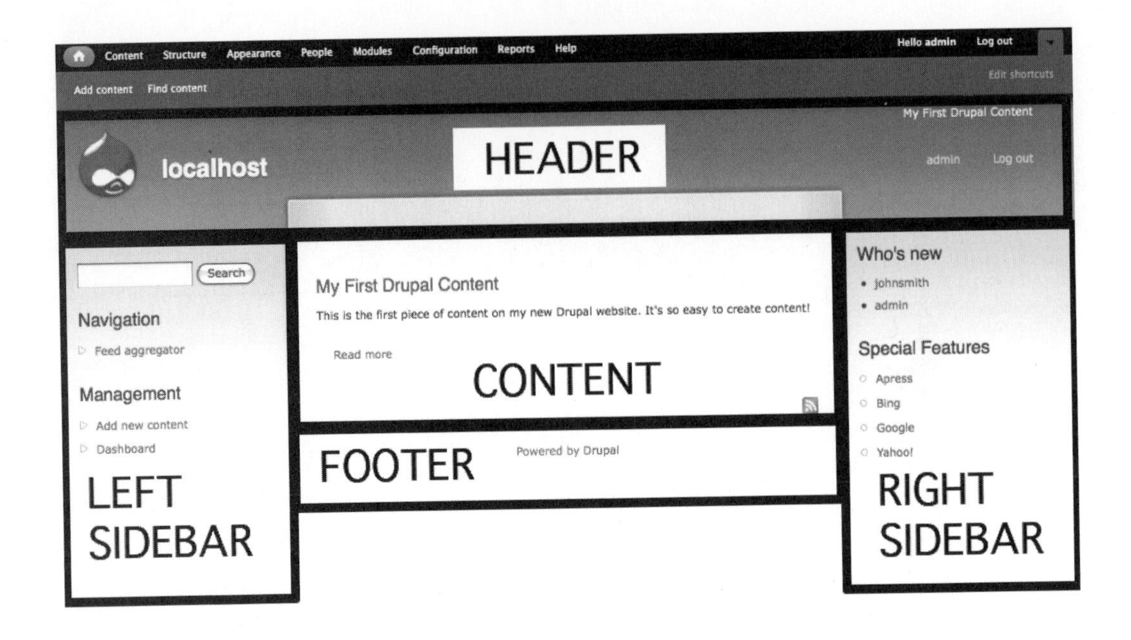

Figure 6-1. The Garland theme

You'll find as you browse through various Drupal themes that many of them follow this same generic layout, which for many people is a negative because it makes them believe that every Drupal site looks nearly identical. The truth of the matter is that yes, many off-the-shelf themes follow this same layout pattern. However, you have the ability to create a layout that significantly deviates from the standard. Figure 6-2 demonstrates how I used the capabilities of Drupal's theme engine to create a Drupal site for the University of Oregon that is used by high school students to manage their electronic portfolio of learning assets and track their progress toward graduation. The area at the top of the page with the brown background is the header, the area in the middle of the page with the green background is the content area, and the brown area at the bottom is the footer.

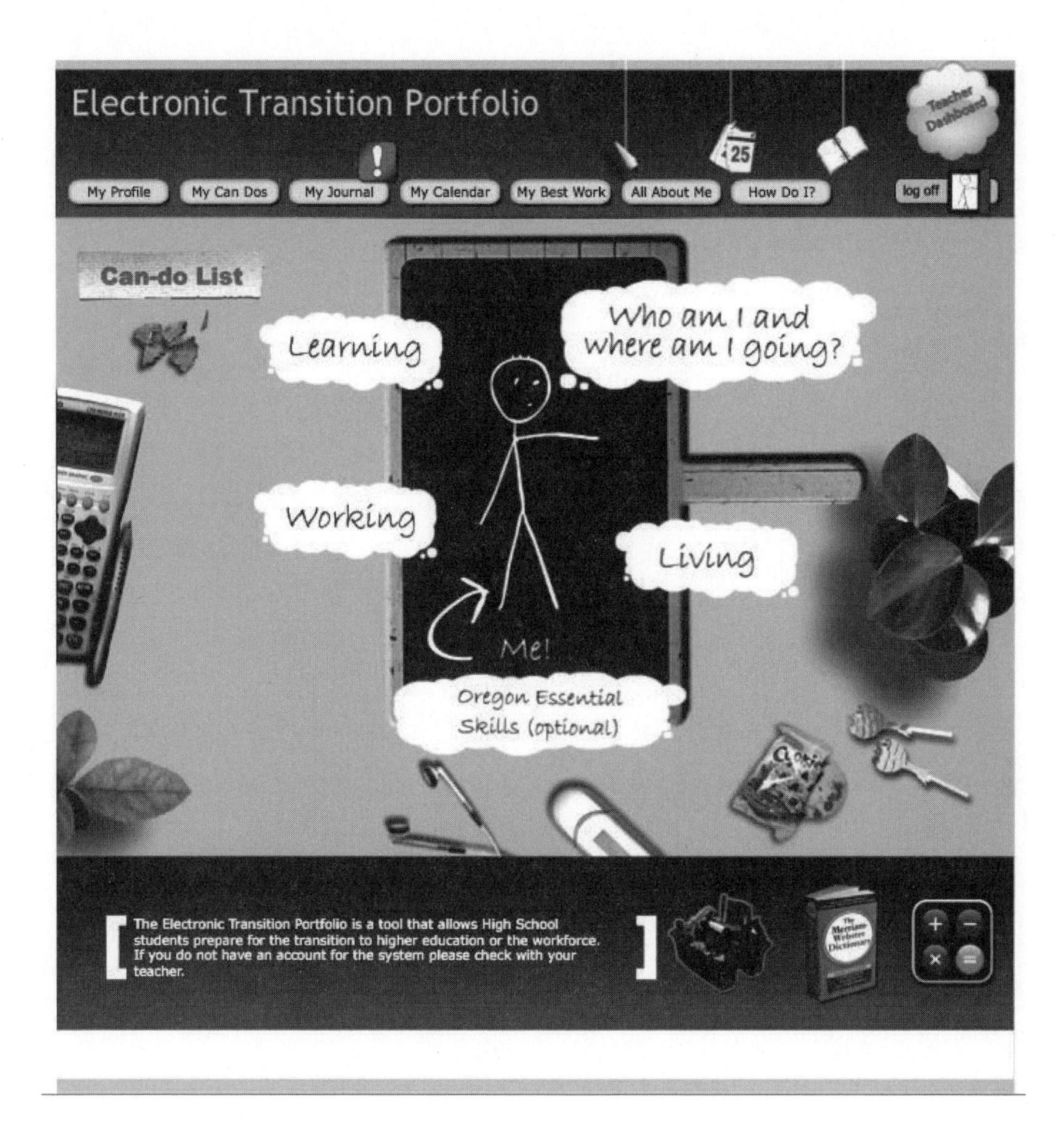

Figure 6-2. *A creative non-traditional Drupal theme*

How a Drupal Theme Works

Understanding some of the basics behind how a Drupal theme works will help lay the foundation for some topics that I will cover in later chapters. The fundamentals of how a theme works can be distilled into a few basic concepts, which I explain here.

As the administrator, you have the ability to pick which theme your site will use. You can either download a stock theme from `http://drupal.org/project/themes`, or you can purchase a commercial theme from various providers that sell Drupal themes. It is likely that you will find something that matches or closely matches what you want from a visual design perspective on the Drupal theme download site. If you scan through the hundreds of themes and can't find one you like, you can always create your own. *Pro Drupal Development*, also published by Apress, covers many of the aspects of creating a theme from scratch.

If you find a theme that you like, download it, expand the downloaded file (just like you did when you downloaded Drupal), and copy the theme to your web server.

Once copied, you enable the theme through the administration features provided in Drupal 7, and voila! Your site is now displayed using the theme.

Once the theme is enabled, Drupal loads it and its associated cascading style sheets and assembles the content. Drupal then renders each page using the structure, style, colors, fonts, and images as you have defined them in your theme.

Finding a New Theme

Drupal 7 ships with the Garland and Stark themes. Although Garland is a great theme, it's likely one that you won't use on your production site (although browsing around the web you'll often run into a site that uses Garland as its production theme). Stark is an extremely plain theme. If you're going for a very clean and text heavy-theme, then Stark may be a good choice for you, but it's likely that you'll want to pick from one of the hundreds of themes that you can freely download and use.

Before you begin your search for a new theme, you should sit down with a blank piece of paper and sketch out the general layout of at least the homepage of your new site. Key concepts to focus on include:

Will your site use horizontal menus and, if so, how many will you have and where will they be placed?

Will your site have a header or banner area? If so, how tall will the header be, and will it span the entire width of your page?

Does your design call for a left or right side bar? Or does your design call for two sidebars on the right or two on the left?

Will your site have a footer and, if so, does the footer span the entire width of the page?

Will you have a fixed width (say, 960px wide), or will the width of the page expand and contract as the visitor expands and contracts the width of their browser?

Answering these questions will help you narrow the choice of themes to only those that support your general layout and design goals.

There are multiple ways to search for themes. The following are two common ways:

- Visit `www.drupal.org/project/themes` and browse through the descriptions of themes that are available for download. See Figure 6-3.
- Visit `http://themegarden.org/` and see each theme listed on Drupal.org in action. Themegarden.org renders its entire site in each of the themes listed on Drupal.org, so you can see how your site might look in each.

Both methods work well. Many people browse through the list on Drupal.org and then visit Themegarden.org to see that theme implemented on a live site. You may choose to use one or both of the sites.

For demonstration purposes, let's search the Drupal.org site for a Drupal 7 theme that matches our intended layout and color scheme. On `www.drupal.org/project/themes`, in the right-hand column, there is a capability for filtering forms based on the version of Drupal that you are using. You'll want to filter the results by Drupal 7, because themes for previous versions will not work on our site.

Drupal will redisplay the list of themes, only listing those that are compatible with Drupal 7. You can also sort the results by title, creation date, last release, or recent activity. Clicking on "Last release" shows all of the newly added themes (or updates to existing themes), which is a nice feature when you visit this page often and want to see what the community has contributed. For this demonstration, let's sort by Title to list the Drupal 7 themes in alphabetical order.

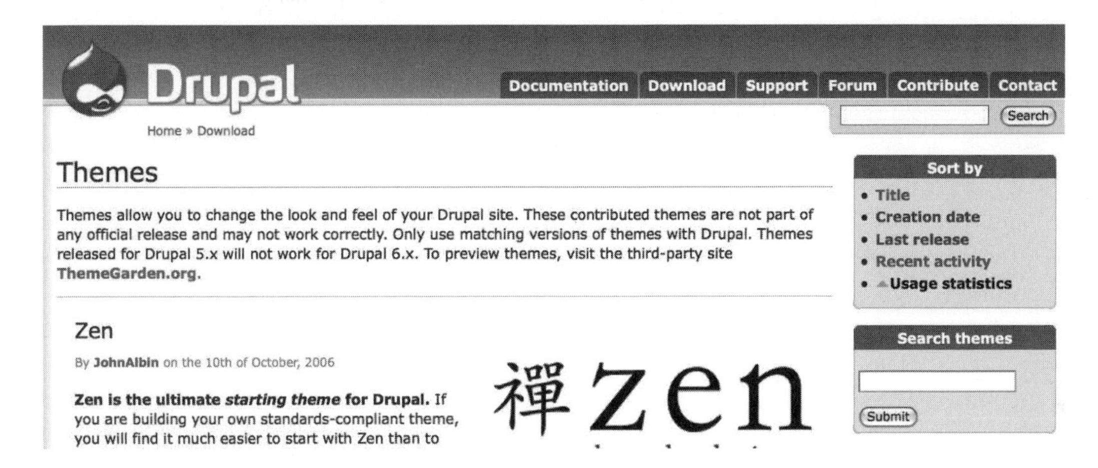

Figure 6-3. Sort options for Drupal themes

Browse through the pages of themes to see the variety that is available. Most theme developers provide a sample screenshot of their design so you can see the general layout and design of their theme. As an example, select the Aberdeen theme (`http://drupal.org/project/aberdeen`), because the visual design and layout varies slightly from the standard layouts (such as Garland) and the colors are nice and subtle. See Figure 6-4.

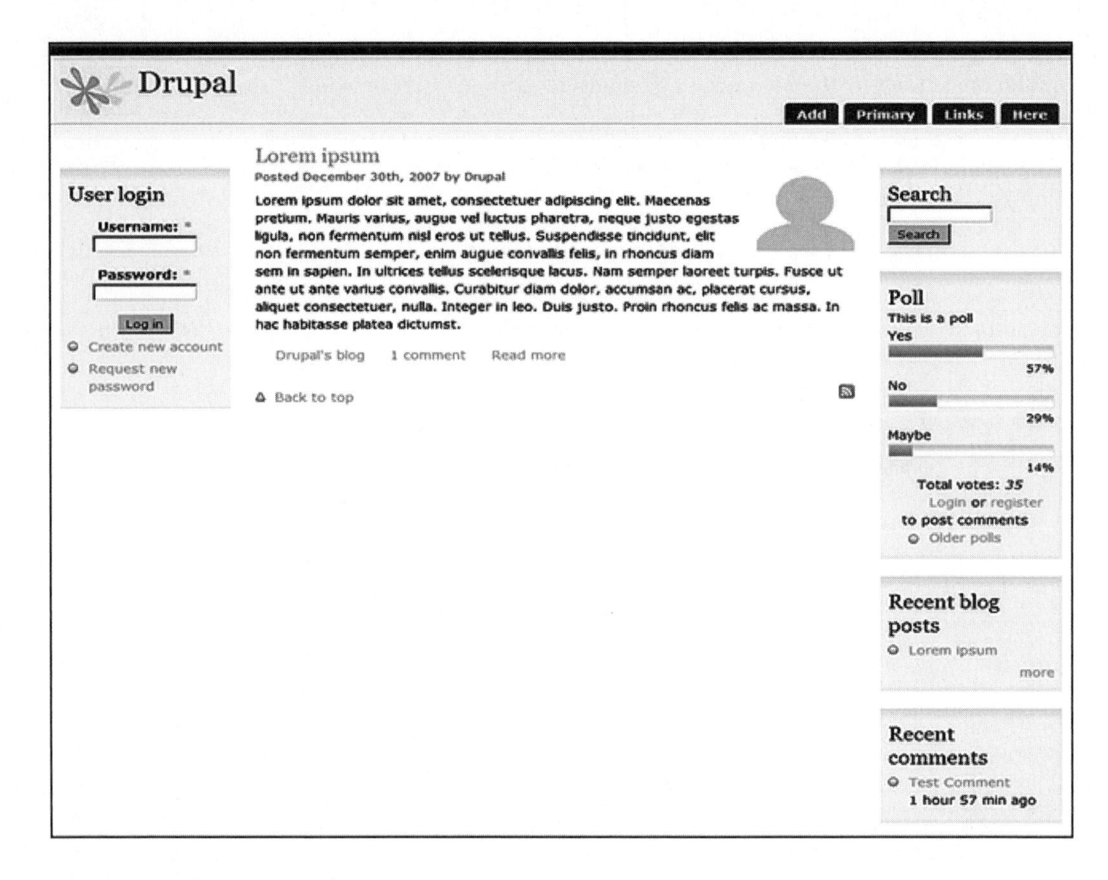

Figure 6-4. *The Aberdeen theme*

Installing a Theme

The next step is to download the theme you want. A new feature in Drupal 7 makes downloading and installing themes a simple task of copying the URL for the theme download file and pasting the URL into a form. To get to this form, first click the Appearance link in the top menu. On the Appearance page, click on the “Install new theme” link. See Figure 6-5.

DISABLED THEMES

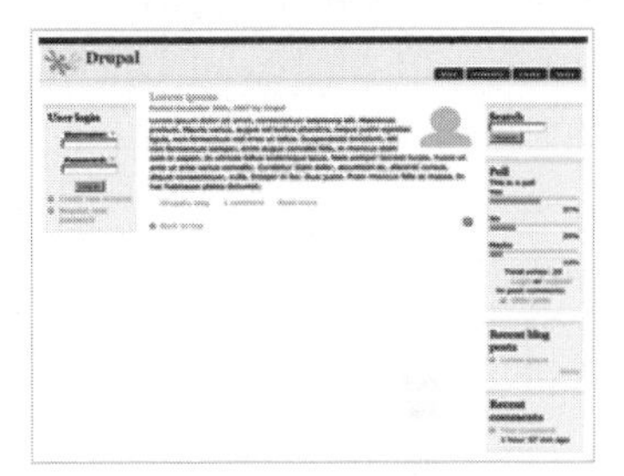

Aberdeen 7.x-1.9

Aberdeen is a fresh design that balances simplicity, soft, neutral background colors, plenty of whitespace and big nice typography

Enable | Enable and set default

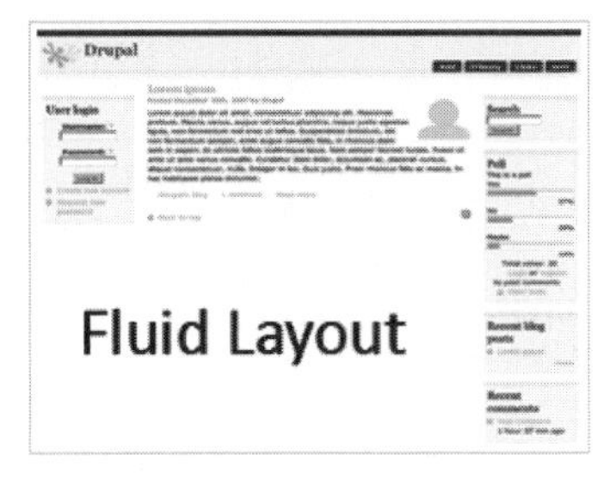

Aberdeen-liquid 7.x-1.9

Aberdeen liquid theme, for a fluid layout.

Enable | Enable and set default

Figure 6-5. Installing a new theme

Clicking on the "Install new theme" link exposes the form that is used to upload and install a new theme. See Figure 6-6.

Appearance

LIST UPDATE SETTINGS

Dashboard » Appearance

To install a new module or theme, either enter the URL of an archive file you wish to install, or upload the archive file that you have downloaded. You can find modules and themes at http://drupal.org. The following archive extensions are supported: *tar, tgz, tar.gz, tar.bz2*

Install from a URL

For example: *http://ftp.drupal.org/files/projects/name.tar.gz*

Or

Upload a module or theme archive to install

Browse...

For example: *name.tar.gz* from your local computer

Install

Figure 6-6. The theme upload/download form

On this form you will see two fields. In the first, you can type (or paste) the URL of the theme's distribution file that you wish to install. Let's do that for this example. Open a new browser window (or a tab) and navigate to the theme that you wish to install (`http://drupal.org/project/themes`). We'll use the Aberdeen theme for Drupal 7 (`http://drupal.org/project/aberdeen`).

Using your mouse, hover over the Download link and right-click on it. In the pop-up window that appears, select the option that allows you to copy the links location (URL). Return to the theme installation form. Right-click in the URL text box and select paste.

With the URL pasted in the text box, you're now ready to click the Install button. Click the button and Drupal downloads the files from the URL specified, copies the files the correct directory, expands (uncompresses) the theme, and makes it available for you to enable.

After downloading, Drupal redisplays the list of themes available on your site, including Aberdeen in the Disabled Themes section of the list. See Figure 6-7.

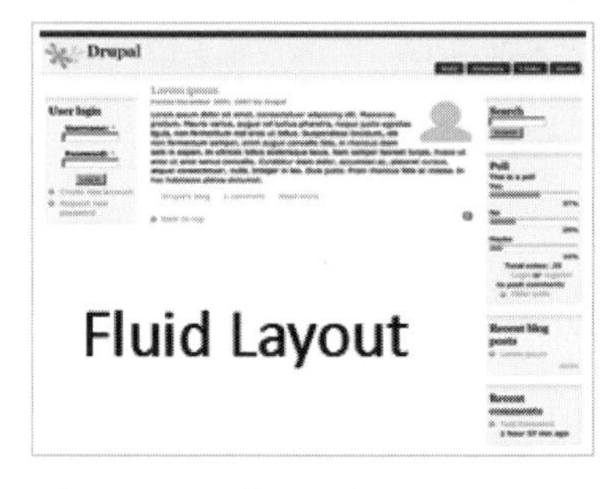

***Figure 6-7.** Disabled themes*

To enable the theme and set it as the default for your site, simply click on the "Enable and set default" link for the theme that you downloaded (we'll use the standard Aberdeen theme, not the fluid layout). At the bottom of the page, click the Save button. Once saved, click on the X in the top right-hand of the Themes page. Return to the home page and click your browsers refresh button. You should now see your site rendered in the new theme. See Figure 6-8.

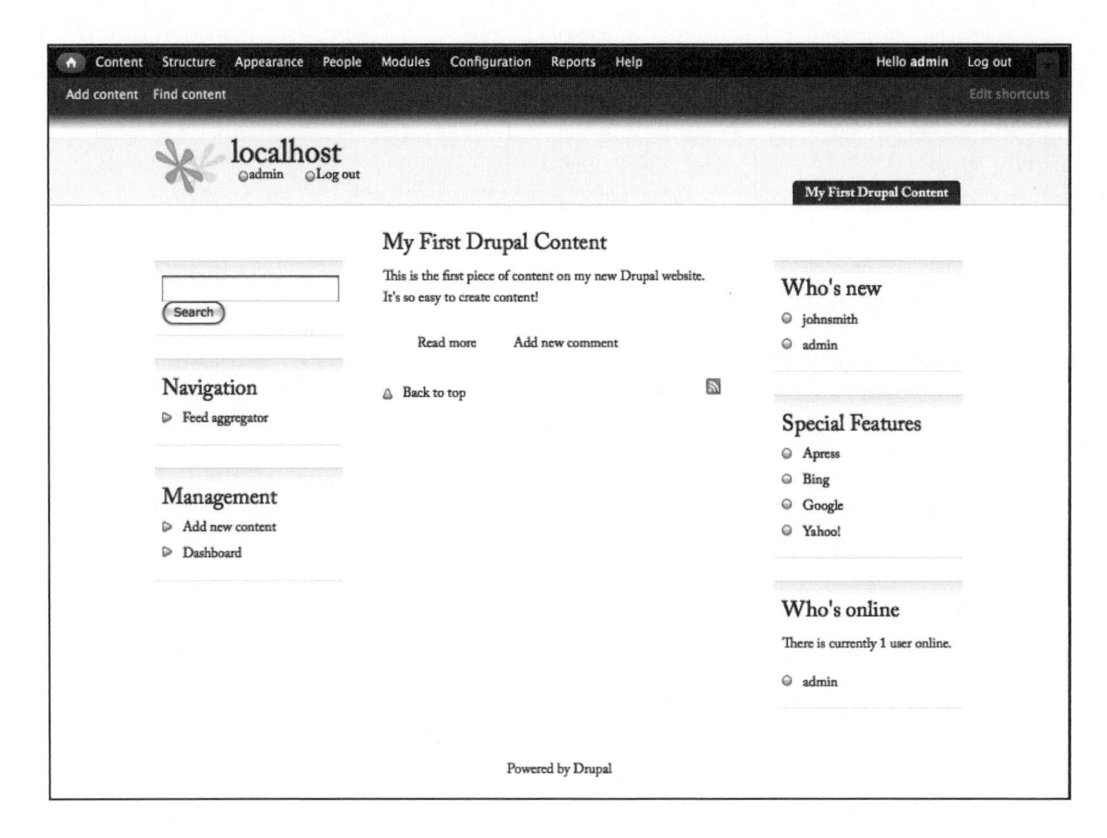

Figure 6-8. *The site rendered in the new theme*

The Administration Theme

Administration forms tend to be wide and long, sometimes not fitting too well within the confines of the content area defined for a given theme. To address this problem, Drupal 7 lets you specify a theme that should be used for administrative functions. You can try your new theme to see if it works for administration screens, or you can pick a different theme to use whenever a site administrator is performing site administration tasks. Typically, a simple clean theme that is at least 960px wide works best as the admin theme. To change the administration theme, simply click on the Appearance menu item at the top of the page and scroll to the bottom. You'll see a section titled Administration Theme. From the list of themes in the drop-down list, select a theme that you know will work with administration forms. By default Drupal 7 enables Seven as the administration theme, because it accommodates administration screens. You may also change the administration theme to any other theme listed in the drop-down list. If you change the value, make sure you click the "Save configuration" button.

Configuration Options

Drupal 7 provides a set of configuration options that, when changed, updates certain aspects of what is displayed within your theme. Depending on whether the theme author adhered to Drupal standards, you can use this form to determine which elements are displayed on the page (Logo, Site Name, Site Slogan, and so on), whether the theme should use its default logo, and whether the shortcut icon should be used (the shortcut icon is also known as the favicon; it's the little logo that appears to the left of your browsers address bar). To get to this screen, simply click on the Appearance menu item in the top menu and click on the Settings tab at the top of the Appearance page. See Figure 6-9.

Figure 6-9. *Appearance configuration options*

■ **Note** A great site to visit to see what others have done with Drupal is Dries Buytaert's personal page. On his site, he lists many of the highest profile sites on the web that are deployed on Drupal. You can find the list at `http://buytaert.net/tag/drupal-sites`.

Summary

In this chapter we stepped into the "wow!" part of building a Drupal-based site: themes. In a matter of minutes, we changed the entire look and feel of our site through a few simple steps. Spend some time browsing through the themes on Drupal.org. You'll be amazed at the breadth of options that are literally a few clicks away from changing the entire look of your site.

CHAPTER 7

■ ■ ■

Drupal Blocks

In this chapter I focus on using blocks to assign content and what are called "widgets" (which include the user login form, latest blog posts, a list of who is currently logged into your site, the current weather conditions, and the like) to specific positions on a page. I will cover standard blocks that ship with Drupal 7, blocks that come with contributed modules, and information on how to build a custom block from scratch. At the end of the chapter you will have the ability to construct a page with some pretty exciting features.

Blocks, Blocks, and More Blocks

A block is a generic term that is applied to any self-contained piece of content, menu, or code. There are standard pre-built blocks that come with Drupal 7: the login block, the search block, the "who's online" block, the "who's new" block, the latest blog postings block, and more. There are also blocks that come with contributed modules, such as blocks that share the latest weather report, your recent Twitter posts, or your current Facebook status. As a site administrator you can construct your own custom blocks, such as a list of upcoming events.

Making Blocks Appear on Pages

In Chapter 6 I covered the structure of themes and how themes define "regions" on a page. Figure 6-1 showed how the theme was divided into left, center, right, and footer regions. I'll now show you how to assign anywhere from one to dozens of blocks to the various regions on your theme, and explain how doing so increases visitor interest in your site by providing interesting and high-value features.

Figure 7-1 is an example of blocks that are assigned to various regions on a page. There are seven blocks that appear on this page.

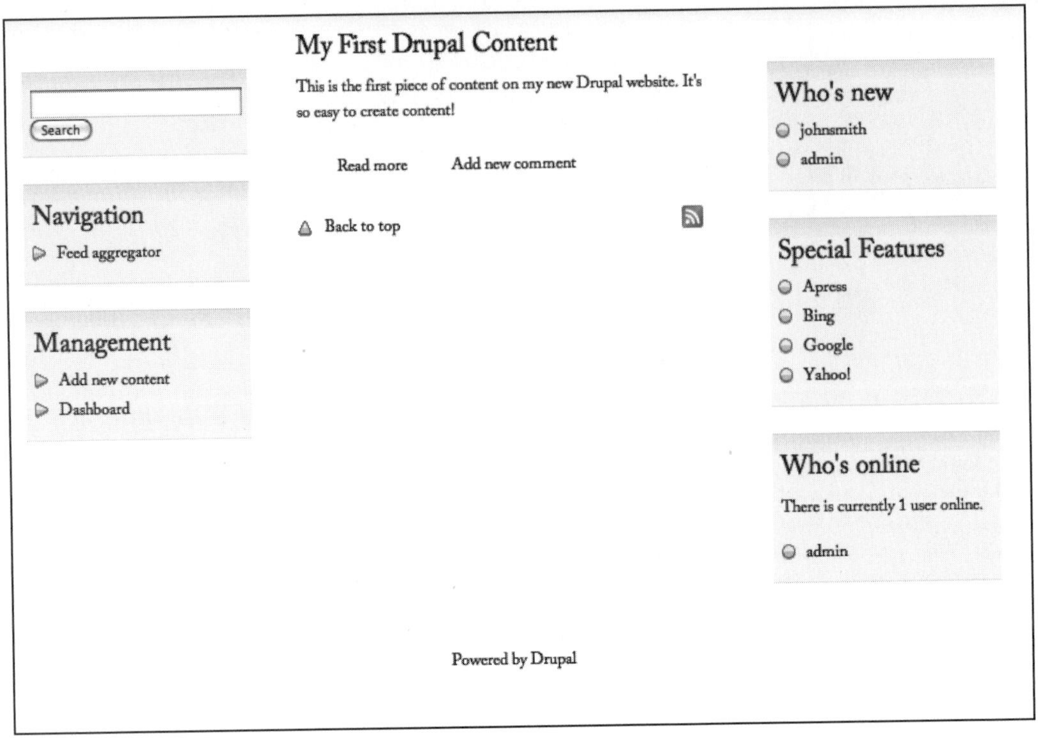

Figure 7-1. See if you can spot the blocks

In this example are blocks that are menus (Navigation, Management, Special Features) as well as interactive blocks (Search), and informational blocks ("Who's new," "Who's online," and "Powered by Drupal").

Let's take a look at the blocks that come with Drupal 7 and assign a few of those blocks to regions on your site. We'll then install a module or two that provide cool blocks that you can add to your site, and then we'll create a custom block from scratch.

Finding the List of Available Blocks

To find the list of blocks that are available for you to use on your new web site, click on the Structure link at the top of the page. This takes you to the Structure page. On the Structure page, click on the Blocks link to reveal the Blocks page, which lists all the defined blocks on your system, including those that are already assigned to regions and those that are not assigned to a region. See Figure 7-2.

Disabled

✣	Powered by Drupal*	<none>	configure
✣	Who's online*	<none>	configure
✣	Special Features*	<none>	configure
✣	Who's new*	<none>	configure
✣	Management*	<none>	configure
✣	User login*	<none>	configure
✣	Navigation*	<none>	configure
✣	Search form*	<none>	configure
✣	Author information	<none>	configure
✣	Main menu	<none>	configure
✣	Recent comments	<none>	configure
✣	Recent content	<none>	configure
✣	Secondary menu	<none>	configure

***Figure 7-2.** The Blocks page*

As you see in Figure 7-2, there are a number of disabled blocks. Enable a few by first picking the region where you want them to show up (click the drop-down that says "<none>") and, after assigning the blocks to regions, click on the "Save blocks" button. If you return to your site's homepage, you'll now see the blocks that you enabled in the regions where you assigned them.

Re-Arranging Blocks

It is likely that, at some point in time, you're going to want to re-order how blocks appear on a page. In the previous example, we may want to have the "Who's new" block appear above the "Who's online" block. To re-order the blocks, navigate to the Blocks page by clicking on the Structure link at the top of the page. On the Structure page, click on the Blocks link. Once on the Blocks page, simply click and hold the plus sign (+) next to the block that you want to move, and drag that block to the position where you want it in the list of blocks for that region. When you release the mouse button, you'll see that Drupal re-ordered the items (temporarily). You'll see a message stating that the changes have not yet been saved. Scroll to the bottom of the page and click Save. Drupal will save the changes and display a message stating that the changes were made. You can now close the Blocks page by clicking on the X in the right-hand corner of the Blocks page. Click your browser's refresh button to update the homepage, which should now display the blocks in the new order that you just defined.

Reassigning and Deactivating Blocks

Drupal also provides the mechanisms for moving a block to a different region and deactivating a block that is already visible on a page. To see this in action, let's deactivate the "Who's new" block and move the "Who's online" block to the Left Sidebar at the bottom of the blocks that already appear in that region. To make the changes, navigate to the Blocks page by clicking on the Structure link at the top of the page and, on the Structure page, click the Blocks link.

On the Blocks page, click on the Region drop-down list for the "Who's new" block and select the <none> option. Immediately upon selecting <none>, that item will disappear from the Right Sidebar section of the Blocks page. Next, click on the Region drop-down for "Who's online" and select the Left Sidebar option. Immediately after selecting the new location, the "Who's online" block will move to the Left Sidebar area of the block listing, and it will appear at the top of the list.

Our task was to move the "Who's online" block to the Left Sidebar at the bottom of the list of blocks, so we need to click and hold the plus sign (+) next to the "Who's online" block and drag the block to the bottom of the list of blocks in the Left Sidebar region. After dropping the block at the bottom of the list, scroll to the bottom of the page and click Save, which commits the changes to the Drupal database. Revisit the home page of your web site, and you will see the changes that you just made.

Configuring Blocks

You can select various configuration setting for blocks on the Blocks Administration page. The configuration options include overriding the title of the block and setting the visibility of the block based on several optional parameters. As an example of how you might use these features in the future, let's change the "Who's online" block so that it only appears on the homepage of your site, and only when the visitor is a user who has logged into the system with a user ID and password. To make these changes, navigate to the Blocks page by clicking on Structure and then clicking on the Blocks link. On the Blocks page, locate the "Who's online" block and click on its configure link. This reveals the block's configuration page. See Figure 7-3.

'*Who's online*' block

Block title

Override the default title for the block. Use *<none>* to display no title, or leave blank to use the default block title.

User activity

15 min

A user is considered online for this long after they have last viewed a page.

User list length

10

Maximum number of currently online users to display.

REGION SETTINGS

Specify in which themes and regions this block is displayed.

Aberdeen

Right Sidebar

Seven

Disabled

Figure 7-3. *The configuration page for the "Who's online" block*

On this form, you can override the default title by entering a value into the "Block title" field. In the "User activity" drop-down you can define the list of users who appear in the "Who's online" block. You do this by selecting the amount of time the person has been logged in for before they appear on the list. In the example, users who have not been logged in for at least 15 minutes will not appear on the list. The next field defines who many people will appear in the list. If you have a site with a significant number of online user and its important to show the names of who is online, then you'll want to increase the user list length to the appropriate value (for example, if you have a social networking site where users interact with each other, you'll want to allow for more names to show).

You can also set the region where the block appears based on the active theme. This is important for sites where different themes are used for example – when a visitor is looking at the site from a device like a PDA instead of a full web browser. You can set a different region for each of the themes on your site.

You will likely want to specify on which pages a block appears. For example, you may want the "Who's online" block to only appear on the homepage of your site. At the bottom of the Block configuration page (see Figure 7-4), you will the Pages tab. To set the block to only appear on the homepage, click on the "Only the listed pages" radio button and enter <front> in the text box (<front> is the special term used to represent the homepage of your site). You could also specify other pages by entering the URL of that page in the text box (for example, /content/). With this option, you can also exclude pages as well as write PHP code to define when the block should appear.

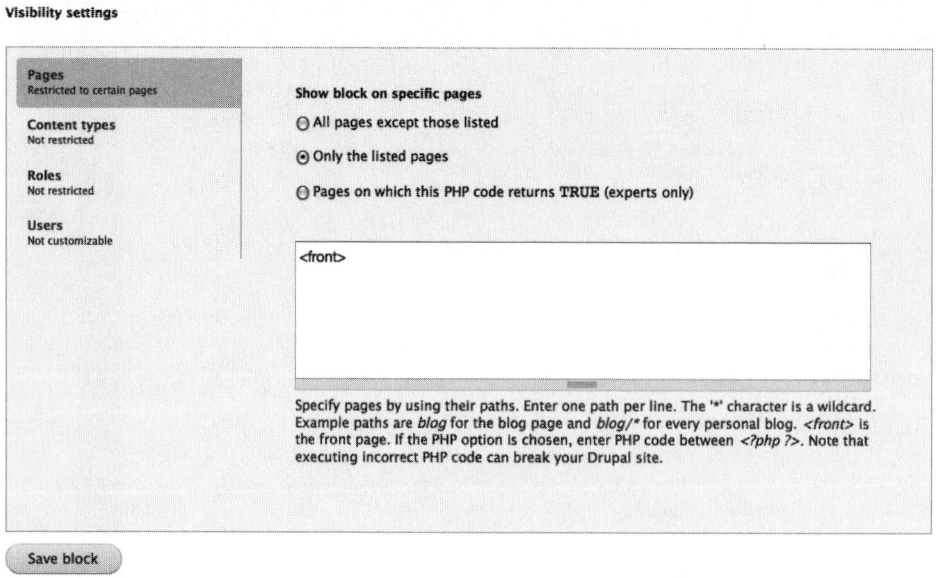

Visibility settings

Pages
Restricted to certain pages

Content types
Not restricted

Roles
Not restricted

Users
Not customizable

Show block on specific pages

○ All pages except those listed

◉ Only the listed pages

○ Pages on which this PHP code returns TRUE (experts only)

<front>

Specify pages by using their paths. Enter one path per line. The '*' character is a wildcard. Example paths are *blog* for the blog page and *blog/** for every personal blog. *<front>* is the front page. If the PHP option is chosen, enter PHP code between *<?php ?>*. Note that executing incorrect PHP code can break your Drupal site.

Save block

Figure 7-4. *Choosing Visibility settings*

It is also possible to set a block so that it only appears for specific types of users based on their assigned roles. Click on the Roles vertical tab to examine and set the visibility by user roles options. As an example, let's set the block to only appear when the person visiting the site is logged in.

Let's also limit the visibility of this block to visitors who are logged onto our site. See Figure 7-5.

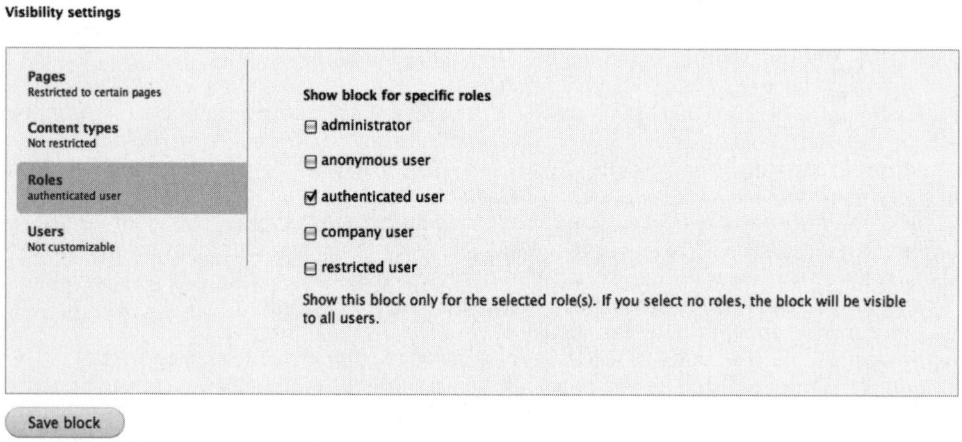

Visibility settings

Pages
Restricted to certain pages

Content types
Not restricted

Roles
authenticated user

Users
Not customizable

Show block for specific roles

☐ administrator

☐ anonymous user

☑ authenticated user

☐ company user

☐ restricted user

Show this block only for the selected role(s). If you select no roles, the block will be visible to all users.

Save block

Figure 7-5. *Choosing roles-based settings*

Once you have clicked the check box, you can now click on the "Save block" button at the bottom of the page and return to the homepage of your site. .

To test your changes, navigate to a page other than the homepage. If you are using the Garland theme, you will see a menu on the right-hand side of your page that lists your user name and a Logout link next to your username. Click on your username. You will be taken to your User Account page. Because you are no longer on your homepage, you will see that the "Who's online" block is no longer displayed, which tells you that your changes were made.

Using Blocks from Contributed Modules

There are literally thousands of contributed modules available for Drupal. Many of them generate blocks as their primary means of displaying information to visitors. Examples of modules that generate blocks include the U.S. Weather Bureau's current weather conditions block, which we'll now install as an example of using a contributed modules blocks.

The first step is to locate the module. You can find the weather service module at `http://drupal.org/project/nws_weather`. Visit the modules project page and right-click on the Download link for the Drupal 7 version, selecting the appropriate copy command for your browser (in this case, Copy Link Location, as shown in Figure 7-6).

Figure 7-6. Copying a module's download link

The next step is to install the module. Click on the Modules link on the administrator's menu at the top of any page. Drupal will display the modules page. On that page, click on the link for installing a new module. You will see the "Install from a URL" text box, which is where you paste the URL you copied in the previous step (see Figure 7-7).

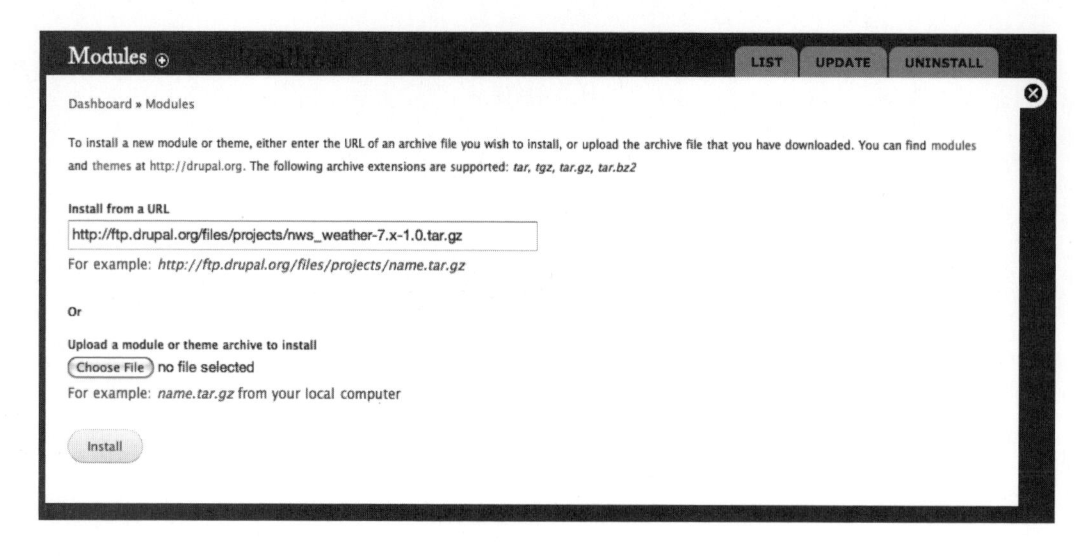

Figure 7-7. Pasting the download link

After pasting the URL, click on the Install button. Drupal downloads the module from the URL you specified and prepares the module for use.

The next step is to enable the module (although the module exists on your site after downloading, Drupal does not automatically enable it as an active module). Click on the List tab at the top of the Modules panel and scroll down until you find the Weather module. When you find it, you'll note that the Enabled check box is unchecked. Click on the check box and then scroll to the bottom of the page and click on the "Save configuration" button. Drupal refreshes the modules page and displays a "The configuration options have been saved" message.

The final step in the process is to assign the module's "Multi Day Forecast" block to a region on your page. Follow the steps from the previous section and assign the block to a region. Remember to click the "Save blocks" button at the bottom of the page. Visit the homepage of your site and you will see the results of your efforts (shown in Figure 7-8): an extended forecast for Seattle Washington (to change the forecast to your home town click on the NWS Weather link in the administrator's menu and follow the directions).

Weather Forecast for Seattle, WA

Sunday, March 21st, 2010

Rain Showers Likely
High Temperature: 56°F
Low Temperature: 43°F

Monday, March 22nd, 2010

Chance Rain Showers
High Temperature: 53°F
Low Temperature: 38°F

Tuesday, March 23rd, 2010

Partly Sunny
High Temperature: 57°F
Low Temperature: 40°F

Figure 7-8. *Seattle's weather (or any other city!), now available on your site*

There are hundreds of modules that generate blocks. Visit `www.drupal.org/project/modules` and browse through the list.

Creating Custom Blocks

There may be cases where you need a block and, even after looking through the list of contributed modules, you can't find anything that meets your specific requirements. In that case, you have the opportunity to create a custom block yourself. Custom blocks can contain any combination of static HTML and PHP code. If you're interested in creating a custom block that requires PHP code, check out *Pro Drupal Development,* published by Apress. It's an excellent reference for developing custom PHP code in a Drupal environment.

To demonstrate creating a custom block, we'll create one that displays static HTML text in the form of "Hello World!" Although it may not be exciting, it does demonstrate the process for creating a new block. The first step is to launch the block creation form, which is accessible from the following URL `http://localhost/admin/structure/block/add` (replace localhost with the appropriate domain name if you are not running Drupal your desktop or laptop). On this form, enter a description of the block in the "Block description field," enter the title you want to appear at the top of the block in the "Block title" field, the text you want to display in the "Block body," and select the region where you want your block to appear in for each of the themes you have enabled on your site. When complete, click on the "Save block" button at the bottom of the page. See Figure 7-9.

Block description *

The Hello World Block

A brief description of your block. Used on the Blocks administration page.

Block title

My First Custom Drupal Block

The title of the block as shown to the user.

Block body *

Hello World!

Text format Filtered HTML   More information about text formats

- Web page addresses and e-mail addresses turn into links automatically.
- Allowed HTML tags: <a> <em> <strong> <cite> <blockquote> <code> <ul> <ol> <li> <dl> <dt> <dd>
- Lines and paragraphs break automatically.

The content of the block as shown to the user.

REGION SETTINGS

Specify in which themes and regions this block is displayed.

Aberdeen

Left Sidebar

Seven

First sidebar

Garland

Left sidebar

Figure 7-9. *Block settings for a custom block*

After saving the block, return to the homepage of your site where you'll see the block you created in the region you specified (see Figure 7-10).

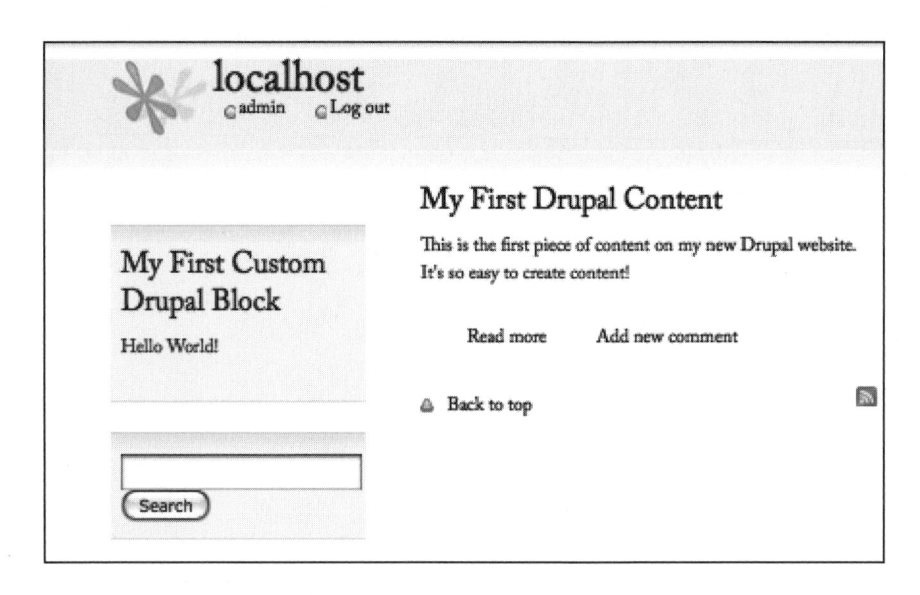

Figure 7-10. Your first custom block

Now let's take your block to the next level by adding a relatively simple block of PHP code that displays the current date, making your block dynamic. To change the block, click on the Structure link in the administrator's menu at the top of the page. On the Structure page, click on the Block's link. On the blocks page, scroll down until you find the block you just created and click on the configure link. Clicking on the link opens the Block edit form where we'll enter the PHP code that displays the current date. Update the Block body by entering the following block of PHP code, immediately following the Hello World! text that you entered previously.

```
<?php
 echo "Today is: ";
 echo date('m/d/Y');
?>
```

After entering the code, change the Text format select list from Filtered HTML to PHP code, directing Drupal to interpret the PHP code you entered, and click the Save block button. Return to the homepage to see the impact of your change.

Summary

Blocks are powerful mechanisms for creating and displaying dynamic content and interactive features on your site. In this chapter we discovered blocks that ship with Drupal 7, how to install a module that provides a weather forecast for your local area, and how to create a custom block from scratch. We will continue to expand on the use of blocks as I cover Views, Panels, and installing additional modules in upcoming chapters.

CHAPTER 8

■ ■ ■

Drupal Modules

Drupal is an amazing product in its off-the-shelf state. The features and functionality provided in Drupal 7 core is often more than adequate to meet the needs of many who build their websites with Drupal. But there are times when you need a feature that isn't possible with Drupal core alone, and in those cases you need look no further than the thousands of contributed modules that have been written to address just about anything you could think of doing on a Drupal based website.

In this chapter you will learn how to find, install, enable, and configure contributed modules. You will go through the process of installing, enabling, and configuring one of the most popular and powerful modules for Drupal: the Views module.

Contributed Modules

A Drupal-contributed module is essentially a program or set of programs that expands Drupal's capabilities beyond what is available in Drupal core. Contributed modules are designed, developed, and provided to the Drupal community free of charge by one or more of the thousands of developers who actively participate in the Drupal community. Modules can be downloaded from Drupal.org and enabled through the Module administration pages. I will cover the process for adding modules in detail in a few moments.

A contributed module can be as simple as providing a mechanism to automatically create the title of an article or as complex as a fully featured eCommerce storefront with product management, inventory management, order management, shipment management, credit card processing, customer management, and returns management. There are thousands modules of every shape and size, covering a wide variety of topics. To find a contributed module, visit `www.drupal.org/project/modules` and browse through the categories of modules. Example categories include (note: the number after the category represents the number of modules that are available for that category).

- Utility (935)
- Content (907)
- Third-party integration (819)
- Administration (561)
- Content Construction Kit (CCK) (422)
- Community (360)

- e-Commerce (316)
- User management (281)
- Import/export (150)
- Multilingual (83)
- Performance and scalability (58)
- Spam prevention (18)
- Mobile (15)

As you can see from these examples, there are thousands of modules that span a wide variety of categories. The general titles of the categories listed here often do not do justice to the rich features that are available in the modules that are buried beneath the titles. It often takes research and patience to scan through the hundreds of modules to find the one that provides the functionality that you need. Complex requirements may also take more than one module to provide the functionally you need to address a larger problem. Understanding which modules do what, which modules work well together, and which modules do not work together is often the hardest challenge of building a complex Drupal website.

A recommended exercise is to visit `www.durpal.org/project/modules` and click on the Release Date link (clicking the link once sorts in date ascending order, clicking the link again sorts the list in date-descending order where the newest module is listed first). Visit the site every day or two and read through the description of the newest modules that were added or updated on the site. It only takes a couple of minutes a day to quickly build up your understanding of the modules and types of solutions that are available through Drupal's contributed modules.

A great third-party website that helps solve the issue of finding the right modules is `www.drupalmodules.com`. This site provides a search feature that makes it easier look for and find the right module for the right job.

How to Download, Install, and Configure a Module

The first step in installing a module is finding the right module to use. As described earlier, there are thousands of modules to pick from; finding the right one is often the biggest challenge. For demonstration purposes, let's pick one of the most popular, powerful, and useful modules: the Views module.

A new feature of Drupal 7 is an administrator's page, which allows you to download and install a module by simply entering the URL of the install file and clicking a button. Drupal handles the task of downloading the modules install file, expanding the install file, moving the files to the correct directory, and installing the module. To access the Modules page, where you can download and install a new Drupal module, simply click on the Modules link in the top menu. Drupal will display the modules configuration page, which at this point shows all of the modules that are shipped as part of Drupal core (see Figure 8-1).

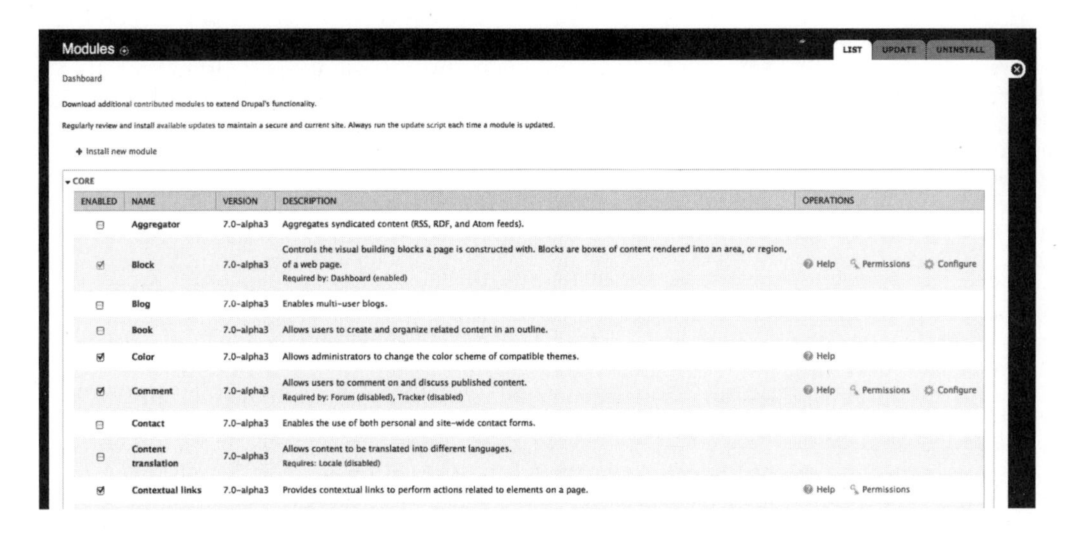

Figure 8-1. Drupal modules

To begin the installation process, click on the "Install new module" link near the top of the page. Clicking on the link reveals the module installation page, shown in Figure 8-2.

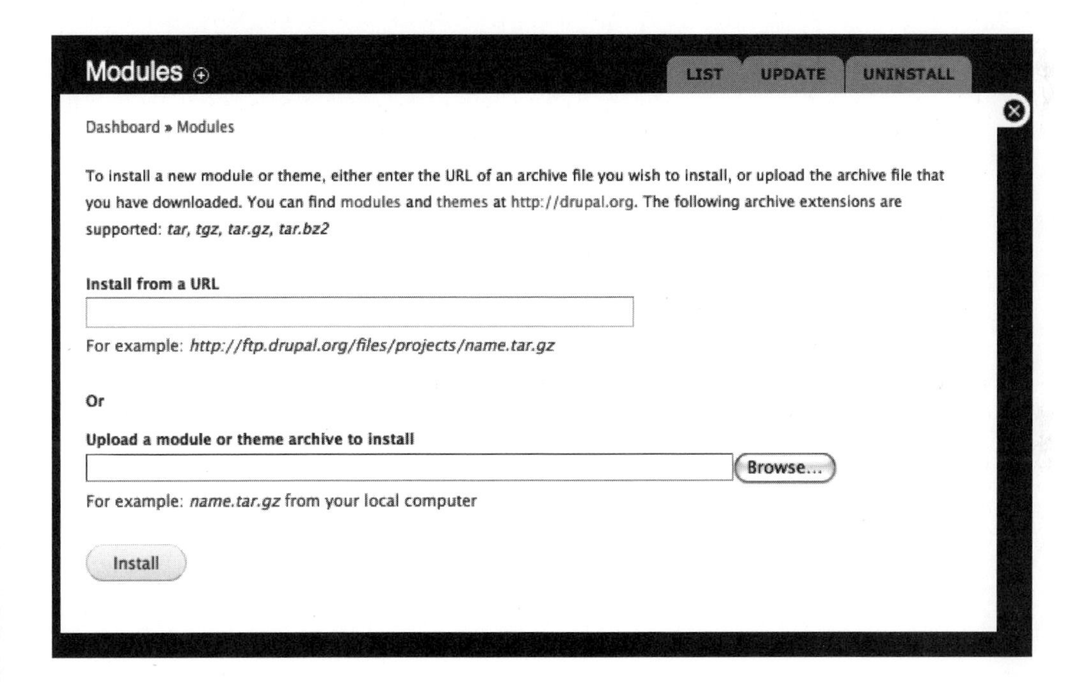

Figure 8-2. The module installation page

On this page, we need to provide either the URL for the module's installation file (from Drupal.org) or, in the case where you downloaded the module to your computer, uploading the file from your computer to the server using the Upload a module or theme feature. To simplify the process, we'll use the first text box to specify the URL of the file that we are going to install. To find the URL of the file visit `www.drupal.org/project` and find the module that you wish to install. In our case the module is the Views module, located at `www.drupal.org/project/views` (each module has its own page on Drupal.org; the URL for each module begins with `www.drupal.org/project/`, followed by the name of the module). Open a new tab in your browser or a new browser window and navigate to the Views page (`www.drupal.org/project/views`). On the Views page, near the bottom, you will find a list of the current versions of the Views module, as shown in Figure 8-3. You should, in most cases, select the current release for the module that you are installing. The current release should be highlighted with a green background. In some cases, you may need to use a module that is still in development because a stable production version is not yet available. Development versions (development, alpha, or beta) are typically highlighted with a yellow background and have a version number that ends in -dev, -alpha, or -beta. You should use pre-production (dev, alpha, beta) versions with caution, as those modules are not yet fully developed and have not been thoroughly tested. In our case, we want the current Drupal 7 version of the module, so locate the 7.x version of the module on the list of available releases.

Views

By **merlinofchaos** on the 25th of November, 2005

The Views module provides a flexible method for Drupal site designers to control how lists and tables of content (nodes in Views 1, almost anything in Views 2) are presented. Traditionally, Drupal has hard-coded most of this, particularly in how taxonomy and tracker lists are formatted.

This tool is essentially a smart query builder that, given enough information, can build the proper query, execute it, and display the results. It has four modes, plus a special mode, and provides an impressive amount of functionality from these modes.

Among other things, Views can be used to generate reports, create summaries, and display collections of images and other content.

Version	Date	Links	Status	
7.x-3.x-dev	2010-Mar-30	Download · Release notes	Development snapshot	⊗
6.x-2.8	2009-Dec-03	Download · Release notes	Recommended for 6.x	✓
5.x-1.6	2007-Jul-14	Download · Release notes	Recommended for 5.x	✓

Find out more · Bugs and feature requests

Figure 8-3. Views module

To capture the URL of the installation file, right click on the Download link for the version you wish to install, and select the appropriate copy link location option from the browser's options menu. Return to the Blocks administration page and paste the URL for the file in the top text box.
You are now ready to install the module. To begin the installation process, click on the Install button. Drupal will download the installation file from Drupal.org, expand the compressed file, move all of the files and directories associated with the module to the appropriate directories on your server, and then run the installation script associated with your module.

The module is now installed but not yet enabled. To use the module, you must enable it by checking the Enabled boxes on the module configuration page and clicking on the "Save configuration" button at the bottom of the page (see Figure 8-4). For Views, you will want to enable Views and Views UI.

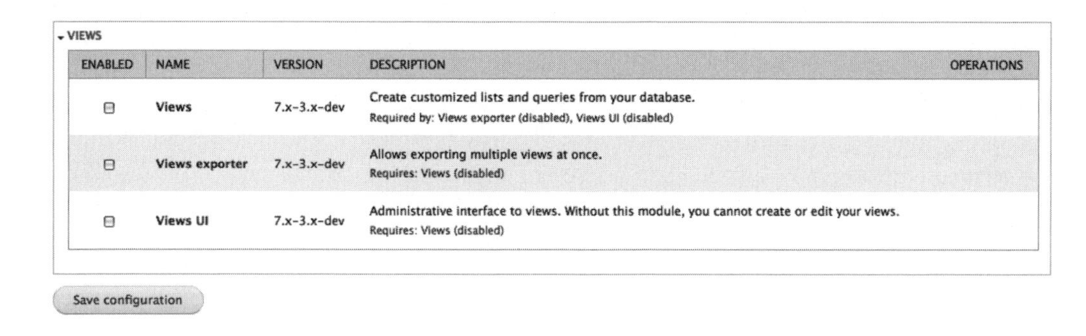

Figure 8-4. The module configuration page

At this point the Views module is installed, enabled, and ready to use. You may now follow the same process to install any contributed module you wish to add to your site.

Configuring Modules and Setting Permissions

Some, although not all modules provide some level of customization and configuration. In the case of the Views module that we just installed, the only configuration tasks are to set the permissions of who can use those modules.

To configure the permissions for the Views click on the Permissions link under the Operations column as shown in Figure 8-5.

VIEWS

ENABLED	NAME	VERSION	DESCRIPTION	OPERATIONS
☑	Views	7.x-3.x-dev	Create customized lists and queries from your database. Required by: Views exporter (disabled), Views UI (enabled)	Permissions
☐	Views exporter	7.x-3.x-dev	Allows exporting multiple views at once. Requires: Views (enabled)	
☑	Views UI	7.x-3.x-dev	Administrative interface to views. Without this module, you cannot create or edit your views. Requires: Views (enabled)	

Save configuration

Figure 8-5. The module configuration page after enabling Views

Permissions for Views, by default, is automatically set to allow Administrators full access to each of the capabilities associated with the module. As you can see from the list in Figure 8-6, the Views module developer defined two types of permissions for this module: the ability to restrict which user roles can administer views and roles that have the ability to bypass access control when accessing views. The default settings meet the requirements for most sites, and we will leave those permissions in their current state.

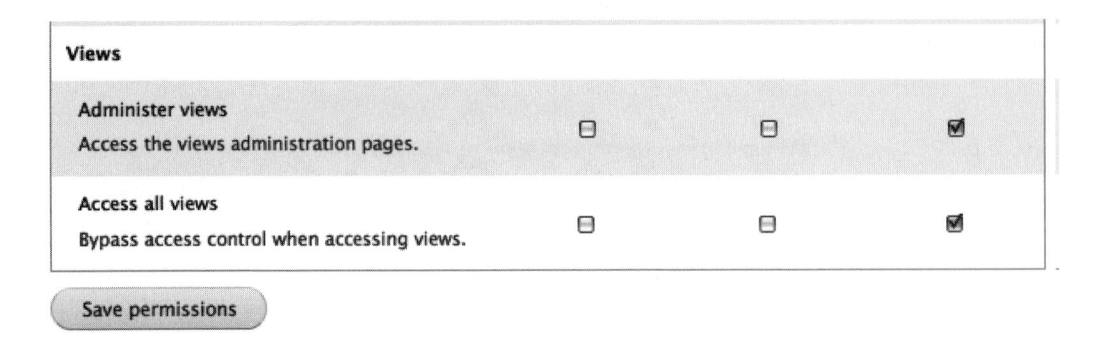

Figure 8-6. Views module permissions settings

As you install and enable other modules remember to review and set the permissions for that module.

Some modules provide the ability to set configuration parameters, such as the Search module (part of Drupal core). When viewing the Module configuration page, you'll notice a Configure link under the Operations column, indicating the module developer provided the ability to set parameters. In Figure 8-7 you can see a few of the Search module's configuration options.

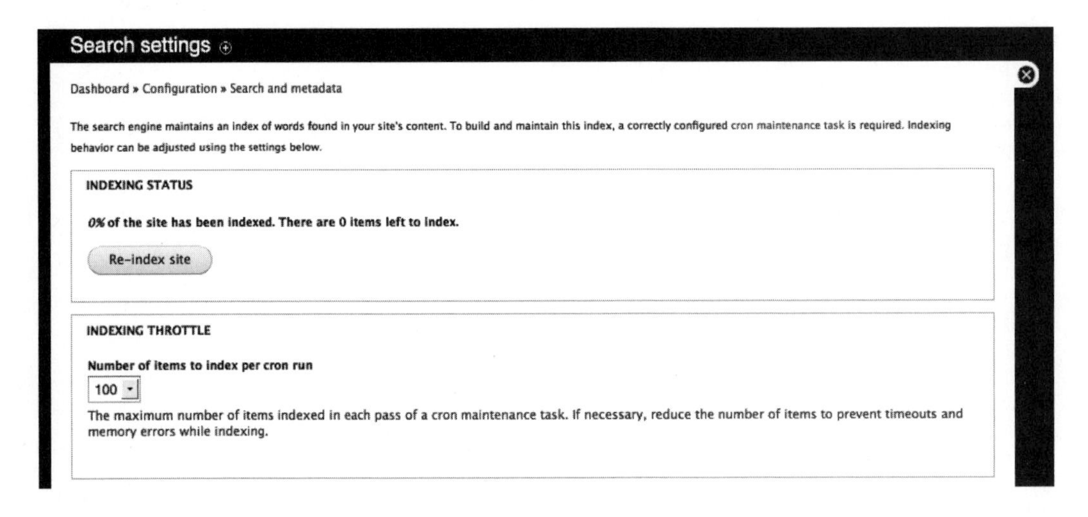

Figure 8-7. Search module configuration options

It is a good idea to review the configuration options for all of your installed and enabled modules to ensure that they are set properly.

Enabling Other Modules

You may "inherit" an existing Drupal site, or you may wish to enable other Drupal modules that already exist on your site (e.g., modules that are part of Drupal core, but not automatically enabled by the Drupal installation process). To see the list of modules that are available on your site simply click on the Modules link at the top of the page, revealing the Modules administration page shown in Figure 8-8.

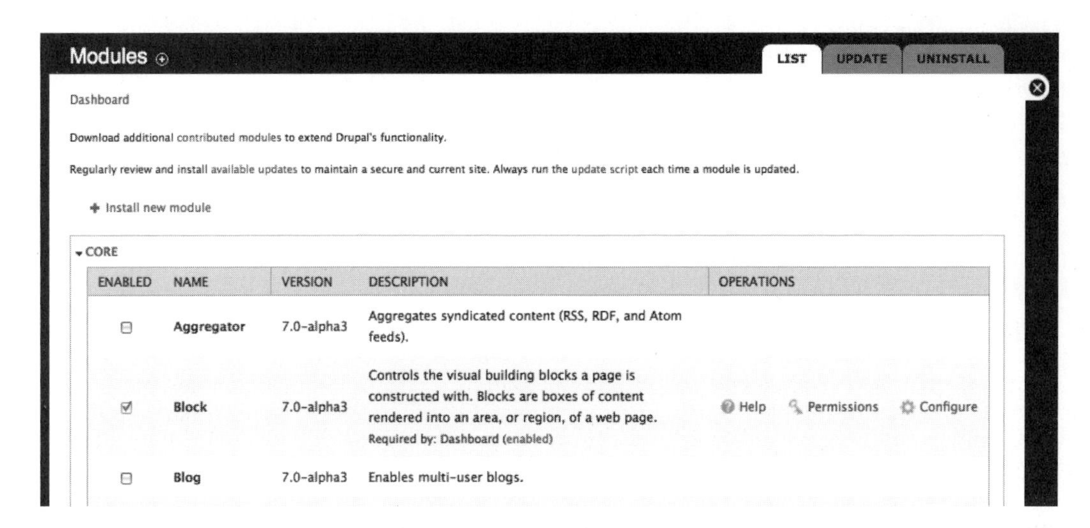

Figure 8-8. Module administration page

Drupal's module administration page is divided into sections, with each section focused on a particular module or group of modules. The modules that are delivered as part of Drupal core can be found in the Core section of the listing. For demonstration purposes, we are going to enable a core module that by default is not enabled by the Drupal install process: the Blog module. As you can see from Figure 8-8, the Blog module is not checked as Enabled. To enable the Blog module, check the Enabled box and scroll to the bottom of the page. Click on the Save button to enable the Blog module so that it can be used on your new site.

After clicking the Save button, Drupal will then redisplay the Module administration page with the successful configuration message at the top of the page. The blog module is now ready for use.

Disabling a Module

There may be cases where a module that you have installed is no longer needed. To disable a module, you simply "uncheck" the enabled check box for that module and click Save at the bottom of the Module administration page. To demonstrate this feature, disable the Blog module that you enabled in a previous step. To disable a module, launch the Module administration page by clicking on the Modules link in the top menu bar and scrolling down to the module that you wish to disable. Uncheck the Enabled check box by clicking on the box, scroll to the bottom, and click the Save button. Drupal will then redisplay the list of modules with a success message at the top.

Upgrading a Module

Drupal modules are often updated with fixes to bugs and new additional features. Drupal 7, fortunately, tells you when a new version of a module has been released, and provides a mechanism for automatically updating that module to the latest version. To view all of the available updates, simply click on the Update tab at the top of the Module configuration page (see Figure 8-9).

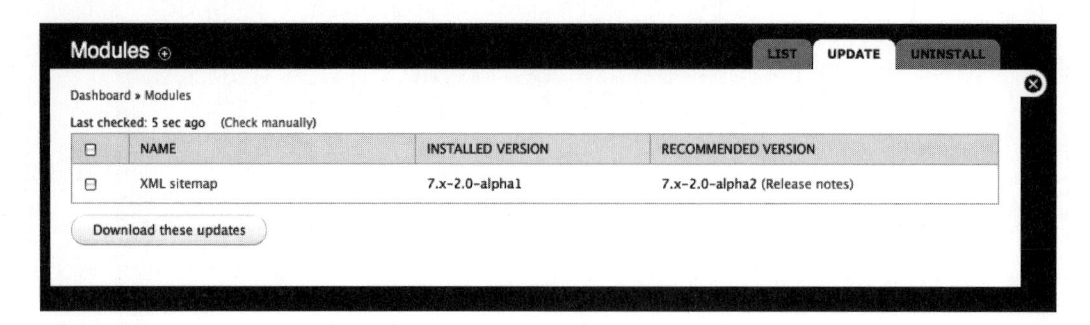

Figure 8-9. List of modules to update

To upgrade a module, click on the check box next to the module's name and the "Download these updates" button.

■ **Note** There may be cases where you don't want to upgrade a module; for example, a case where an upgrade to one module breaks another related module. I suggest that you review the forums on Drupal.org to check to see if anyone has report problems prior to doing the update.

After the update has been downloaded, Drupal directs you to run the update script. Follow the suggestions and backup your site before running the update (see Figure 8-10). Although it's uncommon to have problems due to a module update, there is the possibility that an update causes unforeseen problems with other modules or customizations that you've made on your site. After the update has completed, close the update window and return to your site.

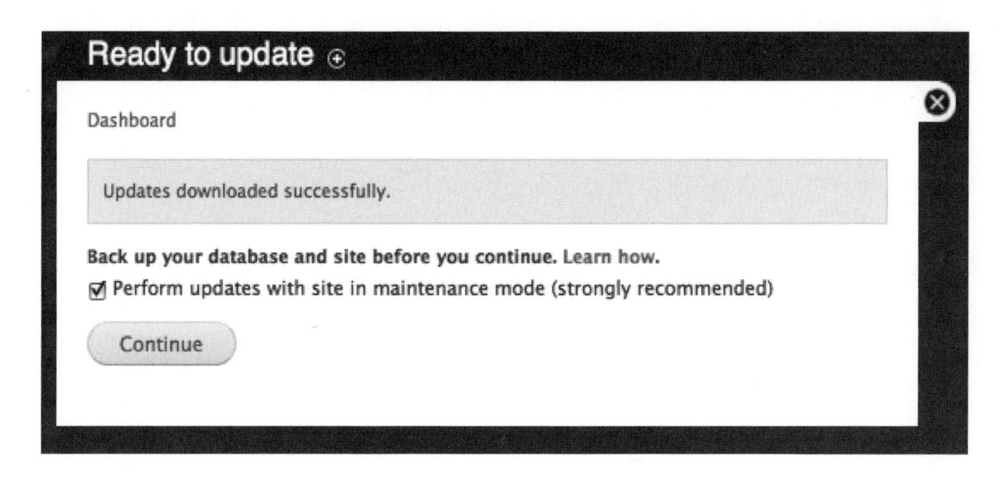

Figure 8-10. Run the update script

Uninstalling a Module

There may be cases where you install a module and it's just not what you thought it would be, or it causes problems on your site. On the Module administration page you will find an Uninstall tab at the top of the page. Clicking on that tab reveals a list of modules that have the capability to automatically uninstall themselves.

■ **Note** Not all modules have the ability to automatically perform an uninstall. It is up to the module developer to create this capability and not all module developers are kind enough to provide this feature.

In the case where automatic un-installation is not available, the process for removing a module is:

1. Disable the module from the Module administration page.
2. Navigate to the Sites ➤ Default ➤ Modules directory on your server.
3. Highlight the folder containing the module and delete the folder.

You should use caution when uninstalling a module, as there are often module dependencies, meaning one module depends on another module to function properly. If you are unsure as to whether a module has dependencies, visit that module's page on Drupal.org and look through the module's description. Modules with dependencies will list those dependencies in the body of their description.

The Top Eleven Modules

There are a few modules that seem to make it to everyone's "favorites" list. For those of us who eat, breathe, drink, and live Drupal, these modules represent our standard "tool belt" that we use on nearly every Drupal project.

Content Construction Kit (CCK)

CCK prior to Drupal 7 was an add-on module that every serious Drupal developer relied on as one of their "killer modules" for Drupal. CCK provides the ability to create custom content types. If you think back in earlier chapters where we created content for our website, we selected from one of two content types that shipped with Drupal 7, the Page and the Article content types. The primary difference between the Page and Article content types was that the Article has an additional field for attaching a picture. CCK provides you the developer with the ability to define new content types with virtually any field that you can think of. You might decide that you really need an Event content type, where an event has a start date, start time, end date, end time, venue, a picture, a seating chart, and a description. You could use the Page content type to create an event, but you would have to rely on the content author to remember to enter into the body field all of the information I just listed. An easier solution is to use CCK to define a custom content type for events and to define each of the fields mentioned as text fields (or radio buttons, check boxes, pop-up calendars for date selection, select lists, and text areas). As of Drupal 7, parts of CCK were moved into core, but not all of CCK made it. There are still additional CCK features that you will likely want to check out, download, and install. We'll describe in detail how to use CCK in Chapter 10.

Views

Views is either the first or second module that comes to mind when you ask experienced Drupal developers what their most favorite module is. The Views module is like a Swiss army knife for selecting and rendering content on your site. Let's say you created 50 pieces of content, each item describing a news event that occurred in the past. Let's say that you want to create a list of those 50 items sorted by the date that each story was published. Views can do that for you. Let's say you want the list of news articles to be listed in tabular format, like an Excel spreadsheet. Views can do that for you. Let's say you want visitors to the page that lists the news article as a table to have the ability to sort the articles by clicking on one of the titles in the table view of articles. Views can do that for you. Let's say you want to provide a filtering mechanism so visitors can pick a subject, person, or location associated with all of your news stories and only see those articles that meet the selected criteria. Views can do that for you. Let's say you want to provide an RSS feed of the news articles to visitors who use feed aggregators. Views can do that for you. Views is an amazingly easy to use module that is extremely powerful and a "must have" on nearly everyone's list. I'll describe how to use Views in Chapter 11.

Panels

A close third to CCK and Views is the Panels module. As we constructed our demonstration site in previous chapters, you saw that we were limited to putting "things" into the left sidebar, right sidebar, or the general content area on a page (beyond the header and footer regions). What if we wanted to divide our page even further into multiple rows and columns, and we wanted a simple to use mechanism for assigning content to each of the columns and rows? The Panels module comes to the rescue. For advanced page layouts, there isn't a tool that is easier to use and more powerful than the Panels module. I will describe how to use Panels in Chapter 12.

Imagecache

This module is another one of those "must haves" that simplifies the process of managing photographs on your website. One of the biggest issues with using pictures is that people take photos with their 12-megapixel cameras. The resulting image is massive, both in dimension and in file size. If you allowed people to upload pictures without scaling the image to the proper dimensions and shrinking the file size to something that doesn't take minutes to download, people would quickly stop visiting your website. Fortunately Imagecache takes care of the issues associated with uploading pictures by automatically scaling a picture to a predefined height and width and downsizing the file size to something that is web friendly. Imagecache also provides the ability to automatically crop pictures, as well as other advanced image manipulation techniques. Imagecache is a lifesaver and a must have for any site that uses photographs.

Nicemenus

Drupal's out-of-the-box menu features provide an easy to use mechanism for creating horizontal and vertical menus, where those menus are restricted to a single level. In many cases you'll want to have the ability to create menus that have drop-downs (for horizontal menus) or fly-outs (for vertical menus). Drupal's menuing system provides the ability to assign menu items in a hierarchical fashion; however, it is up to us, the Drupal developer, to format menus so that items drop down or fly out when a user hovers over a menu item. Fortunately, we have the Nicemenus module that automatically handles the rendering of drop-downs and fly-outs.

Nodequeues

One of the challenges of building a website is to make it easy for content authors to create content and to have that content show up in the right position on the right page. You could give them access to the admin screens for Panels, where they could manually assign each node to a specific position on a page, or you can implement Nodequeues, which provides a simple mechanism for content authors to pick a "queue" where they want their content to appear. You the developer create individual nodequeues, and you assign those nodequeues to a region on a specific page. Content authors just pick the queue where they want their content to show up and click on the assign to queue link. I will touch on the use of nodequeues in the chapter on that describes the use of Panels.

WYSIWYG

Drupal provides a plain text box where authors enter content. Most content authors demand that the site provides some form of "what-you-see-is-what-you-get" (WYSIWYG) editors (such as Microsoft Word-like text editors where what you see on the screen is what you see printed on a piece of paper). The WYSIWYG module provides a simple to use mechanism for installing and configuring one or more of the fully featured editors available for Drupal (e.g., TinyMCE or CKEditor).

Pathauto

One of the key elements of successful search engine optimization is providing URLs on your site that are meaningful. By default, Drupal 7 out-of-the-box URLs look something like http://localhost/node/1. To a search engine, they have no idea what "node/1" means, nor what the content associated with that page may be about just by looking at the URL. Humans visiting the site may also have a difficult time navigating around to pages that are not linked or accessible by a menu, as http://localhost/node/2487 is not very intuitive. Fortunately, we have the Pathauto module, which creates an "Alias URL" to the node being created, and the alias URL takes the form of the title of the node with hyphens used to separate words, and all words are made lowercase. An example might be http://localhost/node/2487. If that node has a title of "Special deals of the month," the URL as generated by Pathauto would be http://localhost/special-deals-month (pathauto removes common words like "the" and "of" from titles when generating URLs). The alias URL becomes the primary path used by Drupal when that page is rendered, and is significantly more user- and SEO-friendly than the http://localhost/node/2487 version.

Webform

The Webform module provides a simple to use interface for creating online forms. You can use online forms to capture virtually any type of information you can think of that would come from a form that a site visitor might fill out. Examples of forms could be an employment application, an information request form, or an event registration form. There are virtually no limits as to what types of forms you can create using the Webform module. The module extends beyond its ability to create and render forms by providing a mechanism for emailing a predefined person the results when someone enters information on a form, a tool for generating reports against the information that is captured on forms, and a tool for exporting information entered in forms to an Excel spreadsheet.

Backup and Migrate

The backup and migrate module automates the task of backing up the information that is stored in your Drupal database based on a schedule that you define (every 12 hours, every 24 hours, and so on). Backup and migrate also provides the ability to manually back up the database (in real time) by simply clicking on a button. You can also restore a backup by selecting a previous back and by clicking on a restore button. Many Drupal administrators sleep better at night knowing that their site is being backed up automatically.

Ubercart

The reason this is not a top-ten module list is I just had to mention Ubercart. It's a bit more specialized, but if you need e-commerce capabilities for your website, Ubercart is the module for you. It provides all of the features and functions required to run an online store, including the ability to sell physical as well as virtual (downloadable) products and collect credit card payments.

As I mentioned before, please take a few minutes a day to visit `hwww.drupal.org/project/modules` and browse through the pages and pages of modules that are available for free!

Summary

In this chapter you learned how to significantly enhance the functionality of your Drupal website through the use of contributed modules. There are literally thousands of free modules to select from, meaning that if there's something you want to do with your Drupal site, there is likely a module that provides the functionality that you need. Coming up next, making your site interactive! The next chapter details how to set up interactive features like blogging, forums, and polls.

CHAPTER 9

■ ■ ■

Enabling Interactive Capabilities

As the owner of your new Drupal site, one of the questions you should be asking yourself is, how are you going to engage site visitors so that they come back frequently? One of the most effective ways of ensuring visitor loyalty is to engage them with interactive features such as blogs, discussion forums, polls, and webforms. Site visitors are more likely to return if they posted a question or comment in a discussion forum on your site, or if they posted a comment to one of your blogs and want to see what others had to say about their comments.

In this chapter I will show you how to enable and configure the three most popular interactive modules that ship with Drupal 7 core, laying the foundation for hooking your site visitors and keeping them coming back for more!

Blogging

Blogging is one of the most prevalent interactive features on the Internet. Blogging is the simple act of recording and publishing your thoughts and ideas about a topic or group of related topics. Many think of blogging as a personal journal or diary, where the "personal" part refers to your thoughts and ideas, not to the visibility of the blog. Blogs are typically open to the general public.

There are websites that are completely dedicated to a specific blog and topic (such as `http://buytaert.net`, the website of the creator of Drupal), and there are websites where blogs represent a small portion of the content (such as whitehouse.gov). Drupal provides the capabilities to do either.

Enabling Blogs

Drupal 7 includes a blog module that makes it easy for users with the proper permissions to author and publish blog entries on your website. To demonstrate how easy it is to set up blogging on your site, let's enable the Blog module and set blogging up so that users assigned to a role of "blogger" have the ability to blog on your new website.

The first step is to enable the Blog module. Click on the Module link in the menu at the top of the page to see the list of modules that are available and enabled on your site. Near the top of the list of Core modules you will see the Blog module. If you have not yet enabled that module, you can do so by clicking on the check box and scrolling to the bottom of the screen, where you will click on "Save configuration."

Clicking on "Save configuration" installs the Blog module and makes all of the capabilities associated with blogging available to those Drupal users on your site who are assigned to a role with the permissions that provides access to Drupal's blogging features.

The next step is to create a "blogger" user role. To create the role, click on the People link in the menu at the top of the page. Once on the People configuration page, click on the Permissions tab. On the Permissions configuration page, click on the Roles link at the top right-hand corner. On the Roles configuration page, enter "blogger" in the blank text box in the Name column and click on "Add role."

Now that you have the role created, the next step is to set the permissions so that a user assigned to the blogger role will have the ability to create and edit blog entries. On the Roles page, click on the "Edit permissions" link for the blogger role to view the Permissions configuration page. On the Permissions page, scroll down and check the boxes for the following permissions:

- Create new *Blog entry* content.
- Edit own *Blog entry* content.
- Delete own *Blog entry* content.

Once these are checked, click on "Save permissions." Next, create a test user account and assign that account to the blogger role. To create the account, click on the People link in the menu at the top of the page. On the People configuration page, click on "Add user." On the Account Information page, enter "testuser" as the username, "test@test.com" as the e-mail address, and "test123" as the password. Then check the blogger role in the list of assigned roles. Finally, click "Create new account" at the bottom of the page.

Creating a Blog Entry

The next step is to log out of your site (you're currently logged in as the administrator) and log in as the test user that you just created. Click on "Log out" at the top of the page and then log back in using the new "testuser" account. Once logged in, click on "Add new content."

■ **Note** Because the testuser account is set up to only create blog postings, clicking on "Add new content" immediately brings up the "Create a blog entry" form. If the testuser account was assigned to roles that allowed that user to create other content types, clicking on "Add new content" link would have brought up a list of content types that the user could create.

Clicking "Add new content" reveals the Create Blog entry page. On this page, you'll find a text field for entering the title of your blog posting and a text area for authoring your blog posting. Create a blog posting that describes how much you enjoy using Drupal. When finished writing, click the Save button at the bottom of the page. Congratulations! You just blogged on your new Drupal website. The sample blog posting that I created is shown in Figure 9-1.

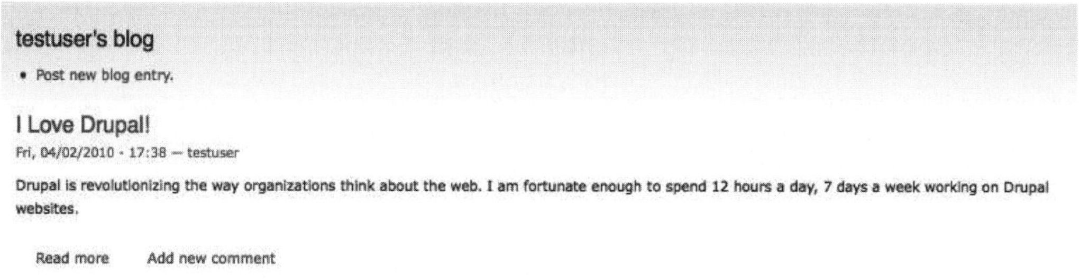

testuser's blog

- Post new blog entry.

I Love Drupal!

Fri, 04/02/2010 - 17:38 — testuser

Drupal is revolutionizing the way organizations think about the web. I am fortunate enough to spend 12 hours a day, 7 days a week working on Drupal websites.

Read more Add new comment

Figure 9-1. *A sample blog posting*

Look at the structure of the post. You'll see that Drupal automatically displays the date and time of the posting, along with the name of the user who wrote it. The blog posting is displayed in Teaser mode, as indicated by the "Read more" link at the bottom. If you wish to adjust the length of the blog-posting teaser, please refer to Chapter 10. Finally, a blog posting permits site visitors to post comments in response—a good way of hooking users to your site by making it interactive.

Displaying Blog Entries

Drupal uses a specific URL structure for displaying blog entries. For example, http://localhost/blog/1. In this URL the keyword "blog" tells Drupal that you wish to render a list of blog entries, while the "1" represents the user ID (UID) of the person who wrote the blog entries. In the example, "1" is the admin user. You can find the UID of any user by simply clicking on the People link in the top menu bar and hovering over the Edit link for that specific user. As you hover over the Edit link, look in the browser's status bar at the bottom of the page, where you will see a URL such as http://localhost/user/2/edit. The value after the "/user/" represents the UID of that user, and the value that you would insert in the URL for viewing that person's blog postings (for example, http://localhost/blog/2). Locate the UID of the testuser account and view the blog-listing page of that user.

Drupal automatically sorts blog postings by the date they were created, with the newest item posted at the top of the list and the oldest item at the bottom. To demonstrate this feature and to see a more complete example of the blogging feature, add two additional blog postings following the steps outlined previously. When complete, visit the blog-listing page for your testuser account. Figure 9-2 shows my blog postings.

testuser's blog

- Post new blog entry.

Preparing my Presentation for InnoTech 2010

Fri, 04/02/2010 - 17:58 — testuser

I have the opportunity to present at InnoTech during the first week of May. The subject of my presentation is "Drupal: revolutionizing how people leverage the web". Its going to be a great presentation!

Read more Add new comment

DrupalCon is Three Weeks Away!

Fri, 04/02/2010 - 17:57 — testuser

DrupalCon 2010 is in San Francisco. I can't wait to see all of the new and exciting things that people are doing with Drupal!

Read more Add new comment

I Love Drupal!

Fri, 04/02/2010 - 17:38 — testuser

Drupal is revolutionizing the way organizations think about the web. I am fortunate enough to spend 12 hours a day, 7 days a week working on Drupal websites.

Read more Add new comment

Figure 9-2. *Sample blog postings page for the test user account*

Adding a List of the Most Recent Blog Entries

Unless your site is purely focused on a blog, you'll likely want to provide site visitors with a mechanism for viewing recent blog posts. The Blog module provides a block that you can place on a page to automatically list the most recent blog postings made on your site. To assign that block to a region on your theme, click the Structure link at the top of the page, followed by the Blocks link on the Structure page.

On the Blocks page, scroll down and locate the "Recent blog posts" block. Change the region from <none> to "Right sidebar" (for demonstration purposes) and click "Save blocks" at the bottom of the page. Return to the homepage of your website (close the blocks page by clicking on the X) and refresh the page. You should then see a new block in the right column that shows your most recent blog posts (see Figure 9-3).

Figure 9-3. *Recent blog postings block*

Visitors can then click on an individual blog posting to read it, or they can click on More to visit a page that shows all of the recent blog entries on your site.

Forums

Forums, or discussion groups, are commonly thought of as one of the earliest forms of interacting on the Web. The Forums module, which is part of Drupal 7 core, provides the features and functions required to support forums on your site. An example of a site that uses Drupal's forums capability is Drupal.org, shown in Figure 9-4.

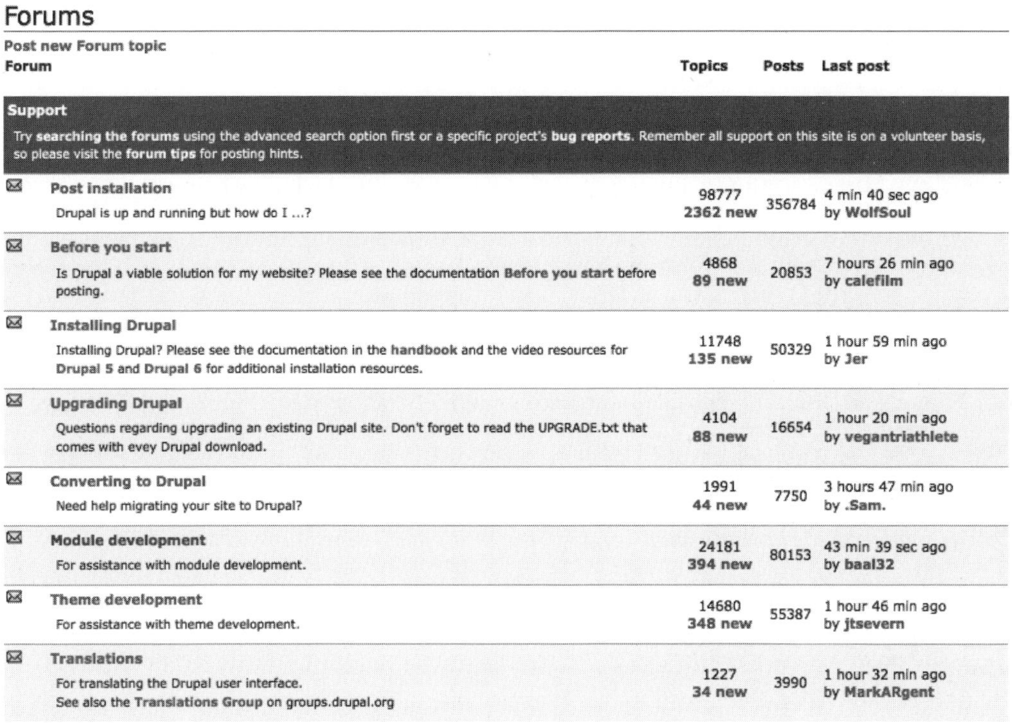

Forums

Post new Forum topic

Forum	Topics	Posts	Last post
Support Try **searching the forums** using the advanced search option first or a specific project's **bug reports**. Remember all support on this site is on a volunteer basis, so please visit the **forum tips** for posting hints.			
Post installation Drupal is up and running but how do I ...?	98777 **2362 new**	356784	4 min 40 sec ago by **WolfSoul**
Before you start Is Drupal a viable solution for my website? Please see the documentation **Before you start** before posting.	4868 **89 new**	20853	7 hours 26 min ago by **calefilm**
Installing Drupal Installing Drupal? Please see the documentation in the **handbook** and the video resources for **Drupal 5** and **Drupal 6** for additional installation resources.	11748 **135 new**	50329	1 hour 59 min ago by **Jer**
Upgrading Drupal Questions regarding upgrading an existing Drupal site. Don't forget to read the UPGRADE.txt that comes with evey Drupal download.	4104 **88 new**	16654	1 hour 20 min ago by **vegantriathlete**
Converting to Drupal Need help migrating your site to Drupal?	1991 **44 new**	7750	3 hours 47 min ago by **.Sam.**
Module development For assistance with module development.	24181 **394 new**	80153	43 min 39 sec ago by **baal32**
Theme development For assistance with theme development.	14680 **348 new**	55387	1 hour 46 min ago by **jtsevern**
Translations For translating the Drupal user interface. See also the **Translations Group** on groups.drupal.org	1227 **34 new**	3990	1 hour 32 min ago by **MarkARgent**

Figure 9-4. *Drupal.org's forums page*

As you can see in Figure 9-4, a forum is made up of one to many topics (e.g., Support in the example above), where site visitors post responses to existing topics or create new sub-topics (e.g., the Post Installation topic above has tens of thousands of sub-topics and posts).

Setting Up Your First Forum

To enable the Forums module, click on the Modules link in the top menu and scroll down the page until you see the Forum module. Check the box associated with the module and click the Save configuration button at the bottom of the page. Drupal will install the Forums module.

The next step in the process is to set permissions for forums. Here are the permissions that you can set:

- Administer forums
- Create new forum topic content
- Edit own forum topic content
- Edit any forum topic content
- Delete own forum topic content
- Delete any forum topic content

Only site administrators should be assigned the ability to "Administer forums," "Edit any forum topic content," and "Delete any forum topic content." If you want users, including anonymous users, to have the ability to post content to your forums, you will need to enable "Create new forum topic content," "Edit own forum topic content," and "Delete own forum topic content" for anonymous users, registered users, or any specific user roles you have defined. For our example site, check the boxes for authenticated users for the Create, Edit, and Delete own forum topics.

Creating forums is a simple two-step process: creating the container that will house your forum topics, and then creating the forum topics that site visitors can respond to.

To create the container, simply click on the Structure link on the top menu. On the Structure page, click on the Forum link. Drupal then displays the Forums administration page. On this page, you have the ability to create new containers and new forum topics. Containers hold topics, and your site can have multiple containers if the need arises. For demonstration purposes, we will create a new container titled "Our Experience with Drupal 7" by clicking on Add container."

As shown in Figure 9-5, on the "Add container" form we only need to enter the title of our container and a brief description of the purpose and content of the forum that we're about to create.

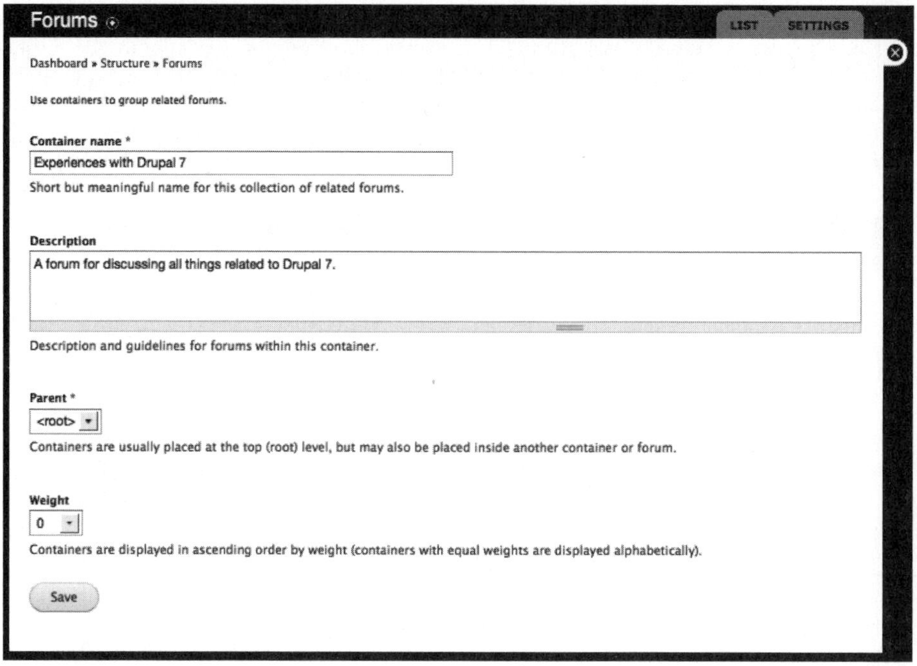

Figure 9-5. Creating a new forum container

After entering the title and the description, click the Save button to create the container. Drupal then redisplays the main Forum configuration page with our new container listed (see Figure 9-6).

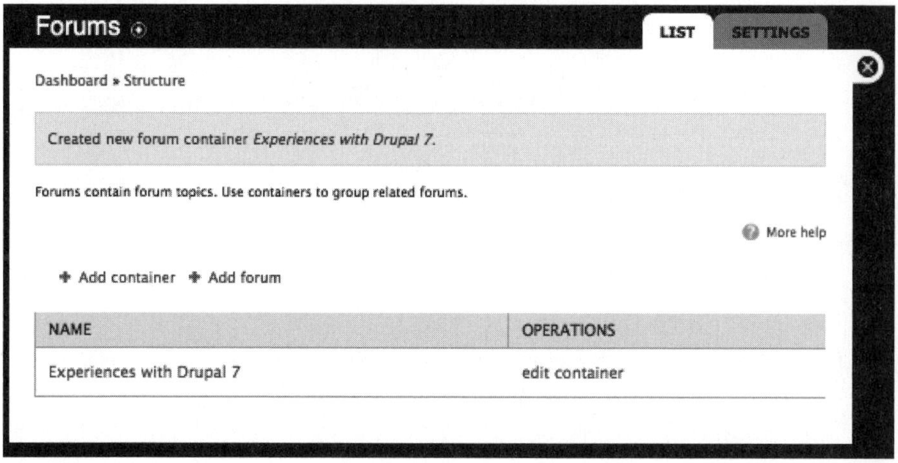

Figure 9-6. A listing of forum containers

With our container in place, we can now add forums to which the site visitors can post questions and responses. Click on "Add forum," which reveals the Forums page. On this page, we specify the name of our forum, provide a brief description of what the purpose of the forum is, and select the container where the forum should reside. See Figure 9-7. After entering the forum name and description, look in the Parent drop-down list for the container that you created in the previous step. When you have selected it, click Save.

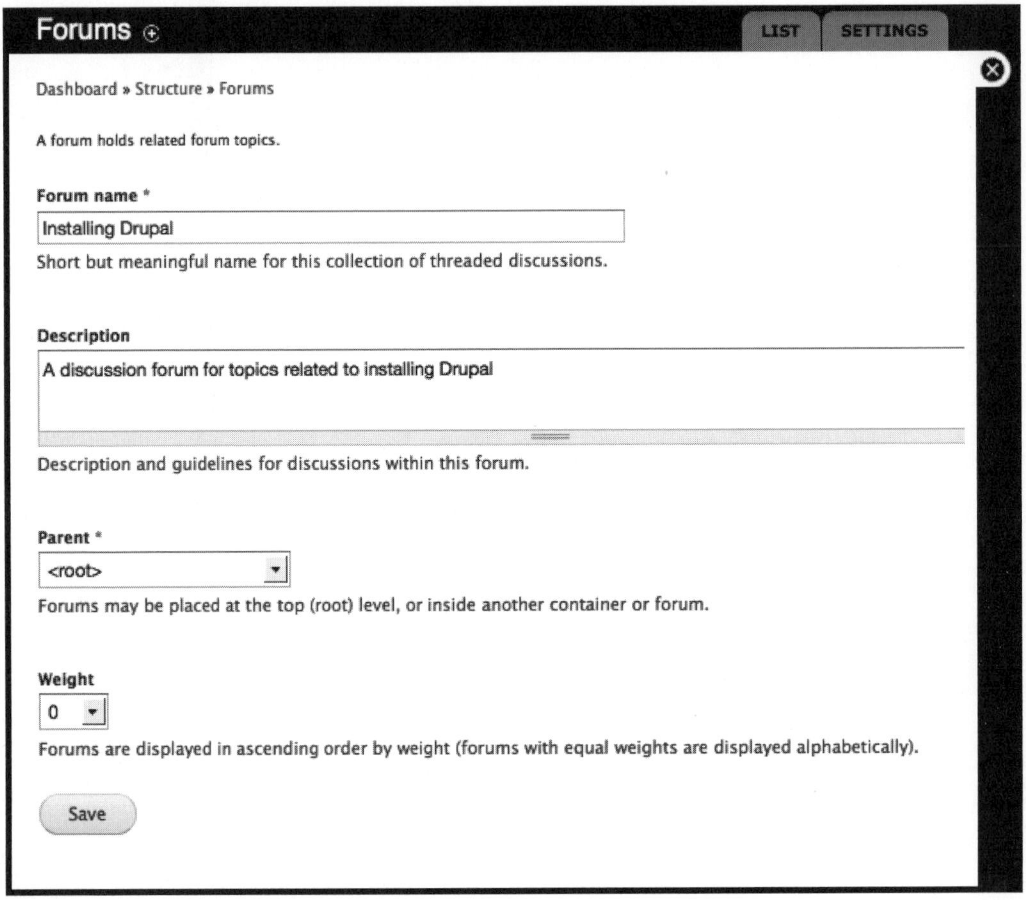

Figure 9-7. *Creating a forum*

Based on the subject area of our container, Drupal 7, there are likely a number of forums that we could create to facilitate online discussions. Continue to add various forums until you feel that you have a broad enough selection to address the common topics that will arise on your forum. Figure 9-8 shows a number of additional forums added to our container, all of which are topics that are appropriate for the general topic of our forums.

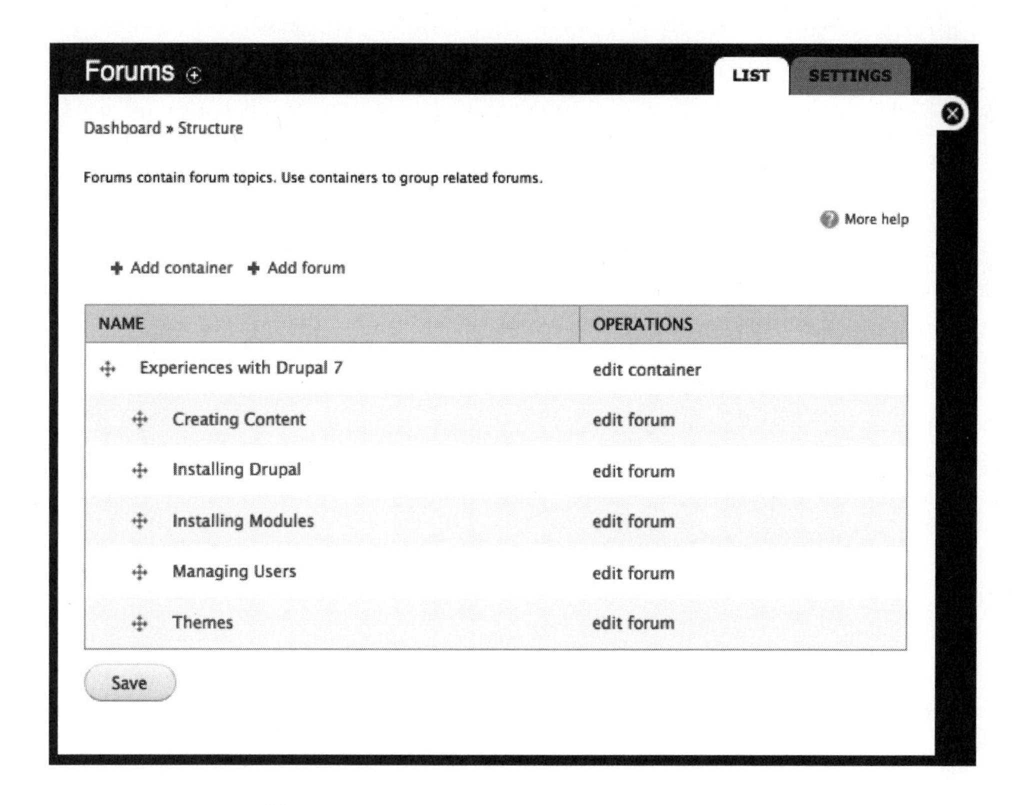

Figure 9-8. Listing of forums

With all of the forums set up, you can visit the Forum page of your website by going to http://localhost/forum. You'll see something like Figure 9-9.

Forums

○ Add new Forum topic

Forum	Topics	Posts	Last post
Experiences with Drupal 7 **A forum for discussing all things related to Drupal 7.**			
Creating Content A forum used to discuss topics related to creating content on a Drupal 7 site.	0	0	n/a
Installing Drupal A discussion forum for topics related to installing Drupal	0	0	n/a
Installing Modules A forum for discussing the installation and configuration of modules.	0	0	n/a
Managing Users A forum for discussing how to manage users on your Drupal site.	0	0	n/a
Themes A forum for discussing Drupal themes.	0	0	n/a

Figure 9-9. The Forums page

Site visitors who are interested in a specific forum, such as the one on installing Drupal, would click on the forum title, revealing all of the related discussion topics. Figure 9-10 demonstrates what the Installing Drupal forum would look like populated with a number of relevant topics.

Installing Drupal

○ Add new Forum topic

Topic	Replies	Last reply
Installing Drupal on Linux By admin 1 min 26 sec ago	0	n/a
Installing Drupal on Windows By admin 58 sec ago	0	n/a
Installing Drupal on Solaris By admin 32 sec ago	0	n/a
Upgrading from Drupal 6 to Drupal 7 By admin 4 sec ago	0	n/a

Figure 9-10. The Installing Drupal Forum

A site visitor with the proper permissions who had something to discuss (like a question about installing Drupal on Ubuntu) could respond to an existing forum topic by clicking on the related topic (Installing Drupal on Linux), revealing a basic form where they can enter the subject and the comment they want to post (see Figure 9-11).

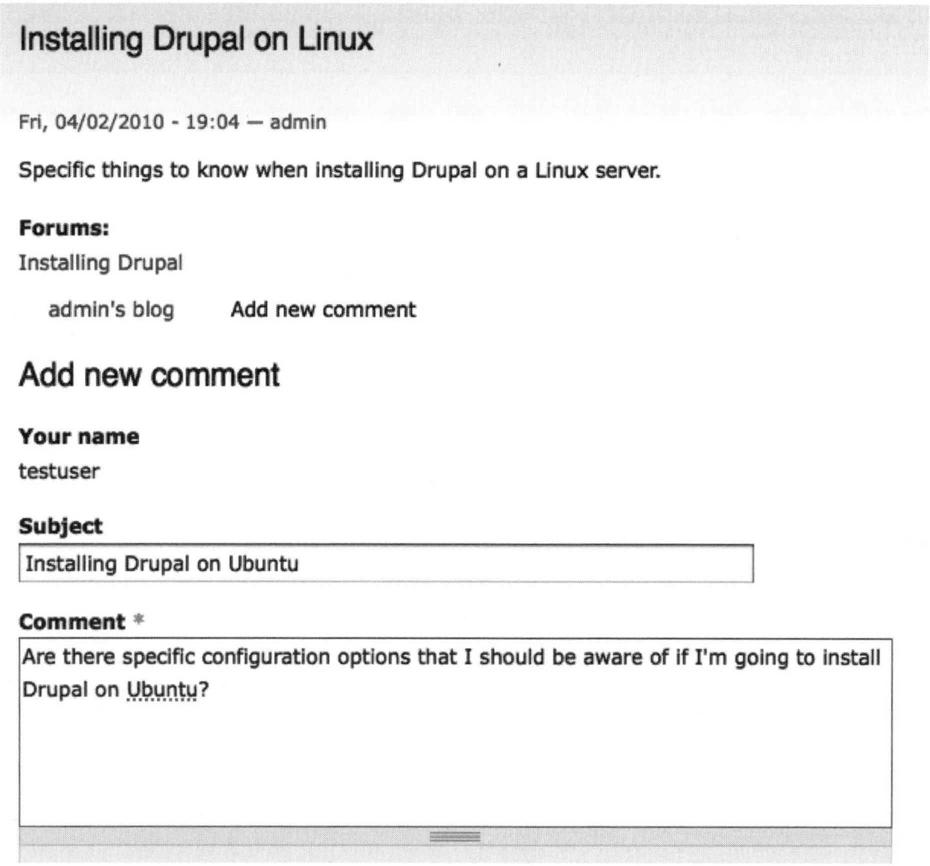

Installing Drupal on Linux

Fri, 04/02/2010 - 19:04 — admin

Specific things to know when installing Drupal on a Linux server.

Forums:
Installing Drupal

admin's blog   Add new comment

Add new comment

Your name
testuser

Subject
Installing Drupal on Ubuntu

Comment *
Are there specific configuration options that I should be aware of if I'm going to install Drupal on Ubuntu?

Figure 9-11. Responding to a Forum Topic as a user

After entering the values and clicking Save, navigate back to the forum for installing Drupal by clicking on the link for Installing Drupal. You can now see in Figure 9-12 that our forum topic has a new comment that visitors can read and post comments to.

Installing Drupal on Linux
Your comment has been posted.
Fri, 04/02/2010 - 19:04 — admin
Specific things to know when installing Drupal on a Linux server.
Forums:
Installing Drupal
admin's blog
Add new comment
Installing Drupal on Ubuntu
Fri, 04/02/2010 - 19:42 — testuser
Are there specific configuration options that I should be aware of if I'm going to install Drupal on Ubuntu?
reply

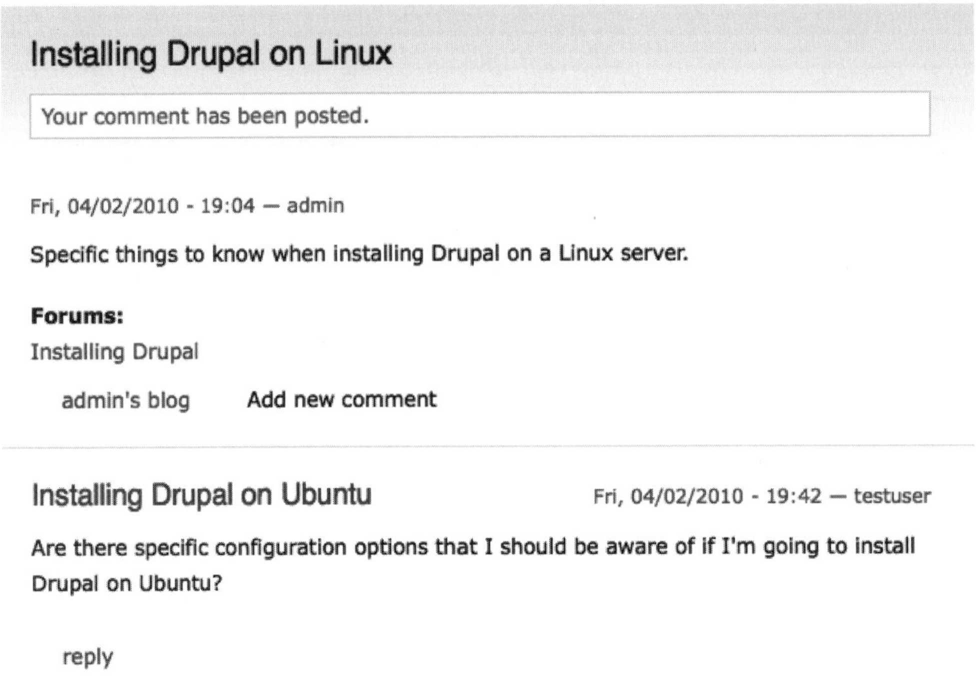

Figure 9-12. *A Forum Topic with a comment*

Drupal core's forum module has a rather limited feature set. A contributed module called "advanced forum" (`http://drupal.org/project/advanced_forum`) provides a number of enhanced features, such as "mark all topics in a single forum or all forums as read," forum statistics including number of topics, posts, users, latest user, and currently online users, shows number of new posts in addition to core's number of new topics, and numerous other features.

Polls

Another common interactive feature is online polls. Polls are used to collect votes from site visitors on a specific subject, such as "should college football adopt a similar playoff structure as the National Football League to determine the national champion?"

To install the Poll module, click on the Modules link in the top of the page menu, revealing the list of all the modules on your site. Scroll down until you find the Poll module and check the check box to enable the module.

Next, click the Save button at the bottom of the page. Clicking "Save configuration" results in Drupal installing the Poll module, making its capabilities immediately available for us to use.

The next step is to set permissions so that visitors can vote on polls. There are two groups of permissions associated with polls: the first group deals with authoring and creating polls, and the second deals with who can vote on polls. For demonstration purposes, we'll leave the first group set to the default values: only the administrator can create and edit polls. Those values include:

- Create new poll content.
- Edit own poll content.
- Edit any poll content.
- Delete own poll content.
- Delete any poll content.

The second group of options should be set so that site visitors can vote on polls. For our example site, set the values so that both anonymous and authenticated users can perform the following three actions:

- Vote on polls.
- Cancel and change own votes.
- View voting results.

Next, click the "Save permissions" button at the bottom of the page.

Creating Your First Poll

To create a poll, click the "Add content" link on your site, which reveals the list of content types that you have enabled on your Drupal installation. On that list, you will now see a content type titled poll (see Figure 9-13).

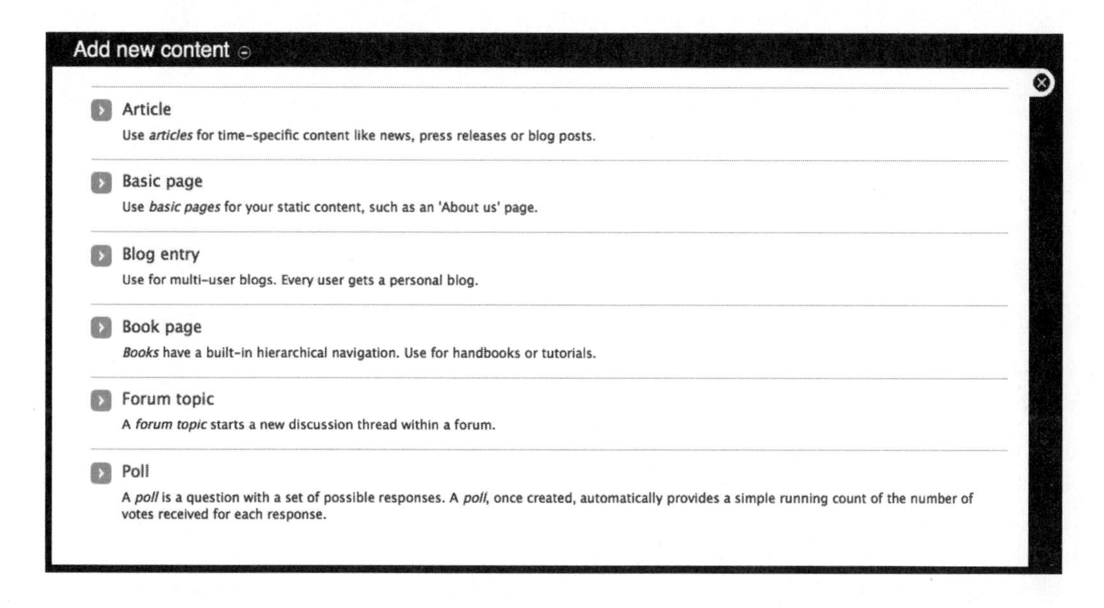

Figure 9-13. *Creating a new poll*

Click on the Poll link, revealing the form that you will use to create the poll. As an example, create a new poll that asks site visitors to vote on whether U.S. college football should adopt a playoff structure like the National Football league. Follow the example in Figure 9-14 and create the poll by entering the question and the answers from which you want visitors to select. Hopefully the fourth answer receives the most votes!

Two key options are also shown in Figure 9-14:

- The status of the poll: Whether it is active or closed. Visitors can still vote if the poll is active, whereas closed polls only display the votes that were tallied while the poll was open.
- The poll's duration: By selecting a value other than Unlimited, Drupal will automatically close the poll when the duration has expired.

For demonstration purposes, you can leave the status as Active and the duration as Unlimited. Click the Save button and voila, you have an online poll!

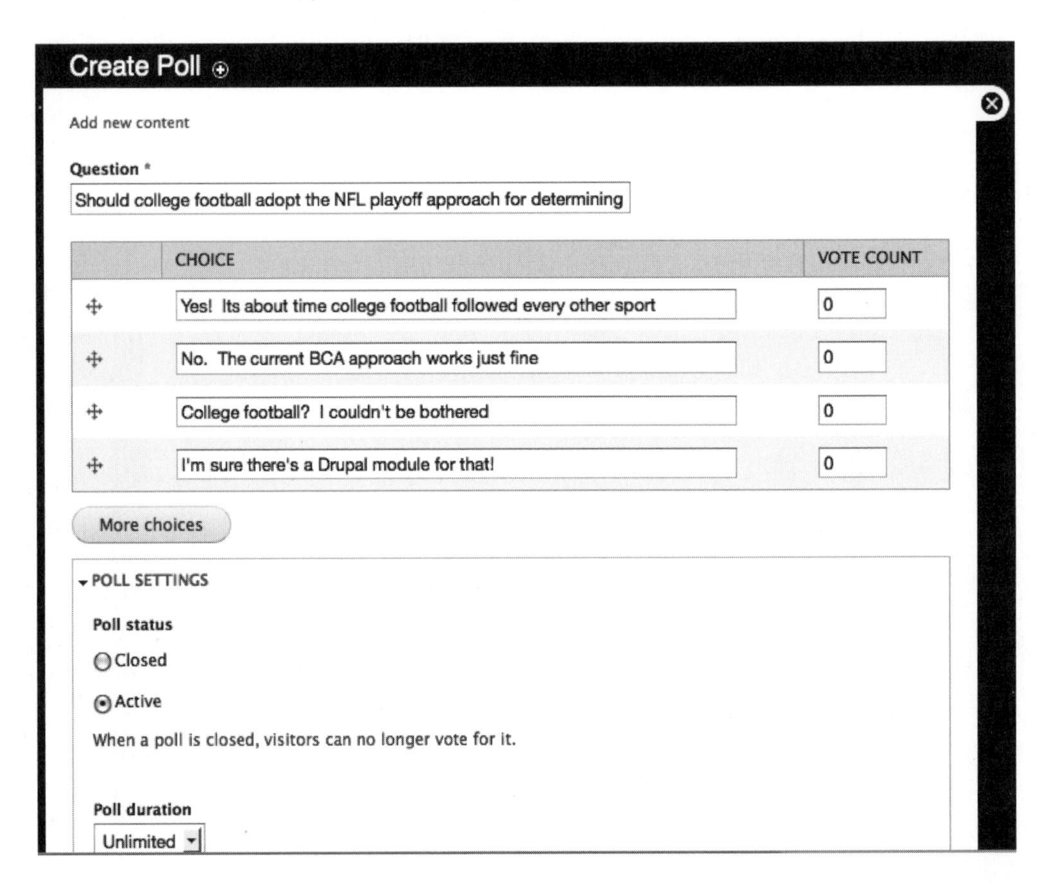

Figure 9-14. Entering the details of a new poll

Drupal displays your new online poll, ready for visitors to place their votes (see Figure 9-15).

Should college football adopt the NFL playoff approach for determining the national championship?
View
Edit
Track
Results
Votes
Your vote was cancelled.
Sat, 04/03/2010 - 08:41 — admin
Yes! Its about time college football followed every other sport
No. The current BCA approach works just fine
College football? I couldn't be bothered
I'm sure there's a Drupal module for that!
Vote

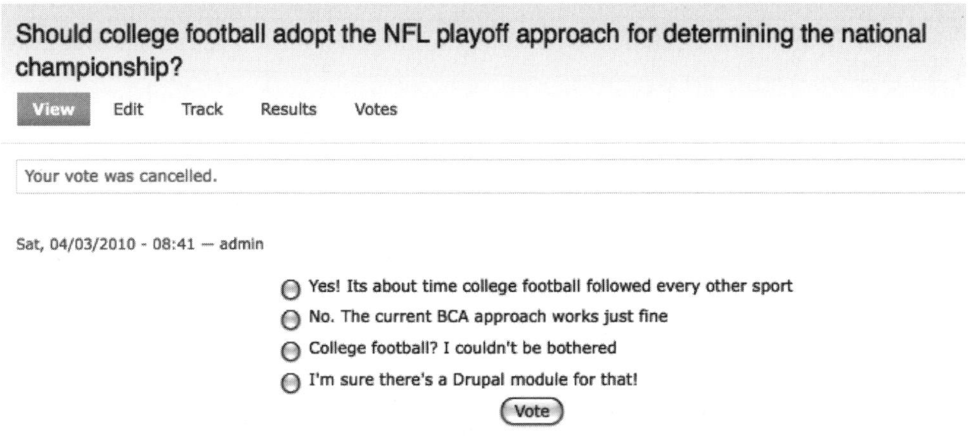

Figure 9-15. *Your first online poll*

You'll notice in Figure 9-15 that there are several links at the top of your poll that allow you the site administrator to manage and monitor the poll. You can do the following:

- View the total number of votes by question by clicking on the View link.
- Edit the poll and change the question and answers.
- Track the poll.
- Click on the Votes link to see who voted for which option.

The Tracker module is a Drupal 7 core module that provides information about the referring site that directed the user to the poll, the user ID of the user if they're logged in on the site, and the date/time they placed their vote. Tracker can be a useful tool if you're trying to analyze what visitors are doing on your site and where they came from. To enable Tracker follow the instructions outlined in Chapter 8.

Select one of the options and click on the Vote button. Drupal displays the total number of votes for each of the options and allows you to cancel your vote if you change your mind. Click through the various links at the top of the page to see the reports that the poll module provides you.

To make your poll visible to site visitors, you could provide a menu link to the poll by using the techniques I described earlier in this book (for example, adding a menu item), or you could use another feature of the polls module, which is a block that lists the latest poll. To enable this feature, click on the Structure link on the top menu, and on the Structure page click on the Blocks link. On the Blocks configuration page, scroll down until you see the "Most recent poll" item, and change the region to either the left or right sidebar. Once you have selected the region, click Save and navigate to the homepage of your website. Your poll is now displayed in the right (or left) sidebar of your website, available for visitors to place their votes.

Web Forms

Collecting information from site visitors through online forms is another key interactive feature that is easy to enable and use on your new site. Using the Webform contributed module, you can create simple forms (such as a form that is used to submit a question) or complex questionnaires using the features enabled through the Webform module. To demonstrate how easy it is, I will walk you through the process of creating an online "suggestion box" where site visitors can enter and submit suggestions to you through a form on your website.

The first step is to install the Webform contributed module. Following the steps outlined in Chapter 8, install and enable the Webform module (`http://drupal.org/project/webform`). After enabling the module, set the permissions for it so that the administrator of the site can access, edit, and delete all of the features listed for the module. You may also wish to enable "Edit own Webform submissions" for anonymous and authenticated users if you want to allow users to update or correct information they previously submitted.

Creating a Webform

The example that we are using is an online forms-based suggestion box. On this form, we will allow site visitors to enter a suggestion, pick from a list of categories that fit their suggestion, indicate whether they would like us to follow up on their suggestion, and require that they provide us with their e-mail address so that we can contact them.

The first step in the creation process is to click on the Content link in the menu at the top of every page, revealing the Content administration page. On this page, click "Add new content." Click on the Webform content type listed on the "Add new content" page's list of content types, bringing you to the first page of the Webform creation process (see Figure 9-16). On this page, enter the title of your Webform, as well as an introduction to what you are asking the user to fill out. For the example, enter Suggestions Box as the title and write a simple introductory statement in the Body field. Then click Save.

Figure 9-16. Create Webform configuration page

The next page you see is for creating the form components or fields (see Figure 9-17). There are three attributes to set for each field: the label that will appear with the field, the type of field you want to display, and an indicator that specifies whether the field is mandatory. The first field that we will create in our example is the text area, where the visitor will enter their suggestion. Enter My Suggestion Is in the text box provided for the label, select Textarea as the type of field we want to use, and set the field to mandatory by checking the box. Then click Add.

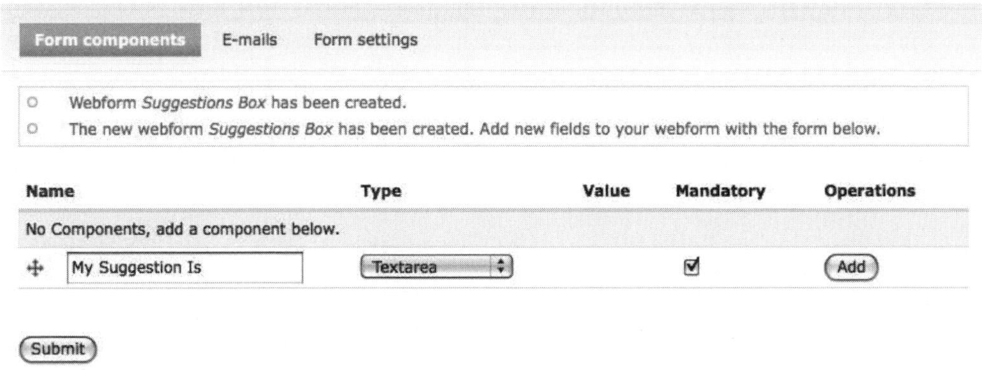

Figure 9-17. Adding a form component

Next you'll see a page that lists options you can set for the new field. On this page you can set the following:

> Label for the field: The module displays what you entered on the previous screen. You may update it here if you wish to change it.
>
> Field key: This is the internal name used by the module to identify this field in the Drupal database. The module automatically creates the name for you. You may override the name is you wish.
>
> Default value: You may want to provide a default value for this field.
>
> Description: The text you enter in this field will be displayed immediately below the form component. Use this field to provide additional instructions to the visitors on what you're asking them to enter or select.
>
> Validation: You can select whether the field is a mandatory one by checking the box.
>
> Display width and height: Depending on the type of component you selected (textbox or textarea), you may see options that allow you to set how wide and how tall a form component will be on the screen.
>
> Resizable: Check the box if you want to allow the visitor to resize the form component (only applicable to textfields and textareas).
>
> Disabled: You can set the field so the user cannot change the value.

For our example, enter this in the Description field: "Please enter your suggestion in the box above. Be as descriptive as possible." After entering the description, click Submit.

After clicking Submit, the module redisplays the Form components page. Using the steps outlined previously, create a "Select options" field that allows the visitor to specify what their suggestion is related to. Enter My Suggestion Is Related To in the label field, pick the Select options value in the Type field, check the Mandatory box, and click the Add button. The page that is displayed after clicking Add has the same elements listed above with the exception of a new field where we enter the options that the visitor can select from (see Figure 9-18) and three configuration options for setting whether you want the Select options component to allow visitors to select multiple items from the list, whether the component should be displayed as a Listbox, and whether the options should be displayed in a random order. For our example, we will leave the Multiple check box unchecked, we'll enter the options as shown in Figure 9-18, and we will check the Listbox checkbox. After updating the values, click Submit.

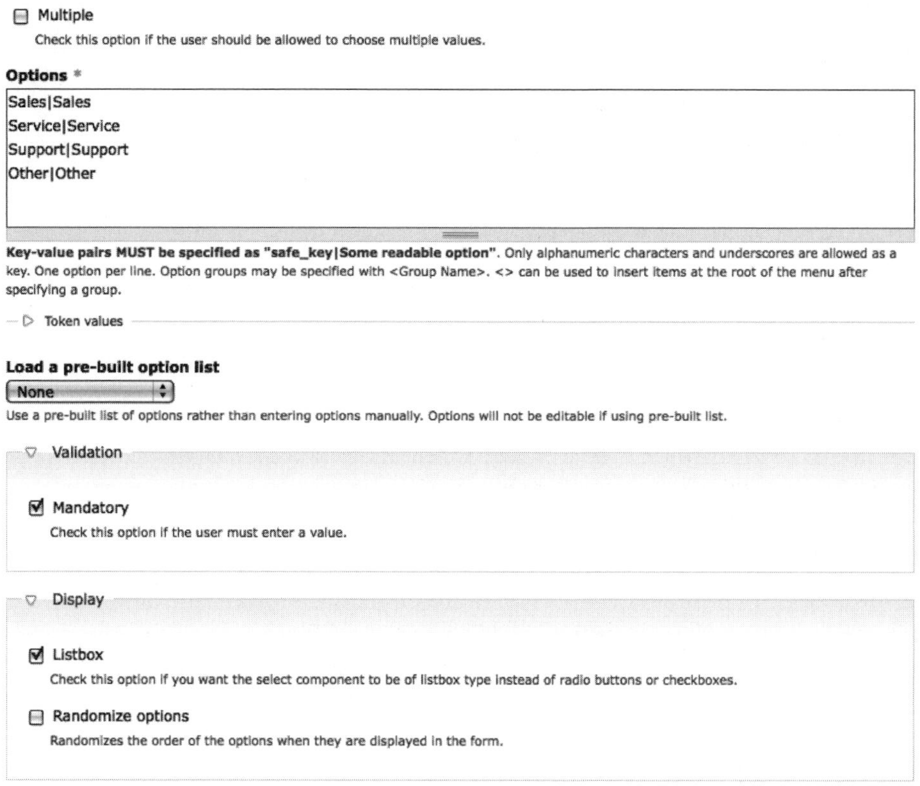

☐ Multiple

Check this option if the user should be allowed to choose multiple values.

Options *

Sales|Sales
Service|Service
Support|Support
Other|Other

Key-value pairs MUST be specified as "safe_key|Some readable option". Only alphanumeric characters and underscores are allowed as a key. One option per line. Option groups may be specified with <Group Name>. <> can be used to insert items at the root of the menu after specifying a group.

▷ Token values

Load a pre-built option list

None

Use a pre-built list of options rather than entering options manually. Options will not be editable if using pre-built list.

▽ Validation

☑ Mandatory

Check this option if the user must enter a value.

▽ Display

☑ Listbox

Check this option if you want the select component to be of listbox type instead of radio buttons or checkboxes.

☐ Randomize options

Randomizes the order of the options when they are displayed in the form.

Figure 9-18. Defining the options for a Select options component

Next, create is a field for entering the visitors' e-mail addresses. Follow the steps outlined above using My Email Address as the label for the field, pick the Textfield value from the list of Types, check the Mandatory check box, and click the Add button. Follow the steps outlined previously on the second screen.

You should now have all of the fields defined for your form. The next step is to set the value for where e-mails should be sent when visitors submit information through your form. Click on the E-mails link near the top of the Webform configuration page, revealing a form where you can define who receives the e-mailed results of a visitor submitting the form. In the Address field, enter your e-mail address as the default recipient of the information. You can also click on the Add button to enable sending the information to more than one person.

The final step in the process is to click on the Form settings link at the top of the Webform configuration page. On this page, you can enter a message that will be displayed on the screen after the visitor submits their form. For our example, enter "Thank you for submitting your suggestion." You may also enter a Redirect URL. Entering a value in this field directs the module to display the page associated with the URL after the users submits the form. You may also set how many forms a visitor may submit, reducing the likelihood of malicious users submitting hundreds of suggestions to your site. When complete, click the "Save configuration" button.

Your form is now ready to be used on your site. You can view the form by clicking on the View link at the top of the Webform configuration page. If you followed the example your form should look something like Figure 9-19.

Suggestions Box View Edit Webform Results

Tue, 04/13/2010 - 16:39 — admin

Please complete all of the information requested below.

My Suggestion Is *

Please enter your suggestion in the box above. Be as descriptive as possible.

My Suggestion Is Related To *

select...

My Email Address *

Submit

Figure 9-19. *The Suggestions Box form*

Give your form a test drive. Enter at least two suggestions, then click on the Results link near the top of the form.

■ **Note** Only users with the permissions set for viewing Webform submissions will see the Results link.

The page that is displayed (see Figure 9-20) provides several tools that you can use to manage the data submitted by visitors. Click through the links (Submissions, Analysis, Table, Download, and Clear) to see what the module has to offer.

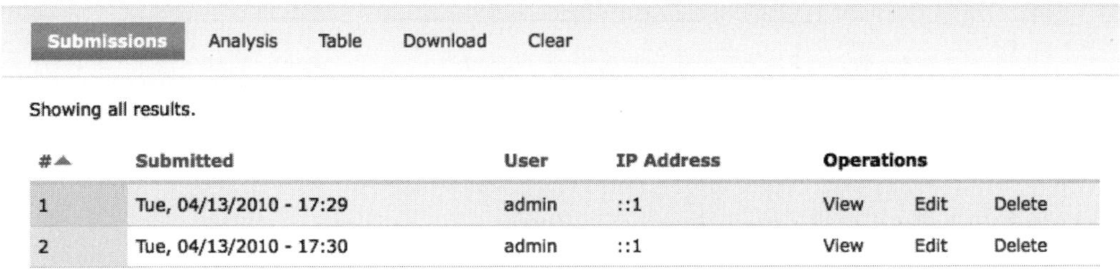

Submissions Analysis Table Download Clear

Showing all results.

#	Submitted	User	IP Address	Operations		
1	Tue, 04/13/2010 - 17:29	admin	::1	View	Edit	Delete
2	Tue, 04/13/2010 - 17:30	admin	::1	View	Edit	Delete

Figure 9-20. Viewing form submissions

Summary

Interactivity is key to attracting and retaining website visitors. By following the steps in this chapter you've moved your site out of the world of "brochureware" sites into the realm of interactive and social networking. Brochureware sites are great if all you are trying to do is communicate information about your organization or products, but hooking and retaining visitors often takes something beyond just displaying text to keep them coming back.

In this chapter you entered into the interactive website world by adding blogs, forums, polls, and webforms. While those are the top four interactive capabilities on the web, there are hundreds of others that you can choose from. Other examples that you may wish to explore and implement on your site include:

> Five Star: A module that provides the ability to rate content on the bases of one to five stars.
>
> Add to Any: A module that allows visitors to post links to your content on social networking sites such as Facebook.

Now that we're interactive, we're going to go through the process of creating custom content types. We've used the basic page and the article in previous chapters.
We will now look at creating your own custom content types for capturing information like an event.

CHAPTER 10

■ ■ ■

Content Types

If you ask Drupal developers what the most powerful feature of Drupal is, many will say it's Drupal's ability to create custom content types. What is a content type? Think of a content type as a template that you provide to users who author content on your site. You may decide that the standard content types that come with Drupal out of the box, the basic page and article, provide all the features you need for your site. But it's likely that you'll encounter situations where you want more control over how users enter information and how that information is displayed on your site, and that's where custom content types come into play. In this chapter I'll show you how simple it is to create a new content type from scratch. Hold on to your tickets, we're about to take off!

The Basic Page and Article Content Types

When you install Drupal 7 you automatically receive two content types that have been defined by the team who maintains Drupal core: the Basic page and Article. If you author a piece of content using the Basic page content type you will see that it provides two basic fields: a title and a body.

An author using the Basic page content type simply enters a title (a required field as indicated by the red asterisk) and the text of their content in the body field. The body field is flexible and can contain whatever the author feels like writing about. The author could:

- Write an entire book in the body field, including HTML markup (headings, tables, CSS, and so on).
- Insert pictures.
- Enter PHP code to extract information from the Drupal database and display the extracted information.
- Write a single sentence.

The Article content type is similar to the Basic page, except it offers the ability to upload a picture and define a set of tags that can be used to categorize the content (see Chapter 4 for details on categorizing content).

Like a Basic page, and Article can be used to author content about any subject, and the body area is allows for entering free form text.

While the Basic page and Article content types are perfect for general content, there will likely be cases where you want to provide some form of structure around the information that is captured. You may want to:

- Require that certain information is entered before the author submits the content item for publishing; for example the start date and time for an event, the address of the venue where the event is being held, and a link to the event on a Google map.
- Have the ability to perform calculations based on the information that is captured in a content item.
- Have the ability to sort content items by specific "fields."
- Have the ability to "filter" or restrict which content items are displayed on a page based on a value in a field.
- Enforce the structure of how a piece of content is rendered on a page; for example, you may want to display information about a book and want the title to be followed by the author, followed by the ISBN, followed by the price, followed by the description of the book.
- While you could publish all of this information in a Basic page or an Article, providing the features for sorting, filtering, making values required, calculating, and structuring how a content item is rendered on a page would be extremely difficult. Fortunately, Drupal's ability to define custom content types makes all of the above possible, and provides many more features that you will find invaluable over time.

Defining a Custom Content Type

A custom content type is defined by you, the Drupal administrator, over and above the Basic page and Article content type. The ability to create custom content types is now included in Drupal 7 core.

To demonstrate the power and flexibility of custom content types, lets create a new custom content type for capturing information about upcoming events. An event could be a concert, a play, a class, a game, or any other activity that is scheduled in advance.

When authoring information about event, you may want to include:

- The name or title of the event
- The date and time when the event begins
- The date and time when the event ends
- The venue or address where the event will be held
- A description of the event
- The price for attending the event

As you will see in a few moments, Drupal provides a simple-to-use administrator's interface for creating and modifying custom content types. As soon as you define a custom content type, it is immediately available to those users who have the proper privileges to author, edit, publish, and delete that specific content type (Drupal provides the ability to restrict access to custom content types by user role).

Creating a Custom Content Type

Creating a custom content type takes two basic steps: sitting down and listing the types of information you want to collect, and building the custom content type using Drupal's custom content type administration screens.

For this example, let's create a custom content type for an event that includes the types of information listed in the previous section.

To get started, click on the Structure link at the top of the page. On the Structure page (shown in Figure 10-1), click on "Content types."

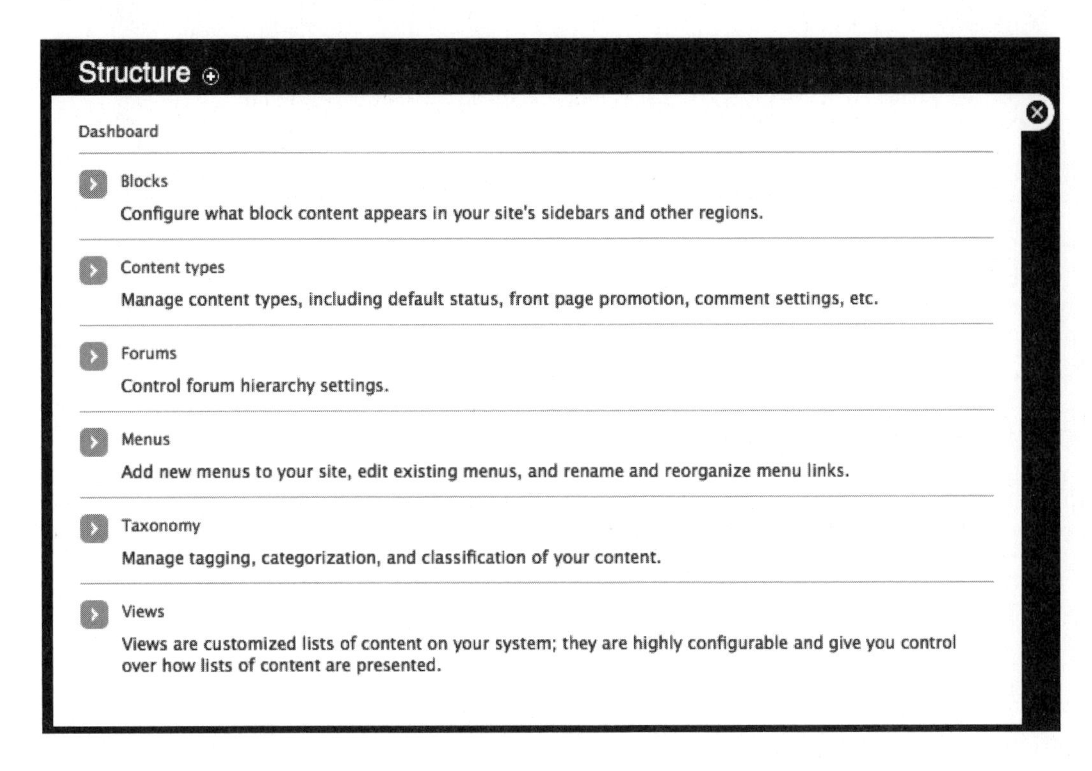

Figure 10-1. Structure page with "Content types" link

The "Content types" screen (shown in Figure 10-2) lists all of the existing content types, which in our case are the Article and Basic page content types that are included with Drupal 7 core, and the Blog, Forum topic, and Poll content types that were created when you enabled those modules in Chapter 9. The Content types page also provides a link to create a new content type. Click on the "Add content type" link to start the process of creating our Event content type.

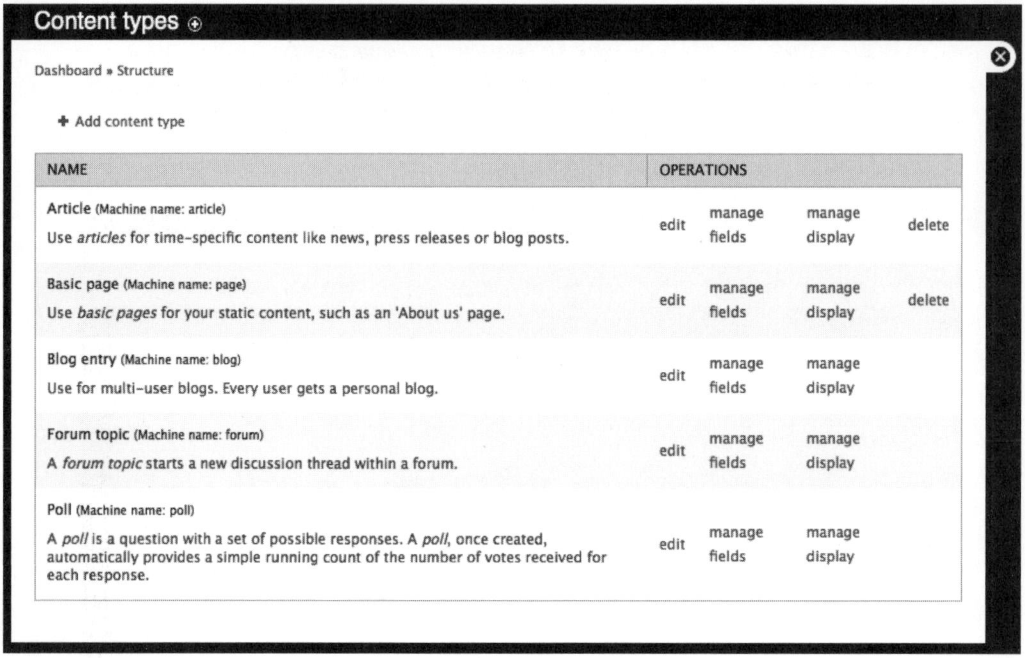

Content types ⊕

Dashboard » Structure

✚ Add content type

NAME	OPERATIONS			
Article (Machine name: article) Use *articles* for time-specific content like news, press releases or blog posts.	edit	manage fields	manage display	delete
Basic page (Machine name: page) Use *basic pages* for your static content, such as an 'About us' page.	edit	manage fields	manage display	delete
Blog entry (Machine name: blog) Use for multi-user blogs. Every user gets a personal blog.	edit	manage fields	manage display	
Forum topic (Machine name: forum) A *forum topic* starts a new discussion thread within a forum.	edit	manage fields	manage display	
Poll (Machine name: poll) A *poll* is a question with a set of possible responses. A *poll*, once created, automatically provides a simple running count of the number of votes received for each response.	edit	manage fields	manage display	

Figure 10-2. *A listing of content types*

The first screen that appears when you click on the "Add content type" link is a form that defines the general characteristics of your new content type (see Figure 10-3). There is a field for the name of the content type, a field for a description that describes the content type (the description is displayed on the author's screen for creating new content), the label for the title field, the label for the body field, and several other configuration options that I will walk you through in detail.

To begin the process, do the following:

- Fill in the Name of the content type, which in our case is Event. The text below the Name field provides a set of guidelines that you should follow when creating a name for a new content type.
- Provide a description of how this content type should be used, such as "A content type used to capture the details about upcoming events."
- Change the "Title field label" from just Title to Event Title, making it more descriptive and intuitive to the author who will be using this template for authoring event information.
- Change the "Body field label" from Body to Event Description, making the label more indicative of the types of information you want the author to enter in this field.
- Leave the "Preview before submitting" setting as Optional.

- Provide a brief explanation of the submission guidelines for this content type. This is an optional value, and may not apply to your content type. For our Event content type, we will use "Please fill out all required fields before submitting the event" as the submission guidelines. You can choose to use or ignore this field when creating new content types.

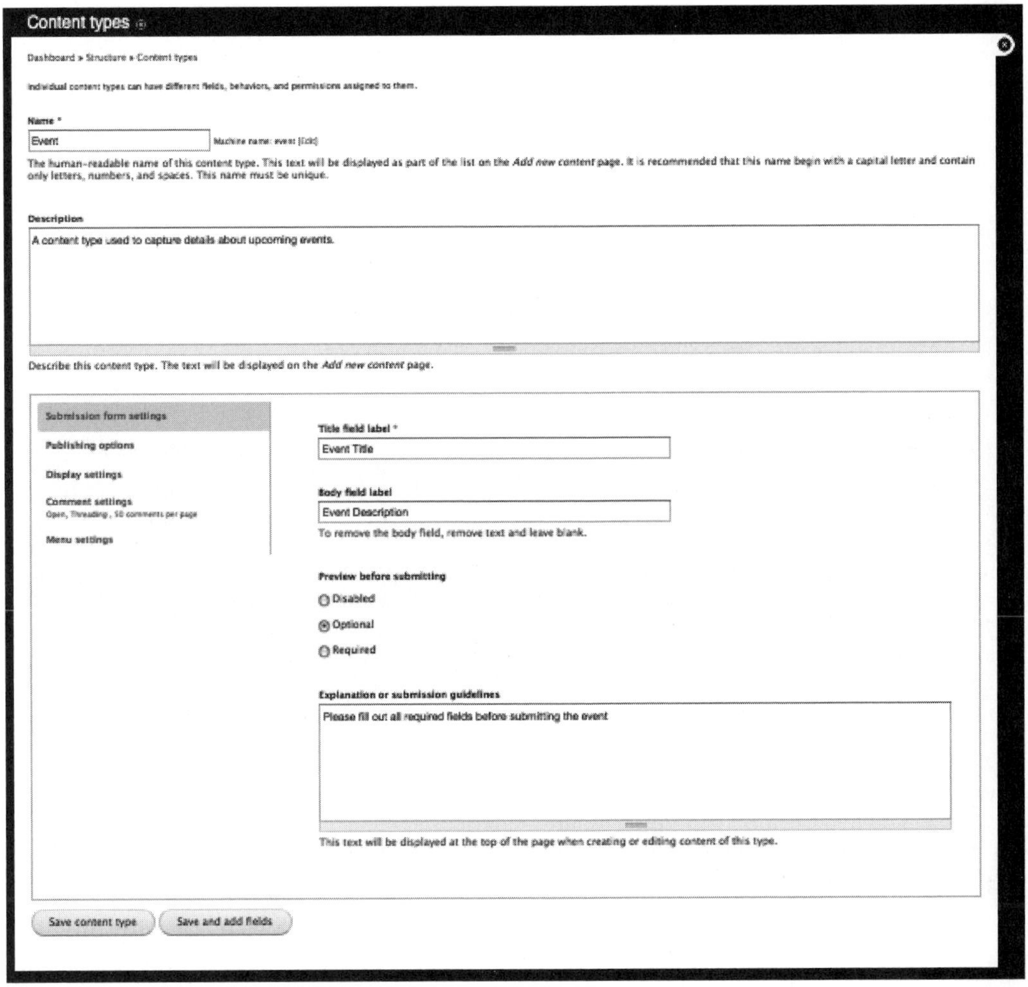

Figure 10-3. Content type creation form

There are other optional settings that you should consider carefully when creating a new content type. First are the Publishing options (see Figure 10-4). In the left vertical menu, click on the "Publishing options."

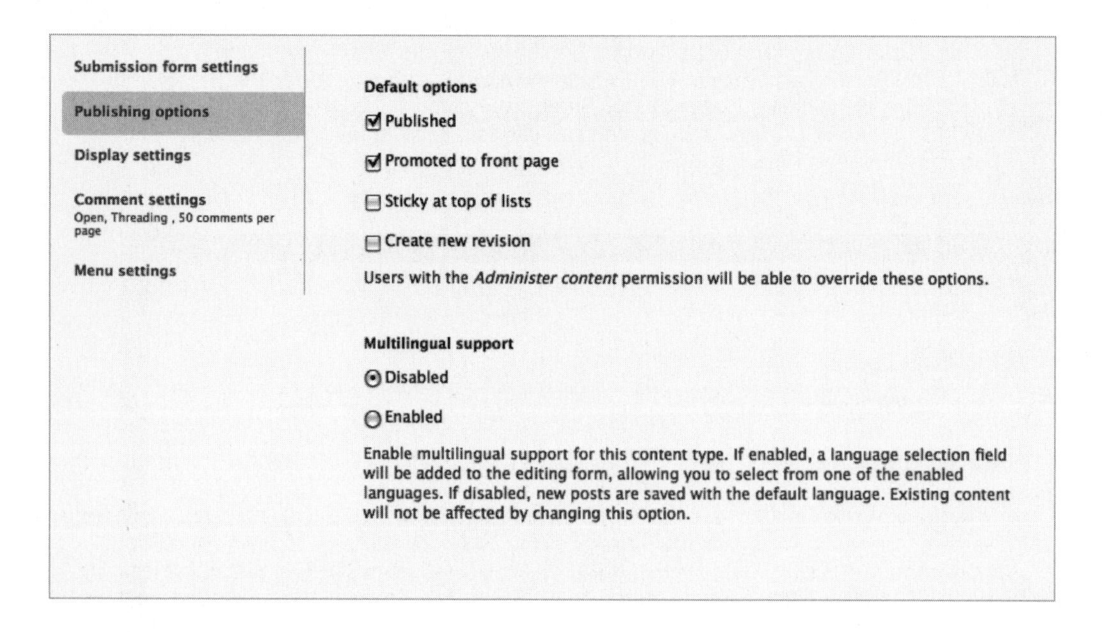

Figure 10-4. Publishing options

Depending on whether you want content to be automatically published (made viewable on your site immediately upon saving) and whether you want the content to automatically appear on the homepage of your website, you may wish to adjust these options. For our Event content type, we want Events to be automatically published when they are saved, but we don't want them to automatically show up on the homepage. So we will uncheck the "Promoted to front page" checkbox. We can also set whether an Event is sticky at the top of lists (meaning that, in a list of various content types on a page, the Event content would always be at the top of the list), and whether we want to automatically create a new version of a content item created as an Event when the author makes an update (typically a good idea, but it depends on whether you want the ability to see the changes made to an individual piece of content over time, and the ability to republish a previous version in the case where the current version is incorrect). For our Event content type, we'll check the "Create new version" checkbox.

The next set of options is for display settings. Click on the "Display settings" tab in the left column to reveal the options that are available with this configuration parameter (see Figure 10-5). You can set whether Drupal should display the name of the author who created the Event content item and the date that the item was authored. Let's say in our case we don't feel that having the author and date published is relevant, so we'll uncheck that box. You may, depending on the type of content being authored, decide that it is important to display the author's name and the date that the content was published. If so, leave the box checked. The second option is to set the length of trimmed posts. Drupal uses the Teaser and Full Node views. Teasers are often used as an introduction to an article. When clicked on, the full version of the article (the Full Node view) is revealed. Teasers are a good way to keep the length of your pages with multiple content items to a reasonable size, and this feature allows you to set how many characters will be displayed in "teaser" mode before a "Read more" link is displayed. For demonstration purposes, we'll leave ours set to the default value of 600.

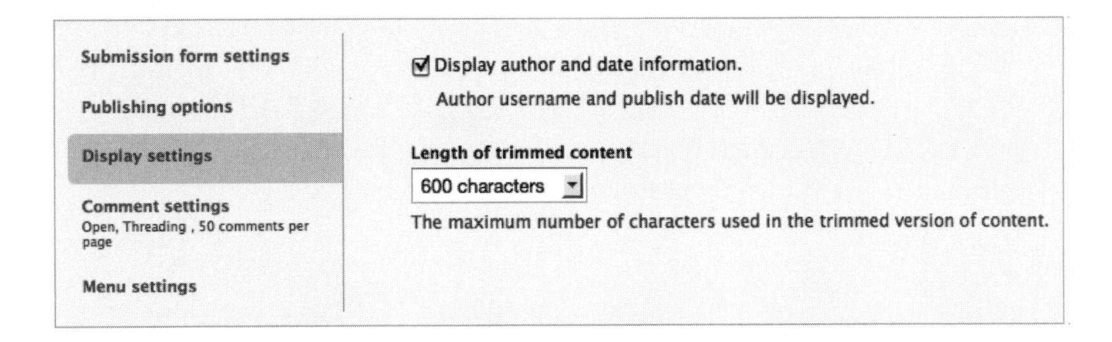

Figure 10-5. Display settings

The next set of parameters deals with how comments are handled for content items created using your content type (see Figure 10-6).

Threading defines how comments are displayed on the page. Threaded comments allow a visitor to respond to another visitor's comment, where their response will appear immediately below the comment they responded to. If you do not select this option, comments are simply listed in the order they were posted. The advantage of threading is that it makes it easier to decipher what the person is responding to (for example, are they responding to the original content or are they responding to another person's comments).

Let's leave the default value of 50, but you may want to decrease that number. The default comment settings for new content allow you to define how comments are handled. The default option is open, meaning that a new content item created using this template will accept new comments. Selecting Closed means that the content will no longer accept comments. Selecting Hidden means that the content will not accept comments, and any existing comments will be hidden from display. The primary difference is that Closed will still display the comment headings below the content, but Hidden hides everything to do with comments from display. We'll select Hidden, as we don't want visitors to have the ability to submit comments about event content.

The "Allow comment title" option allows visitors to enter a title in addition to the body of their comment. You may wish to allow this so people can give a clue as to what their comment says without having to read the whole comment. For example, a title that reads "I loved it" indicates that the body of the comment is from someone who liked your content.

The "Show reply form on the same page as comments" setting means that the form for entering comments is visible on the page at all times. If you uncheck this box, the user will have to click on a link to see the form for entering comments. Generally speaking, most sites do not automatically show the comment box on the page, as it tends to clutter the design.

The "Preview comment" option specifies whether the author of the comment has to preview their comment before it can be published. Disabled means that the user does not have to preview their comment before it is posted, and in fact the option for previewing will not be displayed. Optional means that the user may preview their comments if they wish, but it is not required, and Required means that the user must preview their comment before they publish it.

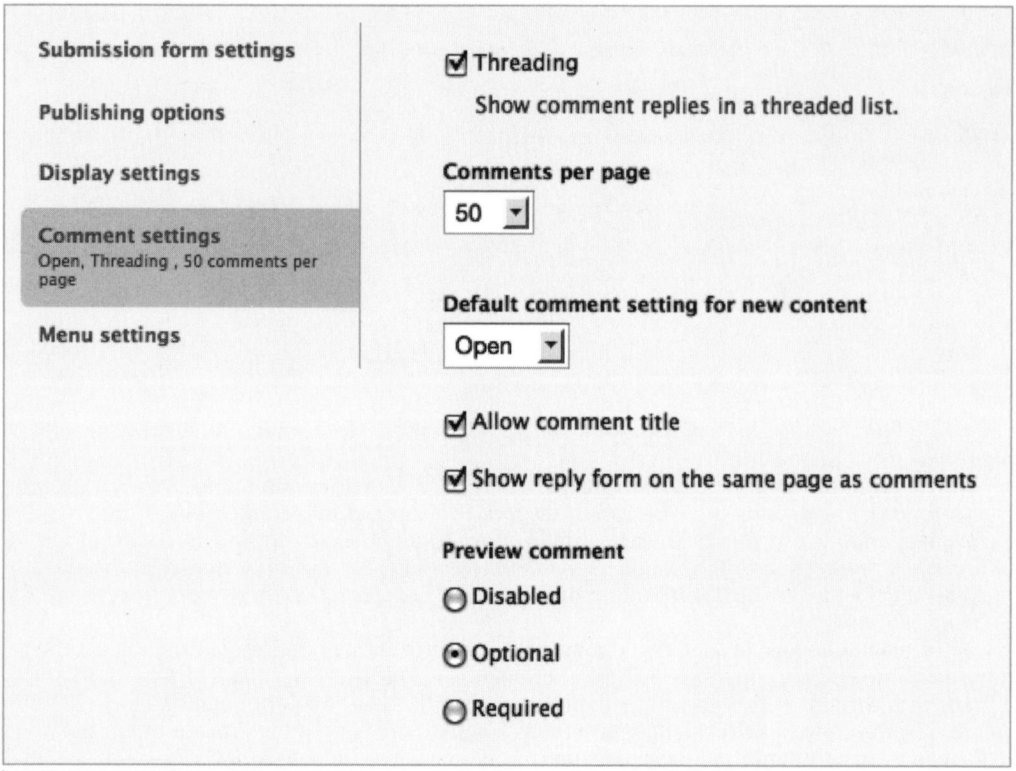

Figure 10-6. *Comment settings*

The final set of parameters defines the menu options that are presented to the author. Click on the "Menu settings" tab to reveal the menu parameters (see Figure 10-7). The list of available menus controls which menus appear as available to assign a new content item to when an author wants to create a menu item for their content item. In the example in Figure 10-7, the only menu that will appear as available is the Main menu. You can uncheck Main to hide all menus from the list that may be selected from, or you can check more than one menu to allow the author to choose from multiple menus. The default parent item option allows you to set which menu is automatically selected when the Menu settings page is displayed when an author creates a new content item from your new content type.

For our example, leave the default values and click Save.

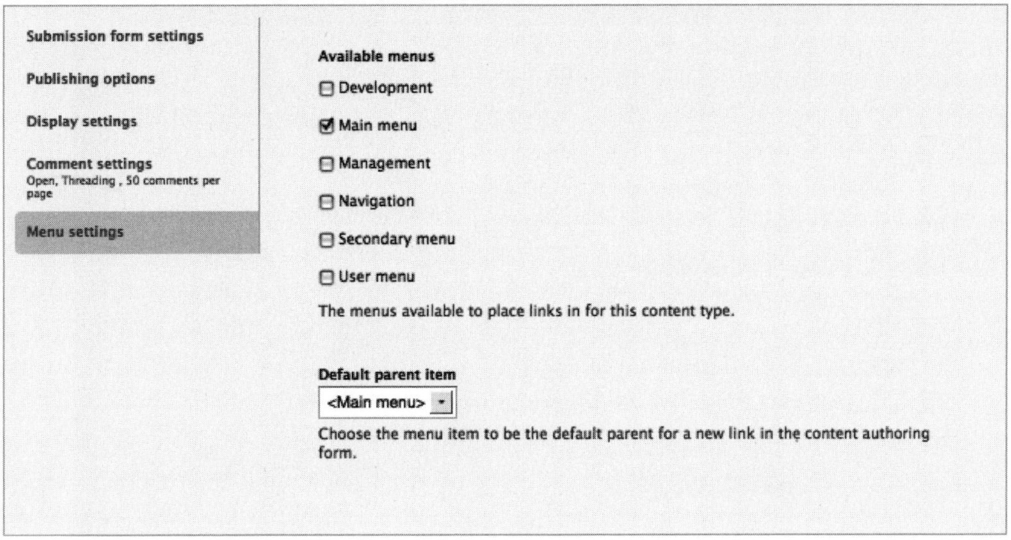

Submission form settings
Publishing options
Display settings
Comment settings
Open, Threading , 50 comments per page
Menu settings

Available menus
Development
Main menu
Management
Navigation
Secondary menu
User menu
The menus available to place links in for this content type.

Default parent item
<Main menu>
Choose the menu item to be the default parent for a new link in the content authoring form.

Figure 10-7. Menu settings

Drupal now redisplays the main Content Type page with your new Event content type listed as one of the options (see Figure 10-8).

Content types

Dashboard » Structure

The content type *Event* has been added.

+ Add content type

NAME	OPERATIONS			
Article (Machine name: article) Use *articles* for time-specific content like news, press releases or blog posts.	edit	manage fields	manage display	delete
Basic page (Machine name: page) Use *basic pages* for your static content, such as an 'About us' page.	edit	manage fields	manage display	delete
Blog entry (Machine name: blog) Use for multi-user blogs. Every user gets a personal blog.	edit	manage fields	manage display	
Event (Machine name: event) A content type used to capture details about upcoming events	edit	manage fields	manage display	delete
Forum topic (Machine name: forum) A *forum topic* starts a new discussion thread within a forum.	edit	manage fields	manage display	
Poll (Machine name: poll) A *poll* is a question with a set of possible responses. A *poll*, once created, automatically provides a simple running count of the number of votes received for each response.	edit	manage fields	manage display	

***Figure 10-8.** Content type list, including the new Event content type*

Customizing Your Form

At this point we could create a new content item using our Event content type. However, the Event content type only has an Event Title and an Event Description field. Our requirements call for a start date, start time, end date, end time, venue/address, a picture, a price, and a link to the registration form. To add these fields, click on "Manage fields." You'll see the screenshot shown in Figure 10-9, in which our Event Title and Event Description fields appear in the list of fields that already exist, as well as a row for adding a new field and a row for adding a field that already exists to our content type (for example, you may have created a Start Date field for another content type, which you can reuse on your Event content type instead of having to create a new field).

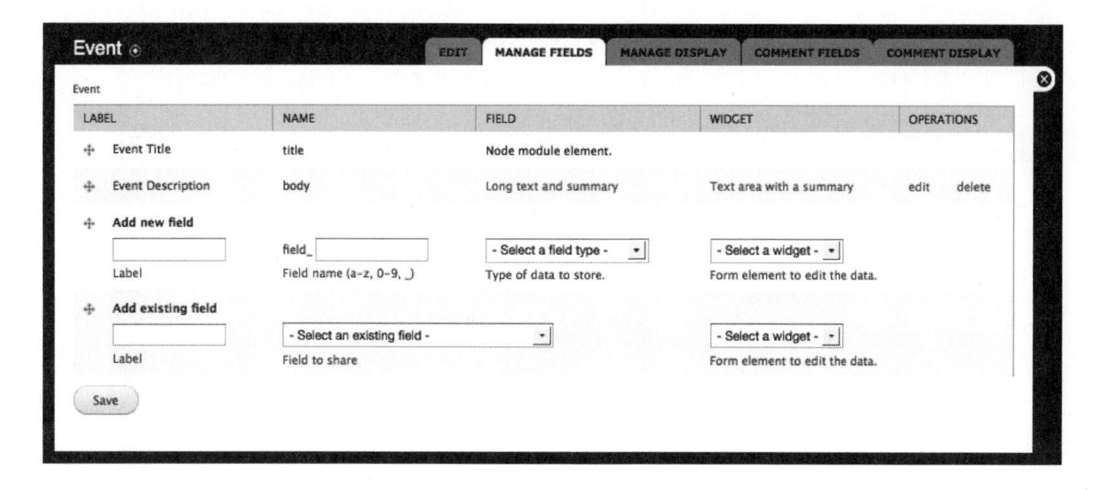

Figure 10-9. The Manage Fields form

We'll start with the Start Date field and add that as the first field after the description field. Enter Start Date in the label field, enter "event_start_date" in the field name (this is the internal name that Drupal uses to identify this field), select Text as the field type, and "Text field" as the widget that we will use to collect the information from the user (see Figure 10-10).

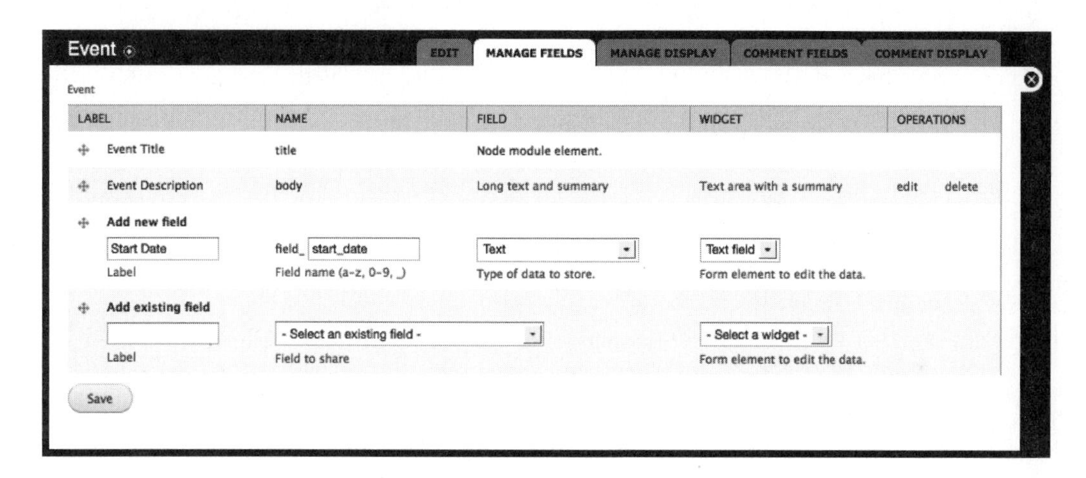

Figure 10-10. Creating the Start Date field

Click Save and you'll see the screen shown in Figure 10-11. The "Maximum length" field defines the maximum number of characters that an author can enter into this field. Because our field is date related, we'll ask the user to enter the date in mm/dd/yyyy format. Using this format, the maximum number of characters that they should be able to enter is 2 (for month) + 1 (for the slash) + 2 (for day) + 1 (for the slash) + 4 (for year) = 10. So we will set the maximum length to 10 instead of 255 (the default value). Next click "Save field settings."

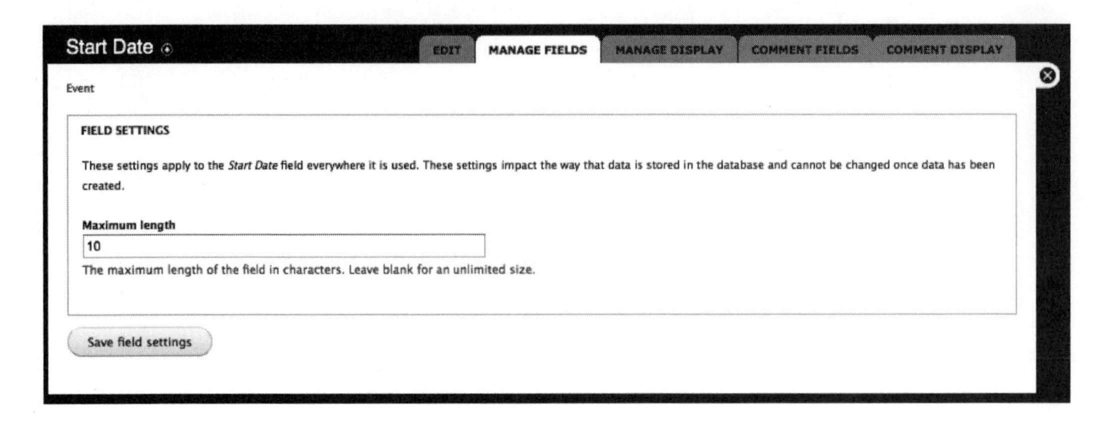

Figure 10-11. *Setting the maximum length*

The next form that Drupal displays (shown in Figure 10-12) enables you to set additional detailed parameters for the event start date field. On this form you have the ability to:

- Change the label that we previously defined for this field. Unless you made a mistake or changed your mind, you can leave the value as it is shown.
- Define whether this field is required. A required field is displayed with a red asterisk, and Drupal forces the user to enter a value in this field before it can be saved. Because our content type is about an Event and dates are important attributes of an Event, you want a date to be required. The size of the text field is used to define how wide the text field is on the screen, and does not affect the number of characters that the user can enter (which is the value we set on the previous page). For our Event type, we can shorten the length, as we only allow the user to enter 10 characters. Changing the length to 15 provides enough room to enter a full date with a little extra space.
- Text processing allows you to set whether the user input will be treated as plain text (meaning that any HTML tags entered by the user in this field will be ignored when the value is rendered on the screen) or filtered text (meaning that HTML tags will be rendered). Because our field is dealing with a date, users should not have the ability to enter an HTML tag, so we will leave the value of plain text.
- The content that you enter in the Help text field will be displayed beneath the text field on the screen. This is a great place to describe requirements for data that will be entered in this field, such as requesting that authors enter dates as mm/dd/yyyy. This is an optional field.

- The Default Value field provides the ability to pre-fill the field with a default value before the content creation screen is displayed to the author. Because our field deals with dates in the future, providing a default value doesn't make sense. There may be cases for other fields where a default value does make sense, such as selecting a seating preference for the event: you may wish to set a default value to "best available." In those cases, this is the place where you would enter the default value.
- The "Number of Values" field provides the ability for the author to dynamically create additional values for this field beyond the first one that is shown on the screen. You might use this feature for fields such as uploading a picture. You might want to provide the user with the ability to attach more than one picture to a piece of content, but you're not sure how many pictures they may want to attach. Setting the value to something greater than 1 results in an "Add another" link appearing below the field. If the author clicks on the "Add another" link, Drupal dynamically adds another field where the author can attach another picture, and they can keep adding another field for attaching another picture until they reach the limit that you set for this field. If the value is set to 1, then the user can only create one instance of this field. Because, by definition, our Events can only start on a single date, we'll leave the value at 1.
- We also have the ability to change the maximum number of characters that the author can enter into this field. We already set the value in the previous screen, but have the opportunity to fix a mistake or change our mind by changing the value in this field. Because the lengths of dates haven't changed since we entered the value on the previous screen, we'll leave the value at 10.

Start Date

EDIT | MANAGE FIELDS | MANAGE DISPLAY | COMMENT FIELDS | COMMENT DISPLAY

Event

EVENT SETTINGS

These settings apply only to the *Start Date* field when used in the *Event* type.

Label *

Start Date

Required field

Size of textfield *

15

Text processing

Plain text

Filtered text (user selects text format)

Help text

Please enter the start date for the event in the form of mm/dd/yyyy

Instructions to present to the user below this field on the editing form.
Allowed HTML tags: <a> <b> <big> <code> <del> <em> <i> <ins> <pre> <q> <small> <span> <strong> <sub> <sup> <tt> <ol> <ul> <li> <p>
 <img>

DEFAULT VALUE

The default value for this field, used when creating new content.

Start Date

START DATE FIELD SETTINGS

These settings apply to the *Start Date* field everywhere it is used.

Number of values

1

Maximum number of values users can enter for this field.
'Unlimited' will provide an 'Add more' button so the users can add as many values as they like.

Maximum length

10

The maximum length of the field in characters. Leave blank for an unlimited size.

Save settings

Figure 10-12. Setting the detailed parameters for the event start date field

We are now ready to click Save to add the field to our content type. Drupal then redisplays the general parameters screen for our content type.

If you click on the Manage Fields tab at the top of the page, you'll see that our new field now appears in the list, just below the Event Description field (see Figure 10-13).

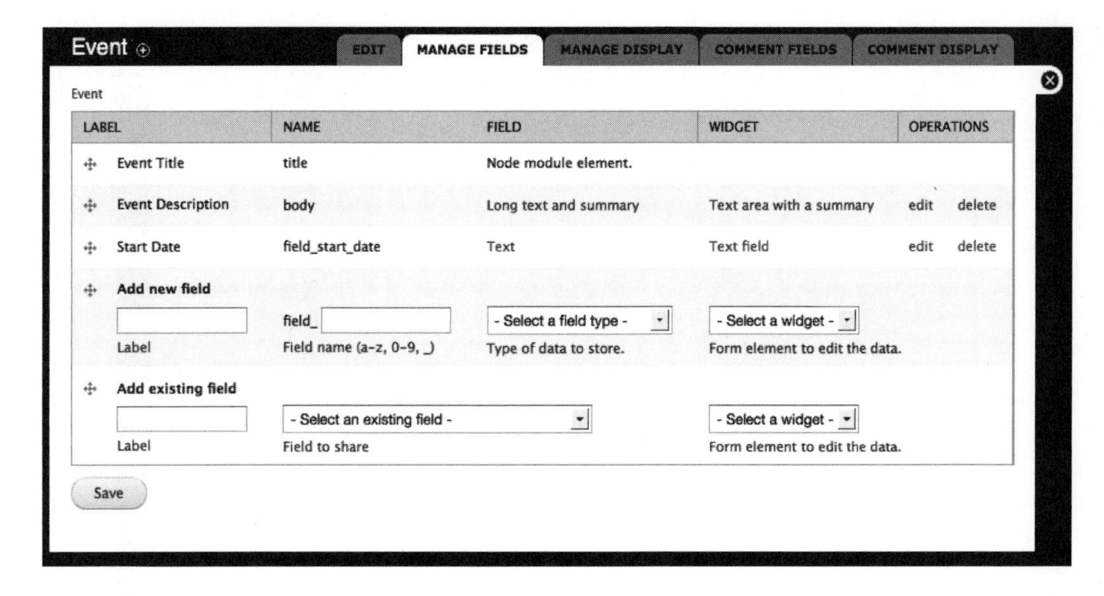

Figure 10-13. *A list of fields for the Event content type including the Start Date*

We are now ready to add the other fields that we defined earlier: the start time, the end date, the end time, and the venue/address. The process for adding the other fields is identical to what we just completed for the start date. Follow the same steps for the other fields, using the appropriate values for label, help text, maximum length, and text field length. When you're complete, your list of fields should look similar to Figure 10-14.

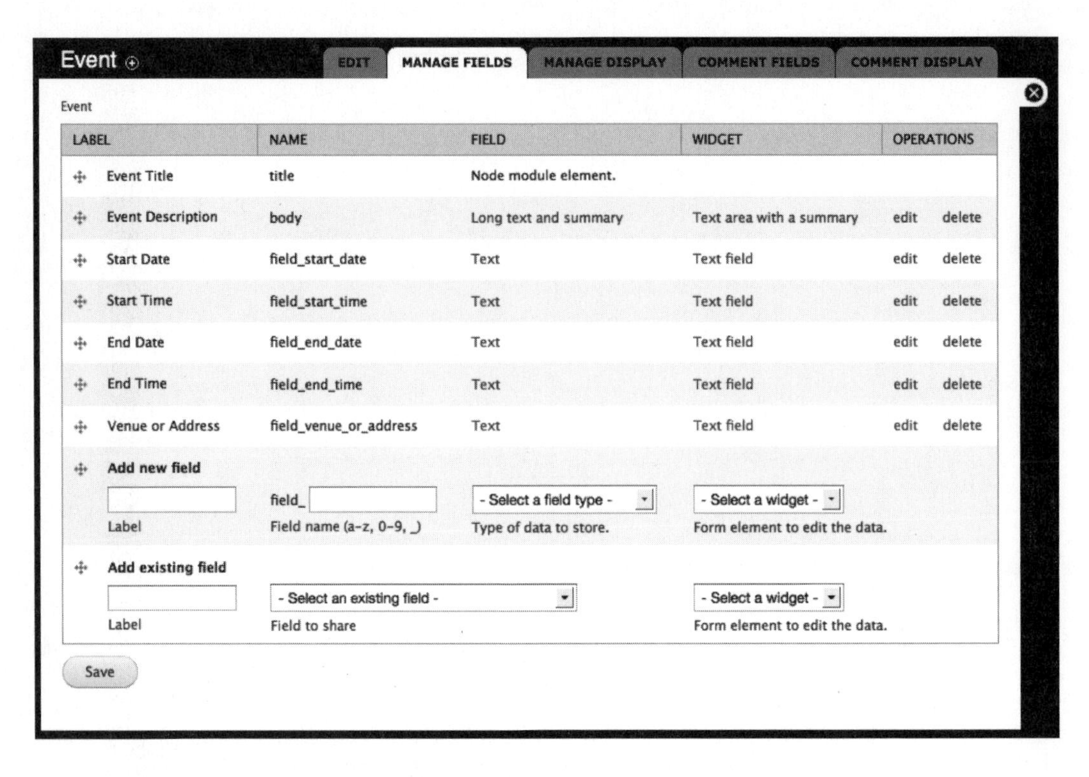

Figure 10-14. All of the event fields are now listed

Our Event content type is now ready for authors to use. To try your new content type, click on the "Add content" link in the gray menu bar, revealing the list of content types that we have available on our site.

Our Event content type appears in the list of available content types. Click on Event to reveal the content creation page for our Event content type (see Figure 10-15). The page shows the Event Title, Event Description, Start Date, Start Time, End Date, End Time, and Venue fields.

Create Event
Add new content
Please fill out all required fields before submitting the event
Event Title *
Event Description (Edit summary)
Text format Filtered HTML
More information about text formats
• Web page addresses and e-mail addresses turn into links automatically.
• Allowed HTML tags: <a> <em> <strong> <cite> <blockquote> <code> <ul> <ol> <li> <dl> <dt> <dd>
• Lines and paragraphs break automatically.
Start Date *
Please enter the start date for the event in the form of mm/dd/yyyy
Start Time *
Enter the start time as hour and minute in the form of HH:MM
End Date *
Enter the end date in the form of mm/dd/yyyy
End Time *
Enter the end time in the form of HH:MM
Venue or Address *
Enter the name of the venue or the street address of the event's location.

***Figure 10-15.** Creating a new event form*

Create a sample event using the event creation form. When you've finished entering values, click Save. Drupal will render your new Event content item using the values you specified. The example Event entered on the form in Figure 10-15 appears as a new Event in Figure 10-16.

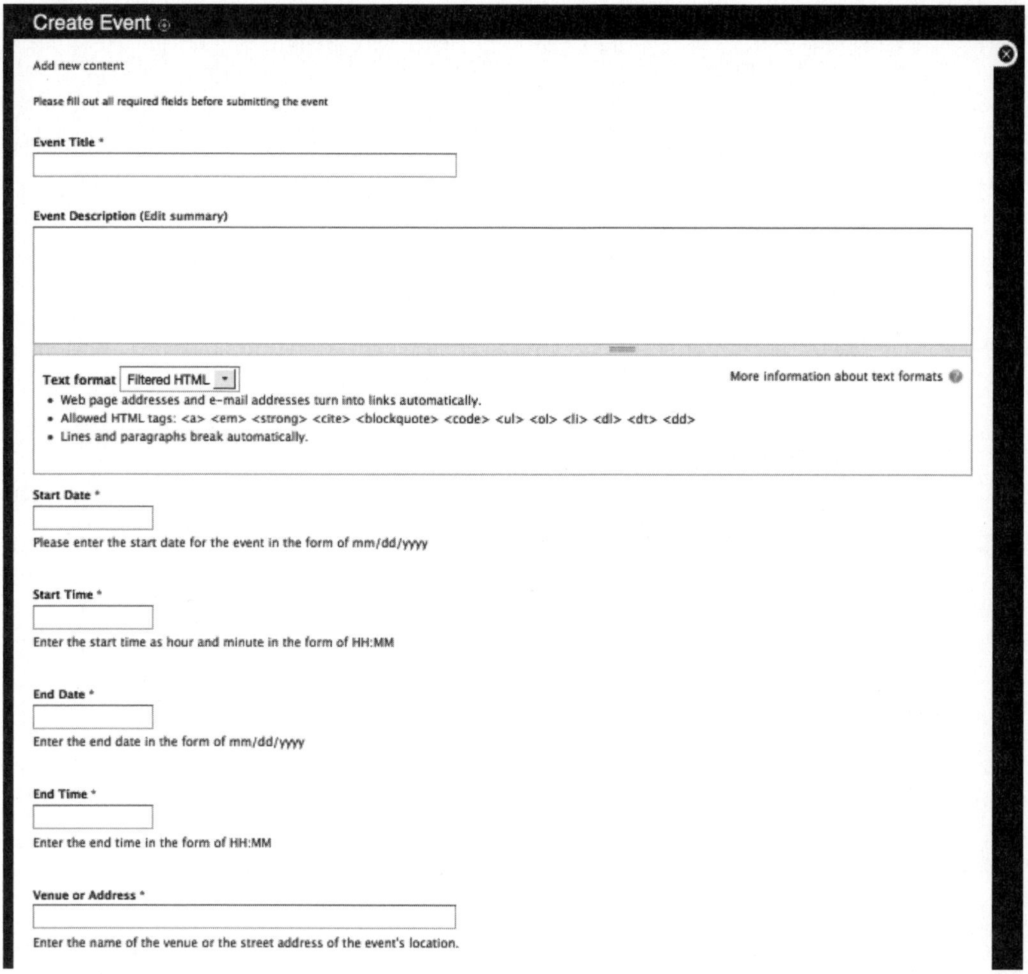

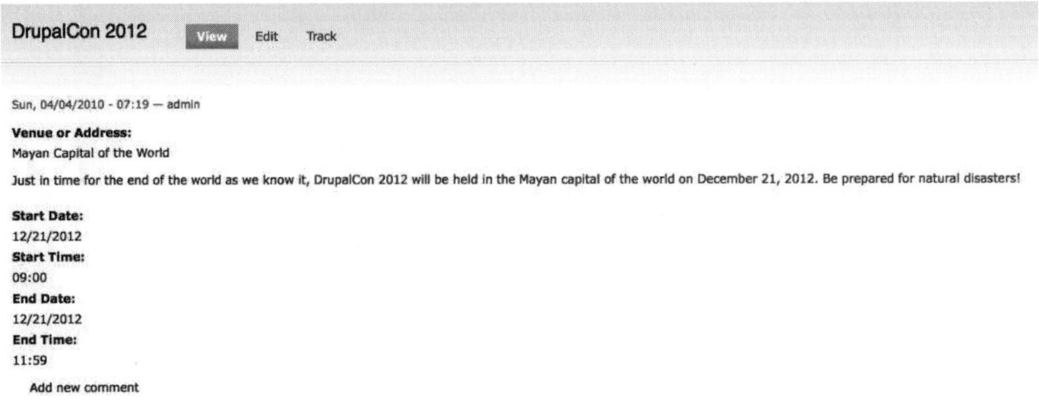

Figure 10-16. *The completed example event*

Other Field Types

In our Event content type, we created a set of text fields for authors to enter values for date, time, and venue. There may be instances where a text field is less effective than using something like:

- Radio buttons: Great for providing a list of options to the author and only allowing the selection of a single item from the list.
- Check boxes: Perfect for providing a list of options to the author, allowing selection of one or more items in the list.
- Select lists: Great for long lists of items to select from, for example all of the countries in the world.
- File uploads: The right field to use when you want to provide the ability to upload and attach a file to a piece of content.
- Text areas (a box with multiple lines): The right field when the author is expected to enter paragraphs of content.
- Numeric fields: Perfect when you want the author to only enter numbers.

The field types listed here are part of Drupal 7 core. There are other custom field types that are available as contributed modules (such as a date field that provides a pop-up calendar, allowing the author to select a date from a calendar instead of entering the date by hand). For a list of those modules please visit `www.drupal.org/project/modules` and click on the Custom Content Type link in the right column list of module categories. You'll find a long list of add-on modules that provide value-added capabilities, like other field types. You can install additional modules by following the process that we described in Chapter 8.

It is likely that you will come across the need to use one of the other field types as you create new content types. We will expand on our Event content type by adding several additional fields using other types of fields.

Radio Buttons

Radio buttons are useful when you want to present the author with a list of values from which they can select only a single item (check boxes are used when you want the author to have the ability to select one or more values). We will expand our Event content type to include the ability to select the type of seating that will be available at the event: either reserved seating or general admission. To start the process, click on the Structure link at the top of the page, followed by the Content type link on the Structure page and the "Manage fields" link for the Event content type. Figure 10-17 shows the values that you will want to enter to create the Type of Seating field.

***Figure 10-17.** Adding a radio button field*

Clicking Save takes us to the second configuration screen for check boxes and radio buttons. On this screen we have to specify the allowed values list, which are the options that will be presented to the author. Drupal requires that options be listed as a "key|label" pair, where "key" is a number representing which option that was selected (the numeric value will be stored in the database), followed by the "pipe" character (press the shift key and \ to enter a pipe character), and "label" is the value that will be displayed on the screen. In the example in Figure 10-18, I used 1|Reserved Seating and 2|General Admission, resulting in the values of 1 or 2 being stored in the database.

***Figure 10-18.** Creating radio button options*

After entering all of the options, click Save to reveal the final configuration page for this field (shown in Figure 10-19). On this form we can:

- Change the label.
- Mark the field as required.
- Create help text.
- Set the default option that will be selected by default when the page is rendered.
- Set the number of values that can be selected from the list. A value of 1 makes the list render as radio buttons, a value of more than 2 renders the list as check boxes.
- Change the list of values from what we created on the previous screen.

Enter help text that will help the visitor understand what this field is about and set the General Admission option as the default value that will be selected automatically when the create new event page is displayed.

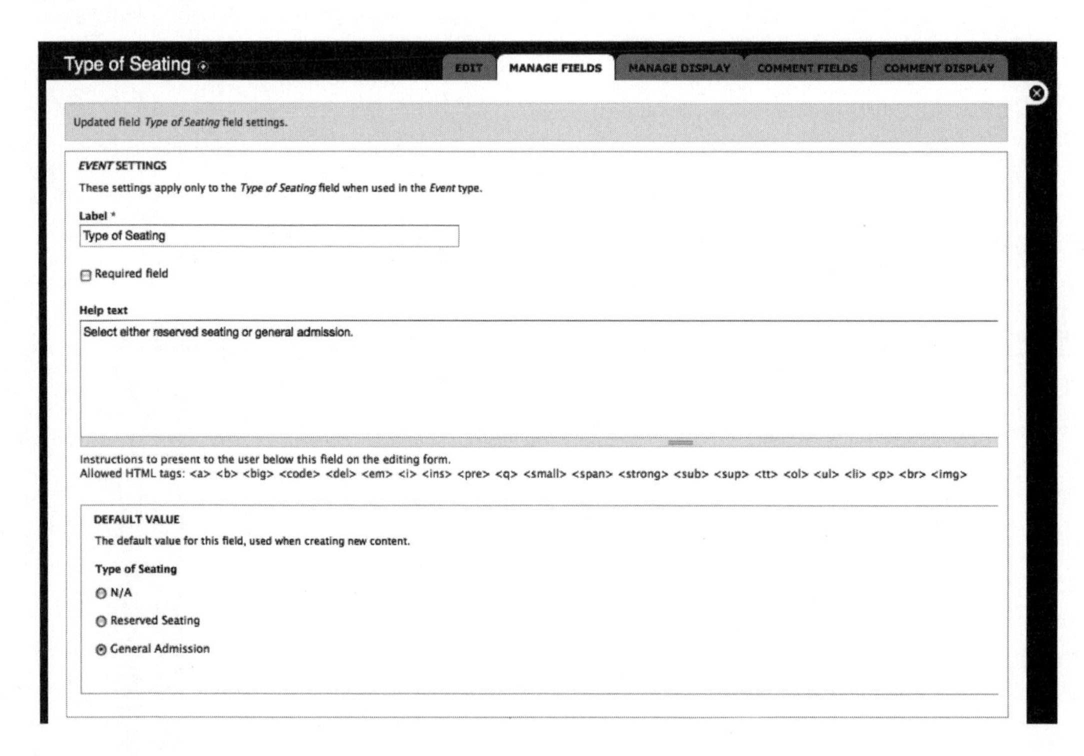

***Figure 10-19.** Configuring a radio button field*

After updating the appropriate values and clicking the Save button, the field is now ready for use. Our radio buttons are shown in Figure 10-20.

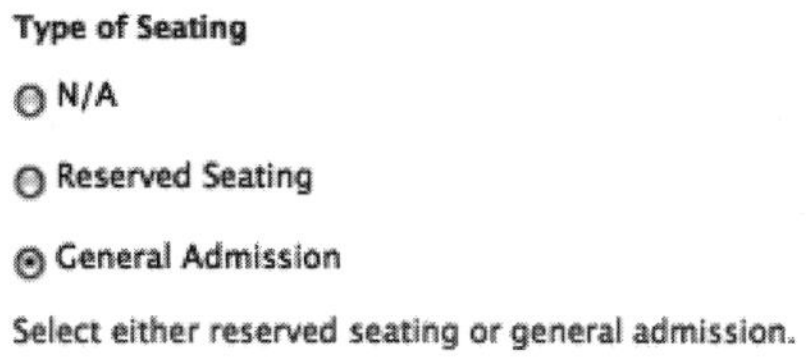

Type of Seating

○ N/A

○ Reserved Seating

◉ General Admission

Select either reserved seating or general admission.

Figure 10-20. The "Type of Seating" radio buttons field

Check Boxes

Check boxes are similar to radio buttons with the one exception: the author can select more than one value from the list. We will now expand on our events content type by adding a list of check boxes that address special accommodations available at this event for attendees with disabilities. We will create check boxes that specify whether audio-assisted devices, visual-assisted devices, and wheelchair seating is available for this event. To define the list of check boxes, return to the Event content type's manage fields page and enter the label (Assistance) and name (assistance), select List from the list of field types, and "Check boxes/radio buttons" from the widget lists (see Figure 10-21).

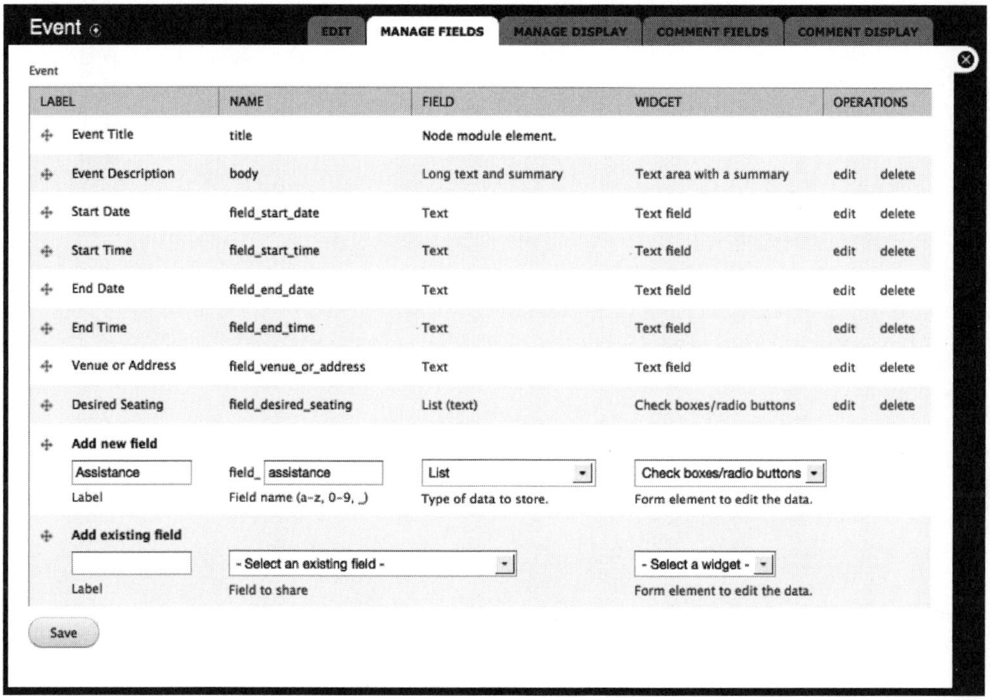

Event

EDIT | MANAGE FIELDS | MANAGE DISPLAY | COMMENT FIELDS | COMMENT DISPLAY

Event

LABEL	NAME	FIELD	WIDGET	OPERATIONS	
Event Title	title	Node module element.			
Event Description	body	Long text and summary	Text area with a summary	edit	delete
Start Date	field_start_date	Text	Text field	edit	delete
Start Time	field_start_time	Text	Text field	edit	delete
End Date	field_end_date	Text	Text field	edit	delete
End Time	field_end_time	Text	Text field	edit	delete
Venue or Address	field_venue_or_address	Text	Text field	edit	delete
Desired Seating	field_desired_seating	List (text)	Check boxes/radio buttons	edit	delete
Add new field					
Assistance Label	field_ assistance Field name (a-z, 0-9, _)	List Type of data to store.	Check boxes/radio buttons Form element to edit the data.		
Add existing field					
Label	- Select an existing field - Field to share		- Select a widget - Form element to edit the data.		

Save

Figure 10-21. Adding checkboxes

After clicking Save, enter the values for the three options, as shown in Figure 10-22.

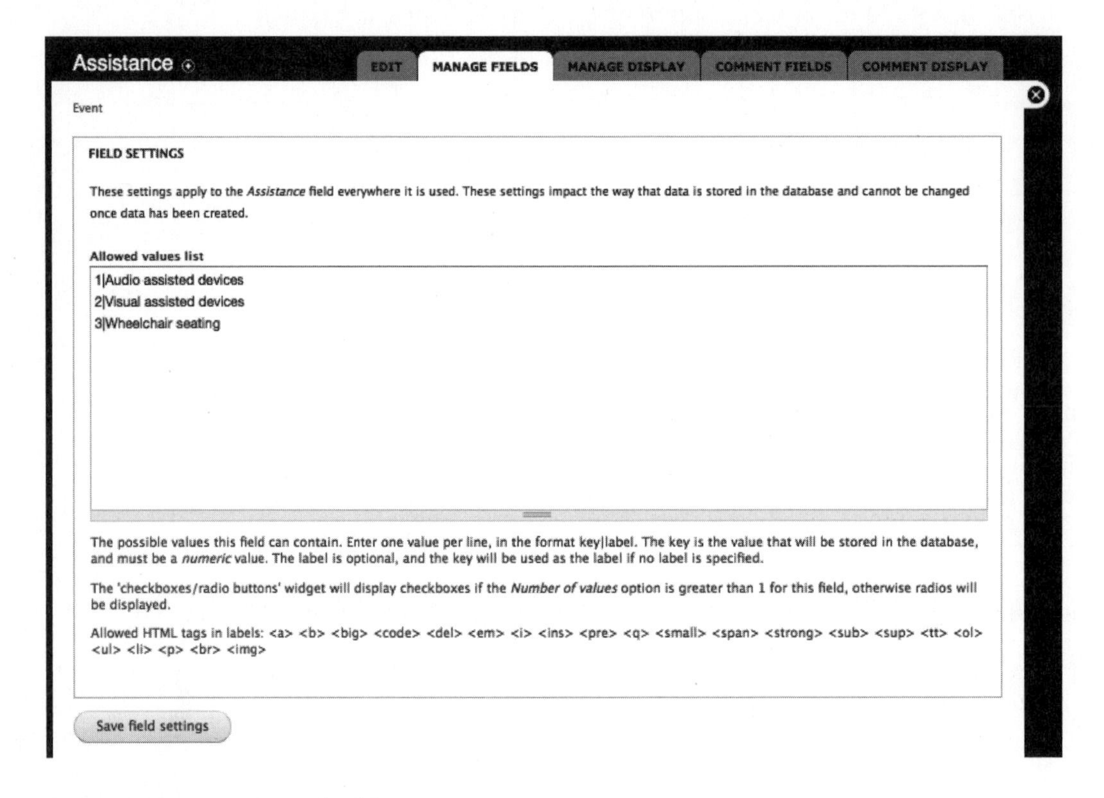

Figure 10-22. *Creating a check box*

The final step in the process is to change the "Number of values" field on the Event settings page. Changing the number of values to any value other than 1 instructs Drupal to render the list as check boxes instead of radio buttons. For our example, we'll allow the visitor to check all of the options, so set the value to Unlimited (see Figure 10-23).

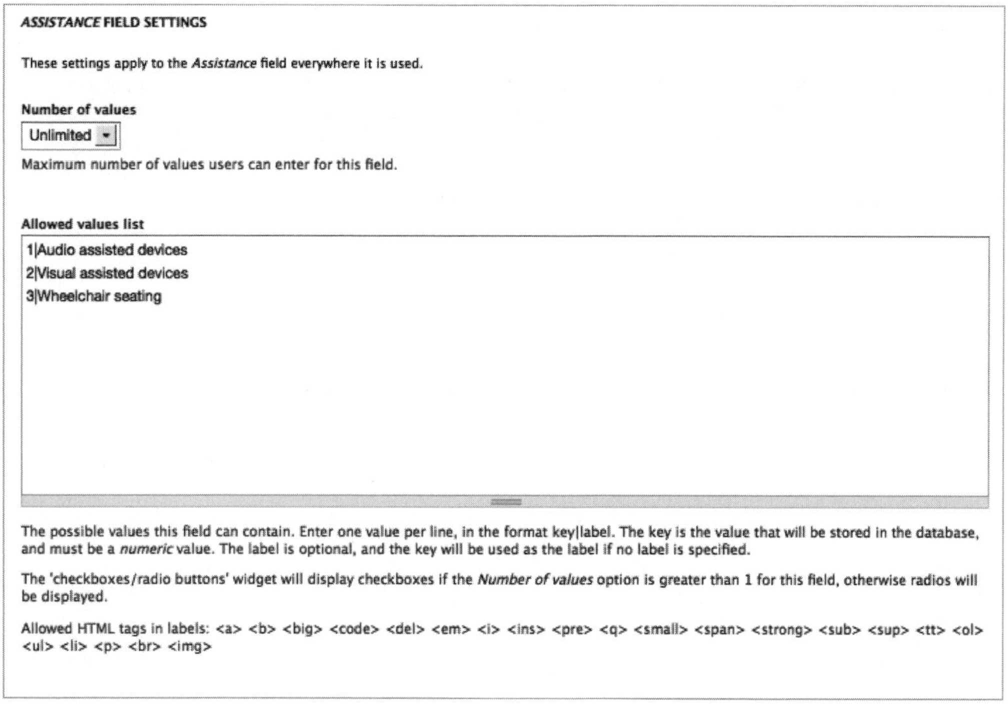

ASSISTANCE **FIELD SETTINGS**

These settings apply to the *Assistance* field everywhere it is used.

Number of values

Unlimited

Maximum number of values users can enter for this field.

Allowed values list

1|Audio assisted devices
2|Visual assisted devices
3|Wheelchair seating

The possible values this field can contain. Enter one value per line, in the format key|label. The key is the value that will be stored in the database, and must be a *numeric* value. The label is optional, and the key will be used as the label if no label is specified.

The 'checkboxes/radio buttons' widget will display checkboxes if the *Number of values* option is greater than 1 for this field, otherwise radios will be displayed.

Allowed HTML tags in labels: <a> <b> <big> <code> <del> <em> <i> <ins> <pre> <q> <small> <span> <strong> <sub> <sup> <tt> <ol> <ul> <li> <p>
 <img>

Figure 10-23. *Setting the Number of values field so the list renders as check boxes*

After updating, at minimum, the “Number of values” field, click Save. The example above will then appear on the content creation form for our content type as a list of check boxes (see Figure 10-24).

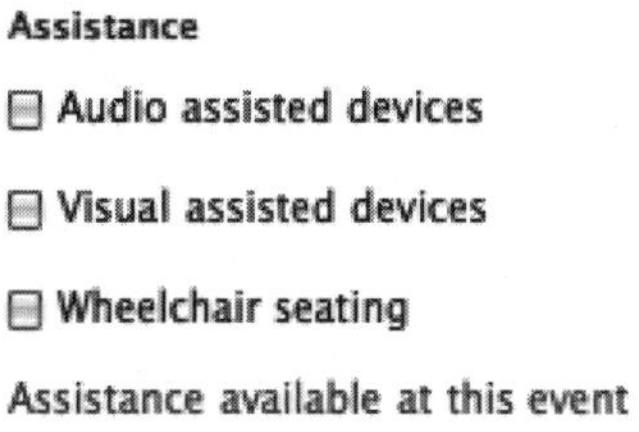

Assistance

- Audio assisted devices
- Visual assisted devices
- Wheelchair seating

Assistance available at this event

Figure 10-24. *The list of check boxes for the Event content type’s Assistance field*

Select Lists

Select lists are often called drop-down lists. To demonstrate select lists, let's create a new field for the Event content type that lists whether the event is a concert, a play, or a lecture. Creating a select list is similar to the previous field types. On the manage fields page for the Event content type, enter "Type of Event" in the Label field, type_of_event in the field name field, choose Select as the type of data to store , and Select as the form element to display. After setting these values click the Save button to proceed with the definition of your new select list field.

On the next screen, as in previous examples, enter the list of values that you want to present to the author as a key|label pair, where the key is a numeric value and the label is the text that is displayed in the select list. For values enter 1|Concert, 2|Play, and 3|Lecture. After entering the list of values, one per line, click Save.

On the final configuration screen, set the default value to 1, as an event can only be one of the types listed in the select list. Click Save after you have set any values that you wish to change on the form. You are now ready to use your new select list field. Figure 10-25 shows what the select list defined in the steps above looks like on a when creating a new event.

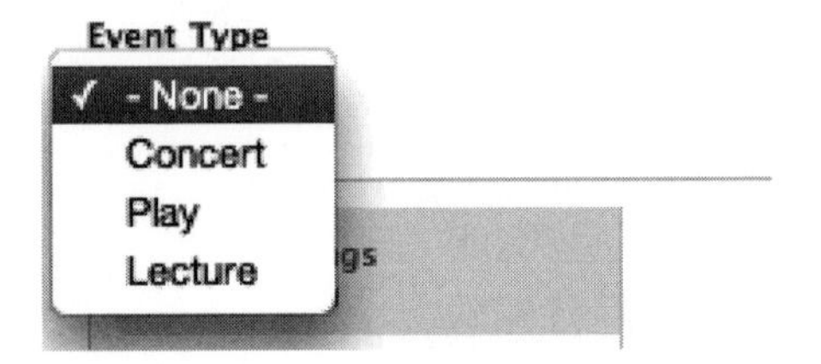

Figure 10-25. *Select list*

File Uploads

The "File upload" field type presents a file browser button that allows an author to browse their local computer for a file to upload to Drupal and attach to the content item that they are creating. Creating a "File upload" field is nearly identical to the steps for other field types. We will expand our Event content type to include the ability to attach the program for the event. As with previous fields, navigate to the Event content type's manage fields page and enter Event Program in the label field, event_program for the field name, select File as the type of data to store, and File as the form element to display.

After setting the values on the form, click Save. You will see the form shown in Figure 10-26. On this form, you can set parameters that define whether the field should be displayed, whether a link to the file should be displayed when a visitor views the content type, and the destination directory where the uploaded files will be stored. Check the "Enable display" option by checking the box, and the "File displayed by default" option. For most purposes, using the "Public files" directory is appropriate, unless the files are sensitive in nature and should be secured, in which case you would select the "Private files" directory (a case where you might want to use Private instead of Public is if you were providing a content type for the human resources department to collect data from field locations, where the field locations attach spreadsheets to the content item they are creating and that spreadsheet contains sensitive employee information). Once the values on this form have been set, click Save.

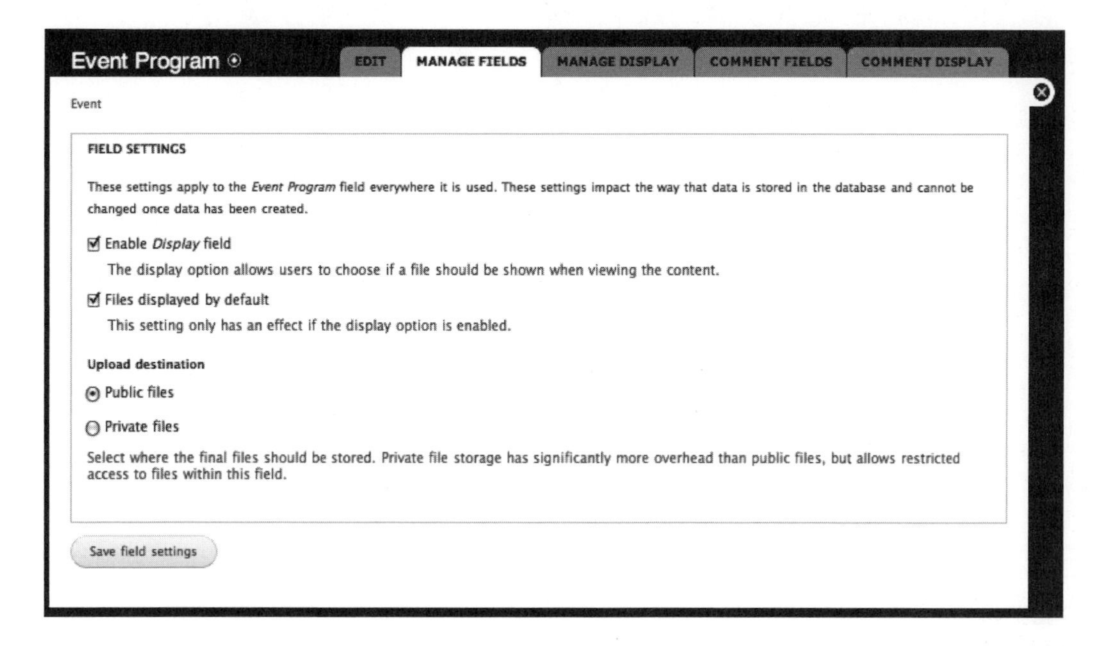

Figure 10-26. *Setting the file upload parameters*

After clicking Save, the final configuration screen is displayed (see Figure 10-27). On this form are three fields that you will want to focus on: the Help text that explains what this field is used for (Upload the events program), the Allowed field extensions (in our case we'll allow an author to upload a file with either a txt, doc, or pdf file extension), and the "Maximum upload size" (for our example we'll allow files up to 1MB to be attached to the event). Once you've updated the values, click on the Save button at the bottom of the form.

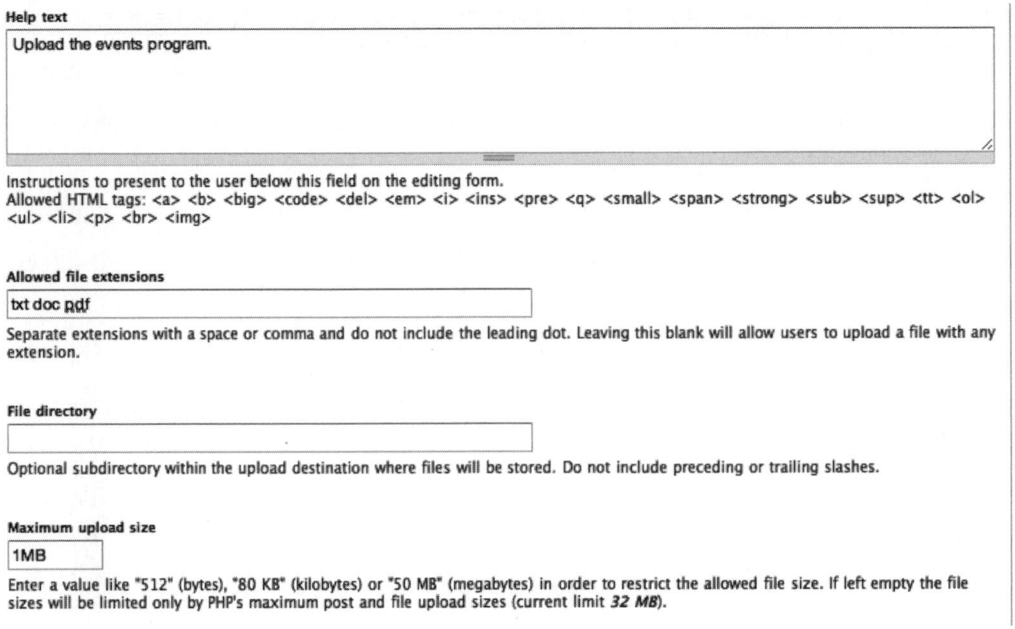

Help text

Upload the events program.

Instructions to present to the user below this field on the editing form.
Allowed HTML tags: <a> <b> <big> <code> <del> <em> <i> <ins> <pre> <q> <small> <span> <strong> <sub> <sup> <tt> <ol> <ul> <li> <p>
 <img>

Allowed file extensions

txt doc pdf

Separate extensions with a space or comma and do not include the leading dot. Leaving this blank will allow users to upload a file with any extension.

File directory

Optional subdirectory within the upload destination where files will be stored. Do not include preceding or trailing slashes.

Maximum upload size

1MB

Enter a value like "512" (bytes), "80 KB" (kilobytes) or "50 MB" (megabytes) in order to restrict the allowed file size. If left empty the file sizes will be limited only by PHP's maximum post and file upload sizes (current limit ***32 MB***).

Figure 10-27. *File upload configuration parameters*

Figure 10-28 shows the new file upload field on the event creation form.

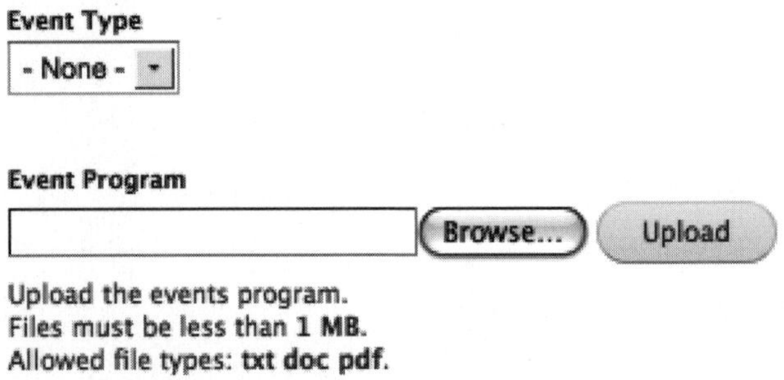

Event Type

- None -

Event Program

Browse... Upload

Upload the events program.
Files must be less than **1 MB**.
Allowed file types: **txt doc pdf**.

Figure 10-28. *File upload field*

Text Area

There will likely be scenarios where you want to provide a field on a content creation form where an author can enter a paragraph or more of text. While you could provide this capability through a text field (a single line text entry box), the more acceptable and standard way is to provide a text area. Extending our event example, let's add a new field that will be used to capture driving directions to the venue. To create a text area, follow the same steps as we used to create other fields. Enter "Driving directions" in the label field and driving_directions in the field name, select "Long text" as the field type, and "Text area" as the widget you will use to collect the content from the author.

After setting the values on the form above, click the Save button to continue to the next screen in the configuration process. This form provides you with the option to specify the maximum length of the content that can be entered into the text box. For demonstration purposes, we'll leave the value blank, an unlimited number of characters, and will continue with the configuration process by clicking on the Save button, revealing the final screen in the configuration process for this field type (see Figure 10-29). On this page, the key values to set for a text area are the Rows and Help text. The value you enter for rows determines how tall the text area will be when rendered on the screen. The default value is 5, which will render a text area the same height as the Help text field shown in Figure 10-29. For the example, leave the value set to 5 and enter Help text (for example, "Enter driving directions to the event's venue").

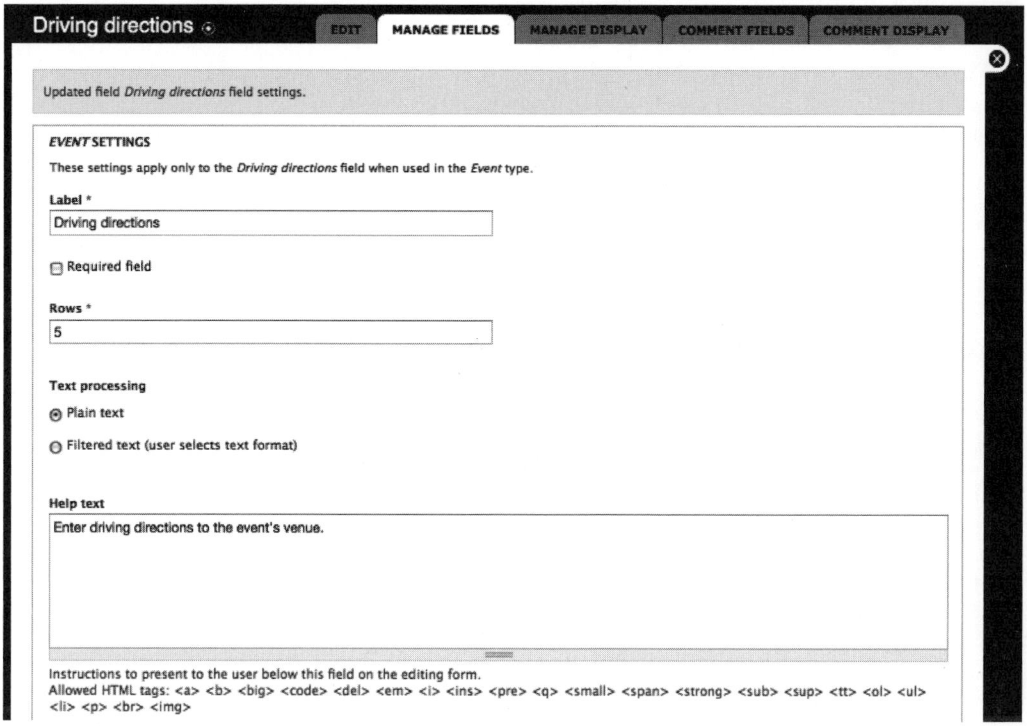

Figure 10-29. Configuring a text area field

After setting the appropriate values and clicking the Save button, the text area field is ready to use. Try creating a new event and you'll see the new text area where you can enter driving directions (see Figure 10-30).

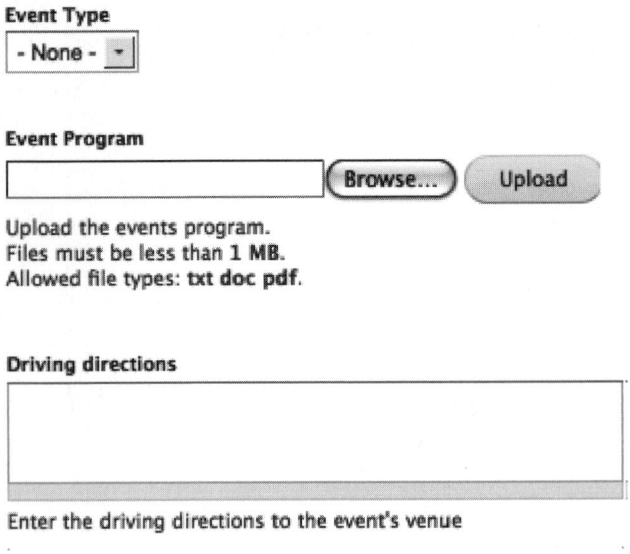

Figure 10-30. The new text area for driving directions

Numeric Fields and Other Field Types

By walking through the various field types listed previously you can see that there is a pattern and a common set of parameters for nearly every field type we created. A numeric field is essentially a text field, but restricted automatically by Drupal so that it will only accept numeric characters (0–9). As you expand on the types of fields that you can create by downloading and enabling contributed Content Construction Kit (CCK) modules, you will find slight variations in the process due to the structure of the fields you are creating. However, the overall process will be the same. If you haven't done so, now is the perfect time to browse the list of CCK modules that are available to extend the capabilities of what is available in Drupal 7 core. Visit `http://drupal.org/project/modules` and click on the Content Construction Kit link in the right column. When you browse, make sure that you're focusing on CCK modules that are built for Drupal 7, as many of the capabilities inherent in CCK are now part of Drupal core, whereas prior to Drupal 7 you had to download an install CCK to do what we just accomplished using Drupal out of the box. To narrow the list to only Drupal 7, click on the "Filter by compatibility" link for Drupal 7 in the right column.

Formatting the Output of a Custom Content Type

There will be times when the visual representation of your new content type doesn't fit with how you would like the content created with your new content type to be rendered on the screen.

Adjusting the order and positioning of the labels in relation to the field can be accomplished by clicking on the "Manage layout" link for the desired content type. To access this feature, click on the Structure link at the top of the page and then click on the "Content type" link on the Structure page. To access the layout feature, click on the "Manage display" link for the content type you wish to modify.

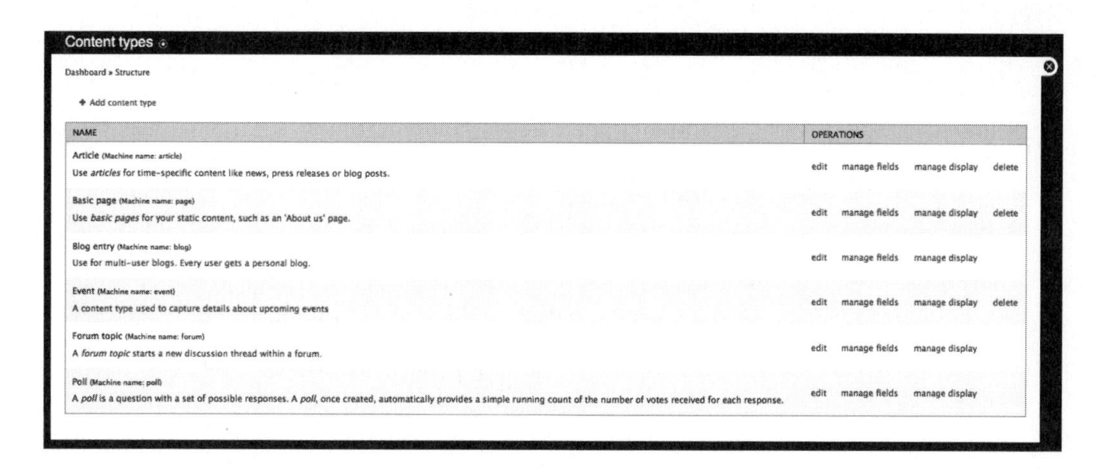

Figure 10-31. *The "Manage display" link on the Content types page*

We will use our Event content type to demonstrate the capabilities. Clicking on "Manage display" reveals the page shown in Figure 10-32.

Event

EDIT | MANAGE FIELDS | MANAGE DISPLAY | COMMENT FIELDS | COMMENT DISPLAY

Event

Basic | RSS | Search

Content items can be displayed using different view modes: Teaser, Full content, Print, RSS, etc. *Teaser* is a short format that is typically used in lists of multiple content items. *Full content* is typically used when the content is displayed on its own page.

Here, you can define which fields are shown and hidden when *Event* content is displayed in each view mode, and define how the fields are displayed in each view mode.

	TEASER		FULL CONTENT	
FIELD	LABEL	FORMAT	LABEL	FORMAT
Event Description	<Hidden>	Summary or trimmed	<Hidden>	Default
Start Date	Above	Default	Above	Default
Start Time	Above	Default	Above	Default
End Date	Above	Default	Above	Default
End Time	Above	Default	Above	Default
Venue or Address	Above	Default	Above	Default
Desired Seating	Above	Default	Above	Default
Assistance	Above	Default	Above	Default
Event Type	Above	Default	Above	Default
Event Program	Above	Generic file	Above	Generic file
Driving directions	Above	Default	Above	Default

Save

Figure 10-32. *"Manage display" page*

This page lists all of the fields that are associated with our content type, and provides the ability to define basic display attributes for the label and content for each of the fields. There are two sets of values that we can set: one for the Teaser view and the Full Node view.

If you click on the select list for Labels, you will find that there are three options:

- Above: The label will be displayed on a line immediately above the widget that you selected for your field.
- Inline: The label will be displayed to the left of your widget, on the same line as the widget.
- Hidden: The label will not be displayed on the screen.

If you click on the select list for the Format of each field, you will see that there are four options:

- Default: The content will be rendered on the screen as you specified when you created the field.
- Plain text: The content will be rendered as plain text, ignoring any HTML characters the author entered as part of the content.
- Trimmed: The content will be "trimmed" to a specified number of characters. If the content is longer than the specified characters, a "Read more" link will be displayed.
- Hidden: The content will not appear on the screen.

If you need to change the order of the fields and how they appear, you can do so by dragging and rearranging the fields on the "Manage fields" page for your content type. You can access this page by clicking on the Structure link at the top of the page, clicking on the "Content types" link on the Structure page, and the "Manage fields" link on the "Content types" page. Clicking through to the "Manage fields" page should reveal a page that looks like Figure 10-33.

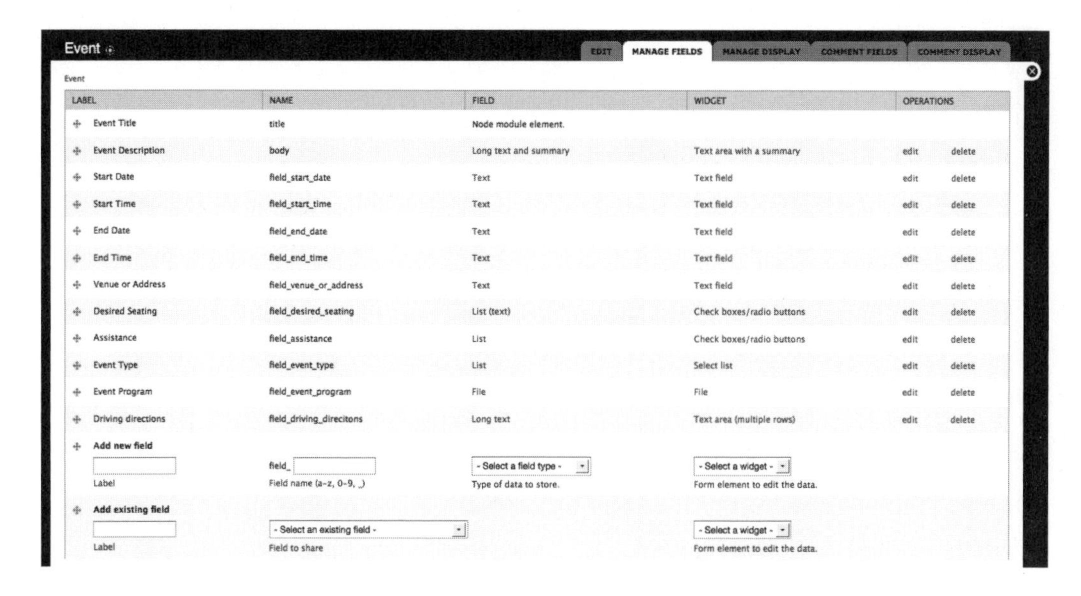

Figure 10-33. Manage fields page

To reposition a field click and hold the plus (+) sign next to the field label of the item you wish to move, drag the field to the position where you want it to appear, and release your mouse button. Remember to click the Save button after you have moved all of the fields to their proper position.

Summary

Content types is one of the "killer app" aspects of Drupal, and is an important concept to understand. While you could construct a Drupal site with just the Basic page and Article content types, it is likely that you'll want to leverage the features and functions provided through the use of custom content types. In this chapter I demonstrated just one of the custom content types that I create for nearly every site that I build for my clients. Other custom content types that I frequently use include customers, products, departments, FAQs, locations, and employees. As you design and develop your new site, I'm sure you'll identify one or more custom content types.

Another powerful feature of custom content types is the ability to develop custom reports or "views" of custom content type data that is stored in the Drupal database. If you think about the Event content type we created in this chapter, it might be valuable to generate a list of events sorted by the start date and time, or a list sorted by venue. Drupal's Views module is a relatively easy to use mechanism for generating lists. In Chapter 11 I will demonstrate how easy it is to generate lists.

CHAPTER 11

■ ■ ■

Views

If you ask anyone who has used Drupal for a while what the "killer module" is, the answer will likely be Views, Panels, or the Content Construction Kit (CCK). Views is usually mentioned first, and it's the module that many users say they can't live without. What does the Views module do that is so special? Simply stated, Views provides an easy-to-use tool for selecting and displaying lists of content on your website. Examples of how you might use Views include:

- Displaying the most recent news articles posted to your website, sorted in descending order by the date of posting.
- Displaying a list of company locations as a table that is sortable by clicking on the titles for the location name, city, state, and country.
- Displaying a photo gallery.
- Displaying a list of blog postings that is filterable by subject.
- Creating an RSS feed that lists the most recent content posted on your website.
- Displaying just about any kind of list that you can think of, created from the content that is stored on your website, as a list, table, or RSS feed.

In chapter 10, we created the Event content type. Let's put it to work by creating lists of events that will be useful to site visitors using the Views module.

Installing the Views Module

Views is a contributed module and must be downloaded, installed, and enabled before you can use it. We used the Views module as an example in Chapter 8, where I covered installing modules. If you did not install Views as part of that exercise, please revisit that chapter and follow the step-by-step instructions.

To verify that Views is installed and enabled, visit the Modules configuration page by clicking on the Modules link in the top menu, which reveals the list of modules that are installed and available on your site. Scroll to the bottom of the list to verify that you have the Views module installed and enabled. See Figure 11-1.

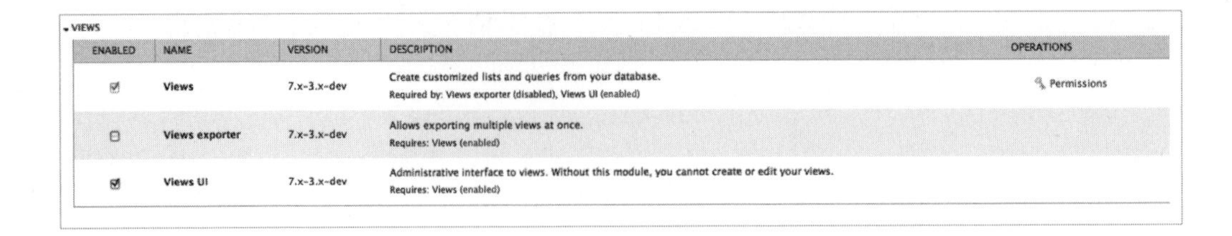

***Figure 11-1.** Verifying that Views is installed and enabled*

The Views components that you will need to work through this chapter are the main Views module (the first item listed) and Views UI. Views Exporter is a good module to use if you want to export the definition of a view and import that definition as a new view. It is not, however, a way to export the data that is rendered in a view. But, there's a module for that, too. Check out `http://drupal.org/project/views_export_xls`.

Creating Your First View

With Views installed and enabled, we're ready to proceed. But a view without content is, well, just a blank page, so the first step is to create some content. In Chapter 10, we created a content type for Events, and a very common use for Views is to create a list of upcoming events. Take a moment to create several Events so you have content to display when you set up your first View.

To create a View, click on the Structure link at the top of the page and click on the Views link, which brings you to the Views administration page. To add a View, click on the Add tab at the top of the page, which reveals the page for creating a new view(see Figure 11-2). On this page, define the following:

- View name: The name must be unique (a name that has not been used for another view on your site), and can only contain alphanumeric characters and underscores (so no blank spaces). It's a good idea to pick a descriptive name that conveys the purpose of the view so that others looking at the list can easily identify the right one to use. For the first view, use upcoming_events as the name.
- View description: This is another field that you can use to provide additional information about the view. For this view, use "A list of upcoming events" as the description.
- View tag: This is an optional field that you can use to provide a list of tags that define what the view is about.
- View type: A list of the types of information stored in the Drupal database that you can use to generate your view. The most common selection is the Node option, as nodes represent a vast majority of the information stored in your Drupal database.

Views ⊕

LIST | ADD | IMPORT | TOOLS

Dashboard » Structure » Views

View name *

upcoming_events

This is the unique name of the view. It must contain only alphanumeric characters and underscores; it is used to identify the view internally and to generate unique theming template names for this view. If overriding a module provided view, the name must not be changed or instead a new view will be created.

View description

A list of upcoming events

This description will appear on the Views administrative UI to tell you what the view is about.

View tag

Enter an optional tag for this view; it is used only to help sort views on the administrative page.

View type

⊙ Node

Nodes are a Drupal site's primary content.

Figure 11-2. *Creating a new View*

Click the Next button to proceed. You'll see the page that is shown in Figure 11-3.

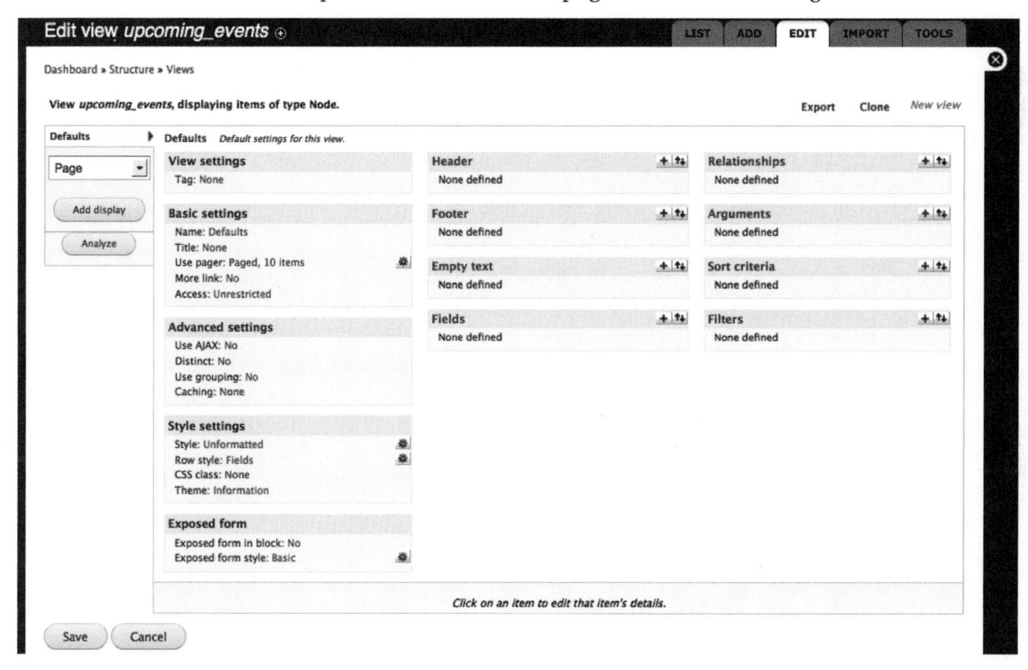

Figure 11-3. *The Views edit page*

At first glance, the form for defining a view looks complex and overwhelming. Fortunately, looks are deceiving.

To define our new view, we'll start with the far left-hand column. At the top of the column, you'll see the word Defaults, which means that any values you set to the right of the column will be treated as the default parameters set for this view. Below Defaults you'll see a drop-down list that includes values for:

- Attachment: Attachments are used to create a view that is a secondary display 'attached' to a primary view. Effectively, they are a simple way to create multiple views within the same view. This is an advanced feature that you can read about at www.drupal.org/project/views.
- Block: I covered blocks in previous chapters, and described a block as a container for content that is assigned to a region on a page. If you want to embed a view on a page in a region, you'll want to use the Block option.
- Feed: Views is the mechanism for automatically generating RSS feeds.
- Page: A page represents a view that is rendered in full-page mode and is accessible through a URL that you define through the configuration process. I will revisit the Page option in a moment.

For now we will leave everything in this column as is.

In the middle column are a number of options that we can set, which I'll discuss in the following sections.

Views Settings

In the Tag field, we can enter a Taxonomy tag that can be used for searching and accessing the view. For this example, leave this value as None. To change the value, simply click on the None link, which exposes a field at the bottom of the configuration form where you can enter a new value.

Basic Settings

In Figure 11-3, you can see that the Basic Settings field includes the Name, Title, Use pager, More link, and Access attributes of your new view. I will explain these here.

Name

You can set the name of the view to something other than Defaults. To change the name, click on the Defaults link and change the value at the bottom of the configuration area. The value entered here is only used for internal uses, and isn't visible to site visitors. For demonstration purposes we'll leave the value as Default.

Title

The value associated with this option is displayed at the top of the list that is generated by Views. To change the value, click on the None link, revealing a text box at the bottom of the Views configuration form where you can change the values. We will change the value to something that is meaningful to a site visitor who is viewing the page where this list is generated. Enter a value such as Upcoming Events.

After changing the value, click on the Update button, which brings you back to the Views configuration page. The value you entered appears next to the Title label.

Use Pager

For lists that will contain dozens or hundreds of items, you can limit the number that appear on a page (usually to 10 or so) and use a "pager" at the bottom of the page instead. A pager looks like this: << previous 1,2,3,4,5,6,7… next >>. Visitors use the pager to navigate through all of the items. Views automatically creates and displays the appropriate pager based on the number of items that are in the complete list. By default, the Views module renders lists using a pager with 10 items per page. You can change this by clicking on the "Paged, 10 items" value. You'll see a list of four options (shown in Figure 11-4). "Display a specified number of items" allows you to specify how many content items will be displayed without a pager being rendered. You might want to use this approach when you only want to list the first three items. I've used this option in cases where I want to display only the last three items created on the site in a "What's New" block. "Display all items" lists every content item that meets the criteria specified in the view definition. This option works well for situations where there are fewer than 25 content items in the list. More than 25, and visitors are unlikely to scroll through them all. "Paged output, full pager" results in a list of items (say,10 items) followed by a pager. A full pager lists other options, such as "Jump to the start of the list," "Jump to the end of the list," "Previous," and "Next." The "Paged output, mini pager" is similar to the full pager, but only provides navigational controls for previous and next.

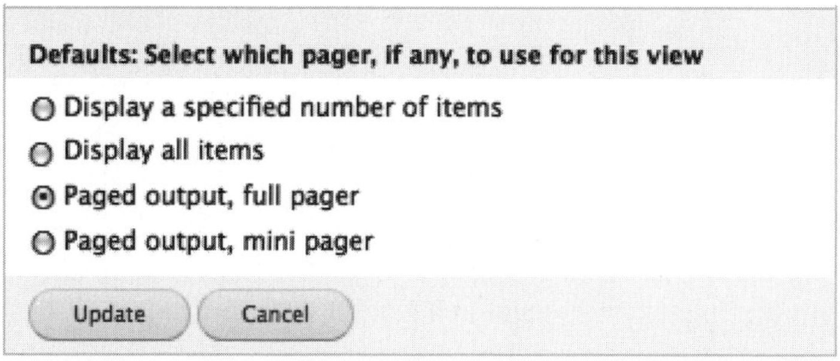

Figure 11-4. *Pager options*

Items Per Page

If you decide to use a pager for your view, you can set the number of items that will appear on each "page" by clicking on the small gear icon to the right of the "Use pager" option. Clicking on the gear reveals a form where you can set the number of items that will be displayed per page, the offset (think of the offset as the starting item for your view; for example, if you want to skip the first 10 items and start at number 11, you would enter 10 in the offset field), the pager ID (in nearly every case you can just leave this value as the default), the number of pages you want to display (in most cases you'll want to leave it as blank to show all pages), and you have the option of exposing the options for the visitor to set the number of items per page and the offset. See Figure 11-5.

Defaults: Pager options

Items per page

10

The number of items to display per page. Enter 0 for no limit.

Offset

0

The number of items to skip. For example, if this field is 3, the first 3 items will be skipped and not displayed.

Pager ID

0

Unless you're experiencing problems with pagers related to this view, you should leave this at 0. If using multiple pagers on one page you may need to set this number to a higher value so as not to conflict within the ?page= array. Large values will add a lot of commas to your URLs, so avoid if possible.

Number of pages

The total number of pages. Leave empty to show all pages.

EXPOSED OPTIONS

Exposing this options allows users to define their values in a exposed form when view is displayed

Expose items per page

When checked, users can determine how many items per page show in a view

Expose Offset

When checked, users can determine how many items should be skipped at the beginning.

Update Cancel

Figure 11-5. Setting the pager options

More

If your view is limited by the items-per-page field to a number that is less than the number you have defined for your view, and you decide not to use a pager, you can provide a "Read more" link, which the visitor can click to see the complete list of items. You can set this value by clicking on No and changing the value on the pop-up form to Yes. For now, let's leave the value at No, as we're using a pager.

Access

We can define which types of visitors have the ability to access the Access view by selecting from the list of user roles or permissions that are defined on our site. You may have a view, for example, that lists information that only people assigned to the Human Resources Department role should be able to access. To set the value, click on the Unlimited link to reveal the configuration options shown in Figure 11-6.

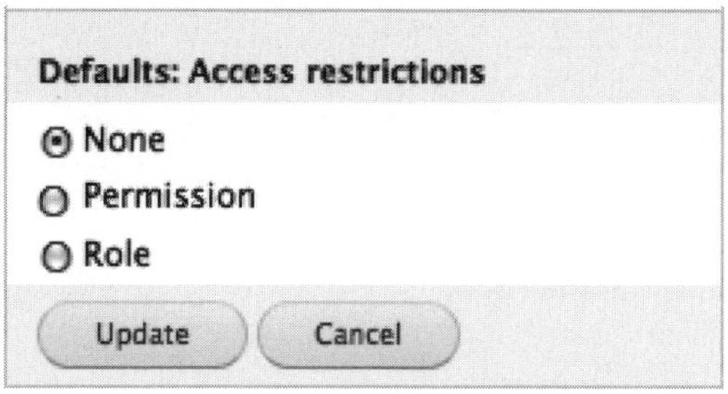

Figure 11-6. Views access restrictions

We can select Permission (for example, we might have a permission that defines the ability to view a particular content type) or Role. Typically, permissions are assigned to roles, and roles are granular enough to define the ability to access a view. There may be cases where you need fine-grained control over who can access a content type, or you have dozens of roles that all have the same permission. In such cases, you can use permissions to restrict instead of having to select dozens of roles. For this example, select Role and then click the Update button, which reveals a page with a list of roles that we can select from. Select the appropriate roles and click Save. For this example, we will select "Authenticated user," which means anyone who has an account and is logged into the site.

Advanced Settings

Advanced settings control features such as the use of Ajax, whether Views should remove duplicate rows, and whether caching should be used.

■ **Note** Ajax is a set of technologies that enable things like sorting and paging through pages of a view, without refreshing the page. It is a nice added feature that makes it quicker for site visitors to manipulate your views. It is, however, optional.

Use Ajax

To enable this feature, click on No and change the value to Yes in the form that appears at the bottom of the Views configuration form. Do this for our example.

Distinct

There may be cases where your view returns duplicate items due to the filters you defined (although it is highly unlikely, it can happen). If you see duplicate items in your list, check this box. To remove duplicates, you can set the Distinct value by clicking on No and checking the box on the form that appears at the bottom of the Views configuration form. In our example, we will leave the value as unchecked.

Use Grouping

Grouping is a powerful feature that allows you to break data returned from a view into separate sections based on a field that is contained in the view. As an example, we could decide that we want to list events grouped by venue, where each venue has its own section of the report that is generated through views. I'll revisit groups in a bit.

Caching

There may be cases where views that return a large number of items take longer than desired to load on the screen. If you have a high-traffic site with views that return large numbers of items, it is advisable to use the caching mechanism provided by Views. Caching causes the view to first check to see if that list exists in cache and, if so, renders it from cache instead of going to the database and retrieving every row that meets the specified criteria. It is a great feature that improves performance. The downside of this feature surfaces if you have content that changes frequently. A highly dynamic list of content using caching may result in items that were added, changed, or removed from the database not appearing as they currently do in the database, as the view was cached and Views did not go to the database to re-read all of the values. It is a helpful feature and something that you should consider using. In our example, the list of events is short and we don't anticipate having a large number of visitors, so we'll leave the value set to None.

Style Settings

This is the "meat and potatoes" section in the first column. These are key settings that impact how the view is rendered on the page. You'll want to pay special attention to these values as you build your view.

Style

Views provides the ability to render the output of your view as a Grid (a good example of a grid is a photo gallery where there are rows and columns of pictures displayed), an HTML list (just a list of items with bullet points), a Table (output that looks like an Excel spreadsheet with rows and columns where each item fills a single row), or unformatted, which renders the content as it would appear on the page in Teaser or Full Node view. We will start with unformatted in our first pass through creating a view, and will update the view to a table later in the chapter.

Row Style

We can define how each item displayed on the screen appears with the Row Style option. To view the configuration options, click on Fields to reveal the configuration options form at the bottom of the Views configuration form. See Figure 11-7.

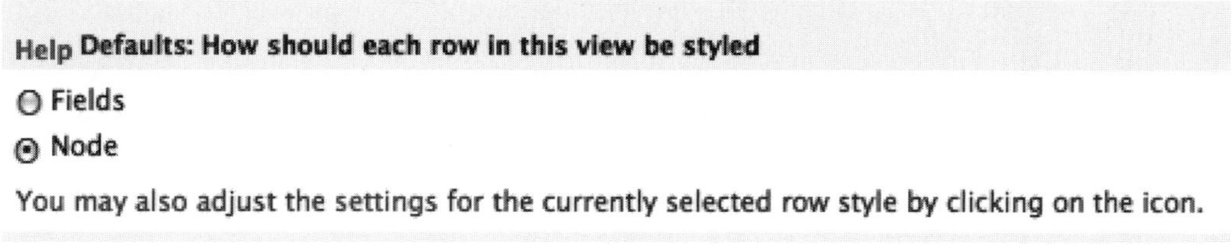

Help Defaults: How should each row in this view be styled

Fields

Node

You may also adjust the settings for the currently selected row style by clicking on the icon.

Figure 11-7. Selecting the row style

We can select the Fields option, which provides the ability to pick individual fields out of our content type to display on the list (you may only want to list the titles of your items in the list and nothing else). Or you may want to display the list of items as a Node, meaning either the Teaser or the Full Node version. When you see lists of the latest news stories, for example, on a site, that would likely be someone using the Node option and rendering the teaser of that node with a "Read more" link to view the entire article). For now, we'll select the Node option.

Since we selected the Node option, we'll want to define whether we want the view to render the Teaser version of our item or the Full Node version. To set that option, select Node to see the Node configuration options at the bottom of the Views configuration form. See Figure 11-8.

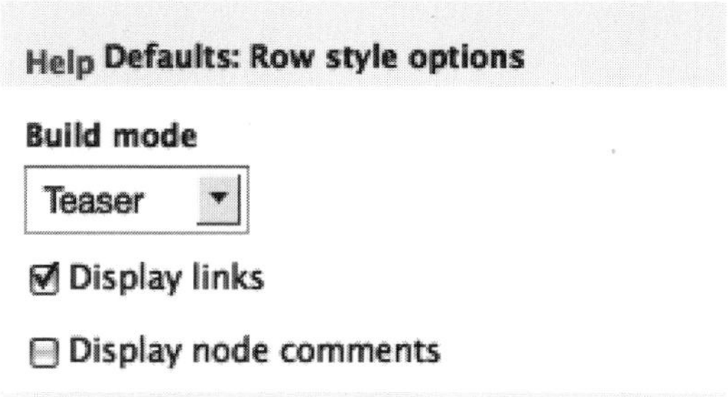

Help Defaults: Row style options

Build mode

Teaser

Display links

Display node comments

Figure 11-8. Node configuration options

On this form, we can select either the Teaser or Full Node mode for how the item will be displayed. For demonstration purposes, we'll leave the option set at Teaser. The "Display links" option provides a mechanism for turning off the "Read more" link for teasers or other links, such as links to file attachments for this node. We'll leave it checked for our example. The "Display node comments" option allows you to specify whether comments associated with each item should be displayed along with the node itself in the list. If comments are an important part of what you are trying to communicate to your visitor, you should check this box. For our example, we do not want to display comments, so we will leave it unchecked. When finished, click on Update to return to the previous screen.

CSS Class

The CSS class option allows you to assign a class attribute to your view. Click on None to access the form where you can change the value from None to the name of a CSS class class.

Theme

The Theme setting is less of a configuration option and more of a helper function for those who are responsible for "themeing" the output of your view. This option displays the CSS tags that are available for styling with your theme. This is an advanced function and beyond the scope of this book.

Exposed Form

The Exposed form provides the ability to separate view controls from the view itself, exposing those controls as a block that you can place elsewhere on your page. You might use this when you have an exposed filter and don't want that filter to appear at the top of the view, but somewhere else as a block (say you provide the ability for the visitor to select options that reduce the number of records that appear in the view, based on a specific criteria; for example, to only show all upcoming events that are taking place at the Civic Center). It's a helpful feature, but an advanced topic that is beyond what I will cover in this chapter.

We've made it through the first column and are ready to tackle the second column. Because we made several changes to our view, it's a good idea to save it before proceeding. If we were to close the window for some reason, all of our changes would be lost. From personal experience, it's a good idea to save often. Before proceeding, click Save.

Header

With this option, you have the ability to author text that will appear at the top of your list. You may want to provide an introductory paragraph that describes the content in the list, or any other static content that you wish to author for this list. To create the content, simply click on the plus (+) sign to the right of the Header title, which reveals a form at the bottom of the Node configuration form where you can select where the header should be applied (either globally on every page or at the top of a specific group, if you defined grouping as an option). For the events example select <All> and check the Global: Text area option. See Figure 11-9.

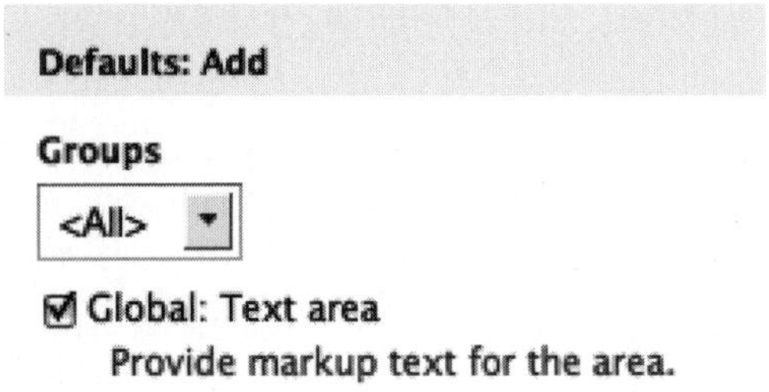

Defaults: Add

Groups

<All>

☑ Global: Text area

Provide markup text for the area.

Figure 11-9. *Selecting the heading type*

After clicking on the Add button, the form shown in Figure 11-10 is displayed. On this form, enter the text that you want to display at the top of your view. For our example, enter "The following is list of upcoming events" and click the Update button.

Defaults: Configure Header *Global: Text area*

Label

The label for this area that will be displayed only administratively.

☐ Display even if view has no result

If checked this area will be rended, even if the views has no results.

The following is a list of upcoming events.

More information about text formats

Text format

Plain text

Figure 11-10. Selecting the heading type

Footer

We can also provide a footer for our view, which is text that will be displayed at the bottom of our list. Creating a footer is the same process as the header. Click on the plus (+) sign to view the form.

Empty Text

The Empty text option provides the ability to display a sentence or paragraph in the case where your view does not return any values. This is a good option to use, as it provides a more user-friendly result in the case where the view is empty. Instead of displaying a blank page, you could display a sentence that says, "We're sorry, we did not find any upcoming events at this time." Go ahead and add this empty text message. To do so, follow the same steps outlined for the header.

Fields

If we had selected Field as the option for Row Style in the first column, we would have been presented with the ability to add the fields that we want to display on our view here. But because we picked Node instead, the concept of fields doesn't apply. I'll revisit this configuration option when we update our view later in this chapter.

We completed the second column, albeit without doing much. It's time to save our view again before proceeding to the last column.

Relationships

The Relationships column provides the ability to "link together" related information. As an example, say you have a content type for an employee, and in it you have a field that is a reference to that employee's location. The address information for the location is stored in the Location content items, and your requirements call for a view that lists employees and their location's address. Because address isn't stored on the Employee content type, you need some method for "linking" the two content types together to display both employee and location information as a single item in the view. Relationships provides that mechanism. For details on using relationships visit the documentation pages for Views at `www.drupal.org/project/views`. Our example view for events doesn't have a relationship, so we'll bypass this setting.

Arguments

Arguments provides a mechanism for passing values to your view, typically through the URL that is used to render the view. An example of how you might use arguments is to limit the values returned for our list of events to a specific venue.

Sort Criteria

One of the "power" features of Views is the ability to sort the output of our view before it is rendered on the screen. You can sort on none, one, or several fields that are associated with your content type. For our example, we want to sort on the list of upcoming events by the title, in ascending order. To set the sort criteria, click on the plus (+) sign in the heading for sort criteria. You'll see the form shown in Figure 11-11.

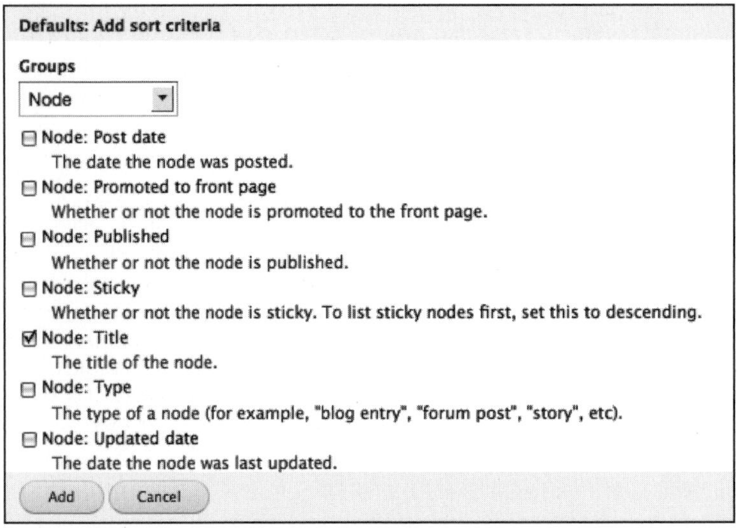

Figure 11-11. *Selecting the sort criteria*

On this page, you will see every field that is defined for any content type that exists on your site. The list is long and will grow over time as you create new content types. Views does provide a filtering mechanism to narrow the list of options based what group the field belongs to. The two primary options that you'll use are <all>, which lists every field, and Node, which lists the Drupal core fields that are associated with a generic node. Since the title field is part of core Drupal, we can select the Node filter to limit the number of fields that are displayed. Check the box next to "Node: Title" and click the Add button at the bottom of the screen. Views then displays another configuration form where we set the order that we want our items to be sorted (see Figure 11-12).

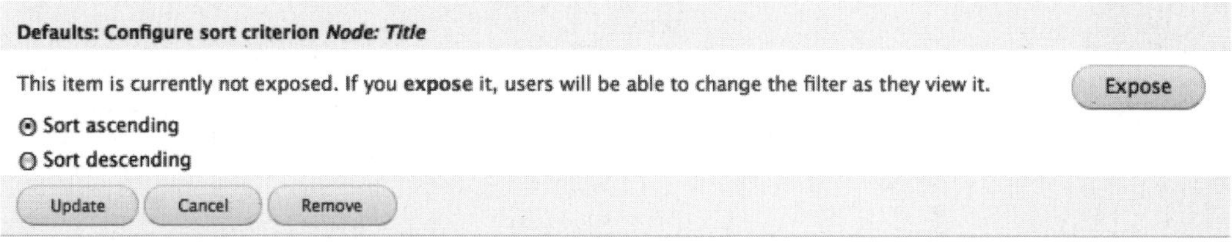

Figure 11-12. *Setting the sort order*

We want our items to be sorted alphabetically in ascending order, so we will use the default option and finish the process by clicking the Update button.

Filters

The last set of configuration options define the filters that Views will use to narrow the list of items that are returned to our view. You can filter the results on every available field for your content type, including the Drupal core fields associated with a node. You could filter by author (as in, only show me articles that were written by John), by published date (only show articles published in the past week), by Taxonomy term (only show me articles about basketball), by content type (only show me Event content), or any other field or combination of fields that are exposed to your content type. For our example, we want to filter the results by content type, as we only want to show nodes that were created as Events. To set that filter, click on the plus (+) sign in the bar associated with the Filter, exposing the same list that appears in Figure 11-11.

To narrow the list of options that are displayed, select Node from the Groups field, as we want to filter by Node Type. After the page is refreshed, scroll down until you see Node: Type and check the box. Click on the Add button to proceed to the next step (see Figure 11-13).

On this screen, we want to limit the types of content that are displayed in our view to only Events. To do this, we simply click on the "is one of" option on the left and check the box next to Event and click on the Update button. If we wanted to provide the option for visitors to select the content type that is rendered, we click Expose. If we had more than one Node type selected, the visitor could select one or more of the values to control what is shown in the list. For our purposes, we only want to show Events, and we don't want to provide visitors with the ability to change that behavior. Check the box next to Event, and click on the Update button to proceed.

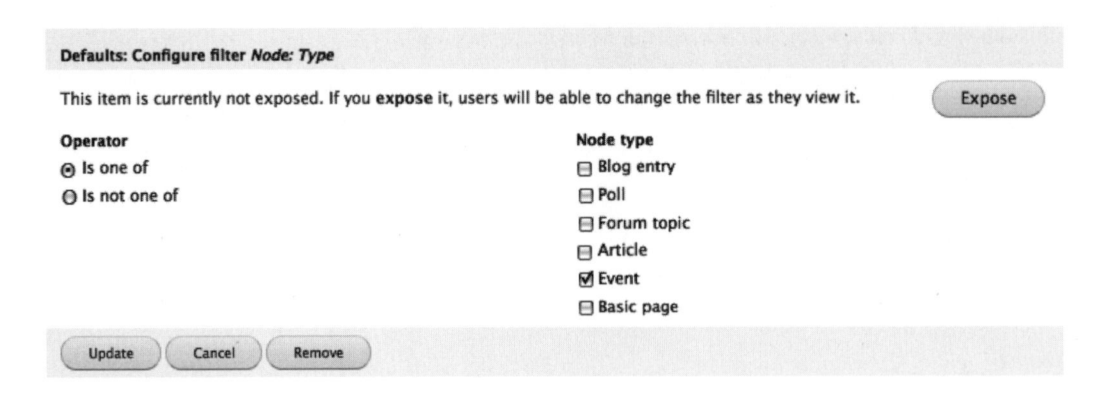

Figure 11-13. Selecting the filter by content type value

At this point your Views configuration screen should look something like Figure 11-14, depending on which options you selected during the previous process.

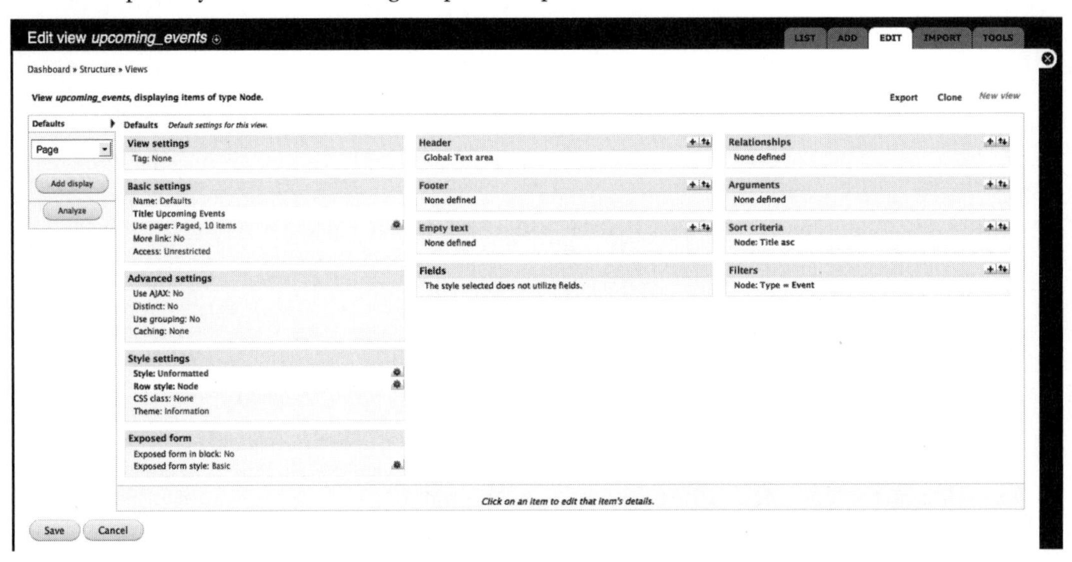

Figure 11-14. The view is configured and ready to test

Click the Save button before proceeding.

Live Preview

You may have noticed a feature at the bottom of the Views configuration page called Live Preview. This allows you to quickly test your view to see if it is displaying the right values in the right order. You can click on the Preview button at any step in the process to see how the view will look on a page. See Figure 11-15.

Live preview

Display: Defaults

Arguments: [ ] Preview

Separate arguments with a / as though they were a URL path.

A list of upcoming events.

A Christmas Carol

- Edit
- Delete

Submitted by admin on Sun, 04/04/2010 - 20:53

Type of Seating:

Reserved Seating

Charles Dickens classic play comes to the Paramount.

Start Date:

12/20/2010

Start Time:

07:00

End Date:

12/20/2010

End Time:

11:00

Venue or Address:

The Paramount

Assistance:

Audio assisted devices

Visual assisted devices

Wheelchair seating

Event Type:

Play

Read more admin's blog Add new comment

Figure 11-15. *Live preview*

Exposing a View as a Page

Views can be embedded in a page as a block, in a node, or they can be their own stand-alone page with their own unique URL (one view per URL). To render a view as a page, we need to add a display type to the view. If you return to the main Views configuration page for the view that we just created (if you are not on that page, you can return to that page by clicking on the Structure link at the top of the page and on the Structure page, clicking on the Views link). Clicking Views presents a list of the views that are defined on your site (see Figure 11-16). Included in this list are default views that are created automatically when you install the Views module, as well as any views that have been created on your site by administrators.

Figure 11-16. List of views

Find the view you want to update in the list and click on the edit link. Our view was the Upcoming Events list. Clicking on the edit tab reveals the Views configuration page.

On this page we want to add a new display, specifically a page display, because page displays have the ability to specify a URL and renders the view in full-page mode. To add the page display, ensure that the value Page is selected in the drop-down list in the far left-hand column of the Views configuration form. Once it is selected, click on the "Add display" button. Views will redisplay the Views configuration page with additional options that are associated with rendering a view as a page. See Figure 11-17.

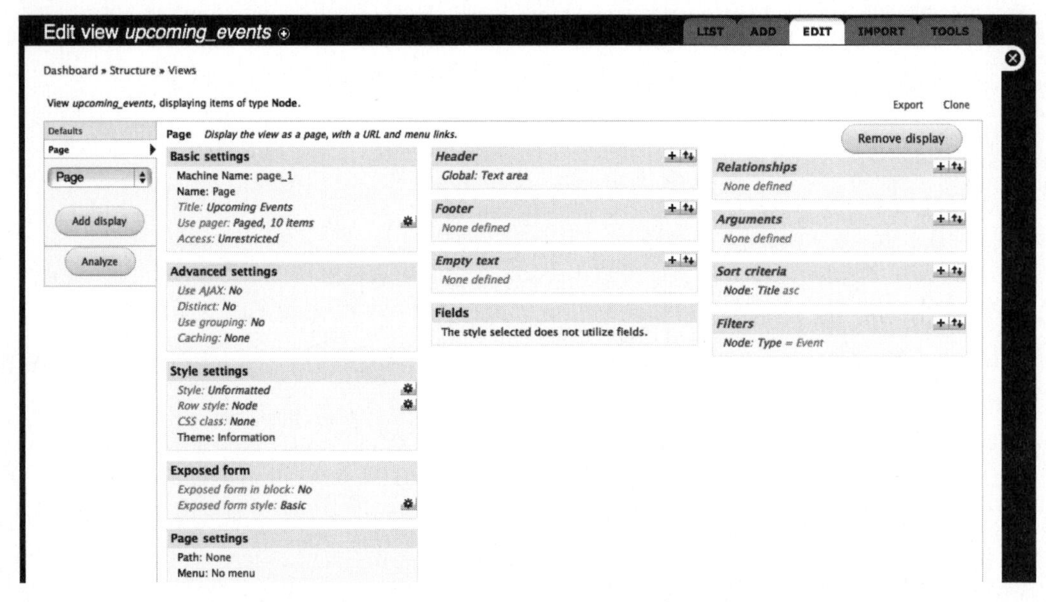

Figure 11-17. Adding a Page display to your view

There are two primary changes to notice on the Views configuration form: first, the left-hand column now has a link for a Page display, and second, there is a new configuration block for Page settings (at the bottom of the middle column). We can now specify the URL for accessing the view and we can add our view to one of the menus on our site.

To specify the URL for this page, click on None next to the Path label, revealing a form at the bottom of the Views configuration form (see Figure 11-18). On this form, you will see that there is a text box for entering the URL that you want to expose that allows a user to see the view in full-page mode. In our example, the new URL is http://localhost/?q=upcoming-events. It is a good practice to use URLs that contain words that are related to the content on that page, using hyphens to separate individual words. Our example creates a human- as well as search-engine-friendly URL for our view. After entering the URL click on the Update button.

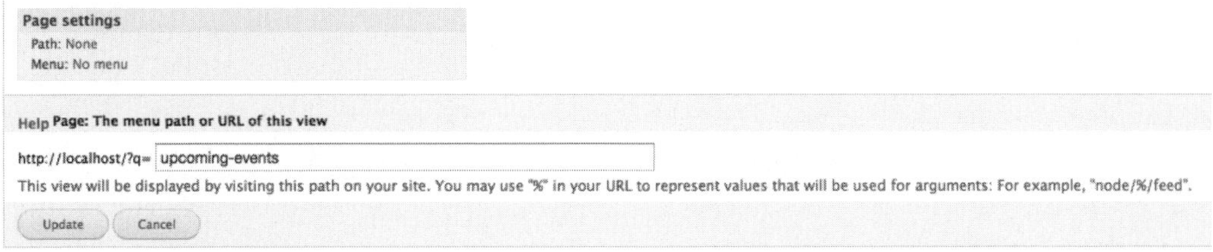

Page settings
Path: None
Menu: No menu

Help Page: The menu path or URL of this view
http://localhost/?q= upcoming-events
This view will be displayed by visiting this path on your site. You may use "%" in your URL to represent values that will be used for arguments: For example, "node/%/feed".
Update Cancel

Figure 11-18. *Specifying a URL*

The second option that we have on this form is to assign our view to a menu. To add our view to a menu, click on the "No menu" link to define the type of menu (a normal menu entry or a tab) and the menu that you want to assign your view to. For our demonstration we will not add our view to a menu.

Remember to save your view before doing anything else! We are now ready to test our view by entering the URL that we just created into the address bar of our browser: `http://localhost/upcoming-events`. After clicking Enter, your view will be rendered on the page. See Figure 11-19.

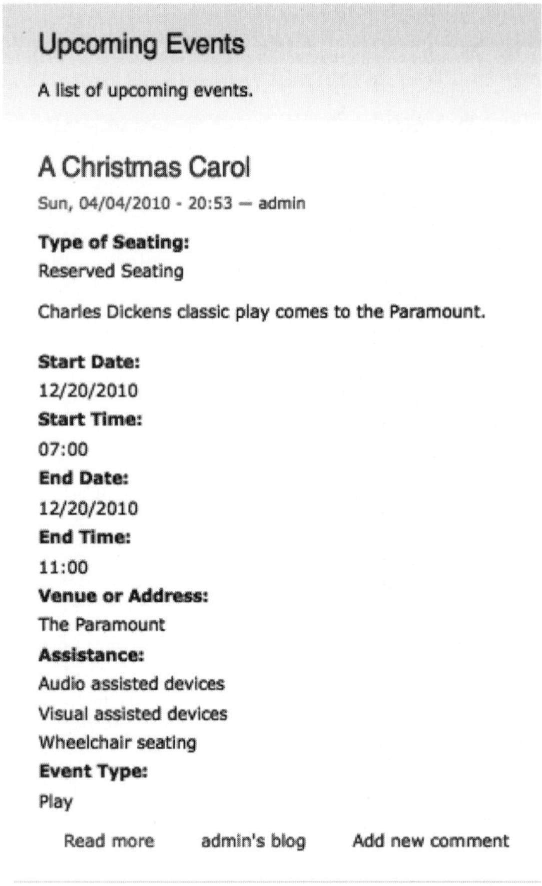

Upcoming Events

A list of upcoming events.

A Christmas Carol

Sun, 04/04/2010 - 20:53 — admin

Type of Seating:
Reserved Seating

Charles Dickens classic play comes to the Paramount.

Start Date:
12/20/2010
Start Time:
07:00
End Date:
12/20/2010
End Time:
11:00
Venue or Address:
The Paramount
Assistance:
Audio assisted devices
Visual assisted devices
Wheelchair seating
Event Type:
Play

Read more   admin's blog   Add new comment

Figure 11-19. Full-page view

Creating Tabular Views

In the previous examples we rendered views as simple nodes. There are likely cases where you will want to render lists as tables. We are going to update our list of upcoming events view that we created in the previous example, changing the output from a list of upcoming event nodes to a list of upcoming events in a table.

The benefits of the table include the ability to render specific fields from your content type and not the whole node, in a format that is sortable by the visitor by clicking on the column titles. Figure 11-20 is an example of how I used a tabular view for one project.

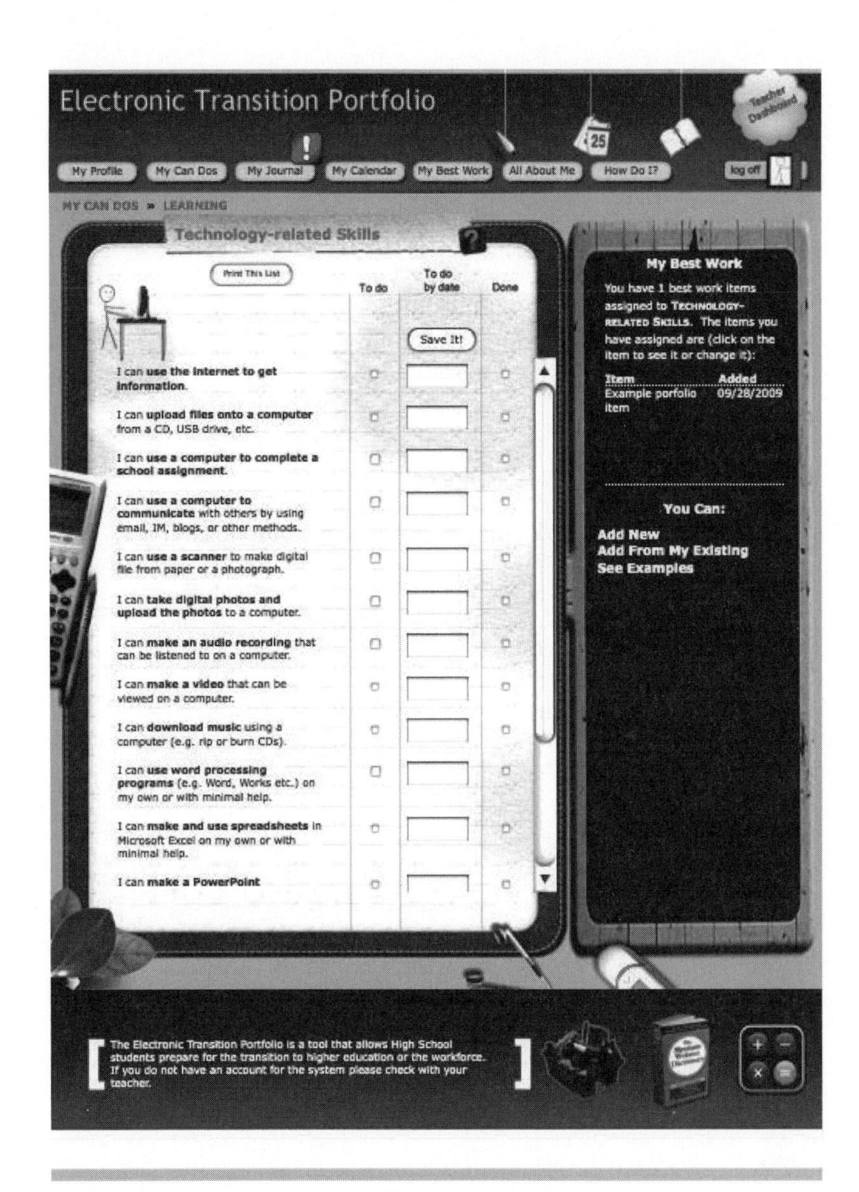

Figure 11-20. *An example of using the table format for a view*

In this example, the author created a view that renders content items as a table on the left, and a list of files that were uploaded as a table in the column on the right. The left column lists several custom content types in a table ("can-do" nodes that capture skills that high school students must demonstrate in order to graduate). This is an advanced version of a table based view, as it allows the student who is using this page to update several nodes at a time by checking boxes next to list items and picking dates from a pop-up calendar. But it is a prime example of a creative way to use tabular views as a mechanism for rendering lists of data as rows and columns.

To update our list of upcoming events view, return to the Views configuration form that we have used in the past (click on the Structure link at the top of the page, click on the Views link on the Structure page, and click Edit next to the Upcoming Events view).

There are two basic changes that we need to make in order to enable our view as a table. First we need to change the Style field from Unformatted to Table, then we need to select the fields that we wish to display in our table.

So first, click on the Unformatted link and, on the configuration form, select Table. See Figure 11-21.

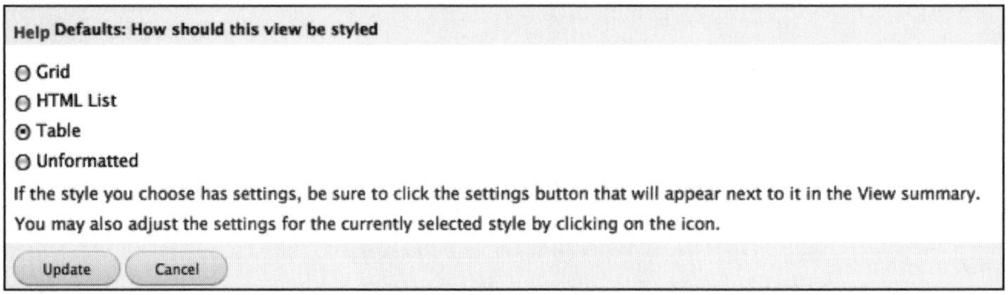

Help Defaults: How should this view be styled

Grid
HTML List
Table
Unformatted

If the style you choose has settings, be sure to click the settings button that will appear next to it in the View summary.
You may also adjust the settings for the currently selected style by clicking on the icon.

Update Cancel

Figure 11-21. Changing the style to table

After changing the value to Table, click on the Update button. The next step is to list the fields that we want to appear as columns in our table. To add the list of fields click on the plus (+) sign in the second column next to the Fields heading to see the screen shown in Figure 11-22.

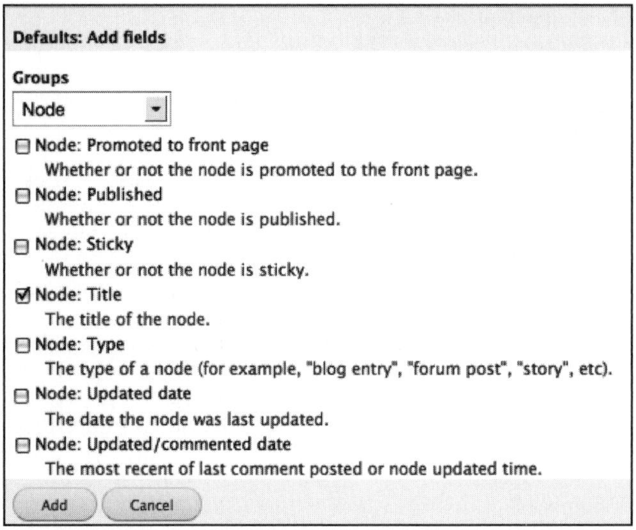

Defaults: Add fields

Groups
Node

Node: Promoted to front page
Whether or not the node is promoted to the front page.
Node: Published
Whether or not the node is published.
Node: Sticky
Whether or not the node is sticky.
Node: Title
The title of the node.
Node: Type
The type of a node (for example, "blog entry", "forum post", "story", etc).
Node: Updated date
The date the node was last updated.
Node: Updated/commented date
The most recent of last comment posted or node updated time.

Add Cancel

Figure 11-22. Selecting fields to display

Scroll down the list and choose the fields that you want to display to your site visitors. Likely candidates include the event title (shown in the list as Node: Title), the event start date, the event end date, and the event venue. Place a checkmark in the box next to each of the fields and then click the Add button at the bottom of the list.

After clicking Add, you will be prompted through a series of screens for setting various attributes of each field that will be displayed. See Figure 11-23.

Defaults: Configure field *Node: Title*

Label

Title

The label for this field that will be displayed to end users if the style requires it.

☐ Exclude from display

Check this box to not display this field, but still load it in the view. Use this option to not show a grouping field in each record, or when doing advanced theming.

☐ Rewrite the output of this field

If checked, you can alter the output of this field by specifying a string of text with replacement tokens that can use any existing field output.

☐ Output this field as a link

If checked, this field will be made into a link. The destination must be given below.

Replacement patterns

The following substitution patterns are available for this display. Use the pattern shown on the left to display the value indicated on the right. Note that due to rendering order, you cannot use fields that come after this field; if you need a field not listed here, rearrange your fields.

- [title] == Node: Title

☐ Trim this field to a maximum length

If checked, this field be trimmed to a maximum length in characters.

☐ Strip HTML tags

If checked, all HTML tags will be stripped.

Empty text

If the field is empty, display this text instead.

☐ Count the number 0 as empty

If the field contains the number zero, display the empty text instead

☐ Hide if empty

Do not display anything for this field if it is empty. Note that the field label may still be displayed. Check style or row style settings to hide labels for empty fields.

☑ Link this field to its node

This will override any other link you have set.

Update | Cancel | Remove

Figure 11-23. *Configuring the field's attributes*

In most cases, you can leave the default values alone and proceed to the next field. The one exception is that you'll likely want the title to be a field that is rendered as a link to the full-node version of that content item. On the form for configuring the title, check the "Link this field to its node" box. Click the Update button for each field until you reach the end of the list. Views then displays the Views configuration page.

There may be scenarios where you want the site visitor to have the ability to sort the data rendered in the view by clicking on the column titles. Clicking on a title will resort the list in ascending (or descending) order, based on the values contained in that column. To enable this feature and to specify which columns should be sortable, click on the gear icon that is to the right of the Style: Table item in the Style settings section of the Views configuration form. Clicking on the gear reveals a spreadsheet-like interface where we can specify which column is sortable by checking the box in the Sortable column. See Figure 11-24.

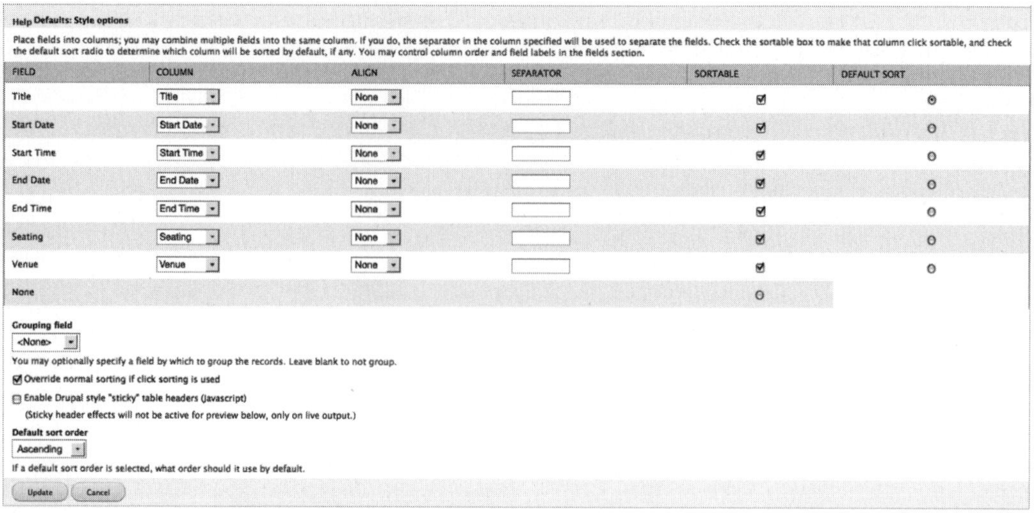

Figure 11-24. Setting sort options by column

We also have the ability to group values in our table by a specific column of information in the view. A good example might be that you want to group all of our Events by venue. Each venue would have its own separate table in the view as it is rendered on the page. A powerful and often overlooked feature!

After clicking the Update button after assigning sort options, make sure you click the Save button for your view.

You are now ready to test your view to see how it looks in table mode. To see the view, enter the URL you created for the page view in your browsers address bar, and click Enter.

Creating RSS Feeds with Views

Another "power" feature of views is the ability to generate RSS feeds from content stored on your site. RSS stands for Real Simple Syndication and is a mechanism that visitors can use to display content from your site in a newsreader like MyYahoo or iGoogle. Any view you create can also become an RSS feed by simply adding the Feed display in the left column of the views configuration form and clicking on the Add display button.

After clicking the Add display button click on the Feed link in the left column to reveal the configuration options for RSS feeds. See Figure 11-25.

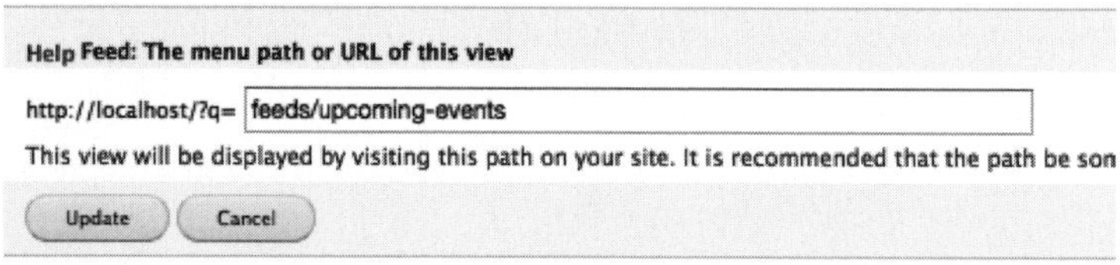

Figure 11-25. Configuring the RSS feed URL

A Feed has the same configuration options as a Page, and requires that you enter a path that a visitor can capture to import into their feed aggregator package. For our example upcoming events view, we'll create a new URL of `http://localhost/?q=feeds/upcoming-events`. We added "feeds" before "upcoming-events" just as a mechanism for organizing all of our feeds into a specific URL structure. The use of "feeds" is purely a personal preference. You can use any URL structure that you wish. After entering the URL, click on the Update button, and after the update, remember to click on the Save button to save all of your changes.

If you followed the example, you can now enter `http://localhost/feeds/upcoming-events` to see that Views generates a standard RSS feed that your users can now use to pull content from your site into their own site or into their RSS reader.

Summary

I've only scratched the surface of how you can use Views on your new site. Views is extremely powerful, and one of the "killer" modules for Drupal. There are also add-on modules for Views that we did not cover in this section. Please visit www.drupal.org/project/modules and click on the Views link in the categories listed in the right column. At the time of writing, there are 299 contributed modules just for Views! Browse through the list (remembering to look to see if there is a Drupal 7 version of the modules you may be interested in). People have created many amazing capabilities for Views.
As part of the "holy trinity" of Drupal modules, Views is even more powerful when used in conjunction with panels. If you think Drupal is awesome, just wait until you see what you can do with Panels and Views!

CHAPTER 12

Panels

The third of the "holy trinity" of must-have Drupal modules is the Panels module. You may have noticed that, up to this point, our page layouts have been constrained to the regions that were defined by the developer of the theme we are using. If you look at the Garland theme shown in Figure 12-1, there are three primary "containers" for elements on our site: the left sidebar, the right sidebar, and the center content area (I exclude the footer and header from this list because you would typically not put dynamic content in either of those regions, although you could if you wanted to).

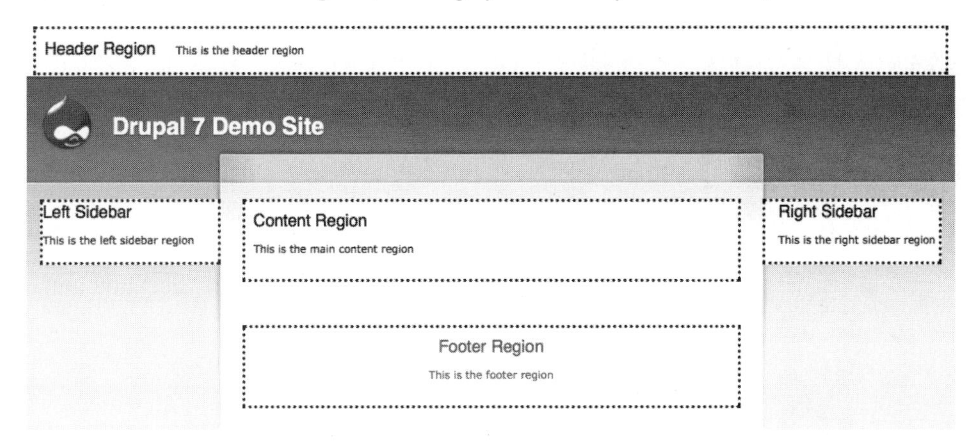

Figure 12-1. The five regions of the Garland theme

The primary container that is used in such a theme is the center content region, which is more or less just a box. Although this layout may work perfectly for every page of your site, there are likely cases where you'll want to divide the content region into multiple "mini-regions." As examples of this, I'll show you two different I've developed, both of which rely heavily on the Panels module.

The first example (see Illustration 12-1) has seven separate "panel panes" (the official name of "mini-regions") divided into six separate "rows":

- The top row has one panel pane that contains the navigation tabs for books, movies, and music.

- The second row has one panel pane for the carousel of items called "Featured Picks."
- The third row has two panel panes, the one of the left is titled "Featured" and shows a featured item from the library, and the one on the right shows a featured story.
- The fourth row is a rotating news banner.
- The fifth row displays another carousel, this time of featured items that are recommended by library staff.
- The sixth row shows a language selection option.

Illustration 12-1. A site using a complex panels layout

The second example (see Illustration 12-2) is less complex, representing a more typical use of panels to divide the content region into multiple panel panes.

Illustration 12-2. A simple two row, three column panels layout

On this page, the content region is divided into two rows, each row having three columns.

Both of these examples make it extremely easy for content authors to place content in a specific panel pane. When creating the site I used Views for each panel pane to define what content should be rendered, how many items should be included in the list, and how those items should be rendered. Using Taxonomy, content authors select the appropriate taxonomy term that is associated with each panel pane, and the content automatically appears in the right spot on the right page. Simply by the author creating a content item and selecting a taxonomy term from a list. I will cover more on putting a solution like this together in a few moments.

Available Layouts

The Panels module provides eight standard layouts and one "flexible" layout for you to use to divide up your content area. Figure 12-3 shows the layouts provided by each option.

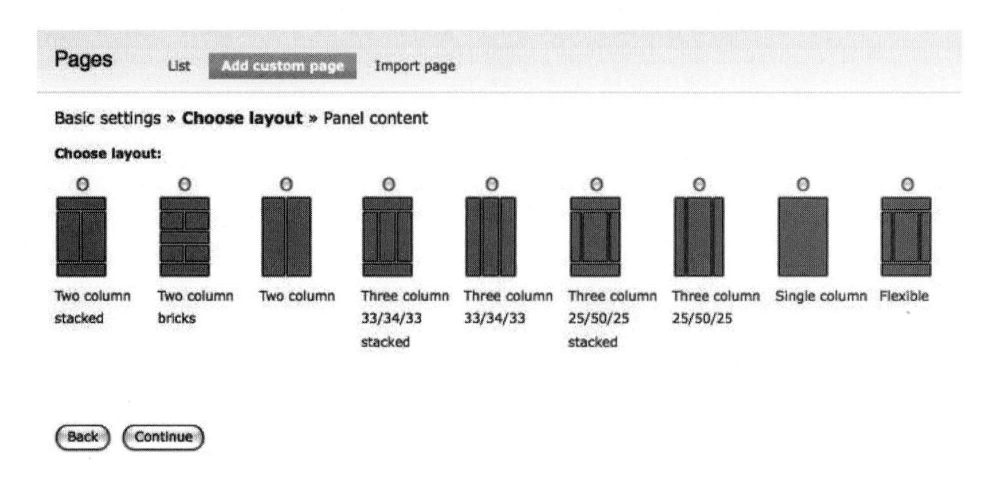

Figure 12-2. Panel layouts

The first eight options are "pre-built" layouts, while the "flexible" option provides the ability create your own layout. I will walk you through examples of using a pre-built and a flexible layout in this chapter.

Is It a Page, a Page, or Is It a Page?

Before creating our first panel page, we need to address an unfortunate case of confusing terminology. Drupal provides a basic, out-of-the-box content type called a Page. You use this content type to create a new page. In the Panels module, you create a page, albeit a panel page. To make it even more confusing, you can assign page content, created using the Page content type to a page built through the Panels module. Confused yet? To minimize the confusion, I will always call pages created through the Panels module "panel pages." I'll call content created using the page content type a "node."

Creating a Panel Page

When creating a panel page, you need to decide what content is going to go on the page, as well as the layout for the page. You can use Figure 12-2 to figure out whether an "off-the-shelf" layout exists that meets your needs. If one of the eight basic layouts doesn't work, you can always create a custom layout using the flexible option. For demonstration purposes, we're going to assume that we want to divide the content region into three rows, with the first row having a single column, the second row having two columns, and the last row having a single column. We could have just as easily picked one of the other layouts, but let's say our requirements called for the layout we just described.

■ **Note** At the time of writing, the Panels module was not ported to Drupal 7. Discussions with the primary developer of the Panels module revealed that the differences between the Drupal 6 and 7 versions of Panels would be minimal. Some of the operations that I describe in the remainder of this chapter may differ slightly from the actual implementation of Panels under Drupal 7. I suggest checking the Apress website and the pages associated with this book for any updates that occur after the book is published. I will provide updates to this chapter on the Apress website once Panels is available for Drupal 7.

To begin creating a new panel page, you must first install the Chaos Tools (`www.drupal.org/project/ctools`) and Panels modules (Panels is dependent on the Ctools module; you can download Panels from `www.drupal.org/project/panels`). To install the modules, follow the step-by-step instructions in Chapter 8. Installing Ctools and Panels is the same as installing any other contributed module in Drupal 7. Make sure that you enable the module after you have installed it. I suggest enabling all of the Panel's module components (Mini panels, Panel nodes, Panel pages), as you will likely use all three types of Panels as you build out your website.

Once the module is installed and ready to use, click on the Structure link on the top menu and click Panels on the Structure page. We will want to create a new custom panel, so select the option for creating a new panel page. The information that we well enter on this page (see Figure 12-3) includes:

- Administrative title: This title appears on the administrator's page that lists all of the panel pages that we have created. This title is not exposed to site visitors, only site administrators. For our example panel page, we'll use "about us panel page" as the administrative title.
- Machine name: This is the internal name that Drupal will use to reference this panel page. The name must be unique, be alphanumeric, and use underscores to separate words (no blank spaces are allowed). For our example panel page, we'll use "about_us_panel_page" as the machine name.
- Administrative description: This is a place to describe the form and its purpose. This description is only viewable by administrators. We'll enter a brief description about the purpose of the page: "This is the panel page that is used for the about us page."
- Path: This is the URL that a user would use to get to the panel page. The URL could also be part of a menu or a link on a page. We'll use "about-us" as the URL for accessing our new panel page.
- Variant type: We will be creating a panel.

- Optional features: Features that we can enable for our panel page include access control (restricting who can see the panel page), visible menu item (putting a link to the panel page on a menu), selection rules, and contexts. Selection rules and contexts are advanced topics that you can read more about at `http://drupal.org/project/panels`. For our demonstration, we will leave all of the optional items unchecked.

Pages
List
Add custom page
Import page
Administrative title:
about us panel page
The name of this page. This will appear in the administrative interface to easily identify it.
Machine name:
about_us_panel_page
The machine readable name of this page. It must be unique, and it must contain only alphanumeric characters and underscores. Once created, you will not be able to change this value!
Administrative description:
This is the panel page that is used for the about us page.
A description of what this page is, does or is for, for administrative use.
Path:
http://localhost/d6/ about-us
The URL path to get to this page. You may create named placeholders for variable parts of the path by using %name for required elements and !name for optional elements. For example: "node/%node/foo", "forum/%forum" or "dashboard/!input". These named placeholders can be turned into contexts on the arguments form.
Make this your site home page.
To set this panel as your home page you must create a unique path name with no % placeholders in the path. The site home page is currently set to /node on the Site Information configuration form.
Variant type:
Panel
Optional features:
Access control
Visible menu item
Selection rules
Contexts
Check any optional features you need to be presented with forms for configuring them. If you do not check them here you will still be able to utilize these features once the new page is created. If you are not sure, leave these unchecked.
Continue

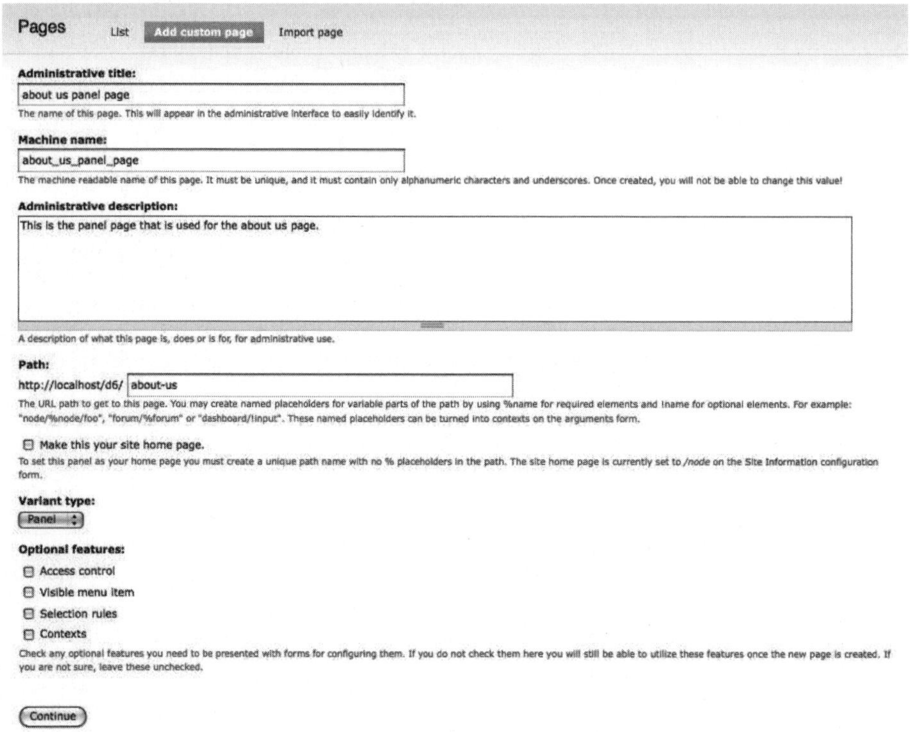

Figure 12-3. Creating a new panel page

After clicking the Continue button, you will be taken to the page shown in Figure 12-4, where you can select the layout that you want to use for your new page. For our example panel page, we'll use the first option, the "Two columns stacked" layout.

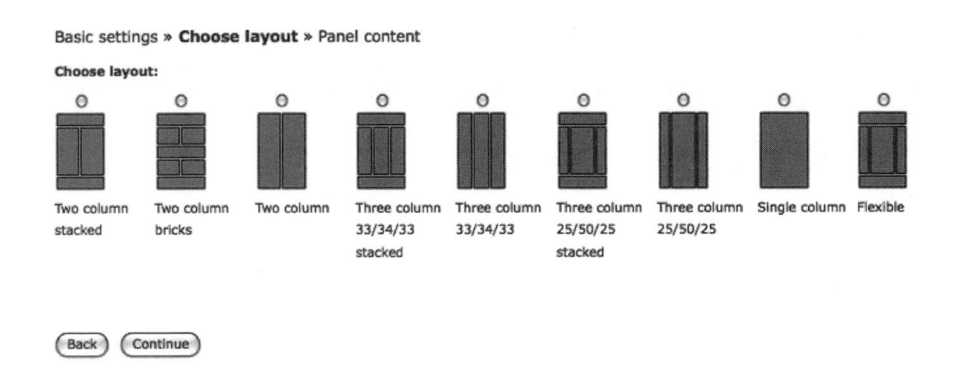

Figure 12-4. List of default panel layouts

After clicking the Continue button, you are taken to the page that you will use to assign "things" to the various panel panes on your new panel page. As you can see from Figure 12-5, you have a panel pane across the top, two columns below the top row, and a single panel pane across the entire panel page at the bottom. Before moving away from this page, click the Finish button to save your panel page, returning you to the main configuration page for this panel page (shown in Figure 12-5). Enter About Us in the title field and click the "Update and save" button.

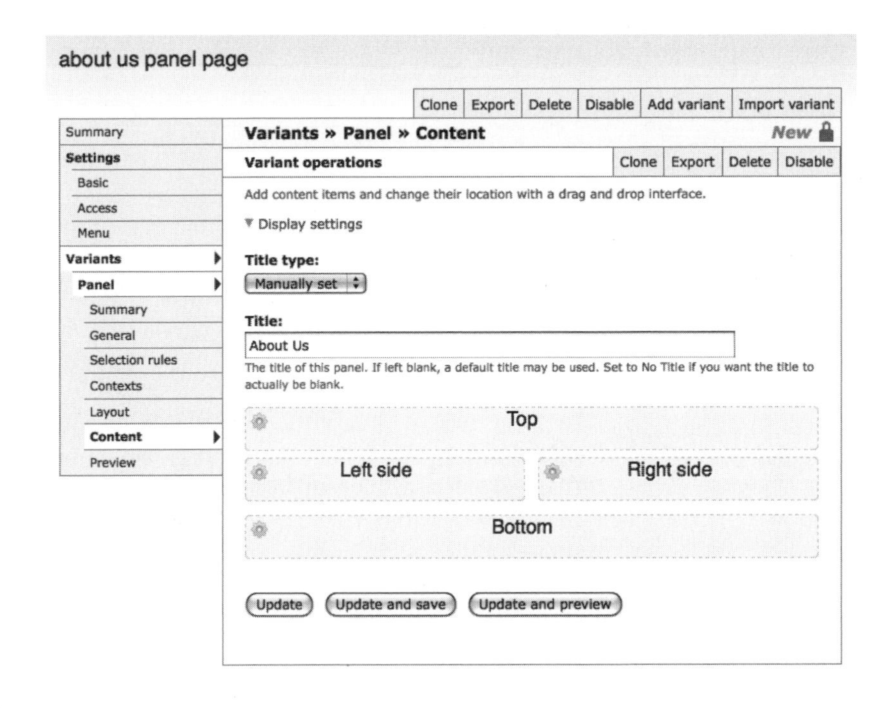

Figure 12-5. Panel page ready to assign content to panes on the page

For our first pass through this exercise, we will create a new node and assign pre-built components that ship with Drupal core into panel panes. To create a new node, either open a new browser window or a new browser tab and use this shortcut URL to get to the content creation form for a new page content type: http://localhost/node/add/page (replace "localhost" with the appropriate domain name if you are not using your desktop/laptop as your server). Enter the URL and click Enter. Add a title and body text, say a paragraph or two. Your new content should look something like Figure 12-6, only with your content and title.

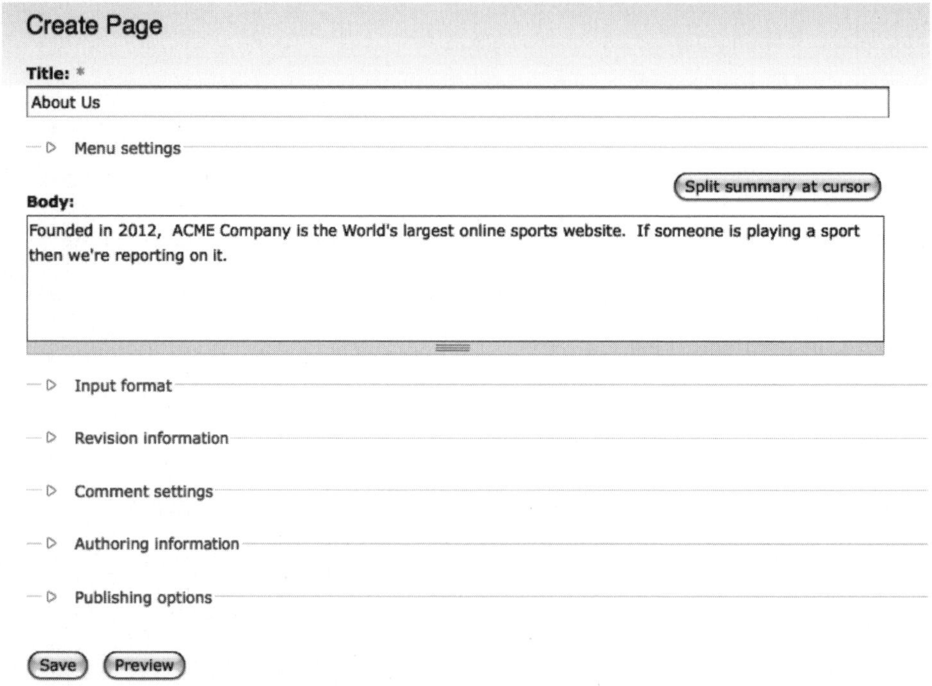

Create Page

Title: *

About Us

▷ Menu settings

Split summary at cursor

Body:

Founded in 2012, ACME Company is the World's largest online sports website. If someone is playing a sport then we're reporting on it.

▷ Input format

▷ Revision information

▷ Comment settings

▷ Authoring information

▷ Publishing options

Save Preview

Figure 12-6. Creating a node to assign to the panel page

Click the Save button to create your new node.

To begin the process of assigning "things" to each of the panel panes (Top, Left side, Right side, and Bottom), click on the gear icon at the left edge of the top panel pane. Clicking on the gear reveals a pop-up menu with an option to assign content and an option to change the style. We want to assign content, so click on the "Assign content" link (see Figure 12-7).

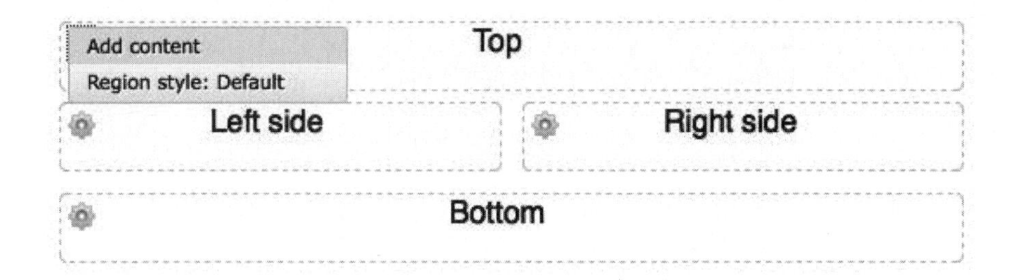

Figure 12-7. The "Add content" link appears after clicking the gear for a pane

Next you see the "Add content to Top page," where "Top" represents the pane that we clicked on to add content. See Figure 12-8.

Figure 12-8. Add Content Screen

Before adding anything to a pane, let's walk through the items that are available for you to assign to a pane. On the "Add content to Top" page (see Figure 12-9) you will see a menu of options in the left column. Click on the Activity link to reveal a list of items that you can assign to the pane.

Figure 12-9. Assigning activity components to a pane

The list of items includes recent comments posted on the site, a list of new users who were recently added to the site ("Who's new"), and a list of currently logged-in users ("Who's online"). If you've installed contributed modules, you may find additional items that are enabled through the additional modules.

Next, click on the Menus link in the left column. This reveals a list of all the menus that are present on the site. The two menus that you can assign to a pane are the Main menu and Secondary links.

Next, select the "Page elements" link in the left menu to reveal the following list of items:

- Breadcrumb is a list of links that represents how the user got to this page. For example, they may have clicked on "About us" on the home page, resulting in a breadcrumb that would just show "Home."
- Help displays the help text associated with an item on the page that provides context-sensitive help.
- Mission displays the mission statement for the organization as defined on the theme configuration option page.
- Page footer message is another item that is defined on the theme configuration options page.
- Page title displays the page title for this page.
- Site slogan is another item that is defined on the theme configuration options page.
- Status messages displays any messages that Drupal or a module generates to represent the results of an action (for example, your updates were successfully saved).
- Finally, tabs. There are various modules that provide a tabbed interface to access various pages on a form.

In most cases, all of these elements are exposed to the visitor through the theme instead of through a panel page. You should consult your theme definition to see if these elements are already included.

The next link in the left column is the Widgets category. Clicking on Widgets displays the following list of items:

- A powered-by-Drupal widget that displays "Powered by Drupal" and the Drupal icon.
- A syndicate widget that provides a site-wide RSS feed showing new content posted on your site.
- A user login widget that provides a form for users to log on to your site.

The links below the Widgets link provide the ability to insert an existing node or add new custom content. To insert the node that we created a few minutes ago, click on the "Existing node" link, revealing the page shown in Figure 12-10.

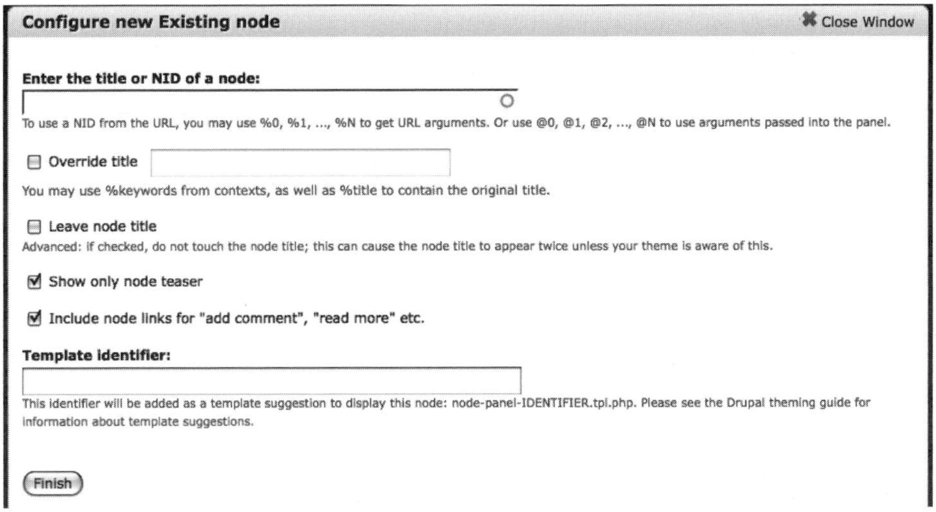

Figure 12-10. Add an existing node

To insert the node that we created earlier, enter the title or, if you don't remember the whole title, enter a word or two that reveals a drop-down list of all nodes with those words in the title. This is a great feature when you have hundreds of nodes to pick from. The example node we created had "About us" as the title, so go ahead and enter that in the "Enter the title or NID of a node" box. (If you know the node ID, you can enter that number instead of the title, but typically the title is the easiest method for assigning a node to a pane.) We'll leave the other options alone, as we don't want to override the title, we don't want to duplicate the node title, we only want to show the teaser, and we want to provide the ability to add a comment. When you've entered the Node ID, you're ready to click the Save button, which brings you back to the main Panel Page configuration page. You'll note in Figure 12-11 that the node that we assigned in the previous step now shows up in the Top pane of the page.

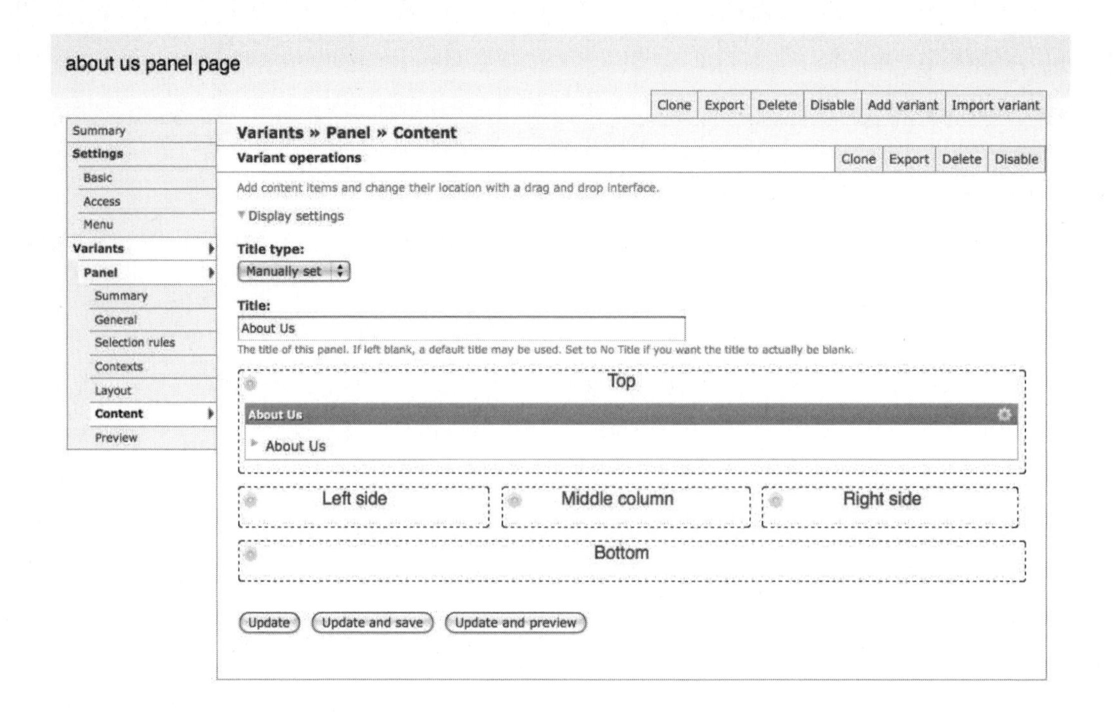

Figure 12-11. The About Us node is assigned to the Top pane of the page

To demonstrate the layout, repeat the process above for the Left side, Right side, and Bottom panel panes. Click on the gear for the Left side pane, then click on the Activity link in the left column and select the "Who's new" item. Leave the title as is and click the Finish button. Do the same for the Right side, only this time select the "Who's online" item. Finally, do the same thing for the Bottom pane, and add the "Powered by Drupal" widget. After you've added your node to each of the other three panel panes, your page should look like Figure 12-12.

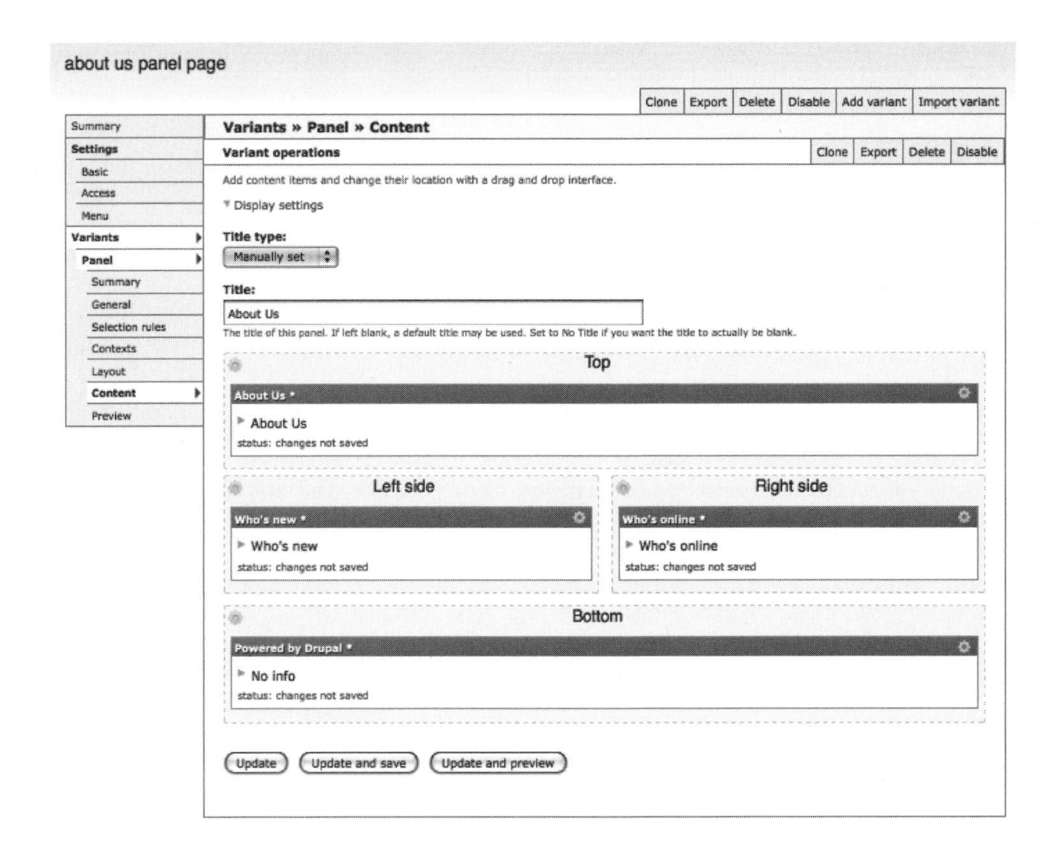

Figure 12-12. The About Us page with items added to each pane

We are now ready to save our panel page and test it. Click on the "Update and save" button to complete the configuration, which returns you to the main Panel Page configuration page. Once saved, we can now test the page. Visit the page at http://localhost/about-us (if you're not running the site on your desktop or laptop, then change "localhost" to the appropriate domain name). The final result should look something like Figure 12-13.

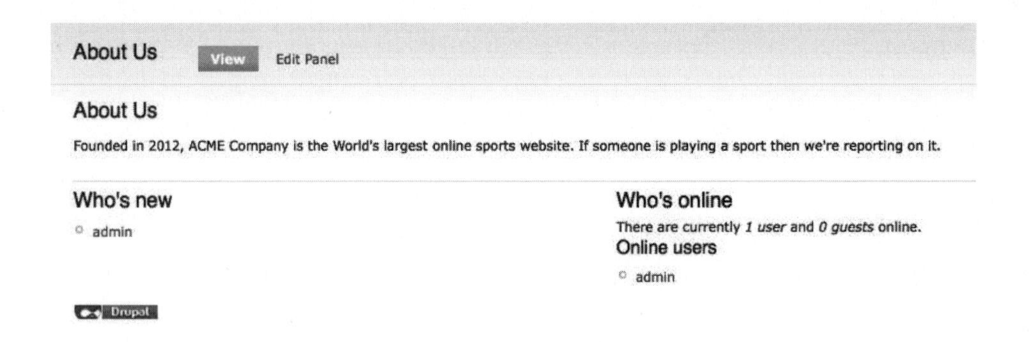

***Figure 12-13.** The completed panel page with content*

Congratulations, you just created your first panel page! The process that we just went through shows how simple it is to create amazing layouts without having to touch a single line of code, HTML, or CSS.

Modifying an Existing Panel Page

Things change, and it is likely that, at some point in the life of your website, you'll want to change the layout of a page, or the content that is on that page. For our example, let's say we decide that we need to

- Insert a second node in the top row under the existing About us node.
- Display the user login form, the "Who's online," and the "Who's new" widgets in the right, center, and left columns. Because we only have two columns, we're going to have to add a third one to meet the new requirements.

To begin the process, we'll click on the Edit Panel link at the top of our page (if you are not on the page that we want to change, enter the URL of the page in your browser's address bar), revealing the Panel Page configuration page, as shown in Figure 12-14.

Before adding the new elements to the page, we'll change the layout so we have a place to put the login form. To change the layout, click on the Layout link in the left column of the panel page configuration area. Clicking this link reveals the standard layout options provided by the Panels module (see Figure 12-4). Select the three column 33/34/33 stacked option. After clicking on the radio button for the new layout option, click on the Continue button at the bottom of the page. You are now presented with a page that asks you where in the new layout you want to move the content that was present in the previous layout.

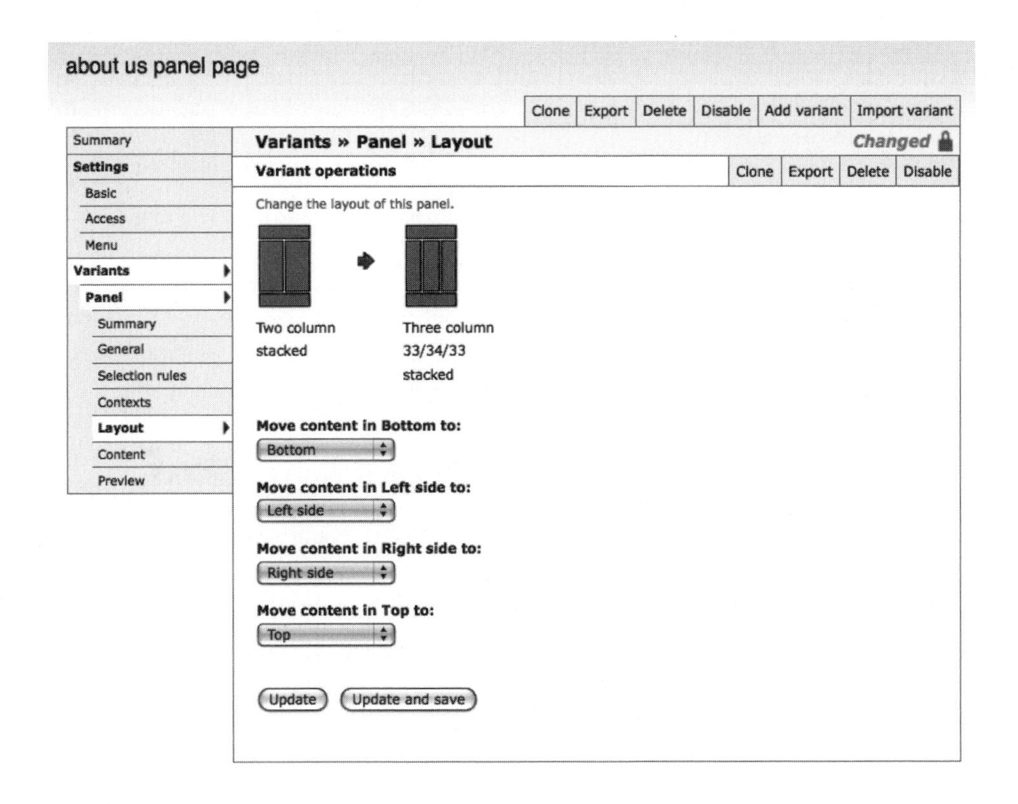

Figure 12-14. Moving content from the old layout to the new

In our example, we'll leave the content that was in the top panel. We'll move the "Who's new" item to the center column by grabbing the title bar of the "Who's new" block and dragging it and dropping it on the center column. The next step is to add the User login component to the left column. Follow the same process that you used in the previous example to add elements to the panel. The User login component is under the Widgets menu item. After adding the widget, it's a good idea to click the "Update and save" button.

The last step in our updates is to add a second node to the top pane. Let's see if you were paying attention in the previous steps. Create a new node and assign it to the top area and arrange it so that it appears under the top item. A good example that you could use is the Company's contact information (e.g., address, phone, fax). After adding the node, don't forget to click the "Update and save" button. The resulting screen should look something like Figure 12-15.

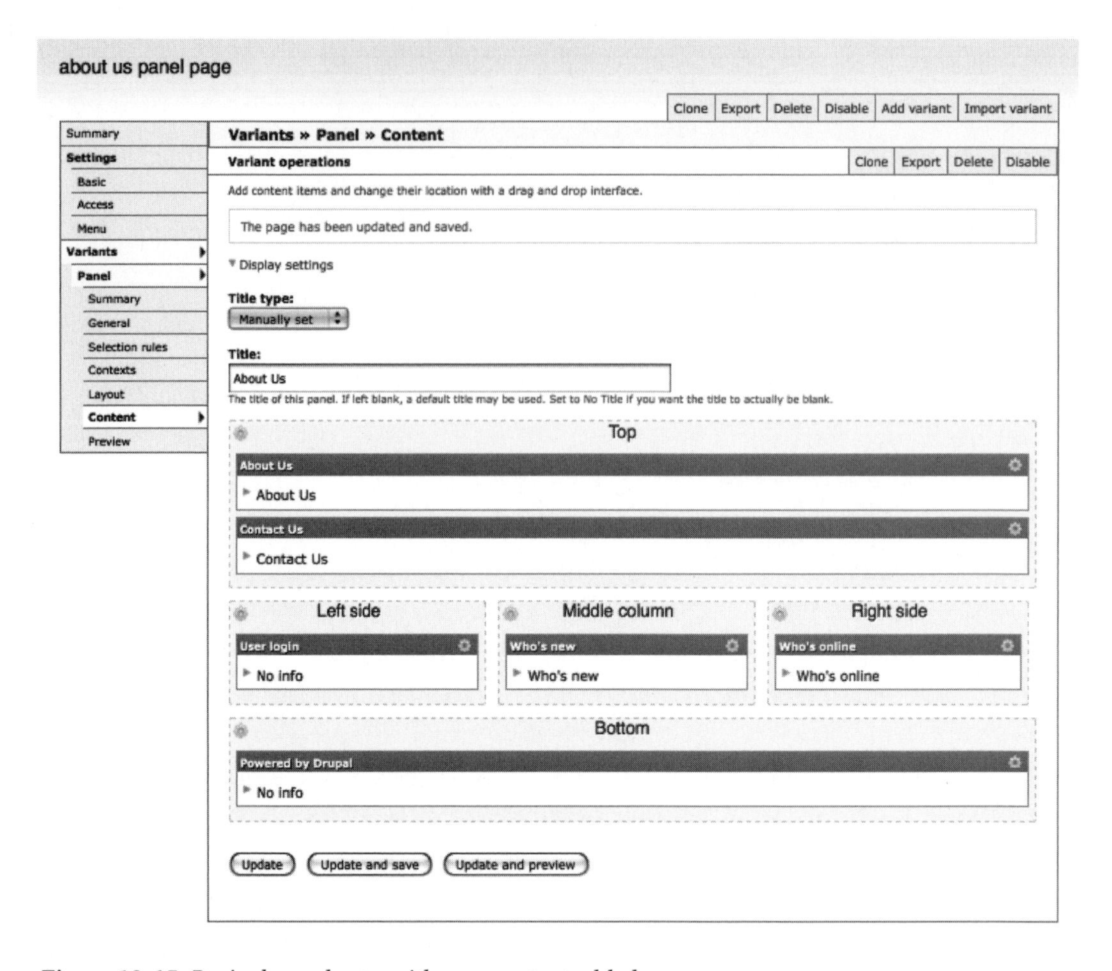

Figure 12-15. Revised panel page with new content added

Clicking "Update and save" takes us back to the Panel Page configuration page, with the Login widget now shown in the right column.

Repeat this process (clicking on the gear icon for the right-side panel pane and clicking the add content link), this time selecting Activity from the left menu instead of Widgets, and select first the "Who's online" item. When that item is added to the right column, repeat the steps for the "Who's new" item.

Before proceeding, click the Update button as a safety measure before proceeding to the process for adding a second node to the top panel pane. We're now ready to add the second node. First create a new node to insert in the top area by either opening a new window or a new tab in your browser and, in the address bar, entering the following URL to get to the Node add form for the Page content type: http://localhost/node/add/page (if you are hosting your Drupal site, you will need to replace "localhost" with the appropriate domain name). On the Page creation form, enter a title and body text. When complete, click the Save button, remembering the title you used for the new node. You can now click the gear icon for the top panel pane and the "Add content" link.

SelectClick the "Existing node" link and then enter either the node ID of the node you just created or the title of the node in the top text box. In Figure 12-16, you can see that entering the first word from the node's title reveals a drop-down list of all nodes with that word in the title. You can select the node from the list by clicking on it. Once selected, you can then skip the other options and click the Finish button.

Configure new Existing node
Close Window

Enter the title or NID of a node:
Welcome to the About Us Page
To use a NID from the URL, you may use %0, %1, ..., %N to get URL arguments. Or use @0, @1, @2, ..., @N to use arguments passed into the panel.

Override title
You may use %keywords from contexts, as well as %title to contain the original title.

Leave node title
Advanced: if checked, do not touch the node title; this can cause the node title to appear twice unless your theme is aware of this.

Show only node teaser

Include node links for "add comment", "read more" etc.

Template identifier:
This identifier will be added as a template suggestion to display this node: node-panel-IDENTIFIER.tpl.php. Please see the Drupal theming guide for information about template suggestions.

Finish

Figure 12-16. *Adding an existing node to a panel pane*

You will be returned to the Panel Page configuration screen, which now shows your second article in the top panel pane, below the previously submitted node.

We have completed the changes that we set out to accomplish, so you can once again click the Update button. Finally, click the Save button at the bottom of the page to complete the updates.

If you return to the About Us page (http://localhost/about-us), you will see results of our changes reflected on the page. See Figure 12-17.

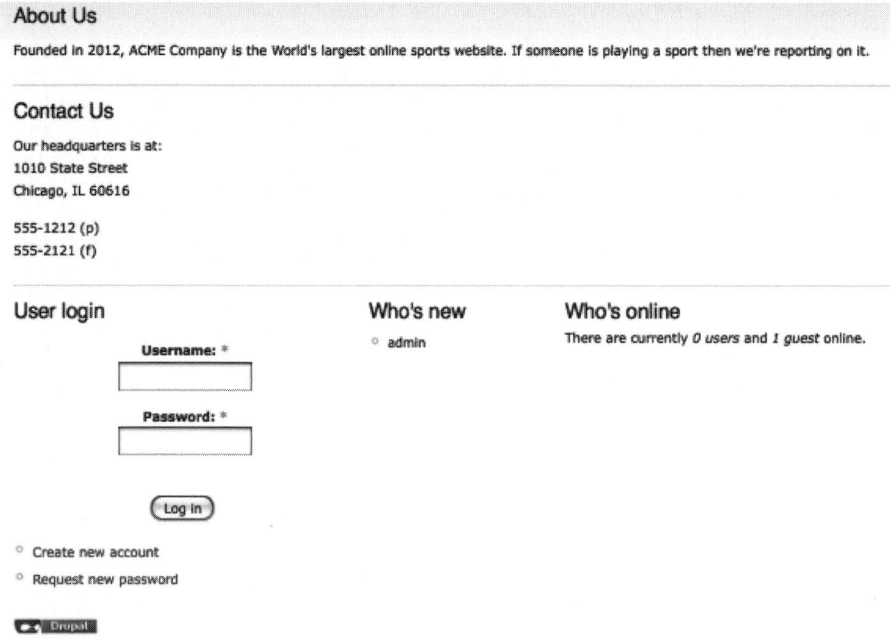

About Us

Founded in 2012, ACME Company is the World's largest online sports website. If someone is playing a sport then we're reporting on it.

Contact Us

Our headquarters is at:
1010 State Street
Chicago, IL 60616

555-1212 (p)
555-2121 (f)

User login

Username: *

Password: *

Log in

- Create new account
- Request new password

Who's new

- admin

Who's online

There are currently *0 users* and *1 guest* online.

Drupal

Figure 12-17. *The revised About Us page*

Note To see the User login form in the left column, you will need to log out. The Login form only displays when you are logged out of the site.

Using the Flexible Layout Option

There may be situations where one of the eight pre-defined layouts available in the Panels module do not meet the layout needs of a particular page. In these situations, you can use the flexible layout option, which provides the ability to create virtually any layout you can imagine. To create a new flexible layout page, follow the steps outlined in the previous section for creating a new panel page (click on the Structure link in the top menu, followed by Panels on the Structure link, and the Add link on the Panels page). Fill out the main panel creation form as we did previously using "Products and services" as the administrative title, "products_and_services" as the Machine name, and "products-and-services" as the URL of the page. Click the continue button revealing the panels layout page. See Figure 12-18.

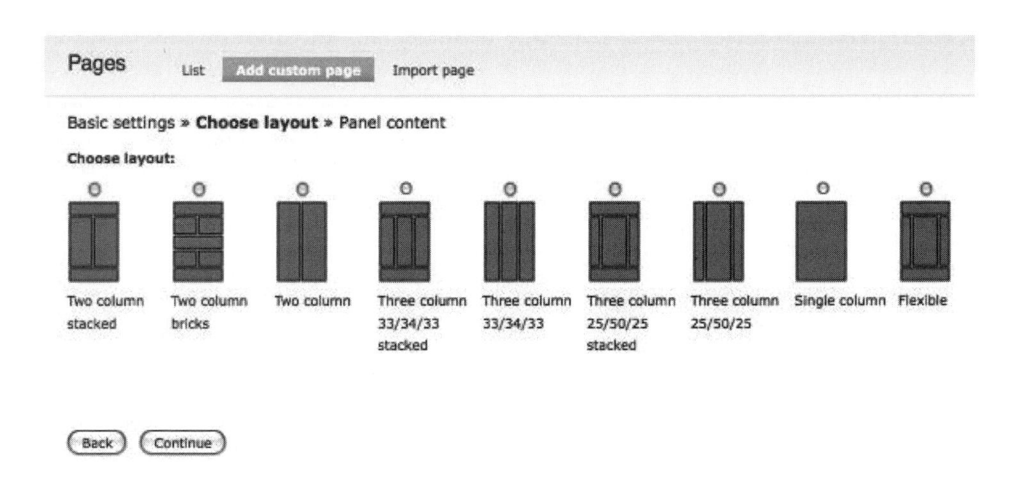

Figure 12-18. Panel page layout options

In the figure, you can see the flexible layout listed as the last option. This option provides you with essentially a blank canvas on which you can "draw" the rows and columns you need on your layout. Clicking Flexible followed by the Continue button brings you to the Flexible Layout configuration page. See Figure 12-19.

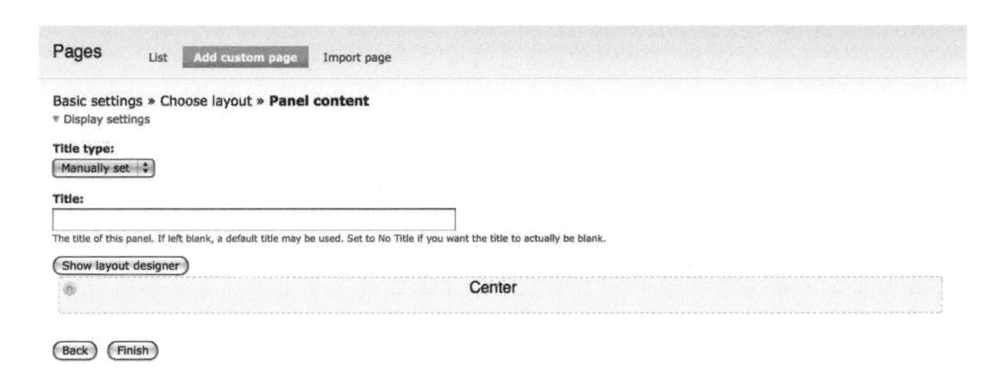

Figure 12-19. Configuring a flexible panel layout

Right now the panel page has a single panel pane (named Center). To add new rows and columns, click on the "Show layout designer" button, revealing the layout designer page shown in Figure 12-20.

Pages List Add custom page Import page

Basic settings » Choose layout » **Panel content**

▾ Display settings

Title type:

Manually set

Title:

The title of this panel. If left blank, a default title may be used. Set to No Title if you want the title to actually be blank.

Hide layout designer

▾ Canvas

▾ Column

▾ Row

▾ Region

Center

Back Finish

Figure 12-20. Flexible panel layout designer

On this page, we can add new regions (for example, we could add a left and right region to the row where our Center region is), new rows, and new columns. If we wanted to add a new region to the left of the existing Center region, we would click on the Row link to expose a list of options. See Figure 12-21.

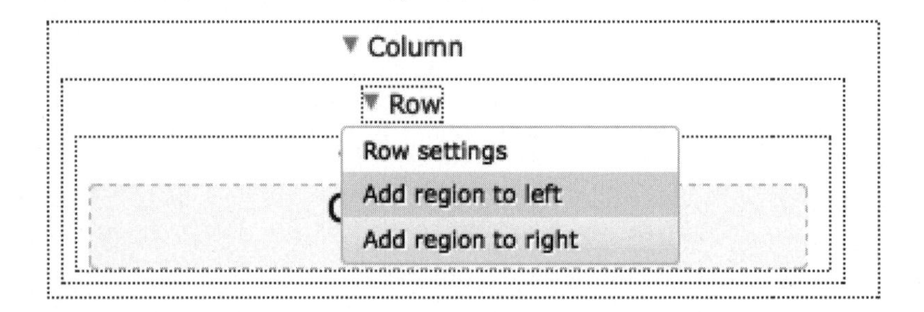

Figure 12-21. Adding a region to a row

The options allow us to add a new region to the left or the right of the existing region. Selecting a new region to the left reveals the configuration options for the new region. In Figure 12-22, the title was set to Left and the width was set to Fluid (the column width will expand or shrink based on the content in that column).

Add region to left

Region title: *

Width:

Fluid

Save

Figure 12-22. Configuring the new region

This results in a layout that now appears like that shown in Figure 12-23.

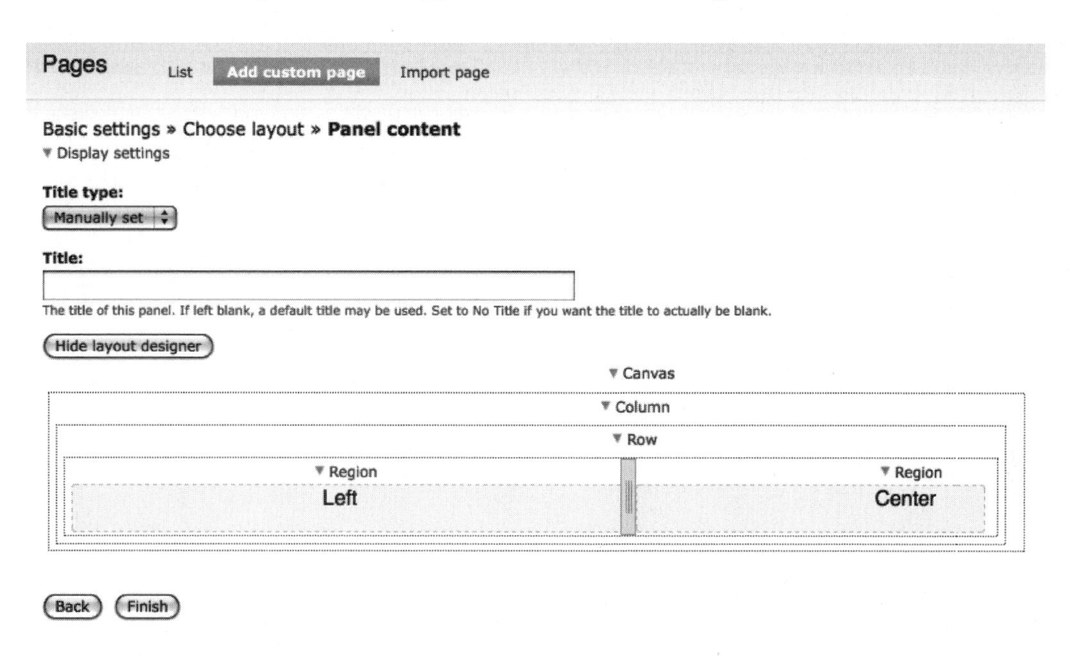

Figure 12-23. Panel configuration page with the new region added to the left

You could continue to add regions to this row, add new rows, and move things around on this form until you have a layout that matches your requirements. Once you have the layout set, click the "Hide layout designer" button to return to the page where you assign items to your various panel panes, just as we did with the stock layouts that we used in previous examples.

Adding Other Things to Panel Panes

There are virtually no limits to what you can assign to panel panes. A common assignment is to insert a view into a panel page. One of the features included in the Chaos Toolset module that we installed in a previous chapter is the ability to assign a view to a panel pane. Once installed and configured, views will appear on the page where you can select items to assign to a panel pane.

Other modules may provide components that you can insert into a panel pane, or you can create your own custom component for a specific panel pane using the "Custom content" option (under "Add existing node").

Summary

Panel pages are a "must have" feature for most websites. The Panels module is one of the contributed modules that will likely become one of your "always install this module before starting a new site" module.

You now have the knowledge required to embark on the journey of creating interesting and creative pages on your new website. With all those interesting pages, you are surely going to see a wave of site visitors. To prepare yourself for the onslaught of activity on your site, I'll take you through the common activities involved in managing your new site in the next chapter.

CHAPTER 13

■ ■ ■

Theming

One of the most significant challenges you are likely to encounter while building your new Drupal site is deciding on the visual design. Using Drupal, the general term that is associated with creating the look of your site is "theming." The concept applies to the overall visual design of your site, as well as to how an individual element on a page is displayed, such as a title. In this chapter I'll walk you through the process of taking an off-the-shelf Drupal theme and customizing the overall look, as well as the look for individual elements on a page. This is your chance to take the concepts covered in this book and apply them to your site, taking it from ho-hum to sizzle!

Picking the Starting Point

To get started, you can do any of the following:

Use an off-the-shelf theme from Drupal.org/project/themes. There are hundreds of free themes that you can download and use on your site. It's likely that you'll find a theme that either matches what you're looking for or is close enough that minor modifications will fulfill your specific requirements.

Use a starter theme from Drupal.org/project/themes. Starter themes are barebones templates that lack any graphical elements, but provide a basic non-graphical skeleton that you can expand on. Think of a start theme as a new house that has been framed and sheet rocked, all ready for you to pick the paint colors, flooring, cabinets, and fixtures.

Create your own theme from scratch. If you can't find a pre-built or starter theme that provides the look or structure that you want, you can build your theme from scratch.

For most beginning to intermediate Drupal developers, the easiest approach is to pick an existing theme and modify it to meet the specific requirements of the site you are building. For situations where you can't find a theme that is close to what you're trying to create, a starter theme may be the best approach. Starter themes provide all of the scaffolding and structure required to create a theme, without having to start from a blank sheet of paper. To start this chapter, I will take you through the steps of using a starter theme. Although slightly more complicated than using an off-the-shelf theme, the concepts you will learn in this chapter will be applicable to modifying an off-the-shelf theme.

A starter theme has all of the elements necessary to create a Drupal theme; it's just missing attributes like colors, fonts, and images. The starter theme that I have picked to demonstrate the theming process is Genesis. There are other Drupal starter themes that you can choose from, and each takes a slightly different approach. Two other popular starter themes are Zen and Fusion. Genesis happens to be my personal favorite, as it is based on a CSS-grid approach and the structure of the theme is easy to understand.

Looking At Starter Themes

There are several starter themes that you can select from. Each provide different capabilities and features. The top three starter themes that you'll find on Drupal.org are:

- Zen: The granddaddy of all starter themes. Zen provides a feature-rich base using a classic CSS tableless design approach.
- Fusion: A feature-rich starter theme that is based on the 960-grid system (a CSS library that makes laying out complex page designs significantly easier). Fusion also provides the ability to use the Skinr module.Genesis: My personal favorite, as it offers a simple structure that is easy to learn, yet powerful enough to develop complex themes.
- Genesis: My personal favorite, as it offers a simple structure that is easy to learn yet powerful enough to develop complex themes.

Before You Get Started

Before taking your first step, there are few things that you'll need to know about theming. Creating or updating a theme does require knowledge of HTML, CSS, and, to some extent, PHP. The complexity of what you are trying to accomplish will drive the depth and breadth of knowledge required to create the desired effects and capabilities in your theme. If you're new to HTML, CSS, or PHP, I suggest picking up *Getting StartED with CSS* by David Powers, *Beginning HTML with CSS and XHTML: Modern Guide and Reference* by David Schultz and Craig Cook, *PHP for Absolute Beginners* by Jason Lengstorf, and *Beginning PHP and MySQL: From Novice to Professional, Third Edition* by W.J. Gilmore. All are excellent references that provide the background knowledge necessary to succeed at Drupal theming.
In the following sections I'll assume that you have at least a basic understanding of HTML and CSS. If you don't, take a quick trip to the bookstore.

The Standard Drupal Theme Files

Drupal themes are composed of several files, all of which reside in a directory with the same name as the theme itself. You can find the Genesis directory in the /sites/all/themes directory of your Drupal installation.

■ **Note** Base themes that are shipped with Drupal 7 core reside in the themes directory at the root of your website. Contributed themes or custom themes that you develop from scratch should reside in the /sites/all/themes directory of your website. This ensures that upgrades to core Drupal do not wipe out your custom themes.

There are several files associated with a Drupal theme. Each file must conform to Drupal's naming and content standards. In the case of the Genesis theme, the key files that we'll be modifying are listed in Table 13-1.

Table 13-1. *Standard Drupal Files*

File	Description
<themename>.info	Every Drupal theme must have a .info file, and the file name must be the same as the name of the theme. For the Genesis theme, the file is named genesis.info. Within the info file, you will define attributes of your theme including the name of the theme (e.g., Genesis), version of Drupal core that the theme supports (e.g., 7.x), name and location for all the CSS files that are required by the theme, name and location of the JavaScript files used by the theme, and names of the regions that are used on the theme (see Chapters 6 and 7 for a description of how regions are used). The key element that we will focus on in this chapter is the list of regions.
page.tpl.php	Each Drupal theme must have a page.tpl.php file. The file contains a mixture of HTML and PHP code, and defines the overall layout and structure of a page on your website. This file also brings other key Drupal core components into your theme through a number of include files. If you look inside the file, you'll see that there are several instances of code that looks like the following: `<?php print $somevariable; ?>`

Continued

File	Description

	Where the value of $somevariable changes depending on where you are in the page.tpl.php file. For example you will find the
	`<?php print $styles; ?>`
	statement in the file. This line of code pulls all of the CSS files defined in the themes .info file into the page as it is rendered by Drupal. Other variables perform similar functions.
	In this chapter I will focus on how the regions defined in your .info file are incorporated and displayed on the site and how the CSS attributes are applied to those regions. An example of how regions are displayed is
	`<?php print render($page['footer']); ?>`
	This code takes the elements assigned to the footer region and renders them on the page at the point where this line of code appears.
	For an in-depth understanding of page.tpl.php file, please visit the theme guide on drupal.org/theme-guide.

node.tpl.php	This file is composed of a combination of HTML and PHP snippets. The contents of the file define how nodes are laid out when displayed on your site; for example, the placement of the title, the author information, the taxonomy terms, the body, and pictures included with the node. In this chapter I will show you how to define the layout for a node.
style.css	All of your sites' CSS markup should be stored in one or more CSS files in your theme directory. A typical Drupal theme will have at minimum a style.css file. You may choose to call the file something else, and you can have multiple CSS files if you wish (e.g., you might want to put CSS overrides for Internet Explorer in its own CSS file).

There may be other optional files in your theme's directory. Examples include theme files (often referred to as .tpl files) for individual components (such as a block). In this chapter I will focus on the core files listed in the table.

Configuring the Genesis Theme

If you haven't done so already, follow the instructions in Chapter 6 and install the Genesis theme (www.drupal.org/project/genesis). You'll notice that the installation process creates two versions of it: Genesis base and Genesis subtheme. A majority of Drupal starter themes use subthemes as the mechanism for creating a new theme based on the foundation provided by the base theme. This allows you to create one or several new themes using the same underlying foundation without having to start from scratch each time you want to create a new theme. I will follow the Drupal standard approach in this chapter, using the off-the-shelf subtheme that is created by during the Genesis installation process. To create a custom subtheme using the Genesis starter theme, you must follow these steps:

1. Copy the genesis_SUBTHEME directory in the /sites/all/themes/genesis directory to your /sites/all/themes directory.
2. Rename the copied directory to genesis_mytheme (I'll use "mytheme" as the name of the new theme that I am creating).
3. In the /sites/all/themes/mytheme directory, rename the genesis_SUBTHEME.info file to genesis_mytheme.info. The .info file must be named the same as the directory in which it resides.
4. Edit the genesis_mytheme.info file and change the following values:
    a. Change the value of name from Genesis SUBTHEME to Genesis mytheme;
    b. Change the description of the theme to My Genesis Subtheme.
5. Edit the template.php file. Using search and replace, change every occurrence of genesis_SUBTHEME to genesis_mytheme.
6. Copy the following files from the /sites/all/themes/genesis/templates directory to your /sites/all/themes/genesis_mytheme directory:
    a. page.tpl.php
    b. node.tpl.php
    c. block.tpl.php
    d. field.tpl.php
    e. region.tpl.php
    f. comment.tpl.php
    g. html.tpl.php

The next step in the process is to enable the Genesis base theme as well as your new Genesis subtheme. Click on the Appearance link in the top menu and scroll down to the "disabled themes" section. You should see three versions of the Genesis theme: base, the off-the-shelf subtheme, and your new derivative of the subtheme named mytheme. Click on the "Enable and set default" link for your new subtheme and return to the home page of your site. Your site should look something close to Figure 13-1.

Skip to main content
genesis
My Drupal 7 Test Site
Search
Management
Add new content
Dashboard
Welcome to My Drupal 7 Test Site
No front page content has been created yet.
Add new content
Secondary menu
Home
Powered by Drupal
Secondary menu
admin
Log out

Figure 13-1. The standard Genesis theme

The Genesis theme is pretty stark in its out-of-the-box state, but that's a positive aspect of using a starter theme. You have the opportunity to create a theme that displays your site exactly how you want, without trying to make an off-the-shelf theme behave the way you want it to. Next I will show you how to use the Genesis starter theme to create a site that looks like Figure 13-2.

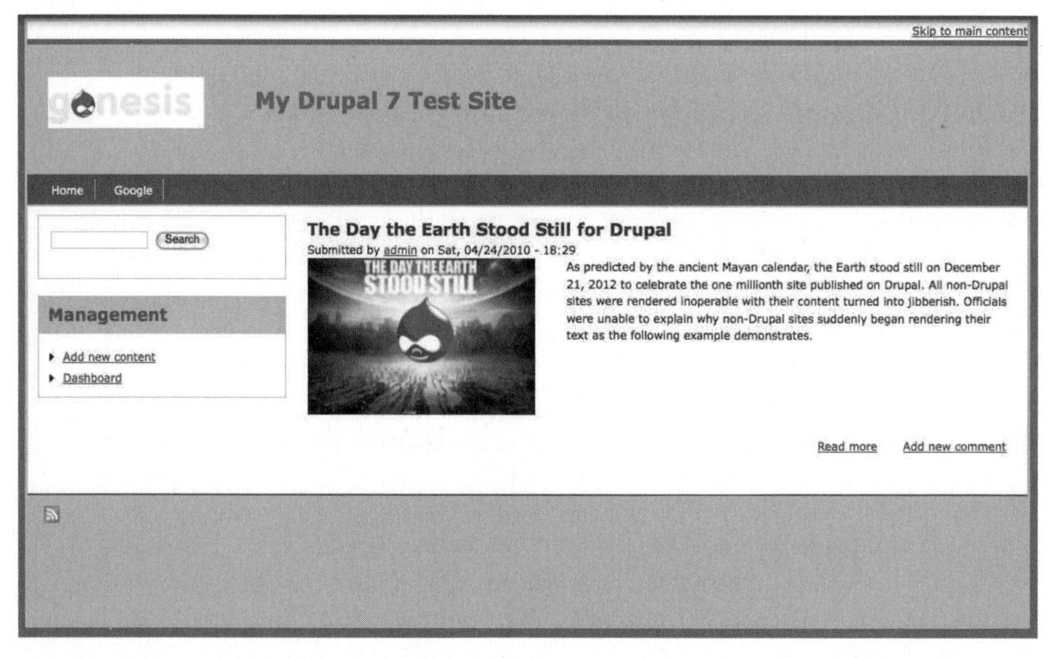
Skip to main content
genesis
My Drupal 7 Test Site
Home
Google
Search
Management
Add new content
Dashboard
The Day the Earth Stood Still for Drupal
Submitted by admin on Sat, 04/24/2010 - 18:29
THE DAY THE EARTH STOOD STILL
As predicted by the ancient Mayan calendar, the Earth stood still on December 21, 2012 to celebrate the one millionth site published on Drupal. All non-Drupal sites were rendered inoperable with their content turned into jibberish. Officials were unable to explain why non-Drupal sites suddenly began rendering their text as the following example demonstrates.
Read more
Add new comment

Figure 13-2. A sample site using the updated theme

Modifying the Base Theme

Before starting the modification process, it's important to understand the basic structure of the starter theme. The first thing that I look at when modifying a theme is the list of regions defined by the starter theme. In the case of Genesis, I open and look at the genesis_mytheme.info file, which can be found in the /sites/all/themes/genesis_mytheme directory. The starter theme defines the following 12 regions:

- Page top
- Leaderboard
- Header
- Help
- Secondary content
- Highlighted content
- Content
- First sidebar
- Second sidebar
- Tertiary content
- Footer
- Page bottom

Figure 13-3 shows the positioning of the standard regions.

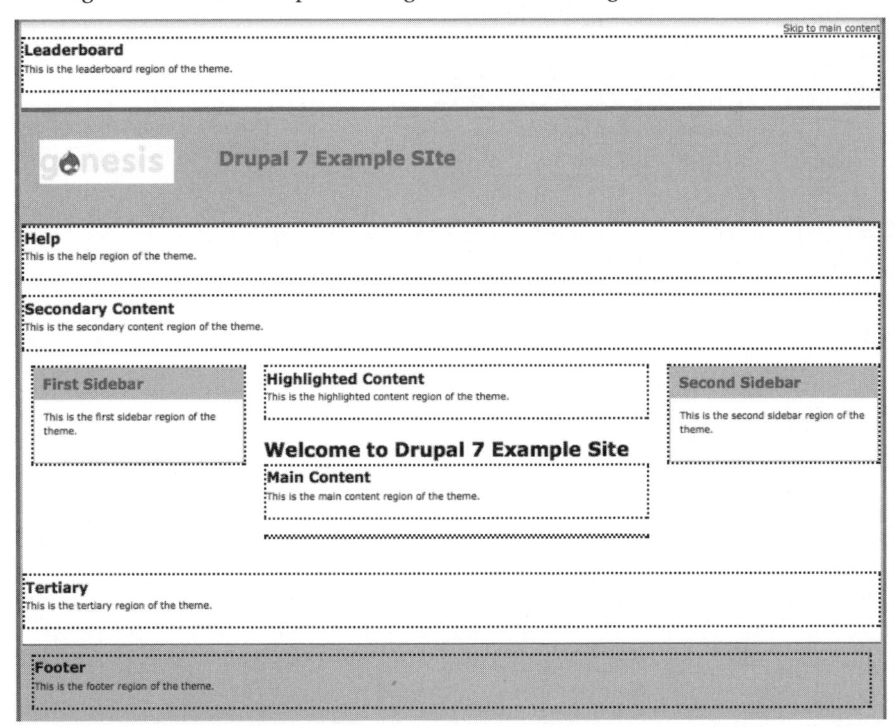

Figure 13-3. Position of the standard Genesis regions on a sample page

One of the reasons that I like the Genesis theme is it provides several powerful features that are simple to use, including the ability to pick the layout of your new site. Genesis provides nine basic layout options in three categories, as shown in Figure 13-4.

genesis-1 Standard 3 column

20em genesis-1a 20em
24.25% genesis-1b 24.25%
240px genesis-1c 240px

genesis-2 Both sidebars on the right

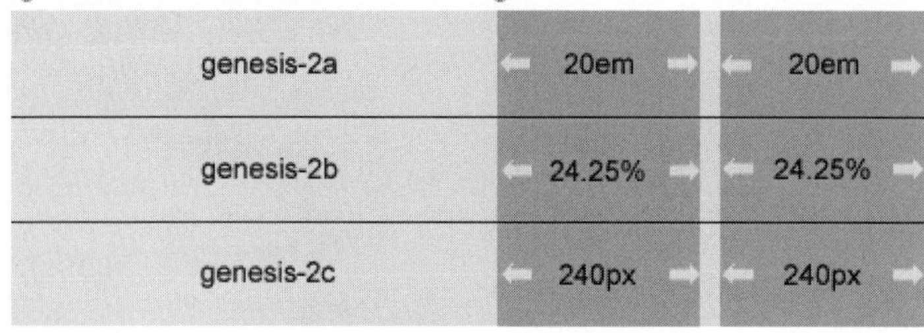

genesis-3 Both sidebars on the left

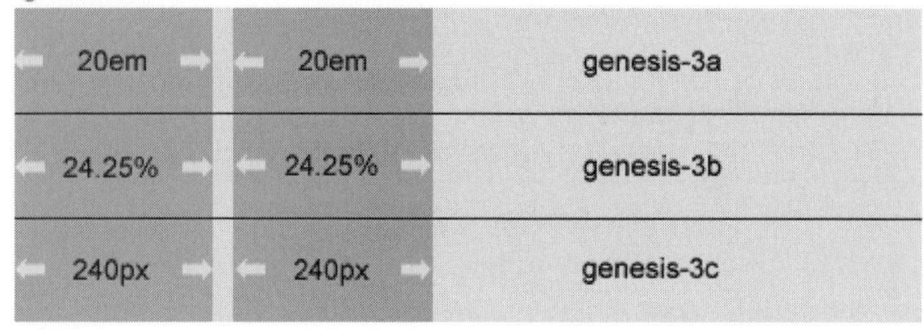

Figure 13-4. *Standard Genesis layout options*

I'll choose the genesis-1c layout. It is a standard three-column layout using fixed-width sidebars. Depending on the requirements for your site, you could select another layout option.

To set the desired layout, I'll edit the html.tpl.php file in the /sites/all/themes/genesis_mytheme directory. In the html.tpl.php file I'll change the CSS ID assigned to the body tag from 1a to 1c, as shown here:

```
<body id="genesis-1c" <?php print $attributes;?>>
```

The next step is to set the width of your theme. By default, Genesis is set to display as a fluid width-based theme, meaning the theme will stretch to the width of the visitor's browser. For demonstration purposes, I'll change the default width from 100% to a fixed width of 960px by updating the page.css file, which is located in the /sites/all/themes/genesis_mytheme/css directory. There are two CSS IDs that you will need to change: one for IE6 and the other for all other browsers. Find the #container CSS ID in the page.css file and change the two definitions to match the following, by changing 100% to 960px:

```
#container {
 width: 960px;      /* Width for IE6 */
}

body > #container {
  width: 960px;      /* Width for all other browsers */
  min-width: 760px; /* set a minimum width */
/*max-width: 960px;    set a maximum width */
}
```

After changing the values, save the file and press refresh on the home page of your site. If your monitor supports a resolution of at least 1024x768, maximize your browser window and you will see the affect of setting the site to a fixed width of 960px. There will now be white space on either side of the main section of your website.

Next I'll jazz up the theme by adding color. I'll create a theme that is based on a green color scheme. One of my favorite tools for creating color schemes is found at http://colorschemedesigner.com/. I used the tool provided on that site to generate a green-based color scheme, and will use these colors:

Primary background color: #528544

Secondary color: #287314

Tertiary color: #9CD88C

I'll set the main body background color to the primary background color, and the main section of the site to white by adding the background color definition to the following CSS elements found in the page.css file:

```
body {
  padding: 0 10px;
  background-color: #528544;
}

#container {
  width: 960px;      /* Width for IE6 */
  background-color: #ffffff;
}
```

After adding the values, save the file and return to your sites home page, clicking the browsers refresh button to reload the CSS file. The updates should have changed the colors on either side of the main section of your website to green, with the main section of your site having a white background.

The next change is to make the header of the site stand out from the rest of the site. I'll add four attributes to the #header CSS definition in the page.css file. I'll add a background color, borders at the top and bottom, and set the height of the header to 120px. After updating the #header definition, you should have something like the following:

```
#header {
   background-color: #9CD88C;
   border-top: 6px solid #528544;
   border-bottom: 3px solid #287314;
   height: 120px;
}
```

After updating and saving the file, reload the homepage of your website to see the effects of the changes you've made.

Next I'll fix the logo and the site title so it renders properly in the header region. I'll first add the following attributes to the #logo CSS id in the page.css file:

```
#logo {
  position: relative;
  float: left;
  margin-left: 20px;
  margin-right: 50px;
  margin-top: 30px;
}
```

Next I'll add the position, float, and margin top attributes as shown here to #site-name CSS id in the page.css file:

```
#site-name {
  font-weight: bold; /* Bold or else the line heights vary. */
  font-size: 2em;
  line-height: 1.5;
  position: relative;
  float: left;
  margin-top: 35px;
}
```

Next I'll change how the site title is displayed. Instead of displaying the title as a hypertext link (underlined and blue), I'll remove the underline and change the text color. In the page.css file, search for the #site-name a:link and #site-name a:visited CSS IDs and add the text-decoration and color attributes as shown here:

```
#site-name a:link    {
   text-decoration: none;
   color: #528544;
}

#site-name a:visited {
   text-decoration: none;
   color: #528544;
}
```

After updating the #logo, #site-name CSS IDs, save the page.css file and press the browser refresh button while on the home page of your website. The revised header layout should now look like Figure 13-5.

***Figure 13-5.** The revised header layout after CSS changes*

Creating a Horizontal Menu

The next requirement for our new theme is to create a horizontal menu that appears below the header. The first step in this process is to add a new region to the theme. To add a new region, edit the genesis_mytheme.info file and add the following line to the end of the list of regions contained within that file:

```
regions[main_menu_links]     = Main Menu Links
```

This code instructs Drupal to include a new region with an internal name of main_menu_links to the list of available regions. The value to the right of the equal sign is the value that will appear in the block configuration page, which we will see in a moment.

The next step is to update the page.tpl.file, where I will add the code that instructs Drupal where to display the main_menu_links region. The code that we need to add includes checking to see whether anything is assigned to the main_menu_links region before attempting to display it on the page. If the region is empty, we don't want Drupal to display it. The second block of code is to instruct Drupal to display the contents of the region. I'll insert the following code right under the "</div><!—header -->" line of code in the page.tpl.php file:

```
<?php if ($page['main_menu_links']): ?>
  <div id="main-menu-wrapper" class="clearfix">
    <div class="main-menu-inner"><?php print render($page['main_menu_links']); ?></div>
  </div>
<?php  endif; ?>
```

The first line of code listed here checks to see if there is anything assigned to the region. If there is something assigned to the region, the next line defines a DIV structure to render the region, in this case a DIV with an ID of main-menu-wrapper. The next line of code declares another DIV structure (main-menu-inner) and uses PHP's Print function to render the contents of the main_menu_links region on the page. The next line closes out the DIV main-menu-wrapper DIV structure, and the last line ends the conditional statement that checks to see whether there is anything assigned to the region. You can use this same approach to create new regions in your theme that are outside of what is provided by the base theme that you began with.

The next step is to update the page.css file with the CSS attributes required to render our new horizontal menu correctly. I'll update the main-menu-wrapper CSS definition in the page.css file by removing the margin attributes that were set in the off-the-shelf version of the page.css file, and adding background-color, border-bottom, and height attributes. The resulting definition should look like the following:

```
#main-menu-wrapper {
  background-color:#287314;
  border-bottom:2px solid #9CD88C;
  height:25px;
}
```

The next step is to add a CSS definition for the main-menu-inner class directly below the main-menu-wrapper. The definition that I created is as follows:

```
.main-menu-inner {
  position: relative;
  float: left;
  height: 25px;
}
```

The next step is to define how the menu items will appear on the menu. Because Drupal menus are rendered vertically as HTML unordered lists, I'll first force the menu items to render horizontally by setting the CSS display attribute to inline. I'll then remove the standard bullet point that is displayed for lists by setting the list-style attribute for the menu items to None, and then to make each menu item stand out I'll add a border to the right of each item and change the padding to offset the borders a bit to the left, right, and bottom. To make those changes, edit the page.css file and add the following CSS class definition:

```
.main-menu-inner ul.menu li {
  display: inline;
  list-style: none;
  border-right: 1px solid #9CD88C;
  padding-right: 10px;
  padding-left: 10px;
  padding-bottom: 3px;
```

For those of you who are new to CSS, this definition applies formatting only to content within HTML LI tags that are contained within the unordered list (ul) with a class definition of menu, within the main-menu-inner DIV tags.

The next step is to clean up the text displayed for each menu item. I'll change the text color to white, and I'll remove the standard underline for HTML links.

```
.main-menu-inner ul.menu li a {
  color: #ffffff;
  text-decoration: none;
}
```

Next I'll add a CSS definition so that when visitors hover over the menu item the text color will change to black, indicating they're hovering over the item. The CSS required to enable this capability is as follows:

```
.main-menu-inner ul.menu li a:hover {
  color: #000;
}
```

The horizontal menu is now set up and ready to enable.

Drupal caches all of the regions defined in the template, meaning changes to your .info file aren't picked up until Drupal refreshes the sites cache. I need to manually reset the cache so that Drupal will recognize the new region I added for the horizontal menu. To do this, click on the Configuration link in the menu at the top of the page. On the Configuration page, click on the Performance link. On the Performance page, click on the "Clear all caches" button. Drupal will now recognize your new region.

The next step in the process is to reassign the Secondary menu from its current position on the page to the new region we created in the previous steps. Click on the Structure link at the top of the page, and on the Structure page click on the Blocks link. On the Blocks page, scroll down until you find the Secondary menu item, and change the block assignment in the drop-down list from its current block to the Main Menu Links block. After making the change, click on the "Save blocks" button at the bottom of the page.

To test the horizontal menu, add another menu item to the Secondary menu following the steps outlined in Chapter 5. For demonstration purposes I've added a new menu item named Google that links to www.google.com. After adding the new menu item to the theme, your new horizontal menu should look something like Figure 13-6.

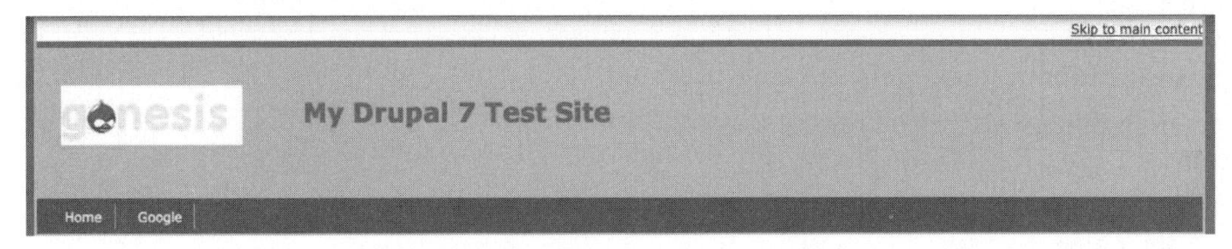

Figure 13-6. Horizontal menu themed

Before moving on to theming the footer, blocks, and nodes that are rendered on the site, there are two minor theming issues that need to be addressed. In its current state, the text rendered in the main body of the site touches the left edge of the body container, and the body container itself needs a little snazzing up around the edges.

To fix the text running into the left edge of the site, I'll add a bit of padding to the DIV that contains all of the main text of the site. The DIV ID that the Genesis theme uses for the main body area is the #columns ID. Locate that CSS ID in the page.css file and add the following line of CSS code:

```
padding-left: 10px;
```

Save the page.css file and refresh the home page of your site. The text in the left column should now render 10 pixels in from the left edge of the main body.

The next step is to add a border to the #container CSS is. I'll use the tertiary color as the borders. Locate the #container ID in the page.css file, and add the following line of CSS code:

```
border: 3px solid #9CD88C;
```

After making the updates, save the page.css file and refresh your browser. Your site should be looking pretty good by now, but we're not done yet. Let's make it even better.

Theming the Footer

The footer of our site is pretty plain at the moment. The only content assigned to that area is the powered by Drupal statement. Let's pretty it up a bit by adding a top and bottom border and changing the background color.

Find the #footer DIV ID in the page.css file. Remove the existing margin definition and add the background-color, height, padding, and border-top definitions as shown here:

```
#footer {
  background-color: #9CD88C;
  height: 100px;
  padding: 10px;
  border-top: 2px solid #287314;
}
```

After making the updates, save the file and refresh your home page. There's one more change that we want to make to the footer, and that is removing the "Powered by Drupal" statement and menu that are shown in the off-the-shelf version of the theme. Our requirements don't include a menu in the footer, nor the "Powered by Drupal" statement. To remove the statement, visit the Blocks page and unassign that item from the footer region by selecting None from the list of options and clicking the "Save blocks" button at the bottom of the Blocks page.

To remove the menu, edit the page.tpl.php file and carefully delete the following lines from the file:

```
<?php if ($secondary_menu_links): ?>
          <div id="secondary-menu-wrapper" class="clearfix">
            <div class="secondary-menu-inner"><?php print $secondary_menu_links; ?></div>
          </div>
<?php endif; ?>
```

After deleting these lines, save the file and refresh your browser. You should now have a clean footer.

At this point you could call it quits and use the theme as is, but there are a few other minor changes that can be made to define how nodes and blocks are themed to make our site just a little bit better.

Theming Nodes

Drupal provides a mechanism for controlling how nodes are displayed on a page. By default, a node is displayed with the title at the top; the author, date, and time below the title; the pictures attached to the node; and then the body of the node. The problem with this approach is that there is a large area taken up by the picture before the visitor sees any text. I'll update the nodes.css file so that the picture will float left of the text, allowing text to begin at the top of the picture, as shown in Figure 13-7. But first I'll take a moment to create a test Article content item and set the publishing option so that the new Article will be displayed on the front page of the site. I'll be sure to attach a picture to the Article using the picture upload feature—any picture will do—and create at least a paragraph of text so you can test the changes that you are about to make.

The Day the Earth Stood Still for Drupal
Submitted by admin on Sat, 04/24/2010 - 18:29
THE DAY THE EARTH
STOOD STILL
As predicted by the ancient Mayan calendar, the Earth stood still on December 21, 2012 to celebrate the one millionth site published on Drupal. All non-Drupal sites were rendered inoperable with their content turned into jibberish. Officials were unable to explain why non-Drupal sites suddenly began rendering their text as the following example demonstrates.
Read more
Add new comment

Figure 13-7. Unthemed node

Next, edit the nodes.css file from the /sites/all/themes/genesis_mytheme/css directory. In the file, search for a CSS class definition named field-type-image. Update the class definition, adding the position, flat, margin-right, and margin-bottom definitions as shown here:

```
.field-type-image {
  position: relative;
  float: left;
  margin-right: 15px;
  margin-bottom: 10px;
}
```

There is another cleanup task, and that is to add some padding to the right edge of nodes. By default, the text will render to the right edge of the DIV container for nodes (node-inner). Search for node-inner in the nodes.css file, and update CSS class so that it includes a padding-right attribute as shown here:

```
.node-inner {
  padding-right: 15px;
}
```

After making the changes, save the file and refresh your browser while on the home page. Your new node layout should look somewhat like Figure 13-8.

The Day the Earth Stood Still for Drupal

Submitted by admin on Sat, 04/24/2010 - 18:29

As predicted by the ancient Mayan calendar, the Earth stood still on December 21, 2012 to celebrate the one millionth site published on Drupal. All non-Drupal sites were rendered inoperable with their content turned into jibberish. Officials were unable to explain why non-Drupal sites suddenly began rendering their text as the following example demonstrates.

Read more   Add new comment

Figure 13-8. Themed node

You could make other changes by updating the node.tpl.php and nodes.css files. I would suggest reading the header of the node.tpl.php file. In the header, you will find a description of the optional elements that you can include in the output generated when Drupal renders a node. For the example theme, the only change that I needed to make was floating the pictures to the left of the text.

Theming Blocks

Another common way to dress up your site is to theme how blocks are displayed. In the out-of-the-box state, a block on our site will be displayed by default as shown in Figure 13-9. As you can see, it's pretty plain.

Management

- Add new content
- Dashboard

Figure 13-9. Unthemed block

A common approach that I use on my clients' sites is to add a background color to the block titles and to wrap the blocks with a border. Fortunately with the Genesis theme, all I'll have to do is to update the blocks.css file with a few additional CSS attributes.

The first CSS class that I'll change is the .sidebar .block .block-content class. I'll add an attribute for padding of 10px around the edges of the block-content container, and a 1px border using the tertiary color. Once changed, the definition should look like the following:

```
.sidebar .block .block-content {
    border: 1px solid #9CD88C;
    padding: 10px;
}
```

The next step is to update the definition for the block title. I will add a background color to the title and change the font color for the title. In the blocks.css file, search for the line that defines the CSS for .sidebar .block h2 and add the attributes shown here:

```
.sidebar .block h2 {
  background-color: #9CD88C;
  padding-left: 10px;
  padding-top: 5px;
  padding-bottom: 5px;
  color: #287314;
}
```

After making the changes, save the blocks.css file and refresh your browser. The changes made to the CSS should result in the themed blocks looking like Figure 13-10—significantly better than the plain look of the default definition for blocks.

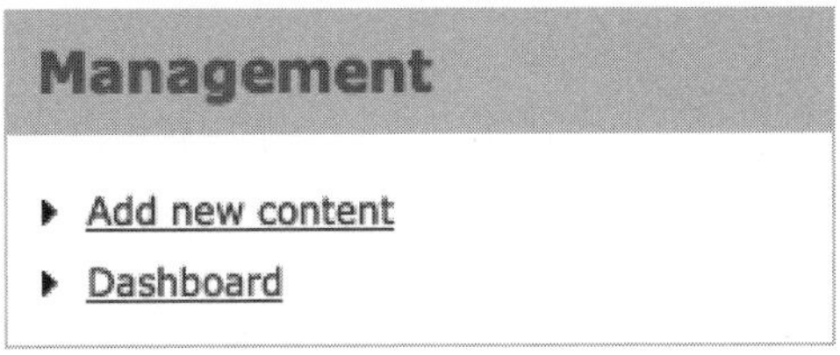

Figure 13-10. *Themed block*

Changing Sitename and Logo

Most Drupal themes adhere to a standard approach for incorporating the logo and the name of the site. To change the logo of the site from the default Genesis logo, click on the Appearance link in the top menu. On the Appearance page, click on the Settings link for your Genesis subtheme. On the Settings page, uncheck the use default logo checkbox. As soon as you uncheck the box, Drupal displays a text field where you can enter the path to the image you wish to use for your logo or have the option to upload a file. Either approach results in a new logo being displayed in place of the default Genesis logo. Be mindful of the dimensions of the logo based on the dimensions of your banner area.

You can also change the site's name by clicking on the Configuration link on the top menu and on the Configuration page clicking on the Site information link. On the Site information page you can change the value in the Site name text field.

A Tool for Helping You Theme Your Site

There is a tool that I use on a daily basis that is indispensible when it comes to theming: Firefox's Firebug plug-in (which is now available for Google Chrome). Firebug provides all of the information you need to identify the right CSS elements to create or modify in order to achieve the look of any item on any page. Firebug provides a simple-to-use mechanism for identifying the CSS ID or class that is assigned to a specific element by simply right-clicking on that element and choosing the inspect element item from the menu. For example, I right-clicked on the site title in the header area and selected the inspect element option. As shown in Figure 13-11, Firebug displayed the HTML used by the theme to render the title and the CSS used by the browser to render that element. Firebug even goes so far as to display the name of the CSS file and the line number within that file where the attributes are defined. It doesn't get much easier than that!

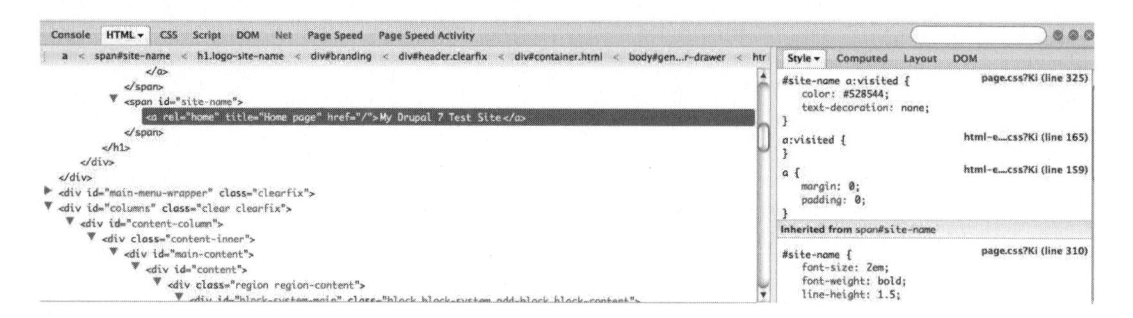

Figure 13-11. *Using Firebug to identify a CSS ID*

Summary

You're now ready to begin creating your own custom themes by either modifying an existing theme, creating a derivative theme from a starter theme like Genesis, or creating a new theme from scratch. There are a number of resources on Drupal.org to help guide you through other more advanced theming topics. A good place to start is Drupal.org/theme-guide and the forums (Drupal.org/forum).

You now have your site themed and ready for its public unveiling, but before you unleash the hordes of people chomping at the bit to see your site, let's make sure you're ready to administer it.

CHAPTER 14

■ ■ ■

Administering Your Drupal Site

If you have followed along in the previous chapters, you now have enough knowledge to build a Drupal 7-based website. Building your website and releasing it to the world is an exciting experience, and one that often brings with it great pride a joy. Whether your site has two or three pages or hundreds, deploying a website and seeing traffic on it is a rewarding and enriching experience. Deploying your website is just a step along the journey; it is by no means the end. As the proud owner of a website, you must monitor it, nurture it, expand it, and support it, all of which are involved in administering your website.

Administering a Drupal website can be a relatively simple task, depending on the size of your site, the number of users, the number of users who have the ability to author content, and the number of modules that you've installed. Over the past several years, I've created a number of personal "pet" project websites that are up and running, and I rarely do anything other than go out and glimpse at the site logs. There are other sites that I have built that require more attention, and the amount of attention really depends on the criteria I just mentioned.

Typical site administration tasks that you will want to consider performing on a periodic basis include:

- Backing up the site so you can restore it should anything disastrous happen.
- Checking the logs to see if there are any errors that you need to address.
- Checking to see if there are any security patches to modules you have installed.
- Checking to see if there are any module upgrades that make sense to deploy on your site.
- Checking to see if there were any Drupal core updates that you need to deploy.
- Approving requests for new user accounts.

In this chapter, I'll describe in detail each of these administrative tasks.

Backing Up Your Site

If you don't do anything else on this list of administrative tasks, at least make sure that your data is safe and recoverable in the case of an unexpected disaster. It's easy to put off backing up your site, as it's likely that you'll rarely need to go back and restore your site from a backup. But speaking from experience, the first time you need to restore your site and you don't have a backup is the last time you won't have backups in place from the start. Take it from the voice of experience: the few minutes it takes to set up backups are well spent.

There are two paths to take to address backups on your new site: you can use utilities that your hosting provider gives to you to backup your database and directories, or you can use a Drupal module called "Backup and Migrate" to automatically back up your site on a defined schedule, and, just as important, to easily restore your site from a previous backup. Both approaches work equally as well, and the "Backup and Migrate" module is a perfect solution for those who are less inclined to use operating-system-level commands to schedule backups and to create the scripts necessary to back up your Drupal site.

You will need to install the module, because it is not part of Drupal core. You can find details for this module at `www.drupal.org/project/backup_migrate`. To install the module, follow the steps covered in Chapter 8.

To access the "Backup and Migrate" configuration page, go to http://localhost/admin/content/backup_migrate (note: replace "localhost" with the appropriate domain name if your site is not running on your local PC). After clicking Enter, you will see the configuration panel for the "Backup and Migrate" module.

The first step in configuring the "Backup and Migrate" module is to define where backup files will be stored on the server. Click on the Destinations tab at the top of the page, revealing the page shown in Figure 14-1. There are two settings for where files will be stored: one for manual backups, where the site administrator clicks on a "Backup now" link to perform the backup, and the automatic backup. I'll explain how to set up automatic backups in a minute. You can also set the database that you want backed up. By default, the module automatically detects the database that your site is running on and sets the parameter. You may choose to override the default directories and database that are set during the process of installing the module, or you may, as I do, leave the defaults.

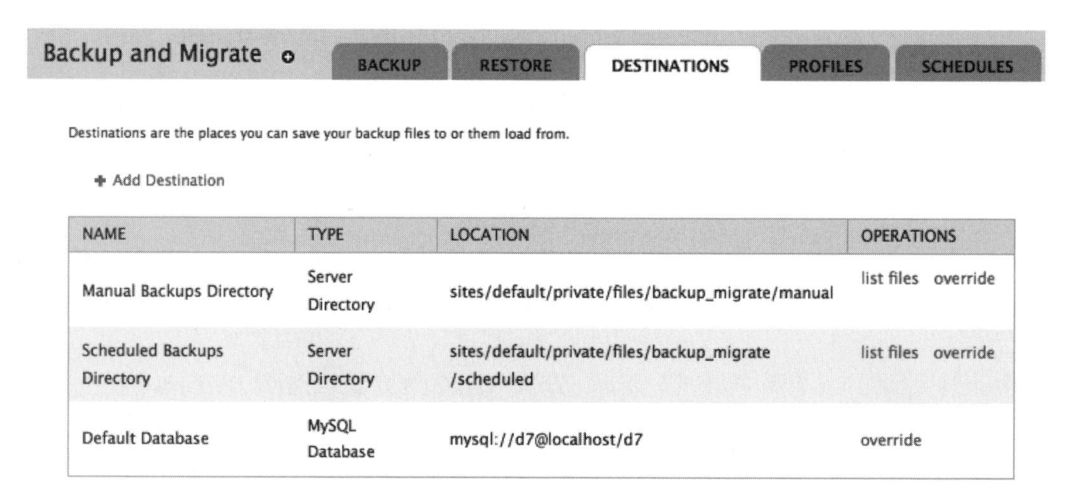

Figure 14-1. *Setting the destination directories for backups*

The next step is to set the schedule for automatic backups. To do so, click on the Schedules tab at the top of the page, revealing the configuration options shown in Figure 14-2. If you haven't set a schedule previously, the page will simply display an "Add schedule" link. Click on that link to view the parameters that you can set for scheduling backups. First, enter a name for the Schedule. We are going to set the backups to be performed on a daily basis, so enter "Daily backups" as the name. Next, set the "Backup every" field to 1 Day(s). Finally, set the "Number of backup files to keep" to 14, meaning Drupal will retain 14 days' of backups before deleting the oldest backup file and storing the newest file. This helps protect you from consuming massive amounts of disk space for old backup files. Set this value carefully. You may have legal requirements in your industry that require that you keep backup files for a certain number of days, weeks, months, or years. Finally, click the "Save schedule" button.

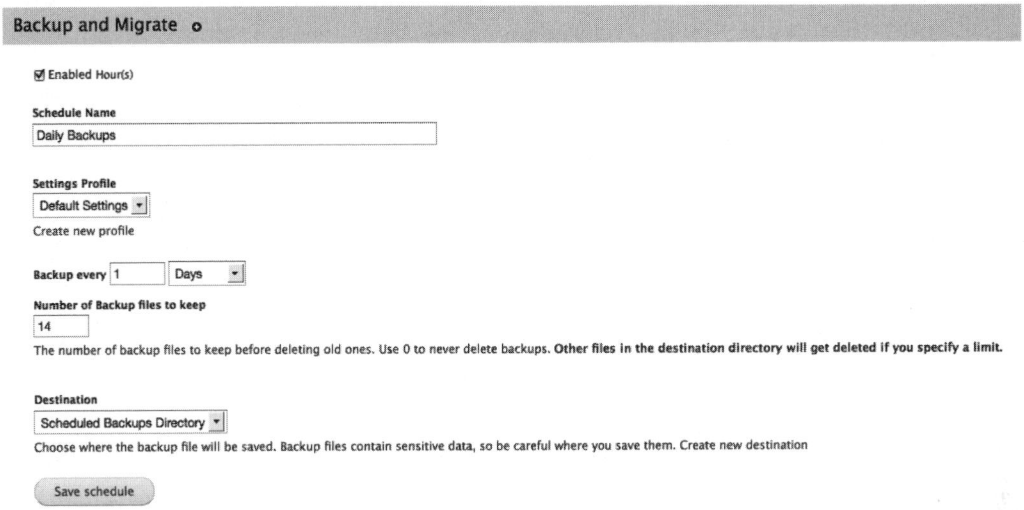

Backup and Migrate

Enabled Hour(s)

Schedule Name

Daily Backups

Settings Profile

Default Settings

Create new profile

Backup every 1 Days

Number of Backup files to keep

14

The number of backup files to keep before deleting old ones. Use 0 to never delete backups. **Other files in the destination directory will get deleted if you specify a limit.**

Destination

Scheduled Backups Directory

Choose where the backup file will be saved. Backup files contain sensitive data, so be careful where you save them. Create new destination

Save schedule

Figure 14-2. Setting up the automatic backup schedule

Drupal will now automatically back up the site on a daily basis. The last step is to perform a manual backup of your site. To do so, click on the Backup tab (see Figure 14-3). On the resulting page, select the Default Database as the database to back up, set the "to" option to the Manual Backups Directory (you can also select Download, which will download the backup to your local computer), and set the "using" option to Default Settings. Finally, click the "Backup now" button.

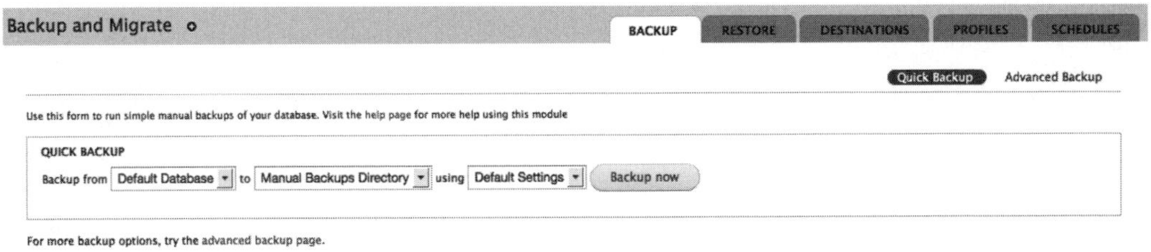

Backup and Migrate

BACKUP RESTORE DESTINATIONS PROFILES SCHEDULES

Quick Backup Advanced Backup

Use this form to run simple manual backups of your database. Visit the help page for more help using this module

QUICK BACKUP

Backup from Default Database to Manual Backups Directory using Default Settings Backup now

For more backup options, try the advanced backup page.

Figure 14-3. Manually backing up your site

When the backup is completed, Drupal will redisplay the screen with information including the name of the backup file that was generated, the directory where it was stored, and how long the backup took to execute.

Restoring a Backup

If, for some reason, you needed to restore your system to a previously backed up state, you can return to the "Backup and Migrate" administration page (http://localhost/admin/content/backup_migrate) and select the backup file to restore. Click on the Destinations tab, revealing the list of destination directories where backups are stored. See Figure 14-4.

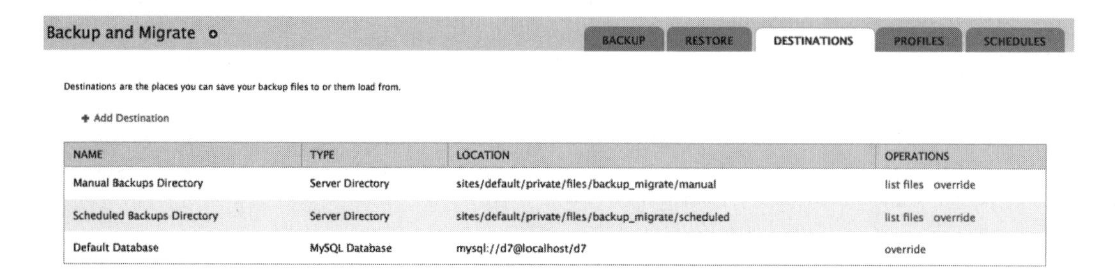

Figure 14-4. Listing the backup directories where backup files are stored

Because we backed up our system using the manual backup process, click on the "List files" link for "Manual Backups Directory," revealing the page shown in Figure 14-5.

<em class="placeholder">Manual Backups Directory</em> Files BACKUP RESTORE DESTINATIONS PROFILES SCHEDULES

FILENAME	DATE	AGE	SIZE	OPERATIONS		
Drupal7DemoSite-2010-04-09T21-38-52.mysql	Fri, 04/09/2010 - 21:38	5 min	702.81 KB	download	restore	delete

Figure 14-5. The manual backups directory and the file to restore

In this example, we could restore our system to the state it was in at the time we did the manual backup by simply clicking on the Restore link for that backup file. If you have scheduled backups enabled and have not manually backed up your system, the process described would be identical, with the exception of selecting the "List files" link for the scheduled backups directory. Clicking that link would reveal a list of backup files that were automatically created based on the schedule that you set in the previous steps.

Backing Up the File System

The "Backup and Migrate" module only backs up the contents of your Drupal database. The Drupal installation itself, meaning Drupal core, all of the contributed modules you have installed, all of the themes you have installed, any customizations you have made to modules, and any files that users have uploaded will not be saved by the "Backup and Migrate" module.

There are several options for backing up the file system, starting with simply copying the entire Drupal directory to another destination (for example, downloading the site to your local PC if you are running on a hosted server), copying the Drupal directory to a USB/CD/DVD if you are running on your local desktop/laptop, or, in the case of a hosted environment, working with your provider to ensure that your Drupal directory is being backed up often enough to ensure minimal disruption in the case of a disaster. Whichever scenario you choose, you should back up the file system on a frequent basis if users are uploading and attaching files to content (even daily, just as you do with your "Backup and Migrate" schedule), and in a case where you do not allow file attachments and uploads, it is still a good idea to back up your file system on at least a weekly basis (due to module updates).

Checking the Log Files

With backups in place, the next administrative task is to periodically check the log files to see if there are errors in the system that need to be corrected (for example, "page not found" errors). To view the log files, click on the Reports link in the top menu, revealing a list of reports that are available to help you administer your new Drupal site. See Figure 14-6.

Figure 14-6. List of standard reports

There are three reports that I will focus on in this chapter (you can easily view the other reports by simply clicking on the links). I will focus on the Recent log entries, Top 'page not found' errors, and the Status report (I'll cover available updates later in this chapter).

Recent Log Entries

Drupal provides a rich framework for recording events in the system that may be of interest to someone who is administering a Drupal site. Module developers and Drupal core maintainers leverage this capability to log any events that they feel are important enough to warrant an entry in the log file. If you click on the "Recent log entries" link, you will see a report that looks similar to Figure 14-7.

Recent log entries
The Database logging module monitors your website, capturing system events in a log (shown here) to be reviewed by an authorized individual at a later time. This log is a list of recorded events containing usage data, performance data, errors, warnings and operational information. It is vital to check the Recent log entries report on a regular basis, as it is often the only way to tell what is going on.
FILTER LOG MESSAGES
CLEAR LOG MESSAGES

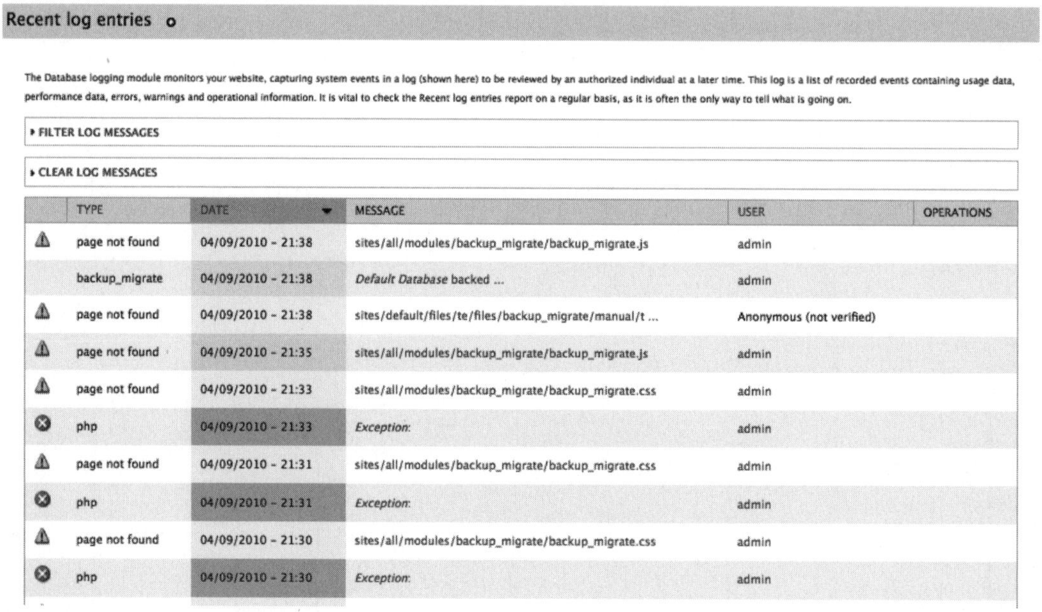

	TYPE	DATE	MESSAGE	USER	OPERATIONS
	page not found	04/09/2010 - 21:38	sites/all/modules/backup_migrate/backup_migrate.js	admin	
	backup_migrate	04/09/2010 - 21:38	*Default Database* backed ...	admin	
	page not found	04/09/2010 - 21:38	sites/default/files/te/files/backup_migrate/manual/t ...	Anonymous (not verified)	
	page not found	04/09/2010 - 21:35	sites/all/modules/backup_migrate/backup_migrate.js	admin	
	page not found	04/09/2010 - 21:33	sites/all/modules/backup_migrate/backup_migrate.css	admin	
	php	04/09/2010 - 21:33	*Exception*:	admin	
	page not found	04/09/2010 - 21:31	sites/all/modules/backup_migrate/backup_migrate.css	admin	
	php	04/09/2010 - 21:31	*Exception*:	admin	
	page not found	04/09/2010 - 21:30	sites/all/modules/backup_migrate/backup_migrate.css	admin	
	php	04/09/2010 - 21:30	*Exception*:	admin	

Figure 14-7. *Recent log entries*

Your entries will be different from those shown in Figure 14-7, because the actions you have performed will have been different. This list of entries includes both errors and successful events (for example, a user logging in to the system results in a log entry that shows the date and time of when they logged in). Simply click on the message to see whatever details the module or Drupal core developer deemed appropriate to share with a site administrator. In Figure 14-7, we see that there are a number of "page not found" errors in for the "Backup and Migrate" module. To address these errors, you may have to download a newer version of the "Backup and Migrate" module, or you may need to visit that module's homepage on Drupal.org to see if there is a workaround. Discussing all of the errors and how to resolve them is beyond the scope of this chapter, because of the breadth of errors that can occur on a Drupal site. The best resource for resolving errors that you may see are the Drupal.org website and the specific module's issue queue that is generating the errors. If you do not find answers on the module's homepage, the next step is to consult the forums on the Drupal.org website. It is highly unlikely that you're the first one to encounter the error, and if you are, posting a request for help in the forum will typically result in a rapid response from someone who knows how to solve the issue.

"Page Not Found" Errors

Returning to the Reports main page and clicking on the "Top page not found" errors reveals a list of "404" errors, or "page not found," errors. See Figure 14-8.

Top 'page not found' errors

COUNT	MESSAGE
8	modules/update/update.manager.js
7	misc/ui/ui.dialog.js
6	misc/ui/ui.core.js
5	sites/all/modules/backup_migrate/backup_migrate.css
4	misc/ui/ui.all.css
4	misc/ui/ui.dialog.css
3	sites/all/modules/backup_migrate/backup_migrate.js
2	upcoming-events
1	admin/structure/types/manage/book/delete
1	about-us
1	sites/default/files/te/files/backup_migrate/manual/t ...

Figure 14-8. *"Page not found" report*

It is important to check this report periodically to see if site visitors are clicking on links that are "broken." In Figure 14-8 you can see that the "Backup and Migrate" module is looking for two files that do not exist in the proper directories, and in the case of the third item, someone attempted to navigate to admin/backup_migrate, which is a destination that does not exist on the site. Resolving the errors listed on this page may take some investigation and analysis on your part. You'll want to focus on errors that have a high count, as they are likely impacting site visitors (in this case, there is a bug in the "Backup and

Migrate" module, which isn't a feature that is visible to site visitors, so resolving that issue may be a lower priority).

Status Report

A general "health" report for your site can be accessed on the list of Reports page by clicking on the Status report link. Clicking this link reveals a page that highlights key areas of your Drupal installation that are of relatively high importance. Items that are checked when you run this report include whether critical configuration files are protected from unauthorized changes and whether the database is up to date. In Drupal 7, with the revised approach for installing modules, it's unlikely that the database will become out of date. If it is reported as out of date, run the http://localhost/update.php script to synchronize the database with the current state of your modules.

You are most likely to see issues regarding the status of Drupal core, contributed modules, and themes. If there is an updated version of Drupal or a contributed module or theme has been updated on Drupal.org, these items will appear as yellow. See Figure 13-9.

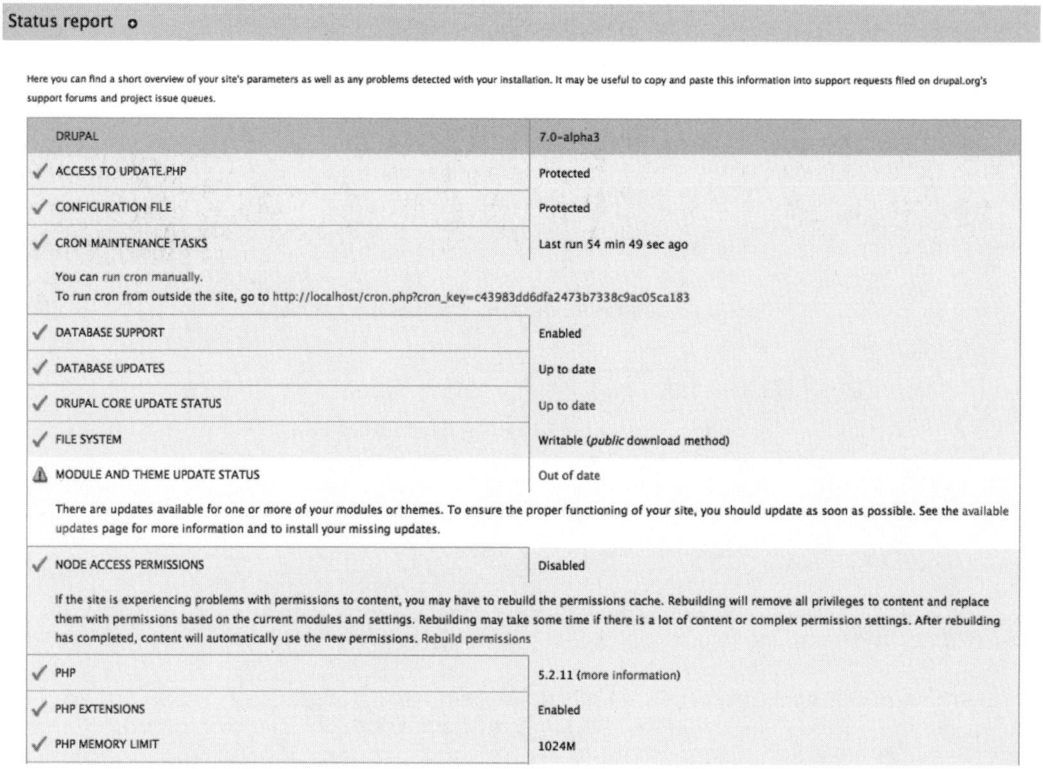

Status report

Here you can find a short overview of your site's parameters as well as any problems detected with your installation. It may be useful to copy and paste this information into support requests filed on drupal.org's support forums and project issue queues.

DRUPAL	7.0-alpha3
✓ ACCESS TO UPDATE.PHP	Protected
✓ CONFIGURATION FILE	Protected
✓ CRON MAINTENANCE TASKS	Last run 54 min 49 sec ago
You can run cron manually. To run cron from outside the site, go to http://localhost/cron.php?cron_key=c43983dd6dfa2473b7338c9ac05ca183	
✓ DATABASE SUPPORT	Enabled
✓ DATABASE UPDATES	Up to date
✓ DRUPAL CORE UPDATE STATUS	Up to date
✓ FILE SYSTEM	Writable (*public* download method)
⚠ MODULE AND THEME UPDATE STATUS	Out of date
There are updates available for one or more of your modules or themes. To ensure the proper functioning of your site, you should update as soon as possible. See the available updates page for more information and to install your missing updates.	
✓ NODE ACCESS PERMISSIONS	Disabled
If the site is experiencing problems with permissions to content, you may have to rebuild the permissions cache. Rebuilding will remove all privileges to content and replace them with permissions based on the current modules and settings. Rebuilding may take some time if there is a lot of content or complex permission settings. After rebuilding has completed, content will automatically use the new permissions. Rebuild permissions	
✓ PHP	5.2.11 (more information)
✓ PHP EXTENSIONS	Enabled
✓ PHP MEMORY LIMIT	1024M

Figure 14-9. *Status report*

Checking for Updates

If the status report shows that there are module or theme updates, you'll want to check to see which types of updates are available. There are three general categories of updates that you will want to pay attention to as you develop your new site and once the site is in production:

- Security updates
- Module updates
- Drupal core updates

In most cases you will want to address security updates as soon as possible, while module updates and Drupal core updates may be something that you address on a monthly, quarterly, or even less frequent basis. Updates typically address bugs that were found in modules and/or new features that were added to the module or Drupal core. As the site administrator, you will need to determine, by looking at the release notes for the each update, whether the update is something you should do immediately (for example, fixing a bug that you have struggled with on your site) or can delay.

To check to see if there are any security patches or updates, click on the "Out of date" link on the status report next to the modules and themes item. The "Out of date" report lists all modules and themes that you have installed on your site that have available updates on Drupal.org. It's a good idea to visit each module's page on Drupal.org to see if there are any critical bugs reported for the new version of the module before you decided to download and install it. I have experienced cases where a new version of a contributed module that I have installed on one of my sites introduced new bugs that I didn't have on the site prior to the upgrade. It's a good idea to check before upgrading.

To install the updates for a theme or module, simply check the box for that module or theme and then click on "Download the updates." Drupal will automatically download, install, and enable the updates. See Figure 14-10.

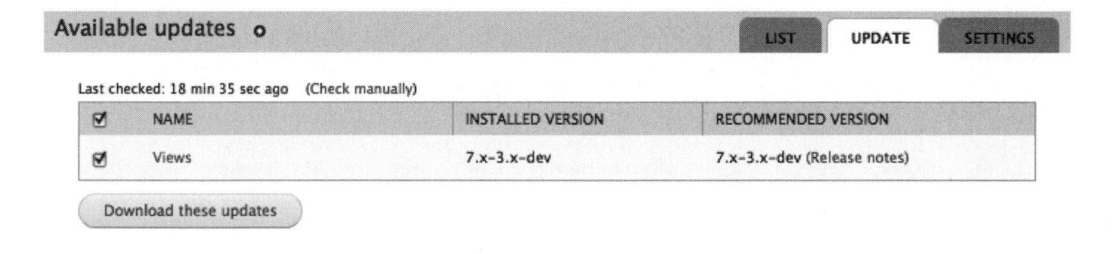

Figure 14-10. *Available module and theme updates*

In a case where Drupal core is updated, the process is slightly more complex. To update Drupal core:

1. Make sure you backup your database!
2. Make sure you backup your entire Drupal directory!
3. Click on the download link for the version that you wish to use, which results in the Drupal .tar file for that version being downloaded to your local PC.

4. Unpackage/expand the Drupal distribution (for Windows users, you may need to download 7zip, a free utility that unpackages tar files on Windows computers).

5. Open the folder that is created when you expand the Drupal distribution (see Figure 4-11).

Name	Date Modified	Size	Kind
themes	Apr 26, 2010, 2:40 PM	--	Folder
sites	Apr 26, 2010, 2:40 PM	--	Folder
scripts	Apr 26, 2010, 2:40 PM	--	Folder
profiles	Apr 26, 2010, 2:40 PM	--	Folder
modules	Apr 26, 2010, 2:40 PM	--	Folder
misc	Apr 26, 2010, 2:40 PM	--	Folder
includes	Apr 26, 2010, 2:40 PM	--	Folder
CHANGELOG.txt	Apr 26, 2010, 2:24 PM	48 KB	Plain text
update.php	Apr 24, 2010, 7:49 AM	20 KB	Plain Text File
authorize.php	Apr 22, 2010, 3:16 AM	8 KB	Plain Text File
UPGRADE.txt	Apr 22, 2010, 1:15 AM	8 KB	Plain text
MAINTAINERS.txt	Apr 20, 2010, 12:13 AM	8 KB	Plain text
web.config	Apr 14, 2010, 8:54 AM	4 KB	Document
.htaccess	Apr 11, 2010, 11:33 AM	8 KB	Plain text
INSTALL.pgsql.txt	Apr 7, 2010, 8:07 AM	4 KB	Plain text
install.php	Feb 16, 2010, 8:19 PM	4 KB	Plain Text File
INSTALL.txt	Feb 13, 2010, 1:35 PM	20 KB	Plain text
INSTALL.mysql.txt	Jan 11, 2010, 8:25 AM	4 KB	Plain text
COPYRIGHT.txt	Jan 2, 2010, 2:20 AM	4 KB	Plain text
xmlrpc.php	Dec 13, 2009, 5:06 AM	4 KB	Plain Text File
INSTALL.sqlite.txt	Nov 10, 2009, 9:27 AM	4 KB	Plain text
cron.php	Nov 1, 2009, 7:30 PM	4 KB	Plain Text File
index.php	Oct 15, 2009, 7:07 AM	4 KB	Plain Text File
robots.txt	Sep 10, 2009, 9:17 PM	4 KB	Plain text
LICENSE.txt	Jan 26, 2009, 6:08 AM	20 KB	Plain text

***Figure 14-11.** Drupal 7 files and folders*

6. If you have Drupal installed on your local computer, delete all of the files *except* the sites directory. It's critical that you keep the sites directory, as it contains all of the files that you've uploaded, all of the backups of your site, and the configuration information for connecting to the database. Next, copy all of the files and directories to your htdocs directory (see Appendix A for a refresher on where you will find this directory for your specific operating system).

7. If you have Drupal installed on a hosted server, use the same mechanism described in Appendix A for transferring the files to that server in the root directory of your hosting account (assuming you installed Drupal in that root directory) after deleting all the files in your root directory *except* the sites directory.

8. Once all of the files have been loaded, enter http://localhost/update.php (note: replace "localhost" with the appropriate domain name if you are hosting this site and not running Drupal on your local PC).

9. Test your site.

Approving Requests for User Accounts

Drupal lets you, the site administrator, determine how user accounts are created on your website. You can:

- Allow site visitors to create their own accounts without approval by a site administrator.
- Allow site visitors to request an account, but require that a site administrator approve it before allowing the visitor to use the account.
- Restrict account creation to only the site administrator.

The approach you use is completely dependent on whether you allow visitors to have their own accounts. There is no reason to provide this feature if you don't provide interactive features on your site. If you provide limited capabilities for authenticated users (for example, if you don't enable permissions for any administrative features to the generic "authenticated users" category) and you don't want to be bothered with enabling user accounts, then allowing visitors to create accounts without approval is appropriate. If you want control over who has an account, then you will want to configure you site so visitors can request an account, but you must approve their requests before their accounts become active.

To set how your site handles user accounts, click on the Configuration link in the top menu, revealing the main configuration page for your site. On this page, you will see a category of options for "People and Permissions." Within this category you will see a link for Account Settings.

Click on the link to reveal the account settings configuration form, shown in Figure 4-11.

REGISTRATION AND CANCELLATION

Who can register accounts?

( ) Administrators only

( ) Visitors

(•) Visitors, but administrator approval is required

[x] Require e-mail verification when a visitor creates an account.

New users will be required to validate their e-mail address prior to logging into the site, and will be assigned a system-generated password. With this setting disabled, users will be logged in immediately upon registering, and may select their own passwords during registration.

When cancelling a user account

(•) Disable the account and keep all content. *

( ) Disable the account and unpublish all content. *

( ) Delete the account and make all content belong to the *Anonymous* user. *

( ) Delete the account and all content. *

Users with the *Select method for cancelling account* or *Administer users* permissions can override this default method.

Figure 14-12. *Account settings page*

On this page, you will find a section titled Registration and Cancellation. In Figure 14-11, the option is set where visitors can request a user account, but administrator approval is required is set.

To see how this feature works, click the "Log out" link at the top right-hand corner of the page, which will return you to your site's homepage as an anonymous user (not logged into the site).

In the left column, you can see that, under the login form, there is a link for "Create new account." Click on that link to see the form where a new user can request a new account.

The visitor needs to provide a username and a valid e-mail address to create a new account. Once these values have been entered and the visitor has clicked "Create new account," Drupal redisplays your site's homepage with a message that their account is pending approval by the site administrator.

You, as the site administrator, must now enable their account. To do so, click on the People link at the top of the page to see the list of users on your site. See Figure 14-13.

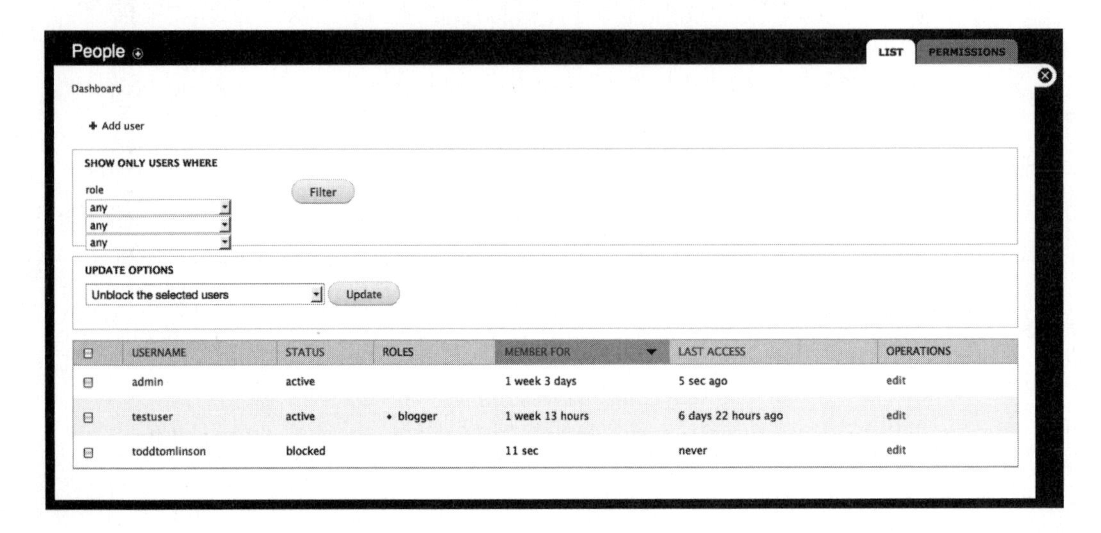

Figure 14-13. *New user listed as blocked*

In Figure 14-12, you can see that a user account was just created for toddtomlinson, and that the user's status is set to "blocked," meaning they are blocked from logging onto the site.

If your site has several user accounts you may wish to filter the list to find only those user accounts that are blocked and hence need to be activated. To filter the list, select the last of the three drop-down menus in the "Show only users where" section, and select "blocked" from the list of options.

Next, click on the Filter button to limit the list of users shown on the page to only those that need to be activated. Click the check box next to each of the users that you wish to activate and make sure that the Update Options select list is set to "Unblock the selected users." When all users have been checked and the appropriate option selected, click on the Update button.

Once the updates have completed, click the Reset button in the "Show only users where" section to redisplay all users. Which shows that our new user, toddtomlinson, is now active. See Figure 14-14.

Figure 14-14. *All users now set to active*

One of the options that you can set on the Account settings page is whether users receive e-mail notifications when their accounts are created. If you have that option enabled, when you enable an account the user is automatically notified via e-mail that their account is now ready for them to log in to the website.

Summary

In this chapter, I covered the basics of administering a Drupal website. I explained the key administrative tasks associated with running your new site.

Depending on the complexity of your site and the features you have deployed, there may be other administrative tasks that are specific to those additional features. This list will get you started down the path to ensuring that your site is backed up, error free, and up to date. For additional Drupal administrative topics, visit the Drupal.org website.

Wow, we've covered a lot of information up to this point. You now have the knowledge necessary to build simple to complex websites on Drupal, and you now know how to administer your new site. That a lot of information to digest, and you may be wondering where to start when setting up a new site. That's the focus on the next and last chapter of the book, helping you navigate through the process of creating a successful Drupal website.

CHAPTER 15

■ ■ ■

Putting It All Together

Reading this book has given you the foundation of knowledge on which to continue to build your Drupal skills. If you are new to the concept of a web content management system, you may not be able to jump in and build a highly complex site as your first endeavor with Drupal. But like all things in life, you have to start somewhere, and you now have the tools and knowledge to begin your journey. For those of you who had content management experience, hopefully the book helped to cast a light on how Drupal works so you can correlate what you know from other CMS platforms with what Drupal provides.

Now What?

Learning anything new takes practice, and with practice comes comfort, and with comfort comes the ability to do new and exciting things. Learning Drupal takes time, study, practice, and patience. One of the best ways to learn Drupal is to find a real-world opportunity to build a web site and do it in Drupal. Whether the site is for your child's sports team, your church, a community group, a non-profit organization, or anything else under the sun, having a project to focus on that you know will benefit a person or organization gives you incentive to learn, which helps in the learning process. How else can you keep up-to-date with your Drupal knowledge?

Look At Other Drupal-Based Sites for Ideas

Although it's hard to look at a site and immediately detect that it is a Drupal site, there is an excellent resource that will help you find sites that were built on Drupal. Dries Buytaert, the creator of Drupal, maintains a fairly up-to-date list of very high-profile web sites that are built on Drupal. You can find that list on his personal web site at `http://buytaert.net/tag/drupal-sites`. Dries does an excellent job of capturing a broad spectrum of sites from various industries and sites from all around the world. The list is updated constantly, so it is a good idea to bookmark that page and to visit it frequently.

By scanning through the list of sites that Dries has compiled (currently well over 100), you can quickly get a sense for the types of sites that people have successfully built on Drupal. By looking at other sites, you can get inspiration for design (the visual look of the site), layout (how the pages are structured), organization (how content is displayed), and the features and functions that have been deployed. Looking at other sites is a common starting point for many people who are embarking on a new Drupal project.

Keep Tabs on Drupal and Contributed Modules

One of the benefits of using Drupal is that it is a constantly evolving platform. As new concepts are defined on the Web, Drupal is often one of the first content management systems to employ those capabilities. Keeping up with the changes is relatively simple: just check `http://drupal.org/project/modules` and look at the latest modules and updates posted to the site. (See Figure15-1.)

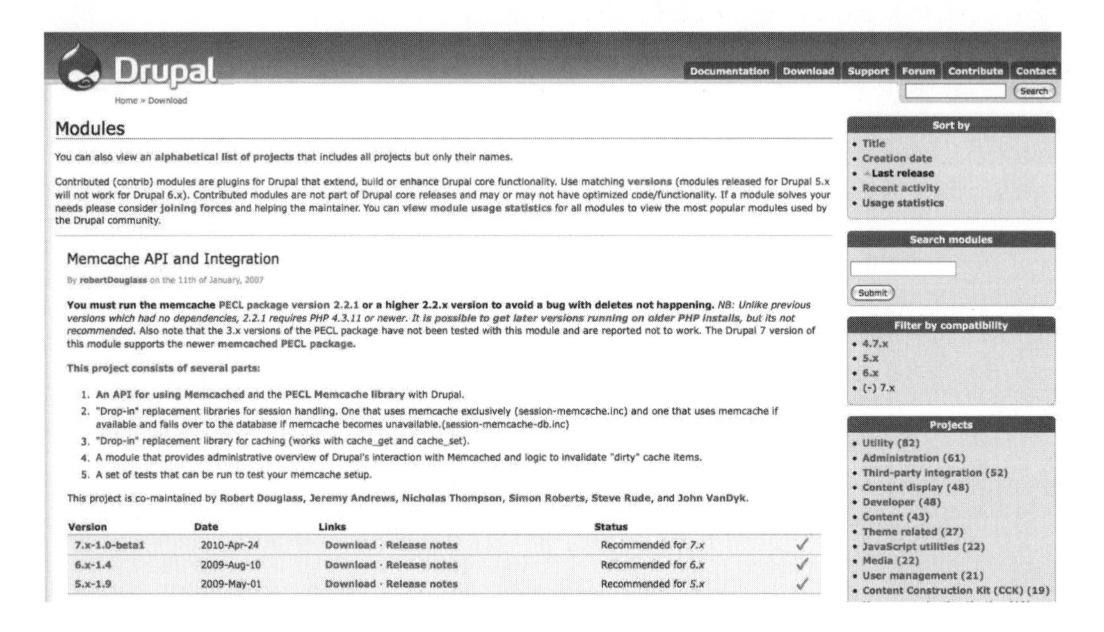

Figure15-1. *List of modules on Drupal.org*

When visiting the page, you'll notice a list of sort-by options in the right column. One of those options is "Last release." Clicking on this option sorts the list of modules in date-descending order, with the last modules posted to the site listed first. Depending on how frequently you visit the site, you may only have to spend a minute or two looking through the list of new modules to see what is available. There is also an RSS feed for module updates that you may want to subscribe to. If you see something of interest, you can click on the title for that module to visit the modules homepage on Drupal.org.

Get Involved in Your Local Drupal Users Group

There are hundreds of Drupal User Groups all around the globe, including regional user groups as well as groups that are focused on specific topics or industries (such as Drupal in Education, Drupal in Libraries, Drupal in Government). Your local Drupal Users Group is a great place to meet others in your community who are also new to Drupal, and to learn, as most groups provide training as part of their periodic meetings. To locate a group near you or a group that is focused on an area that you are interested in, visit `http://groups.drupal.org`.

A Methodology for Building Your Site on Drupal

While there isn't a formal "Drupal Methodology" for building sites on Drupal, there are several industry best practices and processes that you may wish to follow as you embark on the journey of creating a new Drupal web site. The process described in Table15-1 may seem overwhelming and more complex and involved than what you think you need to build your new site, but from experience it's good to at least think about the steps listed and apply and perform the tasks that you think are appropriate, based on the scope and complexity of the site that you are building.

Table15-1. *A Methodoloy for Building Your Drupal Site*

Phase	Task	Activity
I		**Starting Your Project** The tasks listed below are focused on helping you think about and define what your site is going to be. Drupal is a lot like a stack of lumber: you could build virtually any type and style of house with an appropriately sized stack of lumber. You typically wouldn't start picking up boards and nailing them together without first knowing the details of the house that you are going to build. Think of this phase of the project as defining the blueprint of your new site. In this phase, you're documenting key aspects of your site on paper, and not in Drupal. Once you have an understanding of what it is you're going to build, you can embark on the construction activities.
	A	**What is your new web site all about?** Write down, in narrative form, what the purpose of your new site is and, in general, describe the audience that you intend to target with your site. Think of this document as your "elevator pitch," meaning if you met someone in an elevator and they asked you what your web site was about, you could recite this document verbatim before the two of you left the elevator. This activity forces you to define in concise terms what it is you are building and who is going to view the site.
	B	**Identify who is going to visit and use your web site** List the various types of visitors who you intend to target with your new web site. Examples of visitor types for a library site might be children, teens, young adults, adults, jobseekers, and senior citizens. A favorite technique is to use a blank piece of paper and on this paper draw a "box" representing a browser window with your web site in that browser window. Draw a number of stick figures around the box and label each one with the type of visitor that "person" represents.

Continued

Phase	Task	Activity
	C	**Identify the content that you are going to deliver to your visitors** A common mistake in the web site construction process is the "field of dreams" mentality: "if I build it they will come." Well if "they" come to your site, what content are you going to present to "them" so they stay on your site, look around, and bookmark your site for future visits? You may wish to use a blank piece of paper for each visitor type, drawing a stick figure on the left and listing the content that this person would be interested in seeing on your site. There will likely be duplication between various visitor types, and that is okay, but it is important to step into the "shoes" of each visitor type to think about what content you are going to provide each visitor that will make them pay attention and return to your site in the future. Examples of content types might be, for a library website, book reviews, movie reviews, music reviews, recommended reading lists, and a list of upcoming programs at the library.
	D	**Identify the functionality that you are going to deliver to your visitors** Content is typically only one aspect of what constitutes a web site; there may be interactive features that you want to deliver, such as blogs, surveys, videos, audio, discussion forums, online forms, e-commerce, RSS feeds, or other interactive features. In this task list all of the interactive features that you wish to provide to your visitors.
	E	**Define the sites structure** Examine the types of content and functionality documented in the previous steps; you will start to see logical groupings or categories. You may see logical groupings based on a topic or subject, or you may see groupings based on specific visitor types. Using a library site as an example, you might see that there is a logical grouping of content across all visitor types that is focused on book reviews. You might also see a logical grouping of content that is focused on senior citizens and their use of community resources. Each of these logical groupings may, and probably should become a major page on your web site.
	F	**Define custom content types and taxonomy structure** There may be types of content that do not fit the generic Drupal page content type with just a title and body. An example might be that you identified "Events" as a type of content. An Event has a title, a start date, a start time, an end date, an end time, and a location. It might be advantageous to create a custom content type for events that enforces the entry of those additional details rather than relying on the author to remember to enter those values in the body of a generic page. In this step, you should create a list of custom content types and the attributes (such as start date, start time) associated with each content type. While defining content types, it's also time to think about taxonomy and how you are going to categorize content on your site.

Phase	Task	Activity
	G	**Define the navigational structure of your web site** With an understanding of the visitor types, the content that they will want to see on your site, and the logical groupings or major pages that will make up your site, you can now define the navigation (menus) for your site. If you know that a specific visitor type is a primary visitor of your web site, you should make it easy for that visitor to find the information that they are seeking. The typical mechanism for doing that is to provide some form of menu or menus. In this task you would identify all of the links that you wish to provide to your site visitors and how those links should be organized (as menus). Using the library example, you may decide that you want a primary menu at the top of the page that provides links to About the Library, Locations and Hours, and How to Contact the Library. You may decide that you want a secondary menu that links visitors to pages for Books, Movies, Music, and Events. You may decide that you want another menu that helps to direct specific visitor types to pages that are focused on their specific interest areas, such as links for youth, teens, adults, senior citizens, and business owners. You can take the concept to another level of detail by defining drop-down menu items for certain menu links; for example, under the Books menu you may want to provide a link to Recommended Books, What's New, and What's on Order.
II		**Setting Up Your Drupal Environment** Now that you have an understanding of what you're going to build, the next step is to set up your Drupal environment to begin the construction process.
	A	**Decide where you are going to host your new web site** You can easily build your new web site on your desktop or laptop and then deploy that site on a hosted environment, or you can choose to build the site in the environment where you are going to host the production version of your web site. Either approach works well. However, at some point in the near future you are going to want to deploy your site with a commercially viable hosting provider or your organization's own hosting platforms. To find a list of commercial hosting providers that support Drupal, visit `http://drupal.org/hosting`.
	B	**Install and configure Drupal** Following the step-by-step instructions outlined in Appendix A, install Drupal on either your local desktop/laptop or on your hosting providers environment.

Continued

Phase	Task	Activity
III		**Visual Design**
		Picking or designing your Drupal theme is one of those activities that you can choose to do early in the process, mid-way through the development process, or near the end of your efforts. For most people, having a sense of what the site is going to look like helps to visualize the layout as it will look in its final state. There may be mitigating circumstances where you can't pick or design the theme up front, such as the case where the organization you are building the site for doesn't have their branding completed (including logo, colors, iconography, fonts, and so on). In that case it is still possible to continue with the construction activities using a generic theme.
	A	**Look for an existing theme that matches what you are trying to accomplish**
		There are hundreds of themes that are available on Drupal.org and there is likely one that comes close to the layout and design that you would like to use on your site. To see the list of themes visit `www.drupal.org/project/themes`. If you can't find a theme that matches your requirements, you can use one of the various "starter" themes listed on the Drupal site (such as Zen) as a place to start. Revisit Chapter 6 for detailed instructions on how to download and install a Drupal theme.
	B	**Implement your sites specific design elements**
		If you pick an off-the-shelf theme from Drupal.org (versus creating one from scratch), you will likely want to change the themes logo, colors, and so on. The topic of theme development is beyond the scope of this book; however, you can read up on the concepts behind Drupal themes and which files you will want to look in to make changes to customize the them at `http://drupal.org/theme-guide`.
IV		**Downloading and Installing Contributed Modules**
		In step D, Phase you documented the functionality that you want to deliver to your site visitors beyond just content (such as blogs, RSS feeds, video, polls, forums, and e-commerce). In this Phase you will search for, install, and enable the modules that you need to address the desired functionality.

Phase	Task	Activity
	A	**Identify the modules required to address the desired functionality** Some of the functionality may be address by Drupal 7 core modules (such as blogs, the book module, forums, and the like) while other functionality may require searching for an appropriate module. To look for modules visit `http://drupal.org/project/modules`. In the left column you will see several categories of modules. You can start by browsing through the appropriate categories listed in the right column on `http://drupal.org/project/modules`. If you're struggling to find the right module, a good resource to use is the Drupal.org forums. The community is extremely helpful, and posting a quick question asking for advice on which module to use for a specific feature or function may cut down on your research time as well as picking the wrong module for the job.
	B	**Download and install required modules** Once you've identified the right modules to address the required functionality on your site, follow the instructions listed in Chapter 8 for installing, enabling, configuring, and setting permissions for each of the modules.
V		**Creating Custom Content Types** If you identified custom content types in Phase I, E, now is a good time to create those content types. Using the list of content types and the list of attributes for each type, follow the instructions in Chapter 10 for creating new content types.
VI		**Creating Views** There may be pages on which you want to provide a list or table view of content. Now is a good time to construct those views to support creation of pages in the next step. The process for creating views can be found in Chapter 11.
VII		**Creating the Physical Pages** Use the techniques described in this book to create the actual pages (for example, use the Panels module to create complex page layouts). Visit chapter 12 for a description of how to use panels, and Chapter 7 for a description of using blocks. Create the various pages that you defined in Phase I, task E

Continued

Phase	Task	Activity
VIII		**Finishing-Up the Menus on Your Site** With the pages in place, you're now ready to finalize the menus on your site. Revisit the navigational structure you defined in Phase I, task F to ensure that you've addressed all of the navigational requirements for your new site. For a description of how to create menus visit Chapter 5.
IX		**Finalizing the Configuration** At this point, the site should be configured and ready to go. In this phase, make sure that you have created all of the user roles, have assigned the appropriate permissions to those roles, and you have configured how users accounts will be created. Visit Chapter 3 for a description of how to define roles and assign permissions.
X		**Creating Content** Now that we have the site configured, content types created, views defined, panels created, and user roles and permissions defined its the time to create content on your site.
X		**Testing Your Site** With your site nearly ready for production, now is the time to test to make sure that everything works as you expect it to work. Make sure you test the site, as an anonymous user (not logged into the site). It is also a good idea to create test accounts for each of the user roles that you have defined and to visit the site while logged in to each account to ensure that the roles and permissions are working as you had envisioned.
XI		**Deploying to Production** It's now time to deploy your site to your production-hosting environment.
	A.	If you created your site on your desktop or laptop you'll need to copy the entire Drupal directory to your production web server, and you'll need to backup your database and restore the database on your hosting environment. For additional details on this process please see Chapter 13.

Phase	Task	Activity
	B.	If you created your site on a hosting providers platform you are already there and don't need to move your site.
XII		**Administering Your Site**
		As described in Chapter 13, monitor and manage your new Drupal web site.

Summary

In this chapter I covered the methodology for creating a new Drupal site, linking the methodology back to the steps that I covered throughout the rest of the book. Although every web site is different, the steps outlined in the methodology work for virtually any type of web site. It's important to think through everything described in the methodology, and in fact I would suggest that you find a quiet corner and walk through the methodology before starting to build your new site. The methodology forces you to think about what you are trying to accomplish before you build it, minimizing the risk of creating your web site and then finding out that you missed the boat completely.

Your Drupal journey has just begun. Congratulations on taking the first step by completing this book. Drupal is an amazing platform and one that takes time to fully digest. I would suggest continuing the learning process by picking up *Pro Drupal 7 Development,* third edition, by Dave Reid and John van Dyk (Apress, 2010). Although you may not want to be a developer, the book covers several topics that are relevant to site administrators. For a list of other Drupal books please visit `www.apress.com`.

If you have a desire to learn more about programming in PHP or CSS, I suggest picking up *PHP for Absolute Beginners* by Jason Lengstorf (Apress (2009) and *Beginning CSS Web Development* by Simon Collison (Apress, 2006). Both books are fantastic resources and are written for those who are starting to learn development for the web.

I look forward to seeing your new Drupal sites up on the web. Best wishes on your journey, I hope we cross paths at an upcoming DrupalCon!

CHAPTER 16

■ ■ ■

Case Study

In this chapter I will walk you through the process of creating a brand-new Drupal website using the concepts and tools covered in the first 15 chapters of this book. The focus of the case example is designing and developing a website for a non-profit organization that is focused on children with Asperger's syndrome (AS). The organization requested that I build a site that provides its staff with the ability to author and publish content that is focused on parents, teachers, caregivers, and those living with AS.

I'll walk you through the entire process that I went through to create the new site, describing what I did in each step from conceptual design to deployment. You can apply the concepts and approach that I describe in this chapter to create virtually any Drupal website.

Defining and Designing the Site

The first step in creating a new Drupal website is to define and design your new site. Depending on the purpose, scope, and complexity of your new site, the definition and design could be as simple as a few sketches on a napkin or as elaborate as a set of documents that fill up one or more three-inch binders. The key is sitting down and thinking about what you're going to build before you actually start building. If you don't take the time upfront to thoroughly think about what it is you're about to build, you're likely to run into situations where you have to rework portions of your solution to incorporate the concepts that you didn't think about when you started your project.

Target Audience

One of the first steps in defining the site is to think about the types of visitors the site will serve. Understanding the "who" part of the design equation will help you define "what" content and features you need to deploy to attract and retain those visitors. For this new site, I've identified the following key visitor types:

- Parents and grandparents of children with AS
- Parents and grandparents of children who think their child may have AS
- Teachers who have children in their classroom with AS
- Caregivers of children who have AS
- Children, teens, young adults, and adults who have AS
- General visitors who are interested in AS

There may be other "types" that will be visiting the site; however, this list should cover all of the content and functionality required to address the needs of anyone else who visits the site.

Identifying the Content and Functionality Required by Visitors

Using my list of visitor types, the next step is to identify what types of content each visitor type might want to access while on the new site. The simple approach for documenting the content requirements is to list the generate categories of content for each visitor type.

Parents or grandparents of AS children

- A general description of AS
- What to expect from a child with AS
- A list of resources where they can go to get help
- Success stories from other parents of children with AS
- A place to collaborate/communicate with other parents of AS children
- How to help your child's teacher understand the challenges of teaching AS children
- A list of upcoming events related to AS

Parents or grandparents of children who think their child may have AS

- Tools to diagnose whether a child has AS
- A list of resources where they can go for help
- Success stories from other parents of children with AS
- A list of upcoming events related to AS

Teachers who have children with AS in their classrooms

- Tools to diagnose whether a child has AS
- A list of resources for teachers
- A place to collaborate/communicate with other teachers
- A list of upcoming events related to AS

Caregivers of children who have AS

- Tools to diagnose whether a child has AS
- A list of resources where they can go for help
- A list of upcoming events related to AS

Children, teens, young adults, and adults who have AS

- A list of resources where they can go for help
- A place for people with AS to collaborate/communicate
- A list of upcoming events related to AS

General site visitors

A general definition of AS

A list of resources where they can go for help

A list of upcoming events related to AS

The next step in the process is to distill the list of content and functionality into a single list across all visitor types. For the case study site, the types of content include

General descriptive articles about AS (this covers a majority of the content listed by visitor type).

Descriptions of resources with links to the websites where the visitor can find those resources.

Events including the date, time, location, and description of those events.

The functionality required to support the targeted visitors includes

A place for visitors to collaborate and communicate. The tool for supporting this requirement is the Forums module.

Defining the Site's Structure

The next step in the process is to define the overall structure of the new site, where structure refers to the primary pages of the site. From the analysis of our visitors and the type types of content required to address the needs of those visitors, the following pages seem logical:

A home page for the site that provides general information about AS and highlights specific content for each of the major visitor types.

A resources-by-category page. There is enough commonality across visitors and types of resources to combine all of the resources on a single page.

An upcoming events page.

An "about us" page that describes the non-profit organization.

A "contact us" page.

A page for parents of AS children with content that is tagged through taxonomy as related to parenting.

A page for teachers of AS children with content that is tagged through taxonomy as related to teaching.

A page for caregivers of AS children with content that is tagged through taxonomy as related to care giving.

A page for children, teens, young adults, and adults with AS with content that is tagged through taxonomy as related to living with AS.

A discussion forum page.

There may be other pages that I discover I need as I move through the design process, but at the moment, the list appears to address all of the visitor types and content identified in the previous steps.

Defining the Custom Content Types and Taxonomy Structure

I have now identified three basic content types:

> A general content type that will be used for a majority of the content created on the site. The requirements call for a content type that provides the ability to author content that includes a title, body, pictures, and file attachments. The off-the-shelf Article content type provides all of these features. There is also a requirement to allow the author to categorize content by visitor type. I'll add a new taxonomy category for this and link the vocabulary to the Article content type.
>
> A content type used to create a resource. A resource has a title, a description, a category (taxonomy), and a URL that a visitor can click on to view the resource. To meet these requirements, I'll have to create a custom content type.
>
> An Event content type that will be used to capture the start date, start time, end date, end time, location, and description of an event. To meet these requirements, I'll have to create a custom content type.

During the previous steps, I identified two requirements for categorizing or tagging content: the ability to categorize resources and the ability to categorize all content based on targeted visitor type. To fulfill those requirements, I'll create two taxonomy vocabularies: one for visitor type and one for resource category. The terms for visitor type will be easy to define as I created the list of visitor types in previous steps. The terms for resource category might be a more difficult to define, as new types of resources are constantly being created. For that vocabulary, I will use Drupal's tagging feature, allowing the author to use an existing category or create a new category on the fly by simply typing in the new term while creating the resource. I'll start the list with a few categories, and will allow the list to grow organically as new content is added. The starter terms that I will use are: resources for parents, resources for teachers, and resources for caregivers.

Defining the Navigational Structure

With the visitor types, content types, and site structure defined, the next step is to define the navigational structure for the site. Because the site is relatively simple, I'll create a single horizontal menu that lists each of the pages identified during the site structure definition process as the items on the menu. I'll keep it simple at first, and will adjust the navigational structure over time if I find that visitors are unable to find the information they need. The menu items will be Home, Resources, Events, About Us, Contact Us, Parents, Teachers, Caregivers, Living with AS, and Forums.
At this point I have enough information to begin the process of physically creating the new site.

Installing Drupal

The first step in the process of creating the physical website is to install Drupal. For demonstration purposes, I am going to install the site on my laptop and then migrate the completed site to my hosting company. I'll follow the directions outlined in Appendix A to install the current version of Drupal 7.

Visual Design

With Drupal installed, the next step in the process is to pick a visual design. There are three general approaches to this: find an off-the-shelf theme at Drupal.org/project/themes, find a starter theme on Drupal.org, or start from scratch using a Photoshop file. The theme that I created in Chapter 13 is the perfect starting point for this project. The theme is simple, clean, and provides all of the flexibility that I need for this project. I'll copy both the /sites/all/themes/genesis and the /sites/all/themes/genesis_mytheme directories from the sample site used elsewhere in the book to my new site. After copying the folders, I'll need to enable the base Genesis theme. The base theme has attributes and elements that are used by the subtheme that we created. After enabling the base Genesis theme, I'll enable and set the subtheme I created in Chapter 13 as the default theme.

There are a few changes that I need to make to the theme fit my new site. The first is to revise the header. The organization that I am building the site for has a logo that is 960px X 200px, which is wider and taller than the base theme accommodates. There three basic changes that I'll need to make to insert the new logo:

> Most Drupal themes provide a feature whereby the site name specified on the site configuration page automatically renders in the header of the theme. For my site, the logo image includes the name, so I'll need to turn that feature off or the site name will overlay on top of the logo. To turn off that feature, I'll visit the Appearance page and will click on the Settings link for the theme that I am using on the site. On the Settings page is a list of features that you can toggle on or off, including the site name and site slogan. I'll uncheck the boxes for each of the elements that I don't need.
>
> I'll upload the organization's logo using the "Logo image settings" feature provided by Drupal. I'll uncheck the "Use the default logo" box that reveals a file-upload feature. I'll click on the "Choose file" feature and upload the organization's logo. I'll then click on the "Save configuration" button before continuing.
>
> After returning to the home page, I see that the logo image doesn't fit properly in the header of the theme. I'll have to modify the CSS associated with the header to make the theme fit the logo. First I'll update the #header and #logo attributes in the page.css file. The first change is to update the attributes for #header setting the height to 200px so the logo will fit within the boundaries of the header. Next I'll remove the margin attributes from #logo, as the new logo completely fills the header region. After saving page.css I'll return to the home page and see that the logo now fits perfectly within the boundaries of the header.

Next I'll change the color scheme. The logo and colors of the organization that I am supporting are blues, whereas the theme that I am using is based on three colors of green. I'll update page.css using search and replace to change all three green colors that I used in the base theme (see Chapter 13) with the three blue colors from the logo. There are two files that I'll need to update: the page.css and block.css.

Download and Install Contributed Modules

To fulfill the functional requirements for the new site, I'll need to download the following contributed modules:

Views: To create lists of resources and events

Pathauto: To create SEO and user friendly URLs

Backup and migrate: To automatically backup the site

Webform: To create online forms

Date: To enable entering information as date formatted fields

I'll follow the instructions outlined in Chapter 8 and install and configure the modules before moving onto the next step.

With the contributed modules in place, it's time to enable the core and contributed modules that I'll be using to build out the site. To meet the functional requirements, I'll enable all of the features of the contributed modules listed previously and the following Drupal 7 core modules

Aggegrator: I would like to display news feeds from sites that publish articles about AS. The aggregator allows me to take an RSS feed from another site and display it on my site.

Blog: I would like to provide the ability for the staff of the non-profit to blog on the site.

Contact: Instead of building a custom webform for the contact function, I'll use the Drupal core Contact module to enable that functionality.

Database logging: I like having the ability to review activity on the site, specifically error messages that are being generated by Drupal and the contributed modules. Database logging enables the ability to review the errors through Drupal's reporting mechanism (see Chapter 14 for details)

Field UI: I'll be creating custom content types, and the Field UI module provides features that I'll be using throughout that process.

File: I'll allow authors to attach files to content created on the site.

Forum: I'll use the Forum module as the approach for allowing visitors to collaborate and communicate on the site.

Image: I'll allow users to attach images to content types and manipulate those images using the capabilities of the Image module.

Menu: I'll use the standard Drupal menuing system to create, manage, and display menus on the site.

Search: I'll allow visitors to search the site using Drupal's built-in search engine.

Taxonomy: I'll use taxonomy to fulfill the requirements for content categorization and tagging.

With the modules enabled, there is a small cleanup task to do. I want to remove the standard Drupal blocks that are appearing in the left column of my site: the navigation and management blocks and the main content block. The main content block is a standard Drupal feature where new content that is published to the front page (see publishing options on the page used to create content) appears. I want more control over how content is rendered on the front page, so I'll remove that block from my site. I'll visit the blocks page and unassign those blocks from the left column and main content regions by selecting <none> from the list of available regions, saving the updates after I've made the two changes.

Creating User Roles and Setting Permissions

The organization's requirements for user roles and permissions are relatively simple. There are two required roles: staff and site administrator. The staff role has permission to author and publish content, post and administer comments, administer the forums, create web forms, and manage menus. The site administrator's role has all permissions enabled.

Creating the Taxonomy Vocabulary and Terms

With the required modules enabled, the next step is to create the taxonomy vocabularies and terms for visitor types and resources. Following the instructions in Chapter 4, I'll create a new vocabulary for visitor types, and will populate the vocabulary with the following terms: Parents, Teachers, Caregivers, and People with AS. Next I'll create the vocabulary for resources and will populate the vocabulary with the following terms: Resources for parents, Resources for teachers, Resources for Caregivers, and Resources for People with AS.

Creating the Custom Content Types

Following the directions covered in Chapter 10, I'll create new custom content types for resource and event.

The resource content type will allow the author to enter information in the following fields

A title that identifies the resource

A description that provides details about the resource

A URL linking the item to the resource

The taxonomy terms for visitor type

The taxonomy terms for resource category

The event content type will allow the author to enter information in the following fields

The title of the event

The start date for the event

The start time for the event

The end date for the event

The end time for the event

The location or venue for the event

A description of the event

A URL that links to a source for more information about the event

The taxonomy term for visitor type

With the new content types created, the next step is to update the two content types that ship with Drupal 7. I'll want to add the taxonomy terms for visitor types to both the Basic page and Article content types so that authors can easily categorize any content created on the site.

There are other content type cleanup activities that I need to perform. I would like to remove the "Posted by" and "Posted on" information from the Basic page, Articles, Events, and Resources content items. I also want suppress displaying the visitor types and resource types for the same content items. I use those fields to filter the content displayed by views, but it's not something that I want to display to visitors of my site.

To remove those attributes, I'll visit the Content Type configuration page for each of the content types I want to change, and on that page I'll click the "Display options" link near the bottom of the page, revealing the ability to set whether author and date information is displayed. I'll uncheck the option for each of the content types and then click the "Save content type" button. To remove the visitor and resource type fields, I'll click on the "Display options" link for each content type and will set the display option to Hidden for the label and value for both the teaser view and the full content view, as shown in Figure 16-1.

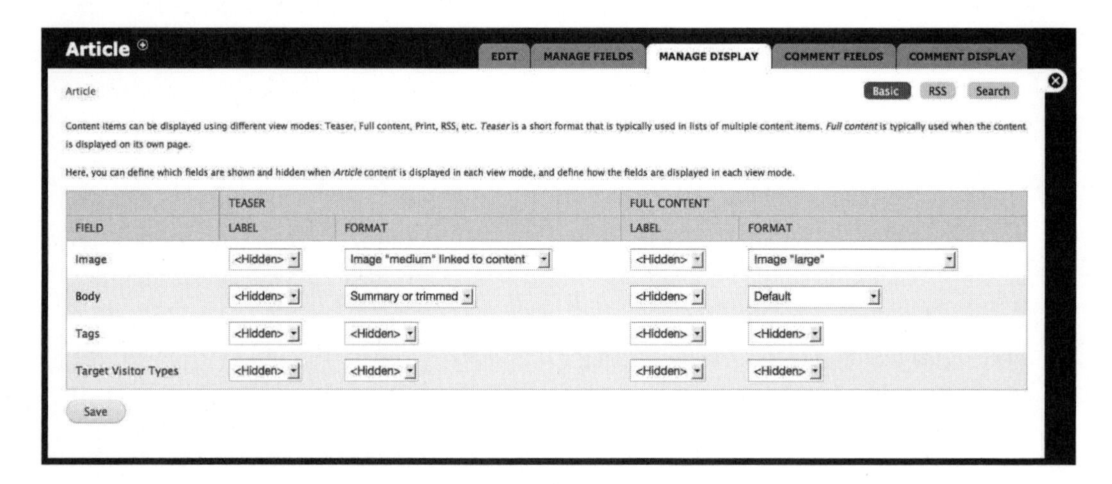

Figure 16-1. *Setting the visibility of the Tags and Target Visitor Types taxonomy terms*

After creating the content types, I'll create two sample content items for Basic page, Article, Event, and Resource so I have some content to work with when creating views in the next step.

Creating Views

The next step is to create the views required to extract and display content on the various pages of the site. Based on the requirements outlined in previous sections, I'll follow the process described in Chapter 11 to create the following views. See Table 16-1 for a list of required views.

Table 16-1. *Inventory of required views*

Description	Attribute / Setting
A view that displays the last five Basic pages and Articles created on the site. I'll use a views argument to restrict the Basic pages and Articles to a specific visitor type. I'll use this view on the home page and will leave the argument blank, which results in the first five new content items displaying, regardless of targeted audience. This view keeps visitors aware of the latest new content posted on the site, as well as making the major pages on the site (e.g., home page, parents, teachers, caregivers, and people with AS pages) dynamic.	1. Title = "Latest Content Posted on the Site" 2. Pager using 5 items per page 3. Rowstyle = node 4. Sort Criteria = node updated date in descending order 5. Arguments = taxonomy term for visitor type 6. Filters = node type Article and Basic page 7. Page views = I'll create multiple page views each with a unique URL. For the parents page, the URL for the page will be /parent, for teachers /teachers, for caregivers /caregivers and for people with AS /people-with-AS (matching the taxonomy term name for each of those categories of visitor types). The value of the URL will be used as the argument to restrict the values returned to content tagged for that visitor type. 8. A block display so that I can include this view on the homepage. I'll assign the block to the Content region and will restrict visibility to this block to the homepage (see Chapter 7 for details).

Continued

Table 16-1. Continued

Description	Attribute / Setting
An upcoming events view that lists the title and date for upcoming events, sorted by the event start date in ascending order. I'll use an argument to filter the events by targeted audience. If there isn't an argument, I'll list all upcoming events. If there is an argument, I'll restrict the items to only those events that match the argument. I'll also use Drupal's content scheduling feature to unpublish events after the event date has passed.	1. Title = "Upcoming events" 2. Rowstyle = fields 3. Fields = node title and event start date 4. Sort criteria = start date in ascending order 5. Arguments = taxonomy term for visitor type 6. Filters = node type of event 7. Block display created so I can place this view in the sidebar of the site
An upcoming events view that renders the complete node for published upcoming events. This will represent the master calendar for all upcoming events regardless of visitor type.	1. Title = "Upcoming events" 2. Rowstyle = nodes using the Full node option 3. Sort criteria = event start date in ascending order 4. Filters = node type of event 5. Page display using a URL of upcoming events
A view that renders resources sorted by resource category and title.	1. Title = "Resources" 2. Rowstyle = nodes using the teaser option 3. Sort criteria = resource category (taxonomy term) and title in ascending order 4. Filters = node type of resource 5. Page display using a URL of resources

With the views determined, I'm ready to create the menu that will direct visitors to the various pages on the site.

Setting Up the Contact Us Feature

One of the required features is a method for visitors to contact the organization. I'll use Drupal core's Contact module as the mechanism for providing this functionality. I'll enable the Contact module by following the directions covered in Chapter 8. After the module is enabled, I'll click on the Configure link on the Modules page for the Contact module, and will follow the directions to create a contact category.

Creating an About Us Page

The organization has requested that I create an About Us page. After discussing the requirements, a simple Basic page provides all of the necessary capabilities. I'll create a Basic page, setting the title to About Us, and will copy and paste the content from the organization's existing About Us page as a starting point for the new page.

Setting Up the Forums

Another key requirement is to provide online discussion forums. The requirements call for the ability for visitors to view and post to the following forum categories:

General topics

Parents

Teachers

Caregivers

Living with AS

Resources

Events

I will follow the steps outlined in Chapter 9 to set up the forum container and topics.

Setting Up the Feed Aggregator

Another of the requirements was to incorporate news articles posted on other sites on the home page. The organization would like to include news articles posted the news-medial.net website related to AS. To create the feed, I'll use Drupal's Aggregator module as the mechanism for collecting and displaying feeds. I'll enable the Aggregator module, and then configure the inbound feeds by clicking on the Configuration link at the top of the page, and the Feed aggregator link on the Configuration page. On the Feed aggregator configuration page, I'll click on the "Add feed" link and enter "Latest AS News" in the title and www.news-medical.net/tag/feed/Aspergers-Syndrome.aspx in the URL field. I'll leave the other settings at their default values and then save the feed.

Creating the Menu Items

With all of the pages created, either through views, nodes, or modules (such as Contact), I'm now ready to create the menu for the site. Based on the theme that I am using, the menu that I'll want to use is the Secondary menu. I'll follow the steps outlined in Chapter 5 to create the menu items listed in Table 16-2.

Table 16-2. Menu items

Menu Item	Links to
Home	<front>
Resources	/resources
Events	/events
About Us	/about-us
Contact Us	/contact
Parents	/parents
Teachers	/teachers
Caregivers	/caregivers
Living with AS	/people-with-AS
Forums	/forum/N where N can be found by clicking on the forum container link on the Structure -> Forums page

After creating the menu items, I'll need to assign the Secondary menu block (a standard block that is part of Drupal core) to the Main Menu Links region.

Wrapping Up the Pages

I now have all of the components required to address the functional requirements of the site. I'll wrap up the process by adding and configuring the blocks for each of the pages on the site, as shown in Table 16-3.

Table 16-3. Adding blocks to pages

Page	Blocks
Homepage	Latest Content block. When I created the latest content view, I created a block display so that I could incorporate that block into the homepage. I'll visit the Block configuration page and will assign the Latest Content block to the Content region. I'll update the block visibility settings so that the block only appears on the homepage by setting the value to <front> Upcoming Events block. When I created the list of upcoming events view, I included a block display. I'll set the upcoming events block to display in the First sidebar region, and I'll set the visibility so that the block appears on the homepage (<front>). Latest news articles collected through the feed aggregator. I'll assign the Latest AS News block to the First sidebar region, and I'll set the visibility so that the block appears on the homepage.
Resources	Latest news articles collected through the feed aggregator. News articles often describe resources, so I'll assign the Latest AS News block to the First sidebar region, and I'll set the visibility so that the block also appears on the Resources page.
Parents, Teachers, Caregivers, and Living with AS	Upcoming Events block. When I created the list of upcoming events view, I included a block display. I'll set the upcoming events block to display in the First sidebar region, and I'll update the block visibility settings to include each of the additional pages.

Testing the Site

With everything in place and ready for production, I'll test the site to ensure that it does everything that the organization wants it to do. To test the site, I'll define a number of scenarios to run through and will document the results of each. To perform the tests, I'll need to set up two user accounts: one assigned to the staff and one assigned to the site administrator role. The scenarios that I have defined to test the site are listed in Table 16-4.

Table 16-4. *Testing scenarios*

Scenario	Description	Expected Result
Create Basic page, Article, and Event content for parents, teachers, caregivers, and living with AS.	1. Log on to the site using the user assigned to the staff role. 2. Create a Basic page and Article for each of the targeted visitor types (one Basic page and one Article per visitor type). 3. Create an Event for each visitor type.	1. Basic pages and Articles appear on the homepage. 2. Basic pages, Articles, and Events assigned to the parents visitor type only appear on the front page and parents page. 3. Basic pages, Articles, and Events assigned to the teacher visitor type only appear on the front page and teachers page. 4. Basic pages, Articles, and Events assigned to the caregiver visitor type only appear on the front page and caregivers page. 5. Basic pages, Articles, and Events assigned to the people with AS visitor type only appear on the front page and living with AS page.
Create at least two Resource content items and assign each to a different category.	1. Log on as a user account with the staff role. 2. Create two resource content items: one assigned to resources for parents and one assigned to resources for teachers.	1. Both content items are successfully saved. 2. Both content items appear on the resources page, sorted by resource type and title.
Attempt to create a Basic page, Article, and Event as an anonymous user.	1. Visit the site as an anonymous user (not logged in). 2. Attempt to create a Basic page, Article, and event.	1. Error message that you are not authorized.
Create a Basic page, Article, Event, and Resource content items while logged in as a site administrator.	1. Log on as a user account with site administrator. 2. Create a Basic page, Article, Event, and Resource content item.	1. Successfully saved each content item.

Continued

Scenario	Description	Expected Result
Visit the Parents page as an anonymous user.	1. Log out of the site if you are already logged on. 2. Visit the Parents page.	1. Upcoming events for parents are displayed. 2. Latest content items assigned to the parents content type are displayed.
Visit the Teachers page as an anonymous user.	1. Log out of the site if you are already logged on. 2. Visit the Teachers page.	1. Upcoming teachers' events are displayed. 2. Latest content items assigned to the teachers content type are displayed.
Visit the Caregivers page as an anonymous user.	1. Log out of the site if you are already logged on. 2. Visit the Caregivers page.	1. Upcoming caregivers' events are displayed. 2. Latest content items assigned to the caregivers content type are displayed.
Visit the Living with AS page as an anonymous user.	1. Log out of the site if you are already logged on. 2. Visit the Living with AS page.	1. Upcoming events are displayed. 2. Latest content items assigned to the living with AS content type are displayed.
Visit the Resources page as an anonymous user.	1. Logout of the site if you are already logged on. 2. Visit the Resources page.	1. Resource content is displayed sorted by resource category and title.
Visit the Contact Us page as an anonymous user.	3. Log out of the site if you are already logged on. 4. Visit the Contact Us page. 5. Fill out and submit a contact request.	2. Contact Us form is displayed. 3. You are allowed to enter contact information. 4. Form saves successfully and displays the thank-you message. 5. Values are received by the person assigned as the recipient of the contact request.

Continued

Scenario	Description	Expected Result
Visit the About Us page as an anonymous user.	1. Log out of the site if you are currently logged on. Click on the About Us menu item.	1. About Us page is displayed.
Visit the Forums page as an anonymous user, and review existing posts, create a new post, and post a response to an existing post.	1. Log out of the site if you are currently logged on. 2. Click on the Forums menu item. 3. Click on one of the forum topics that has an existing posting (as indicated in the number of posts field). 4. Read the posting. 5. Click on "Add a new forum topic" and "Create a new topic." 6. Click on the "Add a new forum topic" link. 7. Enter a subject, select a forum, enter your topic in the body section, and save the item. 8. For the item you just created, create a new comment by entering a subject and comment.	1. Forums page is displayed after clicking on the Forum menu item. 2. A list of forum topics is displayed on the forum page. 3. Clicking on a topic that has a topic count greater than zero displays the topics associated with that item. 4. The new forum topic created is displayed on the site. 5. Posting a comment results in that comment being listed for the topic that the comment was posted against.
Edit an existing content item while logged in as a staff or site administrator.	1. Log on to the site. 2. Click on the title of a content item. 3. Click on the Edit tab. 4. Make a small change to the content item and save it.	1. Edit tab appears at the top of the content item. 2. Allows you to edit the content item. 3. Updates made to the item are displayed on the site.

After testing the site and ensuring that every works as it should I'm ready to deploy the site to production.

Deploying to Production

After testing the site, I'm ready to deploy it to the organization's production server. I developed the site on my laptop, so I'll need to perform the following steps to move the site to the new server:

1. Set up an empty database on the production server.
2. Create a database user account and assign all privileges to that account.

3. Copy the entire site directory from my laptop's hard drive to the product servers document root directory (the location of the document root directory varies by operating system and web server; check with your hosting company or the web server's documentation).
4. Using mysqldump or PHPMyAdmin, back up the database on my laptop and copy that backup file to the production server.
5. Using MySQL's command line interface or PHPMyAdmin, restore the database backup to the new database created in the first step.
6. Edit the /sites/default/settings.php file and update the database settings to reflect the name of the database, the database user name, and the database user password.
7. Visit the site and ensure that everything is up and running. If you followed along in this chapter, you should have a site that looks something like Figure 16-2.

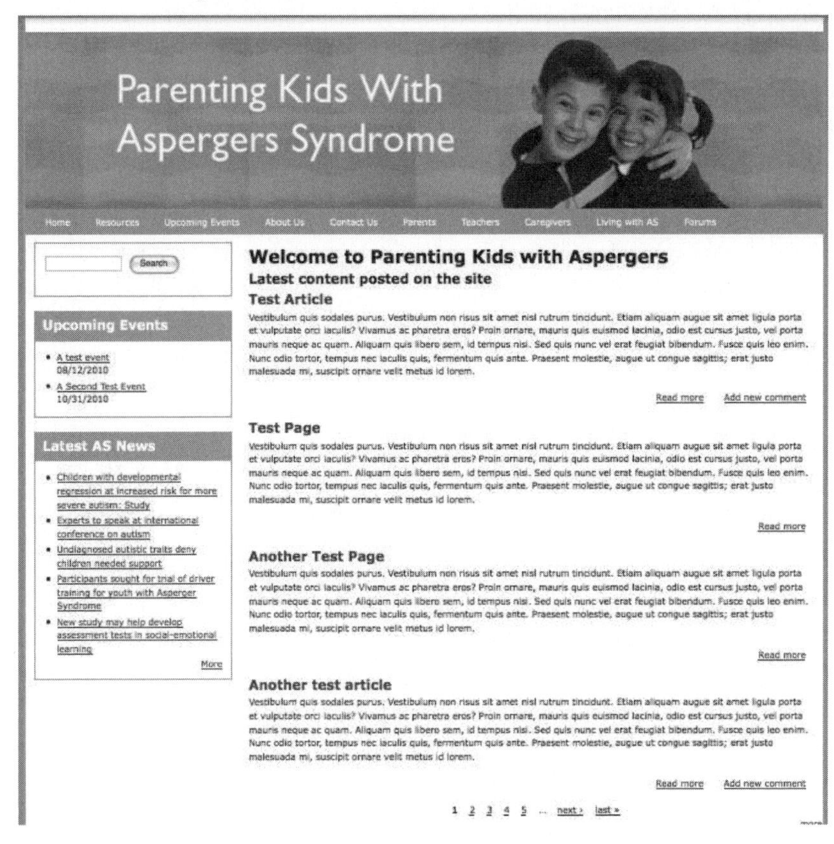

Figure 16-2. The finished site, ready for its first visitors

Create User Accounts

With the new site migrated to the production server, the final step in the process is to create the production user accounts. I'll first delete all of the accounts that I created during the testing phase (with the exception of the administrator's account) and then add the required users and assign each user to the appropriate role. The site is now ready for visitors!

Summary

Congratulations! At this point you have enough knowledge and experience to embark on the journey of creating a new Drupal website from scratch. If you take the time to follow the general pattern described in this chapter, you should be able to create virtually any website on Drupal. The key to success lies in clearly defining what you are building upfront, before you make any attempts at setting up and configuring Drupal.

APPENDIX A

■ ■ ■

Installing Drupal

If you are hosting your Drupal site on a commercial web-hosting provider, it is likely that it has a tool that installs Drupal for you. If that's the case, you can bypass this chapter and follow the directions provided to you by your web-hosting provider. But if you need to install Drupal on your laptop, desktop, or server, then this appendix is for you.

In the sections that follow, I will walk you through the step-by-step process of installing foundational components such as PHP, MySQL, and Apache, as well as the steps for downloading and installing Drupal 7. At the end of this appendix, you will have installed Drupal and will be ready to work through the main body of the book.

The Foundation Required to Install Drupal

Before installing Drupal, you must have access to a server, which must have several pieces of software installed and configured. The type of server you choose is purely a matter of personal preference. You can install and configure Drupal on a Windows, Macintosh, or Linux-based server. Those servers can be either a local machine (your desktop or laptop) or a hosted server (shared or dedicated, hosted by an organization such as Hostmonster).

You will need to have the following components loaded, configured, and running on your server before you begin the Drupal installation process:

- **A web server** (either Apache or Microsoft's Internet Information Server): For the purposes of this book, I will focus on an Apache-based solution, because Apache runs on all of the platforms that Drupal supports. For information on installing and configuring IIS, please consult www.microsoft.com.
- **PHP**: PHP the programming language used by Drupal.
- **A relational database server** (either MySQL or PostgreSQL): For the purposes of simplifying the installation process, I will focus on MySQL. For details on installing and configuring PostgreSQL please consult www.postgresql.org.
- **FTP** (File Transfer Protocol): FTP is used for uploading files to the server.
- **Various libraries** for image handling, secure connections, and mail routing.

If your intent is to run your new Drupal site in a hosted environment, the work of setting up the foundational components has already been done for you by the hosting company. If you are using a hosting company, you can skip to the section on installing Drupal. If your intention is to develop your site on your desktop or laptop and then deploy your site to a server, you will need to install and configure the components required to support Drupal.

Setting Up the Server

Before you install Drupal, you need three basic components in place: the server, the web server, and the database. If you are hosting your site with a commercial hosting company, you can skip to the installing Drupal section, as everything you need is already installed.

Depending on the operating system on your computer, you may already have a few of the required components already installed (for example, OSX comes with Apache and PHP already installed). However, getting all of the components to work together may be more of a challenge than most people want to undertake. Fortunately, a group of very talented people at apachefriends.org created an "all-in-one" software package called XAMPP (XAMPP stands for Apache, MySQL, PHP, and Python) that is very simple for even the least technical person to install and configure. There is an XAMPP distribution for Windows, Macintosh (OSX) , Linux, and Solaris.

The components included in XAMPP that are critical for Drupal are:

- Apache: The web server software package that handles requests for content residing on your server and returning the results of that request back to the person who made it.
- MySQL: The relational database where Drupal stores all of its content.
- PHP & PEAR: The programming language used by the developers who create and maintain Drupal.
- phpMyAdmin: An invaluable tool for creating and managing databases, tables, and data stored in your MySQL database.

There are detailed instructions for installing XAMPP on each of the supported platforms on the `apachefriends.org`.

Installing Drupal

Now that you have the underlying server components installed, you are ready to install Drupal. There are five basic steps associated with installing Drupal on your server, regardless of whether you are running your Drupal site on a Windows, OSX, Linux, or shared-hosting-based server.

1. Download the current Drupal installation package from `http://drupal.org` to your computer.
2. Decompress the Drupal installation package.
3. Copy the files to your web server's root directory.
4. Create the database that you will be using for your new Drupal web site.
5. Launch the Drupal installation script.

Downloading Drupal

Downloading Drupal is a simple matter of visiting **`www.drupal.org`** and picking the latest version and language (such as English or French) of Drupal to download from the homepage. Drupal version numbers change over time, but it is safe to pick the latest version listed on the homepage as the version to download, install, and configure.

To download Drupal, simply click on the homepage link for the latest version, which will take you to the main Drupal download page. On the main download page, click on the link associated with the latest version (for example, 7.0). The compressed file (tar.gz) will automatically download to your computer into the folder you have configured for receiving downloads from the Internet.

Decompressing the Drupal Installation Package

The file downloaded from Drupal.org is a compressed file that has all of the directories and files required to set up and run Drupal on your server. You will need to decompress the tar.gz file into its individual elements, either by double-clicking on the file (this works on OSX and Linux) or by opening the file in a decompression utility (for example, on Windows use a free utility like 7zip). Double-clicking on the file will result in a folder being created on your computer with all of the directories and files expanded to their original pre-compressed state.

■ **Note** Depending on your operating system and your setting for your operating systems file manager, you may or may not see the .htaccess file, as it is classified as a "hidden" file in Linux and OSX. This is a critical file and must be moved in the next step. If you do not see the .htaccess file, please update your file browser's settings to allow you to see hidden files before proceeding to the next step.

Moving the Drupal Distribution to the Root Directory of Your Web Server

The next step is to move the contents of the Drupal folder that you just decompressed in the previous step, to the "root" directory of your web server. If you are using XAMPP, the "root" directory is the folder marked as "htdocs" in the directory where XAMPP is installed. If you are installing Drupal on a hosted platform, the root directory will be that specified by your hosting company (for example, the hosting company that I use names the root directory "public_html"). You should check with your hosting company if you are unsure where to put your Drupal files).

With all of the files in place, you're ready to take the next step of creating the database.

Creating the settings.php File

Drupal uses a file named settings.php to store configuration parameters for your site, such as the name of the database and the userID and password used to access that database. Drupal ships with a default settings.php file that we will use as the starting point for our site's settings.php file. Navigate to the sites/default directory in the location where you copied the Drupal directories and files to in the previous step. In that directory you will find a default.settings.php file. Copy that file and rename the copied version to settings.php.

Next, set the permissions on the settings.php so that anyone can read and update the file. Drupal must have the ability to update this file during the update process. Check your operating systems directions for setting permissions if you're unsure on how to do this.

Creating the Drupal Database

Creating the database is a relatively simple process. If you are using XAMPP or a hosting provider, you should have access to the phpmyadmin administrators tool. To access the admin tool, visit http://localhost/xampp page. In the Tools section, you will see a link to "phpmyadmin." Please click on that link to launch the phpmyadmin administrator's page.

On this page, locate the text box that is right below the "Create new database" label. In this text box, type in a name that is easy for you to remember and is representative of what your web site is about (using this approach makes it easier in the future to figure out which database goes with which web site, especially when you have multiple Drupal sites running on your server). MySQL is extremely flexible, and you can name your databases anything that you wish; however, there are generally accepted standards that you may wish to follow:

- Only use lowercase characters.
- Separate words with underscores.
- Keep the database name shorter than 64 characters (a MySQL restriction).

For demonstration purposes, I have created a new database named "drupal7testsite." After entering the database name, click on the Create button. See Figure A-1.

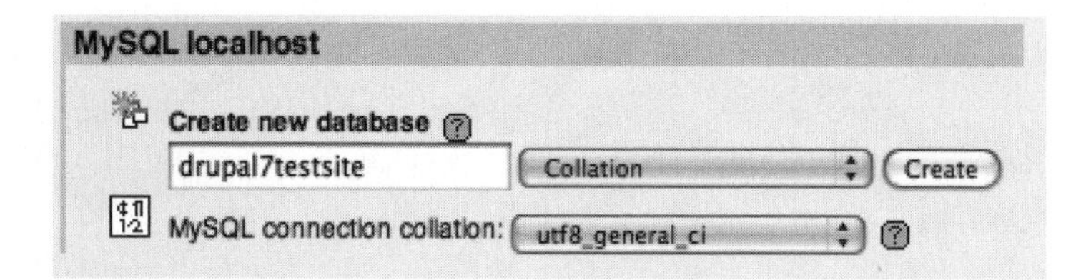

***Figure A-1.** Creating a new MySQL database*

The next screen that appears shows that the database was created. We don't have to create any tables, which is what this screen can be used for, because Drupal will create the tables for us as part of the installation script.

Creating a User Account

The next step is to create a MySQL user who will be associated with the database that we just created. You can use the "root" account that is created automatically when MySQL is installed. However, for security purposes, it is a better practice to create a user account that can only access this database. To access the user account creation screens, simply click on the Privileges tab. This screen lists all existing user accounts. Click on the "Add a New User" link at the bottom of the page.

There are four fields on this screen that we need to fill to create our new user account (see Figure A-2):

- User ID: This is the unique value that represents our database user and will be used by Drupal to log onto the database. For our example enter drupal7.
- Host: This field provides the ability to restrict which system the user can log in from. For security purposes, we want to set this value to "localhost" by selecting the Local option from the drop-down list. Localhost is your web server; we don't want that user to have the ability to log in from any system other than the server.
- Password: Create a password and enter that same password in the "Re-type" field.
- Database for User: Here, leave the default option, which is to grant all privileges on the database that we just created, and then press the Go button at the bottom of the form.

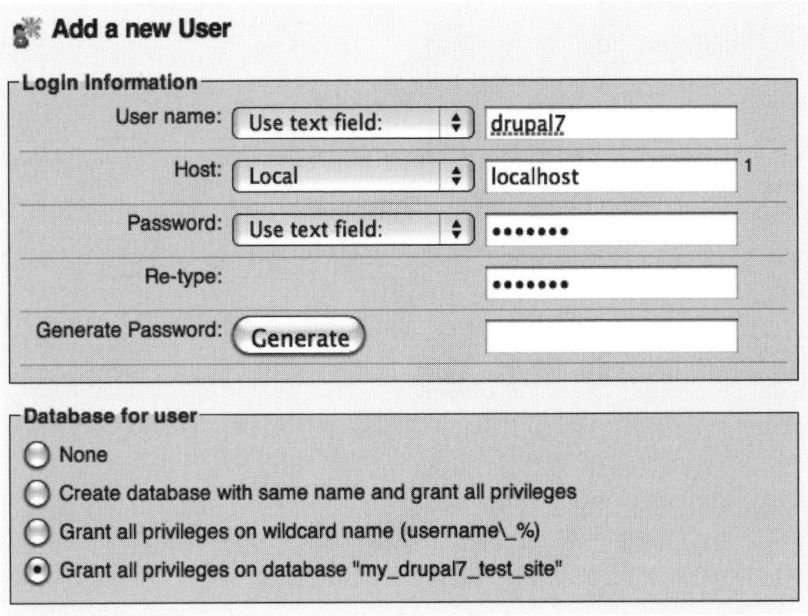

Figure A-2. Creating a new database user

One you press the Go button, phpMyAdmin creates your user account and grants the user the required privileges to use your new database. You are now ready to start the Drupal configuration process.

Configuring Drupal

To start the configuration process, simply open a web browser and type http://localhost in the address bar. The first page lists two installation profile options (see Figure A-3). The Standard option installs the complete version of Drupal with all of the core modules that I describe and use throughout the book. The Minimal profile installs a bare bones version of Drupal, without many of the core modules that I describe elsewhere in this book (for example, it does not install forums, blogs, and polls). For a vast majority of Drupal site owners, the Standard version is the correct one to select. If you're developing a custom platform (your own distribution profile with specific modules) you may wish to start with the Minimal profile. For our case select the Standard option and click Save and continue.

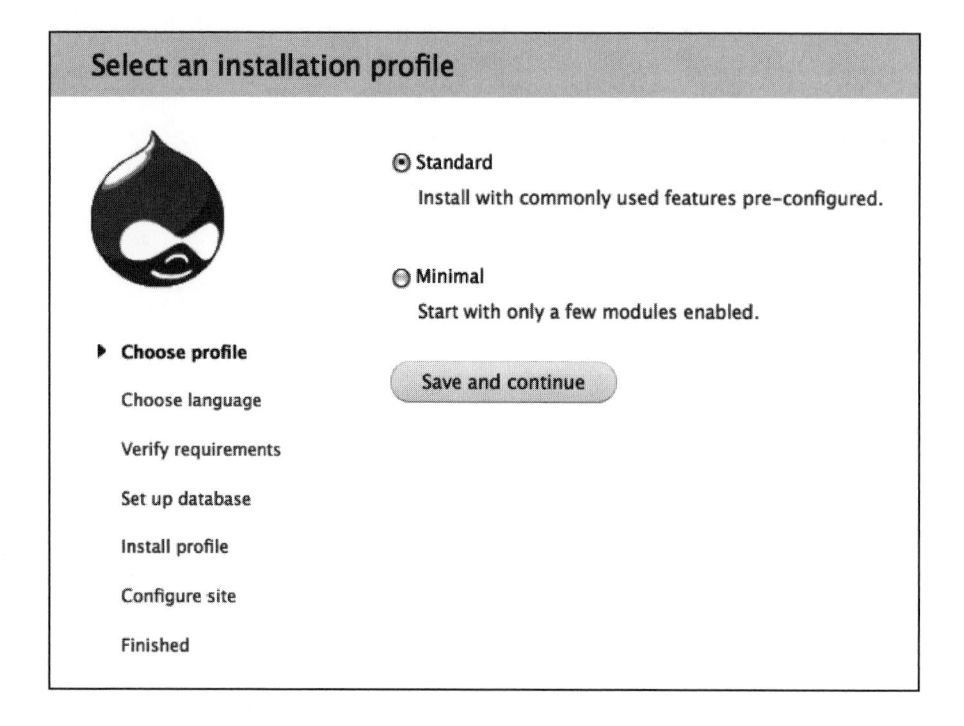

Figure A-3. *Selecting the installation profile*

The next screen in the process asks for the details of the database that you created in the create database process. On this screen (shown in Figure A-4) enter:

- Database name: Enter the name you used when you created the database.
- Database username: Enter the user ID you used when you created the new user.
- Database password: Enter the password you used when you created the new user.

If you've forgotten what you used for any of the above values, you can look them up through phpmyadmin.

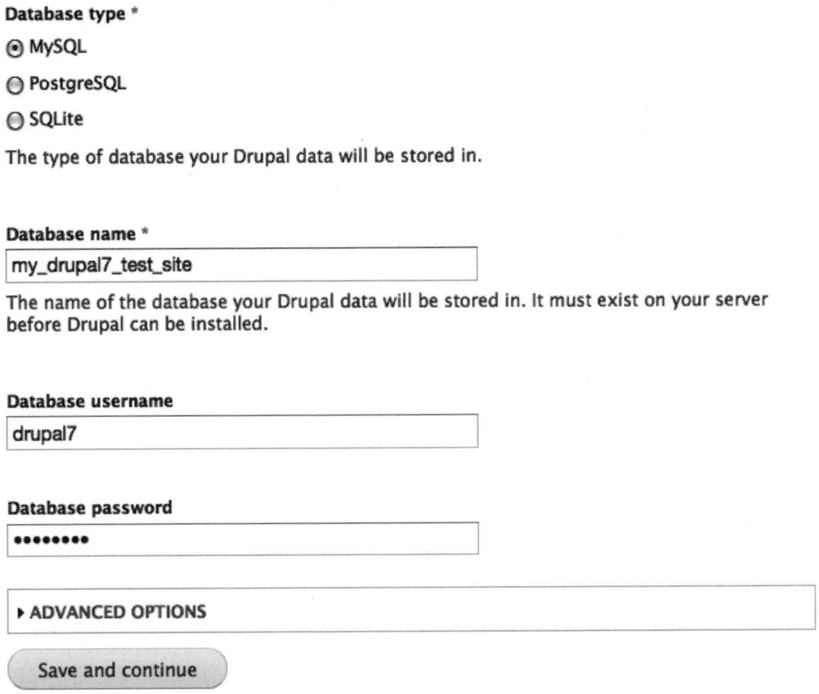

Database type *

◉ MySQL

○ PostgreSQL

○ SQLite

The type of database your Drupal data will be stored in.

Database name *

my_drupal7_test_site

The name of the database your Drupal data will be stored in. It must exist on your server before Drupal can be installed.

Database username

drupal7

Database password

••••••••

▸ ADVANCED OPTIONS

Save and continue

Figure A-4. Setting the database parameters

If you entered the correct values, Drupal will run the installation scripts. After Drupal creates the database tables required to support your new site, we're ready to set a few simple configuration parameters (see Figure A-5).

All necessary changes to *./sites/default* and *./sites/default/settings.php* have been made. They have been set to read-only for security.

SITE INFORMATION

Site name *

localhost

Site e-mail address *

Automated e-mails, such as registration information, will be sent from this address. Use an address ending in your site's domain to help prevent these e-mails from being flagged as spam.

SITE MAINTENANCE ACCOUNT

Username *

Spaces are allowed; punctuation is not allowed except for periods, hyphens, and underscores.

E-mail address *

Figure A-5. *The site configuration form*

On this form enter the following values:

- Site Information

  Site name: The name or title of your site.

  Site e-mail address: This is the default e-mail address that will be used by Drupal for any outbound e-mails generated by the system.

- Site Maintenance Account

  Username: This is the username of the administrators account for your new web site. Use something that is easy for you to remember.

E-mail address: the e-mail address where administrator related emails will be sent

Password: Enter the password for the administrator's account.

Confirm password: Re-enter the password you entered in the password field.

- **Server Settings**

  Default country: The country where you reside (or leave the no default country value if you do not want to specify the default country; this is an optional field).

  Default time zone: Select the appropriate time zone for your web site.

- **Update Notifications**

  Check for updates automatically: If checked, this feature looks for updates to Drupal core and any contributed modules you have installed and highlights cases where a new version or a security patch has been released. It's a good idea to check this, as it makes the task of tracking updates to modules much easier than having to manually check each module's status.

  Receive e-mail notifications: If checked, this directs Drupal to send an e-mail to the administrator when new versions of modules are detected.

Once you've updated the values, simply click on the "Save and continue" button. The result of clicking that button should be a screen that indicates that you have successfully installed Drupal!

Click on the "Visit your new site" link at the bottom of the page to see the homepage of your new Drupal web site.

Summary

In this appendix, I covered the process for setting up the server and installing Drupal. You're now ready to begin the journey of creating an incredible web site using the Drupal 7 platform!

APPENDIX B

Additional Resources

As you begin (and continue) your journey of learning Drupal, there will likely be times when you'll need to find a Drupal module, a Drupal theme, additional details about specific Drupal technologies (such as theming), and operating system level commands (like backing up the site from the command line). The following is a list of recommended web sites where you can find additional resources to help you along your journey.

Drupal Modules

The primary site for finding modules is the Drupal.org web site (`http://drupal.org/project/modules`). Every Drupal contributed module has its own "homepage" that describes the module, provides links for downloading the various versions of the module, and, in most cases, links to additional documentation and examples.

Another site that provides a slightly more user-friendly interface is the Drupal Modules site (`www.drupalmodules.com`). This site provides a friendly search interface, user reviews, user ratings, most downloaded, most favored, and other value added services.

Drupal Themes

The primary source of Drupal themes is the Drupal.org web site (`http://drupal.org/project/themes`). You can browse through dozens of themes, see screenshots of each, and download the themes you like from Drupal.org.

Another useful site is the Theme Garden site (`http://themegarden.org/drupal6/`). Note: I assume that Theme Garden will develop a Drupal 7 site. This site is unique in that it is a Drupal site that allows you to change the theme of the site on the fly to see how a site looks using the various themes that are available on Drupal.org.

Drupal Documentation

The Drupal community has assembled a number of online handbooks (`http://drupal.org/handbooks`)

that are chock-full of information about Drupal. You will find handbooks that cover topics such as:

- Getting Started
    - Understanding Drupal
    - Installation Guide
    - Administration Guide
- Creating a Site
    - Structure Guide
    - Site Building Guide
    - Theming Guide
- Writing Your Own Code
    - Developing for Drupal
    - API Reference
- Reference
    - Code snippets
    - Troubleshooting
    - FAQs
- Tutorials
    - Drupal Cookbook
    - Tutorials
    - Videos and Slides
- Community
    - About Drupal
    - Getting Involved
    - Documentation Team

Where to Go When you Have Problems

One of the best sources for Drupal help is the forums on the Drupal.org web site (`http://drupal.org/forum`). There are hundreds of thousands of postings on just about every conceivable topic. If you run into an issue, you're likely to find that the solution to your problem is already documented in the forums. If you can't find a solution, you can post a question to the forums and receive a solution to your problem often within hours of posting the issue.

How to Backup Your Drupal Site

In Chapter 13 I talked about using the backup and migrate module as a means of backing up the database. You will also want to backup the directories on your server. There is a detailed description of how to do this on the Drupal.org web site (`http://drupal.org/node/22281`).

Where to Host Your Drupal Site

If you are looking for a place to host your web site, an excellent resource is the Drupal.org site (`http://drupal.org/hosting`). The hosting page lists a number of companies that are known to support Drupal.

Where to go to Learn HTML and CSS

A great resource to help you learn HTML and CSS is the W3Schools web site (`www.w3schools.com/`). You'll find easy-to-understand tutorials and excellent examples.

Video Tutorials

There are thousands of YouTube (`www.youtube.com`) videos that cover a wide variety of Drupal topics. It is a great source for learning various aspects of Drupal. Enter Drupal in YouTube's search box and you'll see a very long list of Drupal related videos.

Drupal Podcasts

Another great source for learning Drupal is podcasts. There are a number podcasts that cover Drupal on iTunes.

APPENDIX C

■ ■ ■

Social Networking

We are in the middle of a fundamental shift in how websites interact with visitors. We've moved from designing and developing websites that allow visitors to look at content to sites that allow visitors to participate in the process of creating content and sharing that content with the their circle of friends. While the general term used for this is "social networking," I like to think of it as the concept of the participative web.

In this appendix, I'll show you how to leverage Drupal's core capabilities as well as contributed modules to extend the reach of your website by enabling your visitors to participate in the content creation process and share their experience and content on your site with their circle of influence. I'll show you how to put your face on Facebook, tweet your expertise on Twitter, picture things on Flickr, and avail of other social networking capabilities.

■ **Note** The capabilities discussed here were not available in Drupal 7 at the time the book was written, but are available in Drupal 6 and will be ported to Drupal 7 at some point in the future.

Expanding Your Reach by Sharing

One of the easiest mechanisms for embracing social networking on your Drupal site is to allow visitors to post content they find interesting on your site to one or more social networking sites. It's a feature that enables visitors to say, "hey, look what I found" by posting your content on one or more of the sites shown in Figure C-1.

AIM	AOL Mail	Allvoices	Amazon Wish List	Arto	Ask.com MyStuff
Backflip	Bebo	BibSonomy	Bitty Browser	Blinklist	BlogMarks
Blogger Post	Bookmarks.fr	Box.net	BuddyMarks	Care2 News	CiteULike
Connotea	Current	DZone	DailyMe	Delicious	Digg
Diglog	Diigo	Evernote	Expression	Facebook	Fark
Faves	Folkd	Foxiewire	FriendFeed	FunP	Gabbr
Google Bookmarks	Google Buzz	Google Gmail	Google Reader	Health Ranker	HelloTxt
Hemidemi	Hotmail	Hugg	Hyves	Identi.ca	Imera Brazil
Instapaper	Jamespot	Jumptags	Khabbr	Kledy	LinkaGoGo
Linkatopia	LinkedIn	LiveJournal	MSDN	Maple	Meneame
MindBodyGreen	Mister-Wong	Mixx	Mozillaca	Multiply	MyLinkVault
MySpace	Netlog	Netvibes Share	Netvouz	NewsTrust	NewsVine
NowPublic	Oneview	Orkut	PhoneFavs	Ping	Plaxo Pulse
Plurk	Posterous	PrintFriendly	Propeller	Protopage Bookmarks	Pusha
Read It Later	Reddit	Segnalo	Shoutwire	Simpy	SiteJot
Slashdot	SmakNews	Sphere	Sphinn	Spurl	Squidoo
StartAid	Strands	StumbleUpon	Stumpedia	Symbaloo Feeds	Taggly
Tagza	Tailrank	TechNet	Technorati Favorites	Technotizie	Tipd
Tumblr	Twiddla	Twitter	TypePad Post	Viadeo	VodPod
Webnews	Windows Live Favorite:	Windows Live Spaces	Wink	Wists	WordPress
Xerpi	Yahoo Bookmarks	Yahoo Buzz	Yahoo Mail	Yahoo Messenger	Yample
YIGG	Yoolink	YouMob	unalog		

Figure C-1. *The social networking sites to which your visitors can post your content*

Allowing visitors to post your content on their favorite social networking sites turns your visitors into marketing engines for your site. If a visitor likes something on your website, they will likely post it on one or more social networking sites. The great aspect of social networking is that people of similar interests tend to congregate on the same sites. The potential result for you is new visitors that you didn't have to search for yourself. It's a powerful capability that you should not overlook.

To provide the ability to easily share your content with social networking sites, all you have to do is install and configure the Add to Any Share/Bookmark module (Drupal.org/project/addtoany). After installing and configuring the module, Drupal will automatically render a small button beneath each content item on your site. When a visitor clicks on the button, a list of social networking sites that you have selected appears, allowing the visitor to click and submit your content item to a social networking site (see Figure C-2). The module also provides the ability to e-mail the content item to a friend and bookmark the page.

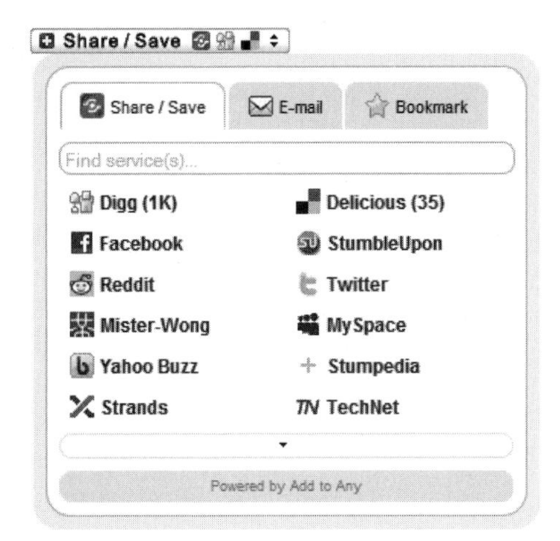

***Figure C-2.** The Add to Any widget*

Integrating Your Site with Social Networking Sites

Linking content to social networking sites is only one dimension of the capabilities you have with Drupal. Another approach is to integrate the content from various social networking sites into your Drupal site and automatically post new content items created on your site on various social networking sites. There are several Drupal contributed modules for integrating your site with social networking sites like Facebook, Twitter, Flickr, and YouTube.

Integrating Drupal with Facebook

With over 400 million users and 200 million users who sign on daily, Facebook is the granddaddy of all social networking sites. Tapping the Facebook community with your Drupal site is a relatively simple process that involves the use of two Drupal modules.

The Facebook Status Module (`drupal.org/project/fbstatus`). This module provides the ability to display Facebook status updates from your Facebook account on your Drupal site. Using Facebook's RSS feed capability, status updates from your Facebook profile are automatically captured and displayed on your Drupal site in a block.

The Drupal for Facebook Module (`drupal.org/project/fb`). This module provides a powerful set of features that allow you to essentially embed your Drupal website within Facebook as a Facebook application. Using this module you can deploy all the content, features, and functionality of your Drupal website as a Facebook application. You can see a demonstration of the capabilities enabled by this module at `http://apps.facebook.com/drupalforfacebook/`.

Integrating Drupal with Twitter

The Twitter module (`http://drupal.org/project/twitter`) provides the ability to display your tweets in a block on your Drupal site and the ability to post tweets whenever a new content item is created on your site. Figure C-3 demonstrates the ability to post a tweet when you create a new content item and the display of tweets in a block.

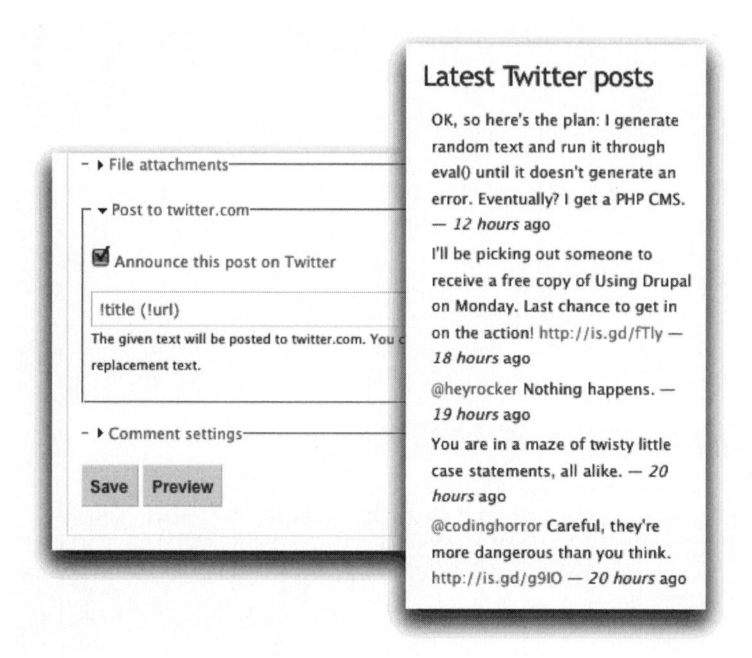

Figure C-3. *Posting a tweet*

Integrating Drupal with Flickr

There are several Drupal modules that provide the ability to integrate your site with Flickr. Examples of modules that you may wish to use include:

> **The Flickr module** (`http://drupal.org/project/flickr`) provides the ability to download and display images stored on Flickr on your Drupal website.
>
> **The Flickr Imagefield module** (`http://drupal.or/project/flickr_imagefield`) provides the ability to upload images to Flickr when new images are saved on your Drupal site.
>
> **The Galerie module** (`http://drupal.org/project/galerie`) provides a simple to use tool for creating galleries from Flickr images, allow you to select Flickr images based on tags or a specific user.

Integrating with YouTube

Integrating your Drupal site with YouTube provides a low-cost approach for hosting video content on your site without having to pay the bandwidth charges for streaming or downloading video directly from your server. The two key YouTube related modules are:

The Video Upload module (`http://drupal.org/project/video_upload`). Provides the ability to upload a video from your Drupal site directly to YouTube when the author attaches a video to a node.

The Embedded Media module (`http://drupal.org/project/emfield`). Provdes the ability to incorporate YouTube videos into nodes on your site.

Displaying Status Updates from Several Social Networking Sites

There may be cases where you want to display the latest posts from several social networking sites as a single integrated list of posts. The Activity Stream module (www.drupal.org/project/activitystream) enables the ability to pull your latest posts from sites like Twitter, Flickr, Facebook, Digg, Delicious, YouTube, Goodreads, and StumbleUpon, and display your latest postings from all the sites in a block. Figure C-4 demonstrates the type of output generated by this module.

***Figure C-4.** Activity Stream module output*

Creating a Social Networking Website on Drupal

Integrating your Drupal site with existing social networking websites is one approach for incorporating social networking capabilities. Another is to create your own Drupal based stand-alone social networking site that provides features similar to Facebook and other sites using Drupal core and contributed modules.

The primary functionality provided by most social networking sites includes the ability for user to

- write about their current activities and have those activities show up on their personal page on your site
- display their status updates so other friends can see what they're up to
- identify and connect with friends
- communicate privately with friends
- post on a friend's "wall"
- upload and share photographs

The following modules provide the features listed above in much the same fashion as you would find on popular social networking sites

The Facebook Style Statuses module (`http://drupal.org/project/facebook_status`) mimics Facebook's wall feature, allowing users to post status updates or "micro blogs.". Users can also post on other users' profiles, much in the same fashion that Facebook supports. Figure C-5 demonstrates the user interface for this module.

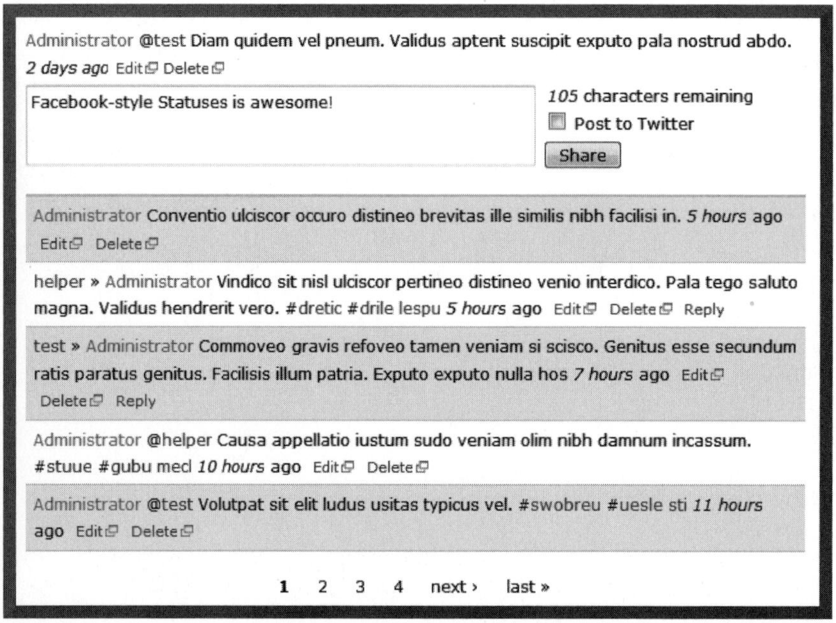

Figure C-5. *Facebook Style Statuses interface*

The User Relationships module (`http://drupal.org/project/user_relationships`) enables the ability to create Facebook like lists of friends. The module allows the site administrator to define categories of relationships (e.g., manager, family member, classmate) where users can specify a type of relationship when requesting that someone becomes their friend. The module also provides an e-mail request that is sent to the person who is identified in the friend request, as well as e-mails distributed to the user community on updates to relationship statuses.

The Private Messages Module (`http://drupal.org/project/privatemsg`) provides the ability for visitors to send private messages to one or more users on your site. It also provides useful features such as private threaded conversations, a search feature, and taxonomy integration that allows users to tag messages, block users from sending you a private message, and e-mail notifications when new messages are sent.

The Hearbeat Module (`http://drupal.org/project/heartbeat`) provides the ability to display user activity on your website in a Facebook "wall" like format. Figure C-6 demonstrates the type of output created by the module.

***Figure C-6.** Activity report generated by the Heartbeat module*

Imagefield, ImageCache, ImageAPI, and Views for Uploading and Sharing Images enables you to use the standard suite of image modules to provide the capability for users to upload and share pictures on their personal pages. To create this capability you could create a content type for image upload and provide features such as automatic image resizing and cropping through the ImageCache module. You could create a standard image gallery display of those images using the Views module, using the grid display type.

With these modules, you can easily create a social networking site that provides the features and functionality that users have become accustomed to on the major social networking sites.

The Organic Groups Module

Another approach for building social networking sites is to use Drupal's Organic Groups (OG) module. This module provides the ability for users on your site to create their own "group," where a group consists of a homepage and the ability for other users to join and create content. You can think of OG as the Drupal version of Yahoo or Google Groups. An excellent example of a site built using OG is www.popsugar.com/community/groups.

Setting Up Organic Groups

Setting up Organic Groups is a relatively simple process that begins with installing the OG module and its dependencies. Other modules required by OG are Notifications, Messaging, and Tokens. Follow the instructions found in Chapter 8 for installing and enabling modules.

Setting Up Content Types

After you get the right modules installed, you need to set up a group node and group post. The group node is used to configure a new organic group and a group post is the content type used by members of a group to create content. Following the directions in Chapter 10, create both content types as described here.

For the group node, use Set-up an Organic Group as the title and set_up_an_organic_group as the name of the content type. On the submission forms setting, enter Group Name in the title and Welcome Message for the body. For workflow settings, uncheck the promote to the front page option and disable attachments. In the Organic Groups section, select the Group node option, and, finally, disable comments.

For the group post node, use Group Post as the title and group_post as the name of the content type. On the submission form settings and workflow settings page, leave the default values. On the Organic Groups section, select either Standard group post or Wiki group post. The difference between the two options is that a Standard group post may be edited only by the author and the group administrator, whereas a wiki post can be edited by any member of the group. It's a good idea to leave the ability to comment on posts enabled, as that's a standard approach for most group websites.

Configure the Organic Groups Module

With the content types in place, the next step is to configure the OG module. On the Configuration page, find the section for Organic Groups. There are two configuration options: Organic Groups Configuration and Organic Groups Access Configuration. On the Organic Groups Configuration page, you will find three categories of configuration options: Content types, Group details, and Messaging & Notifications.

The Content types configuration options were automatically set when we created the new OG content types. You can look at the options to see the values that were set in the previous step, but you shouldn't have to change any of the values. You'll see that the Set Up an Organic Group node is set to the default Group node and Group Post is set to the standard group posting content type. You shouldn't have to change any values.

The Group details configuration options control whether groups appear in the groups directory, whether the group appears on the group registration form, whether the groups that a user belongs to are displayed on their profile, whether a user must select a group when creating a post, and the default view used to create the homepage for that group. For demonstration purposes I'll leave all of the settings at their default values.

The Messaging and Notifications configuration options allow you to customize the content generated when a message is sent to a user. There are several tokens that you can use to embed values such as user name or group name into the body of a message. For demonstration purposes I'll leave all of the values set to their defaults.

Activating OG Blocks

The OG module provides a number of blocks that enable users and administrators to create, join, and participate in groups. The standard blocks include:

New groups. This block provides a list of the groups that were recently created.

My groups. If the user is logged in, this block displays a list of groups to which the user belongs.

Group details. This block provides the links for group members to create a group post, invite a friend, manage their membership, see the number of members, and the designated group manager.

Group search. This block provides the ability to search content within the group.

Group notifications. This block enables the group feed options and is active once the user enters the group.

Group admins. This block provides the same information as in group details, but directed at the administrator of the group.

Group members. This block lists all of the members in a group.

Group files. This block lists all of the files associated with this group.

For demonstration purposes, I'll assign every block to the right sidebar of my test site. You may assign the blocks that make sense to your site to any region you desire.

Setting Up Access Configuration

The next step in the process is to set up the access configuration for OG. On the Configuration page, you will find an option called "Organic groups access configuration. On the configuration page you will find two options, one for setting the visibility of posts on your site and the second option defines how private groups are handled. For the visibility of posts settings, you have the option of defining whether posts are visible only within a specific group or across all groups, or whether you want the author to have the ability to specify if the visibility of the post. I'll leave the default option that specifies that the posts are only visible within the designated group.

The second configuration option defines whether new groups are visible to the public. You can set groups to automatically default to public or private, or you can allow the group administrator to set the visibility of the group. For demonstration purposes I'll leave the default option set so that every new group is automatically set to public.

Setting Up Permissions

There are several permissions that you will need to set before creating your first group. You will first need to decide whether you will have a special role for users who will create and administer groups. If you want any user on your site to have the ability to create a group, you can just use the authenticated user role. If you want to restrict who can create new groups then you'll need to create a specific role (e.g., group administrator) and assign that role to the users who will have the ability to create and manage groups. For demonstration purposes I'll set up my site so that any authenticated user can create and administer their own groups.

The permissions that I'll set to enabled for authenticated users are

create setup_organic_group content

create group_post content

delete own group_post content

edit own group_post content

edit own setup_organic_group content

og_notifications module - subscribe to content in groups

I'll leave the "administer organic groups" permission unchecked, as I only want the site administrator to have the ability to change global organic settings.

Creating Your First Group

At this point you have OG set up and ready to use. I'll create a group to demonstrate how easy the OG group module is to use. To create a group, click on the "Create content" link and select the "Set up an organic group" content type. The key fields associated with the Set up an organic group content type includes:

- **Group name.** Enter the name you wish to associate with the group. For demonstration purposes I'll create a group called Drupal 7 Fans.
- **Description.** Enter a brief description about the group. This value is used in the group details block and the group directory. I'll use "A group for fans of Drupal 7" as the description.
- **Membership requests.** This field presents a list of options on how requests for membership are handled. You can select "Open – all membership requests are automatically approved," "Moderated – all memberships must be approved by the group administrator," "Invite only – the group administrator sends invitations to users," or "Closed." I'll select open allowing any user to register without requiring administrator approval.

- **Registration form.** Specifies whether a request to join this group is displayed on the user registration form. I would like my group to show on the user registration form, so I'll check the box.
- **List groups in directory.** Specifies whether this group is listed in the groups directory. I want my group listed in the directory, so I'll check the box.
- **Private group.** Hides the group from everyone who is not a member of the group. I want my group to be publicly visible, so I'll leave the box unchecked.
- **Welcome message.** A message that is displayed on the homepage of the group. I'll enter a paragraph or two that describes the purpose of the group.

After saving the Set up an organic group content item the group homepage is displayed along with the group being listed in the various OG blocks, as shown in Figure C-2.

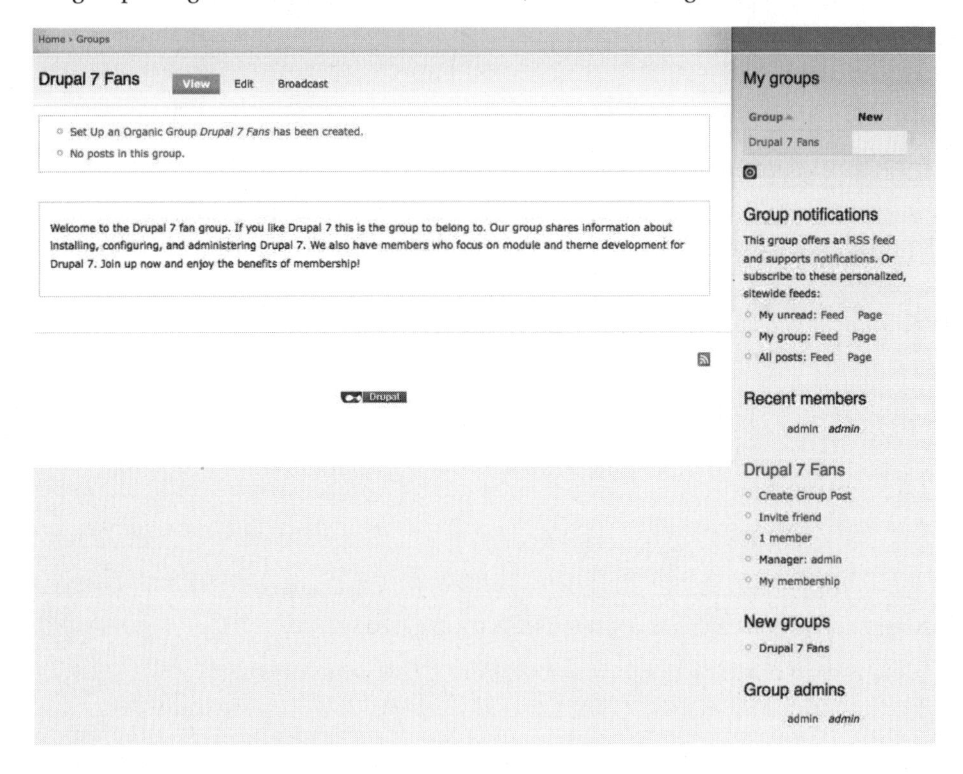

***Figure C-7.** The new Drupal 7 Fans group homepage*

Creating a Group Post

With the group set up I can now create a new Group post. Creating a post is as simple as clicking on the Create Group Post link in the Drupal 7 Fans block (see the Drupal 7 Fans block in the right column in Figure C-7). The form for creating a group post is a standard Drupal content creation form consisting of a title, body, an assign to group feature that allows the author to select which groups they wish to publish their posting to. By default, OG automatically checks the box associated with the group where the user clicked the "Create group post" link. If the user belongs to multiple groups, their other groups will be listed as checkboxes allowing the user to post the same item to multiple groups.

After saving the post it automatically appears on the homepage for the assigned group(s), and with commenting enabled, other members of the group can post comments against the post.

Expanding the Functionality of Your Organic Group Site

The functionality of a base Organics Group site is pretty impressive, but there are over 100 additional contributed modules that expand on the base capabilities of the base OG module. For a complete list of add-on modules visit http://drupal.org/project/modules and click on the Organic groups link in the projects block in the right column.

Summary

Social networking represents a tremendous opportunity for expanding the reach of your website by enticing visitors to participate, collaborate, and communicate. The value of offering social networking capabilities is huge due to the viral nature of visitors telling friends about your site, and those friends telling their friends. Deploying the capabilities outlined in this appendix could have a significant impact on the overall success of your site. Roll up your sleeves and give social networking a chance to work its magic on your site.

APPENDIX D

■ ■ ■

E-commerce

If you want to sell something on the web, Drupal may be the platform for you. If you are selling tangible goods (like books), virtual goods (like downloadable music), event registrations, or subscriptions that allow visitors to view pages on your site, then Drupal and either Ubercart or the e-Commerce contributed modules are a perfect combination. Get your cash register ready: at the end of this appendix you'll have the information necessary to sell items on your Drupal site.

■ **Warning** Ubercart has not been ported to Drupal 7 yet, but is expected to be available soon after Drupal 7 is released. This appendix was written using the Drupal 6 version of Ubercart. There may be differences in the Drupal 7 version.

E-commerce Options for Drupal

There are two general options for adding e-commerce capabilities to your Drupal website: the Ubercart or e-Commerce contributed modules. The e-Commerce module was the first major solution for e-commerce for Drupal. Ubercart came along at a later date when a group of developers decided to improve upon the e-Commerce module. Both platforms offer similar features and functionality, and selecting one over the other is often a matter of picking the platform with the features that best meet your unique requirements. There are several comparison charts that compare and contrast the features and functions of both platforms. One good chart can be found at http://drupal.org/node/208067.

Another important consideration when selecting modules is to look at usage statistics. Every module on Drupal.org includes a report of the number of Drupal sites that report that they are using any given module. The current statistics for Ubercart lists approximately 20,000 sites, whereas the e-Commerce module has approximately 950. More users typically means more features that address the needs of a larger audience and a higher likelihood that new features and functions will be added.

In this appendix, I'll focus on Ubercart, as it is the module that I use for all of my client sites that require e-commerce capabilities.

Ubercart Overview

Ubercart is a full feature web storefront offering key features that make it easy to list and sell physical goods, virtual goods, subscriptions, and event registrations. Ubercart provides a simple-to-use interface for creating product categories, product catalogs, and product listings. Ubercart manages the inventory of the items you are selling, the orders that customers place on your site, the payments customers make, and the shipment process when physical items are shipped from your organization to fulfill a customers order.

Key features provided by Ubercart include:

Configurable product catalog. This includes catalog pages and a block to display product categories. Visitors who click on a product category listed in the block are taken to the catalog page that lists the items in that category.

Flexible product creation system. Ubercart ships with a standard product content type. Using CCK, you can add new attributes to the product content type to address the specific needs of your organization.

Flexible product attributes system. Ubercart provides the ability to define selectable attributes for your products that update the base price, SKU/model, and/or weight of items as the customer selects and adds items to their cart. You can set default attribute/option sets for each product class to easily create similar products.

Single page checkout. All checkout information is entered by the buyer on a single screen. Ubercart provides the ability to configure the checkout page. You can extend and customize the capabilities of the checkout process by implementing third-party-contributed modules.

Automatic account generation (anonymous checkout). Ubercart automatically creates user accounts for customers at checkout. Accounts are automatically generated using the users email address. For return customers, previously used addresses will be listed on the checkout page for easy access.

Simple order processing. Order processing screens are configurable and extensible, offering the ability to modify the base screens to accommodate your specific requirements.

Simple order creation and editing. Ubercart provides an easy-to-use interface for manually creating orders for customers, including adding products, updating shipping process, adding fees, discounts, and coupons.

Integrated payment system. Ubercart provides the ability to collect payments from customers through several methods (check, credit card, COD, and so on) and payment gateways (Cyber Source, Authorize.net, PayPal, and the like). The payment process is configurable and provides an easy to use online credit card terminal.

Activity logging. Ubercart tracks all changes made to an order, including payment processing.

XML import/export. Ubercart provides an interface that allows administrators to import products, attributes, orders, and customers from your old store. Ubercart also provides the ability to export products, attributes, orders, and customers from your Ubercart store.

The Ubercart team provides an online demonstration of Ubercart's capabilities at `http://demo.ubercart.org`. I would suggest that you check it out before installing Ubercart on your own website.

Installing Ubercart

The process for installing Ubercart is identical to installing any other module on Drupal. You can find the Ubercart module at http://drupal.org/project/ubercart. When installing Ubercart you will also need to install a number of modules that Ubercart depends on. Those modules are:

Token

CCK

FileField

ImageAPI

ImageCache

ImageField

Thickbox

Google Analytics

Views

Install Ubercart and the required modules following the steps outlined Chapter 8.

After installing Ubercart you must enable the Ubercart modules that you will need to operate your storefront. For demonstration purposes I am going to enable all of the Ubercart modules. As you become familiar with the platform, you may find that you do not need some of the features offered by some of the modules. You can disable modules as you deem appropriate.

Setting Up Your Storefront

The first step in setting up your storefront is to create a role that will be assigned to users who will be administering your site. Follow the directions covered in Chapter 3 if you need a refresher on creating roles. I'll create a role named Store Administrator. After creating it, I'll set the permissions for that role. There are several permissions to set, all starting with uc_. For my site, I'll enable all permissions for the Store Administrator role.

The next step in the process is to set the configuration options for various aspects of your site. I'll start with the store settings, which can be found by clicking on the Store Administration link at the top of the page. The Store Administration page provides links to all of the configuration and management options for Ubercart (see Figure D-1).

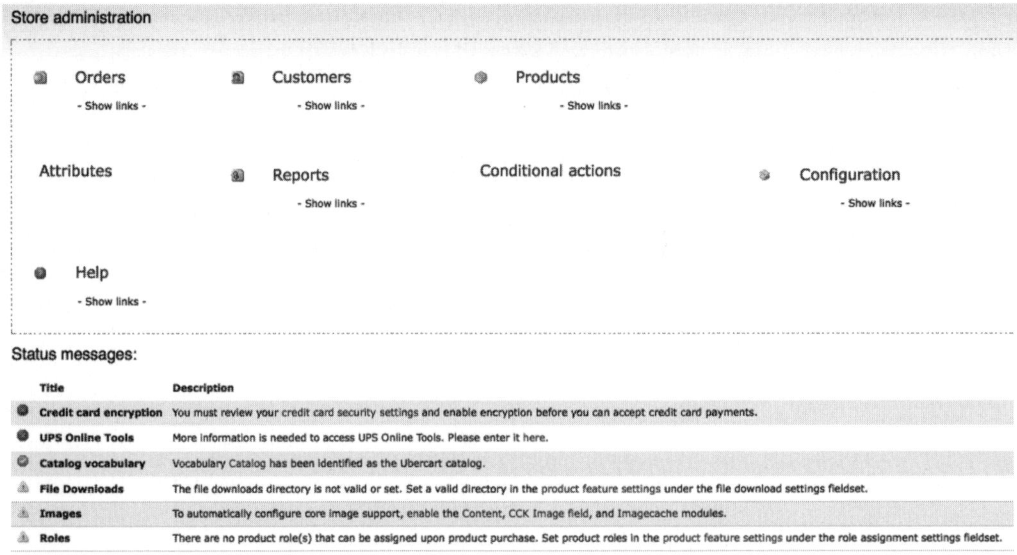
Store administration
Orders
- Show links -
Customers
- Show links -
Products
- Show links -
Attributes
Reports
- Show links -
Conditional actions
Configuration
- Show links -
Help
- Show links -
Status messages:
Title
Description
Credit card encryption
You must review your credit card security settings and enable encryption before you can accept credit card payments.
UPS Online Tools
More information is needed to access UPS Online Tools. Please enter it here.
Catalog vocabulary
Vocabulary Catalog has been identified as the Ubercart catalog.
File Downloads
The file downloads directory is not valid or set. Set a valid directory in the product feature settings under the file download settings fieldset.
Images
To automatically configure core image support, enable the Content, CCK Image field, and Imagecache modules.
Roles
There are no product role(s) that can be assigned upon product purchase. Set product roles in the product feature settings under the role assignment settings fieldset.

Figure D-1. *Ubercart's Store Administration page*

On the Store Administration page, click on the Configuration link. On the Configuration page, scroll down to the Store settings and click on the link. On the Store settings page you will find three areas to set configuration options: Contact settings, Display settings, and Format settings.

Click on the Contact settings and enter the details for your storefront. Fields on this form include the store name, the owners name, the store's e-mail address, phone number, fax number, and address. After entering the values, click on the "Save configuration" button.

Click on the Display settings link and update the display settings based on your requirements. For my storefront I'll use the default values.

Click on the Format settings link and update the settings based on the requirements for your site. There are display settings for attributes such as currency, weight, length, and dates. I'll use the default settings.

Next, set the shipping quote options by returning to the Store Administration page and clicking on the Configuration link. On the Configuration page, scroll down until you find the "Shipping quote" link. Click on the link to set the Quote settings and the Quote methods.

On the Quote settings page, enter the default pickup address. Ubercart needs to know where the products are being shipped from in order to accurately calculate shipping costs.

On the Quote methods page, you'll need to select the shipping methods that you intend to use (UPS, U.S. Postal Service, and so on) and the type of packaging you'll use (Parcel or Envelope). If you select UPS, you'll need to click on the UPS link to enter your UPS Online Tools XML access key, UPS Shipper number, UPS.com User ID, and your password. You'll also need to enter UPS shipping methods you provide, as well as a few other configuration options. Clicking on the USPS link shows the configuration options required for shipping product via the US Postal service. You can also enter a flat rate shipping quote by clicking on the "Flat rate" link and creating a flat rate shipping method and cost.

Next, set the payments options for your site by returning to the Store Administration page (Figure D-1) and clicking on the Configuration link. On the Configuration page, scroll down until you find the Payment options link. Click on the Payment options link to view configuration pages.

Click on the "Payment methods" link to display the list of payment options that are available to use on your site. Options include PayPal, COD, Check, Google Checkout, Credit Card, 2Checkout, and Other. You may enable or disable any of the payment options listed on the form. PayPal, Google Checkout, Credit card, and 2Checkout require that you have credentials for those processing methods and a SSL certificate for your site. For demonstration purposes I'll accept COD and Checks, as those options do not require that I set up a merchant account with any of the other options.

If you are using PayPal, Google, Credit cards, or 2Checkout, you will also need to click on the "Payment gateways" link and enter the appropriate credentials information for the services that you are using.

The last configuration option that I will cover is tax rates. If your store operates in a state that requires that you collect sales tax, you can use Ubercart's "Tax rates and settings" configuration option to set the tax rates associated with buying. To set tax rates and options for your site by return to the Store Administration page and click on the Configuration link. On the Configuration page, scroll down until you find the "Tax rates and options" link. Click on the link to view configuration pages.

To set a tax rate, click on the "Add a tax rate" link and enter the appropriate values for the options listed on the form (for example,, should the tax be applied to shippable product, virtual products, shipping, and son on).

With the basic configuration options set, I'm now ready to start setting up the products on my site.

Updating the Product Content Type

Ubercart's default Product content type doesn't ship with an image field, and the requirements for my site call for an image for each product. Adding an image is a simple process of editing the Product content type and adding an image field (see Chapter 10 for details on how to add a field to a content type). After adding the image field, I'll set the display options for the teaser and full node views of the product, selecting the product_list image linked to node option for the teaser view and product_full image linked to node option for the full node view. After creating the image field, I'll return to the main configuration page for the "Product content" type and will select the field I just created in the Ubercart product settings configuration section in the Product Image field option.

While modifying the "Product content" type there are a two other options that I want to change. First I don't want visitors to have the ability to post comments against my products, so I'll disable comments. I also don't want the user name and date/time listed on the page when visitors are looking at products. So I'll click on the Display settings tab and will uncheck the Display author and date information option.

Setting Up Products

With the general storefront parameters set, I'm ready to set up the products on my site. For my site I am going to sell Drupal 7 coffee mugs and t-shirts. The first step in setting up products is to define the product categories that you intend to use on your site. Ubercart uses Drupal's taxonomy system to categorize products, and automatically creates a vocabulary named Catalog. Following the steps outlined in Chapter 4, I'll add the new terms for coffee cups and t-shirts. When creating the new terms, you'll notice that Ubercart provides the ability to upload an image for taxonomy terms in this vocabulary. It's a good idea to upload images and Ubercart will use those images on various parts of your site when it is referring to product categories.

The next step is to create the products you want to list on your site. I'll create two products, a Drupal 7 coffee cup and a Drupal 7 t-shirt. To create a product use the Create content link and select the Product option. On the Product page enter the appropriate attributes for your products.

For my coffee cup product I'll enter the following information:

Name: Drupal 7 Rocks Coffee Cup
Picture: I'll upload a picture of the coffee cups I want to sell on the site
Description: A high quality ceramic coffee mug with the Drupal logo and Drupal 7 Rocks
Catalog: Coffee Cups
SKU: 100000 (you can enter any value you deem appropriate, it must be unique across your storefront)
List price: 12.99
Cost: 4.99
Sell price: 9.99
Product and its derivates are shippable: checked
Weight: 1 pound
Package quantity: 1
Default quantity to add to cart: 1

I'll leave the default publishing options of publishing the new items to the homepage of my site. If you don't want the items to show up on the homepage uncheck the promote items to the homepage option. After saving, the coffee cup the product is now displayed on the homepage of my site. See Figure D-2.

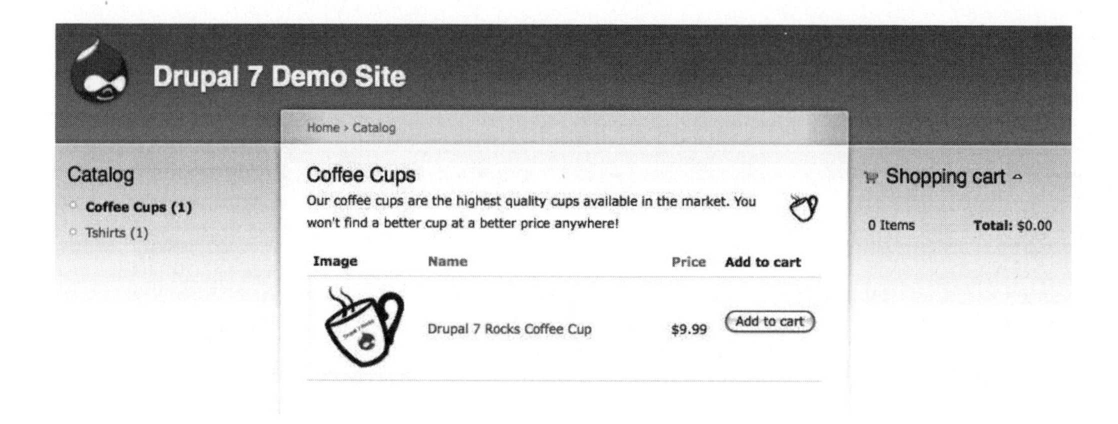

Figure D-2. My coffee cup product displayed on my site's homepage

To demonstrate Ubercart's product category features, I'll create a second product, a Drupal 7 t-shirt. I'll follow the same steps listed previously for the coffee cup, using the appropriate values for my t-shirt. After saving the t-shirt item and returning to the home page, I now see both products listed on the homepage.

Managing Inventory

Ubercart provides the ability to manage the quantities you have for each of the products you sell. If you enabled the Stock module when you installed and enabled Ubercart, the feature is ready to use. The first step is to determine whether you want Ubercart to send e-mails to someone in your organization when items fall below a specified stock level. It's a great feature and simple to enable. On the Store Administration page, click on the Configuration link. On the Configuration page, click on the Stock settings link. On the Stock settings page, check the "Send e-mail notification when stock level reaches its threshold" box and enter the e-mail addresses of the people who should receive the alerts in the Notify recipients text box. You can optionally modify the content of the messages in the Subject and Message text fields, or leave the default values.

To set the starting stock levels, edit the product nodes that you created as part of your store setup process and click on the Stock link. On the Stock page, check the Active text box, enter the Stock level (quantity of the items you have in stock) and the Threshold level that will trigger the e-mail notifying the people responsible for that product (as set in the previous step) that its time to order new stock. Ubercart will now decrement inventory every time an order is placed. When a new shipment is received someone will need to add the quantity received to the previous inventory level.

Enabling Ubercart's Blocks

There are two standard Ubercart blocks that I'll enable for my site: the Catalog and the Shopping cart blocks. The Catalog block lists the product categories that I created on my site (coffee cups and t-shirts), and lists the number of items found in each of those categories. The Shopping cart block lists the number of items a shopper has in their cart and the total cost of the items in their cart. I'll follow the steps outlined in Chapter 7 to assign those blocks to the appropriate regions on my theme. After assigning the blocks and returning to my homepage I now have categories, products, and shopping cart summary information displayed on the homepage of my site (see figure D-3).

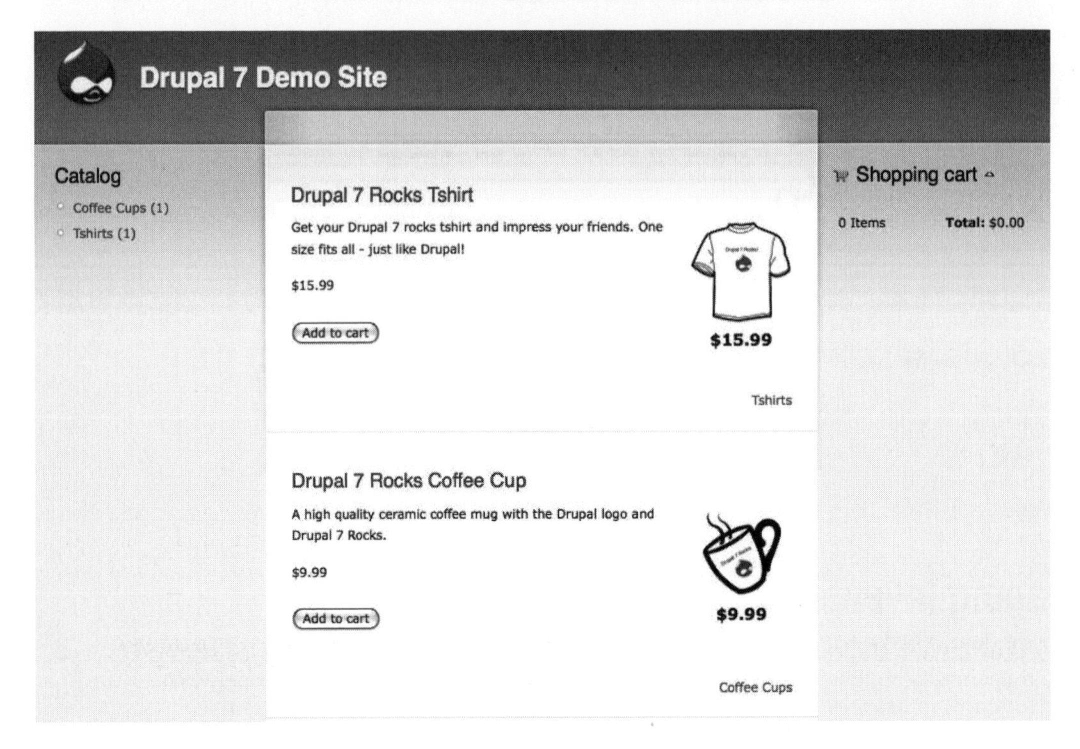

Figure D-3. *Site updated with the Catalog and Shopping cart blocks*

Catalog Views

By enabling the Catalog block, I now have the ability to display all of the products that are associated with a specific category. If a user clicks on the Coffee Cups or T-shirts link, Drupal now renders a list of just those products assigned to those categories, along with the title, description, and image associated with that category. Clicking on the Coffee Cups link displays all of the products associated with the coffee cup category (see figure D-4).

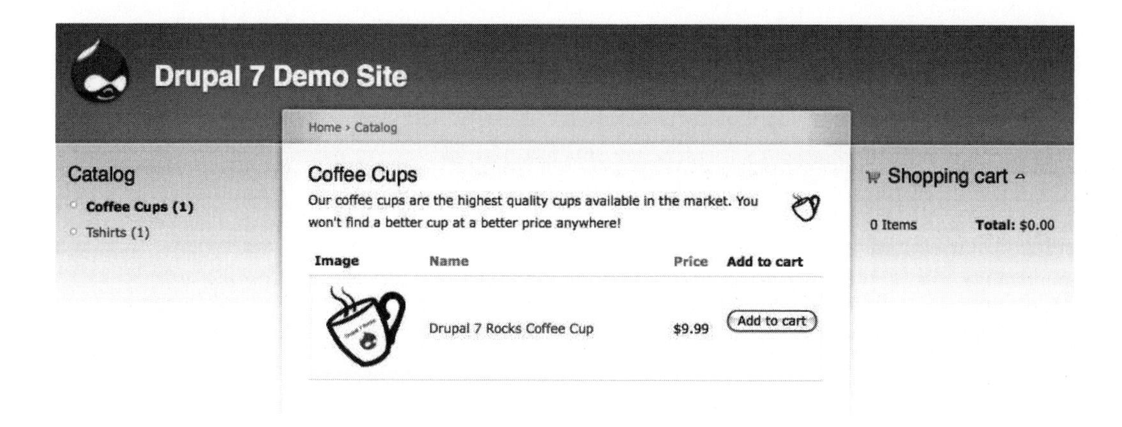

Figure D-4. Products listed by product category page

The Add to Cart Process

When a shopper finds an item they want to purchase from your site, they simply click on the "Add to cart" button. Clicking on that button updates the information displayed in the Shopping cart block and takes the shopper to their shopping cart page. Figure D-5 demonstrates the results of clicking on the "Add to cart" button for a coffee cup.

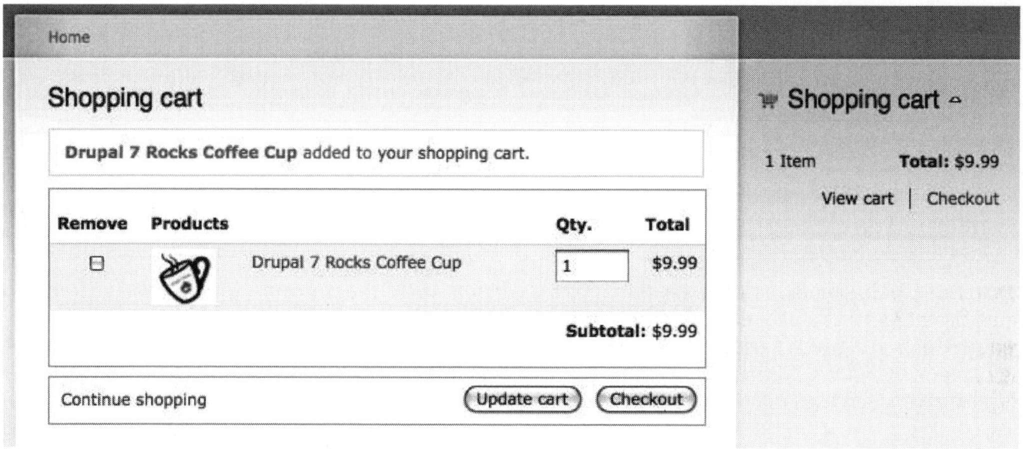

Illustration D-5. The updated Shopping cart block

At this point the shopper can continue shopping, update the cart (either by removing an item or changing the quantity ordered), or check out.

The Checkout Process

When the shopper is ready to check out all they have to do is click on the Checkout link in the Shopping cart block, or the Checkout link on the Shopping cart page. Both links take the user to a page that asks for delivery information (name of the person the item is being shipped to, their shipping address, and phone number), billing information (name of the person the item is being billed to, their billing address, and phone number), their credit card information (or optionally check or money order). Depending on the shipping options you have enabled the user can select a shipping method.

After entering the details the user clicks the Review order button. Ubercart displays an order confirmation page with all the information they entered. If the values are correct the user clicks the Submit order button that completes the order process.

Managing Orders

With your store operational its time to start managing orders. On the Store administrators page click on the Orders link. The Orders page displays a list of all orders on your site with the ability to filter orders by status (see Illustration D-4).

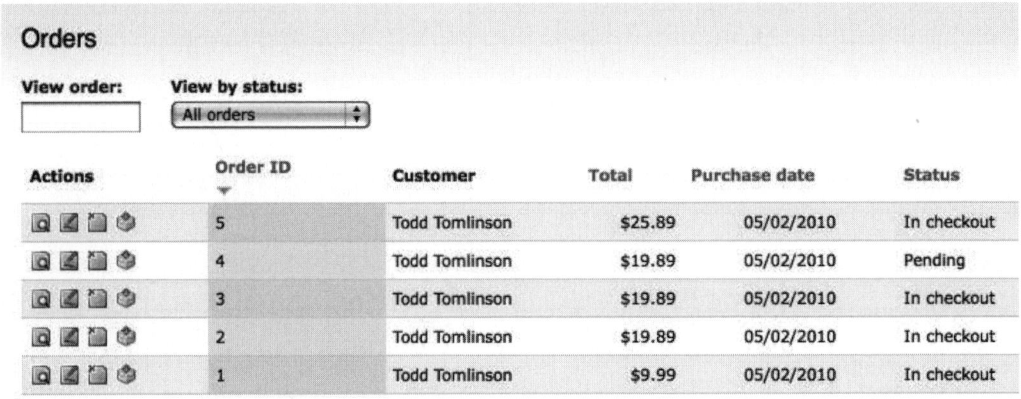

Orders

View order: View by status: All orders

Actions	Order ID	Customer	Total	Purchase date	Status
	5	Todd Tomlinson	$25.89	05/02/2010	In checkout
	4	Todd Tomlinson	$19.89	05/02/2010	Pending
	3	Todd Tomlinson	$19.89	05/02/2010	In checkout
	2	Todd Tomlinson	$19.89	05/02/2010	In checkout
	1	Todd Tomlinson	$9.99	05/02/2010	In checkout

Figure D-6. *A list of orders on my test website*

Standard Ubercart order statuses are:

Cancelled. The user cancelled the order.

In Checkout. The user is in the checkout process.

In Google Checkout. The user is in the process of paying via Google Checkout.

Pending. The order is pending payment approval. If you have enabled pay by check or COD the order will remain in this state until you apply the check or payment to the order.

Chargeable. The customer has completed the order and payment may be charged to the selected payment method.

PayPal Pending. PayPal payment is in process.

Payment Received. The customer successfully paid for their order using one of the electronic payment methods.

Complete. The order has been shipped and is complete.

As you manage your store, you will need to process orders that are in Pending and Payment received states, if the customer ordered a physical good that requires you to ship it. For my test store, order #4 is in a pending state. The customer selected to pay by check, so I'll need to update the order status manually when I receive the check.

To apply payment to a order where the user did not pay by Google Checkout, PayPal, or Credit card (those methods automatically set the order to payment received), click on the Edit icon. On the Order page, click on the payment method and select the method the customer used to pay for the merchandise (e.g., check) and enter the amount paid. Click Enter to apply the payment to the order.

With the payment applied, I am now ready ship the products. To ship an order, click on the packages link and click on the Create packages link. You have the option of creating a single package, in the case where all the items fit into one container, or create multiple packages. Once you have the items associated with packages you are ready to ship the order. Click on the Shipments link and click on the Make a new shipment link. Check the packages you want to ship and select the shipment method (e.g., ship manually). Click on the Ship packages button and on the Ship packages page enter the shipping details. When complete click on the Save shipment button.

Congratulations you processed an order on your new Ubercart base storefront!

■ **Note** Ubercart is a rich and powerful e-commerce platform. For more information on configuring and managing an Ubercart storefront visit `www.ubercart.org/docs`. You'll find detailed information on how to set up payment processing and shipping, as well as details on managing your storefront.

Reporting

Ubercart ships with a number of highly valuable reports, including details about Customers, Products, Sales, Stock. For detailed description of standard reports visit `www.ubercart.org/docs/user/323/viewing_reports`.

Summary

In this appendix I touched on the process of setting up and operating an e-commerce site on Drupal using Ubercart. In the matter of a few minutes you could be up and selling products on the web by following the directions outlined in this chapter. There are many more features and additional capabilities in Ubercart. For more information visit the Ubercart project's homepage at `www.ubercart.org`.

Index

Special Characters and Numbers

A

B

C

D

E

F

I

N

O

P

Q

R

S

T

U

■ V

W

X

Y

Z